David Thom

Sermons preached in Liverpool, with a memoir of his life

David Thom

Sermons preached in Liverpool, with a memoir of his life

ISBN/EAN: 9783337086060

Printed in Europe, USA, Canada, Australia, Japan

Cover: Foto ©Lupo / pixelio.de

More available books at **www.hansebooks.com**

LIST OF SUBSCRIBERS.

Name	Copies	Name	Copies	Name	Copies
Abercrombie, George	2	Cureton, Miss	4	Hindle, John	1
Affleck, Thomas	1	Curphey, John	1	Hinton, J., M.R.C.S.	1
A Friend	2			Hinton, Richard	1
Angus, William	1	Daly, Denis	2	Hodge, Mrs.	1
Aspinall, Rev. G., Ph.D.	1	Davies, Rev. E. T.	1	Horsfall, John	1
		Davies, Thomas	1	Houghton,—	1
Balloch, Archibald	1	Dawson, Rev. Thomas	1	Houghton, Richard, Jun.	1
Baruchson, Arnold	1	Day, Miss	8	Houston, John	1
Beer, Edward	1	Dewrance, Mrs.	12	Howard, Bernard	1
Bell, Jonathan	1	Dickie, J.	4	Howard, Mrs.	2
Bell, Joseph	1	Dickie, W.	2	Howell, Edward	1
Bennett, John	2	Dickinson, J., M.D.	1	Hudson, J. H.	1
Bennett, Richard	5	Dimma, Mrs.	1	Hume, Rev. A., D.C.L.,	
Bennett, Robert	5	Downey, John	3	LL.D.	1
Best, Joseph	1			Hunt, George	1
Binning, John	1	Eldridge, Miss	1	Hutchins, Charles	1
Birrell, Rev. Charles M.	1	Ellams, James	1	Hynde, Miss	2
Black, James	1	Ellis, John	1	Hynde, Miss M.	1
Boult, Joseph	1	Ellison, Miss	1		
Boyd, Andrew	3	England, Rev. J., A.M.	1	Inlach, Henry, M.D.	1
Braby, Frederick	1	Evans, Mrs. John	5	Innes, Mrs.	1
Brown, Rev. H. S.	1			Irvine, Miss	1
Brown, James R.	1	Fawcett, Lieut.-Col.	3	Irving, John	3
Brown, Miss	1	Ferguson, A.	1		
G. M. B.	1	Figgins, Rev. J. L.	1	Jackson, William	1
Bruce, James H., M.D.	1	Fordyce, George	1	Johnson, Edward	1
Buchanan, A., M.D.	1	Forfar, Rev. Pat. T.	1	Johnson, James	2
Buchanan, Moses	1	Fraser, John	6	Johnstone, Robert	1
Buck, John M.	1	Fraser, Wm. Newby	1	Jones, Evan	1
Buck, Rev. W. F.	1	Freer, Mrs. Charles	2	Jones, Mrs. Morgan	1
Butterfield, John	1	Fyfe, Miss	1		
Buxton, David	1			Keith, William	1
Byrd, Mrs. D.	1	Games, John, M.D	1	Kellock, Hugh	1
		Gardener, Mrs.	3	Kelly, Rev. John	1
		Gardener, John, Jun.	10	Kent, David	1
Callow, William	2	Gaskell, James	1	Ker, Stewart	1
Cameron, D., LL.D.	1	Gates, John	2	Kerfoot, Mrs.	1
Cameron, John, M.D.	1	Geddes, David	1	Kerr, Mrs. James	1
Campbell, Miss	1	Gelston, Miss	4	King, Miss E.	1
Carbery, John	1	Gerrand, Miss	1		
Cariss, Astrup	1	Gibson, Mrs. T.	1	Lamb, David	2
Carpi, B.	1	Gibson, Mrs. W.	2	Lewis, Rev. E. C.	3
Charles, George	3	Giddens, Henry	1	Lewis, H. K.	12
Chatterton, J.	1	Gordon, William	3	Lewis, Miss	1
Chatterton, J. G.	1	Graham, Rev. J., D.D.	1	Long, James	1
Clark, John	1	Grindlay, John	1	Lowden, Samuel	1
Clason, Rev. P., D.D.	1			Lowe, Rev. J. B., D.D.	1
Clayton, Frank	2	Hackney Miss Alice	1	Lupton, Bannister	3
Coghill, Alexander	3	Haddock, —	1		
Coghill, Harry	3	Haddon, Miss C.	1	Macalpine, Hugh B.	2
Copeland, Dr. J.	1	Haigh, Benjamin	1	Macalpine, Miss	1
Corlett, John	1	Hall, Robert Henry	1	Mc Bryde, Anthony	2
Corrie, Joseph and Son	1	Hamlyn, Richard	1	Mc Bryde, John	1
Coubrough, Henry	1	Hastings, John	1	Mc Clellan, David	2
Cowan, Miss	1	Havercroft, G. T.	1	Mc Clellan, John	2
Coward, Mrs. F.	1	Haydon, H. W.	1	Mc Culloch, S., LL.D.	1
Cox, Henry T.	2	Haywood, George	1	Mc Donnell, Mrs.	2
Coxon, Miss	8	Heap, Robert	2	Mc Ewan, James	2
Crosby, Mrs.	1	Higgins, Mr. & Mrs. C.	2	Mc Ewan, Miss	1

	Copies		Copies		Copies
Mc George, David	2	Price, Mrs.	1	Stromeyer, Mrs.	1
Mc George, Mrs. James	1	Procter, Mrs. James	2	Sugg, James	1
Mc George, Thomas	5			Swallow, Miss L.	1
Mc George, William	8	Ramsden, Mrs.	1	Swinden, Wm.	1
Mc Gregor, Daniel	1	Rawlins, C. E., Jun.	1		
MacIlveen, Mrs.	1	Read, —	1	Tait, Wm.	1
Macintyre, James	6	Rees, Rev. William	1	Talbot, F. C.	1
Macintyre, Louis H.	2	Richardson, Richard	1	Thompson, Miss E.	5
Macintyre, Peter, M.D.	3	Richardson, Samuel	1	Thompson, Mrs.	1
Mc Keand, J.	1	Ronn, William	1	Thompson, William	1
Mackenzie, John	3	Roberts, Humphrey	1	Thompson, William	1
Mackenzie, Simon	1	Robertson, John	1	Tilston, James	1
Mc Kinnell, Jas. H.	1	Robinson, Andrew	3	Titherington, W.	1
Mc Kittrick, Thos. C.	2	Rockliff, Robert	1	Tod, James	1
Mc Kittrick, W. L.	1	Rogers, Mrs.	1	Tomkinson, William	2
Macrae, James Hardie	1	Ronald, Byron Lord	1	Tomlinson, Miss	2
Macrae, John Wrigley	1	Ronald, Lionel Knowles	1	Topham, R.	1
Mc Whinnie, J. C.	1	Ronald, Robert W.	10	Trevitt, Rev. James	1
Marples, David	2	Rowell, William	1		
Marshall, Edward	1	Rudd, Henry V.	2	Underhill, James	1
Mashiter, Mrs.	1	Rule, Alexander	1	Urquhart, Thomas	1
Mather, James	1	Rushton, William, M.A.	1		
Mayer, J., F.S.A., &c.	1			Wade, Christopher	1
Metcalf, S.	1	Salt, Charles F.	1	Waldie, David	4
Middleton, —	1	Sandland, John D.	2	Waldie, James	2
Miller, John	2	Scarff, Henry	1	Walmsley, Mrs	1
Mitchell, John	3	Scott, Mrs.	1	Walter, Miss A. J.	1
Molyneux, John	1	Scott, Mrs. Christine	1	Wands, Robert	1
Morgan, Mrs.	1	Sharp, William	1	Wannop, Mr. and Mrs.	2
Morrison, Duncan	1	Shaw, Thomas K.	2	War, James	1
Mott, Albert J.	1	Sherlock, Mrs. M.A.	1	Whitby, John	1
Muir, John	1	Sherwood, Mrs. E.	1	White, Rev. V.M., LL.D	1
Muir, Thomas	1	Sidgreaves, Charles	1	Whitney, Thomas	2
Musgrove, Edgar	1	Sinclair, John, M.D.	1	Wilkinson, Daniel	1
		Sloan, Peter	1	Williams, Mrs. Bell	2
Napier, William	1	Smith, Boyle	1	Williams, Josiah P.	1
		Smith, David	1	Williams, Mrs. Thomas	1
Orr, Rev. John	1	Smith, J. (Seaforth)	20	Wilson, Rev. Andrew	1
Owen, Miss H.	1	Smith, James	1	Wilson, John	1
		Smith, William	1	Wilson, Joseph	1
Page, Henry	1	Sparham, T. H.	1	Wilson, Richard	2
Pannell, Mrs. Joseph	2	Stewart, Andrew	1	Wilson, Mrs. Robert	1
Park, Mrs.	1	Stewart, David Thom	1	Wishart, Mrs.	1
Parkinson, Rev. H. W.	1	Stewart, James G.	1	Woolsey, H.	1
Pattison, William	1	Stewart, Robert	1	Wright, James	1
Picton, James A. (F.A. & A.S., &c.)	1	Stewart, Mrs. William	1		
		Stockil, Miss	1	Yuill, John	4
Pollard, John W.	1	Stockil, Miss E.	1		
Poynter, John	1	Stockil, William	1	Zimmerman, H. W.	1

SERMONS

PREACHED IN BOLD-STREET, AND CROWN-STREET CHAPELS,

LIVERPOOL,

BY THE LATE
REV. DAVID THOM, D.D., Ph.D.

WITH A BRIEF MEMOIR OF HIS LIFE.

LONDON:
H. K. LEWIS, 15, GOWER STREET NORTH.
1863.

SONNETS.

IN MEMORY OF DAVID THOM.

A CHRISTIAN hero! great and bold of speech;
   No praise he asked, he feared from man no blame:
His soul no arrows of reproach could reach;
   Ever his tongue proclaimed the Saviour's name.
Far into things divine he looked, and sought
   The mines of holy truth for gems divîne:
Bright joy, sweet peace, hope stedfast, love unbought,
   These gifts of God unmasked, O man, are thine!
He mixed not earth with heaven, nor vainly thought
   To find God's life among the dead in crime:
He walked with God, and from his Spirit caught
   Those rays of heaven which visit few in Time.
Of Truth's prevailing power a witness, he
Alike in life and death sought strength to be.

Birkenhead, April 5, 1862.

Another noble spirit hath been ta'en
   To swell the names in Heaven's triumphal band!
Dear THOM, that spirit is *thine own*, the gain
   To thee how great—a seat at God's right hand!
A purer atmosphere than this of ours
   Thou breathest now; and that unbounded love
Whose proclamation here evok'd thy pow'rs
   For ever wilt thou realise above.
No chains of *Shiboleth* had strength to take
   Thy judgement captive or to fetter thee,
A mental Samson—thine it was to break
   The withes like tow, and bid thy soul go free.
Dead Samson, as we weep beside thy pall,
Well may we ask on whom Elijah's cloak shall fall!

Wick, March 4th, 1862.

TO THE READER.

The publication of a volume of Sermons is a very common occurrence, and if it happen to go forth to the world as the production of some well-known and popular theological "authority," may prove a profitable speculation. The publication of this volume, however, was not induced by a view to profit (understanding the term in its mercantile signification), but by a different motive, and with a very different object; and the Editor may inform the Reader that the theological "authority" of the preacher was recognised by only a very limited number, and these consisted chiefly of persons in the humbler walks of life; and that "authority" was only recognised by them, in so far as they found the doctrines proclaimed by the preacher to be consistent with the Oracles of Truth.

Dr. Thom was not known to the world, nor even in the immediate neighbourhood of his ministerial labours, as a popular preacher, but the reverse. For the last thirty years of his ministry, his congregation never at any time amounted to more than from 150 to 200 individuals; but most of these were warm and attached friends, who recognised in him an "honest man" and a "true Christian," and were delighted to listen to the revealed truths of Scripture, as they fell like "heavenly manna" in honeyed accents from his lips. Well might he be respected and even loved by those who knew him, for he was at all times as accessible to the poorest as to the richest of his Christian brethren, and was ever ready to do good to all men as the Lord gave him opportunity.

The history of the publication of this volume of Sermons is simply this. It occurred to a few of Dr. Thom's congregation (and the Editor was not one of them) to employ a short-hand writer to report some of his religious Services, and after his decease this fact became known to his friends generally, and many of them expressed a strong desire to have the Sermons published. It was the privilege of the Editor to be one of the Doctor's hearers for upwards of thirty years, and also to be one of his most intimate friends. He was believed to be well acquainted with the Doctor's religious sentiments, and was requested and induced to undertake the task of revising the Sermons for publication.

Dr. Thom was an exceedingly rapid speaker (he gave utterance to at least ten more words per minute than the average of recognised rapid public speakers), and it was therefore not an easy task for any short-hand writer to keep pace with him correctly. The reporter may, probably, not have been intimately acquainted with the Doctor's theology, and it may readily be conceived that, without any fault on his part, there were many errors to be corrected, and many blanks to be filled up in the manuscripts, as they came into the hands of the Editor. But further (and those who were his constant hearers can testify to the fact), such was the Doctor's anxiety to make himself thoroughly understood, that he would often repeat, usually in somewhat different phraseology, the same idea; this frequently made him exceedingly tautotogical, which, in publishing, had as far as possible to be avoided. The Editor does not pretend to say, that the reader will find the Sermons altogether free from this defect.

Under the circumstances related, it may be conceived that it has been a tedious task to the Editor to get the work into a shape suitable for publication. He is happy however to say, that he has succeeded in revising all the Sermons of the Doctor that were reported, and thinks that those readers who attended his ministry will recognise them, and ventures to assure the general reader that he may take them, as affording a faithful transcript of Dr. Thom's theological sentiments.

For the last seven or eight years of Dr. Thom's life, he was deprived, through blindness, of the usual facilities for the composition of his discourses, and his general health during that period was far from satisfactory. He was, however, very careful whenever circumstances permitted, to devote a certain period of the day to out-door exercise, and he had several very favorite walks.—It was during his long, silent walks, that he composed and arranged his Lord's-day's Discourses, and their perspicuity and method attest the strength of his mind and the retentiveness of his memory.

It is very probable that the readers of these Sermons may not be numerous, but to such of them as understand and rejoice in the glorious Scriptural truths which run though every page of the volume, the Editor feels assured that its perusal will afford infinite delight.

THE EDITOR.

Liverpool, March 3rd, 1863.

TABLE OF CONTENTS.

	PAGE.
BRIEF MEMOIR OF THE AUTHOR'S LIFE.	i—lxviii

SERMONS.

I.
THE WEAPONS OF A CHRISTIAN'S WARFARE. . . . 10

II.
THE MESSAGE OF GLAD TIDINGS AND PEACE. . . 33

III.
THE CHRISTIAN NOT HIS OWN.—THE PURCHASE AND THE PRICE. 55

IV.
THE GLORIFICATION OF GOD, BY THE BELIEVERS OF HIS REVEALED TRUTH. 68

V.
THE STABILITY OF THE DIVINE FOUNDATION.—FIRST SEAL: "THE LORD KNOWETH THEM THAT ARE HIS." . 80

VI.
THE STABILITY OF THE DIVINE FOUNDATION.—SECOND SEAL: "LET EVERY ONE THAT NAMETH THE NAME OF CHRIST, DEPART FROM INIQUITY". 94

VII.
THE CONFLICT AND TRIUMPH OF CHRIST JESUS. . 106

VIII.
THE SCRIPTURE DECLARATION—"IT IS WRITTEN"—THE HIGHEST OF ALL AUTHORITY. 129

IX.
THE RIGHT OF PRIVATE JUDGMENT,—ITS SPHERE AND ITS LIMITS. 135

X.
JESUS CHRIST, "THE WORD" MANIFEST IN FLESH. 149

XI.
THE RESURRECTION OF CHRIST. . 163

SERMON XII.
DIVINE KNOWLEDGE AND ITS RELATION TO DIVINE FAITH. . 176

XIII.
FAITH—ITS SUPER-HUMAN ACHIEVEMENTS. . . 189

XIV.
"THE LORD IS MY HELPER." THE CHRISTIAN'S UNFAILING RESOURCE, AND THE GROUND OF HIS UNWAVERING CONFIDENCE 200

XV.
DESPERATION, CONSIDERED AS A PRINCIPLE OF HUMAN CONDUCT. 246

XVI.
THE LIBERATING POWER OF THE LAW OF THE SPIRIT OF LIFE IN CHRIST JESUS. 223

XVII.
LOOKING UNTO JESUS, THE BELIEVER'S SALVATION. . . 235

XVIII.
THE MIRACULOUS MANIFESTATION OF GOD'S GLORY IN APOSTOLIC TIMES. 246

XIX.
THE CORRUPTING TENDENCIES OF THE HUMAN HEART IN ITS DEALINGS WITH SPIRITUAL THINGS. . . . 260

XX.
THE RENEWING AND PURIFYING INFLUENCES OF THE GOSPEL. 275

XXI.
THE OMNIPRESENCE OF CHRIST. 288

XXII.
CONFORMITY IN SUFFERING BETWEEN CHRIST AND THE MEMBERS OF HIS CHURCH. 300

XXIII.
THE INFINITELY-DISTANT—THE MOST INTIMATELY-PRESENT GOD. 312

FUNERAL SERVICE. 325

BRIEF MEMOIR

OF THE

LIFE OF DAVID THOM, D.D., Ph.D.

David Thom, the first-born of a family of nine children, was a native of Glasgow. February 19th, 1795, witnessed his entrance into the world. His father, John Thom, a merchant of that city, was married to Jean Falconer, the eldest daughter of William Falconer, also of Glasgow. From a memoir, by his son David, contributed to the pages of a periodical, to which we shall have occasion hereafter to make further allusion, we learn that John Thom, having been matriculated in the University of Glasgow, was compelled, shortly after, to exchange the congenial pursuits of the University for the bustle of the market. His activity, intelligence, integrity and business-like habits, secured for him the notice, respect and confidence of his fellow-citizens: and his local influence was manifest in the positions of social responsibility which he occupied, and the many private trusts which were eagerly pressed upon him,—trusts which were generously accepted, and conscientiously and humanely discharged. While avowing himself a follower of Jesus Christ in the Communion of the Church of Scotland, John Thom's unselfish, Christian life, afforded, to all who had the opportunity of observing his conduct, most adequate testimony to the vitality of his faith, and the power of that Christian principle by which he was actuated. Such, in few words, was the father of David Thom.

Of his mother, who, with natural endowments of a high order and considerable mental cultivation, combined a devout recognition of her responsibilities as a pious parent, David, ever reflecting her tender affection in his own breast, writes, as many as four years after her departure at an advanced age—when himself the father of a large family—"respecting his excellent, Christian, and much-endeared mother, who was born at Glasgow, Jan. 22, 1768, and finished her course at Liverpool, Dec. 6th, 1847, his feelings are still too keenly sensitive, to permit the writer to say a word more."

Guided by the worthy example of such a father, and encompassed by the solicitude of such a mother, David passed his childhood and youth.

Among his earliest reminiscences, was a circumstance which, on a very recent occasion, he made known to his family, and it is recorded, as affording an illustration of the extraordinary retentiveness of his memory. Mr. Marshall, the second husband of his great grandmother,—aged, infirm, and helpless,—was seen by little David, sitting in a corner of the apartment, and being fed with a spoon. Though he was then but *twenty months old*, an indelible impression was made. The fact then observed, must have been food for, as well as a stimulus to, subsequent reflection, and the exercise of his judgment; for the sight of an old man being treated as an infant, led to the suspicion that, after all, men must be only babies of a larger growth: and the remembrance of the fact was deepened, probably, by a consideration so subversive of the preconceptions of childhood.

On another "flat," in the same house, three weeks after the birth of David, his cousin and early companion, William Falconer, was born, to whom he bore a strong resemblance and with whom an affectionate intimacy was maintained till death removed him in February, 1861. Though like in features, they were judged to be very different in disposition by their grandmother Falconer, who, on one occasion, when they were two or three years old, summoned them to her bedside and presented each with a sugared almond. David Thom, without any hesitation, popped his into his mouth; but William Falconer, laid his in the palm of his hand, and after cautiously turning it over and over, put it down on the bed. After narrowly examining both the boys, Mrs. Falconer, addressing David's mother, observed, "Jean, take care of David, and open windows." David never forgot the strange feeling that possessed him when under the gaze of the clear, grey, hawk-like eyes of his grandmother Falconer. Yet a truer perception of his cautious nature might have spared her the dread that, if left near an open window, he might, some day, through rashness or fearlessness, throw himself out.*

To musical impressions he must have been susceptible in no ordinary degree. Music of a mournful strain affected him to tears. One Sunday, when quite a little boy, he was sitting in church, and the precentor struck up a very melancholy psalm-tune. David endured it for a few minutes; then, no longer able to restrain himself, cried out aloud, "that'll do; that'll do." His mother much shocked, tried in vain to subdue his excitement. She turned away her head in despair, and somebody led him out of church.

On attaining his sixth year, 1801, David Thom entered the English school under Mr. Banks, Glassford Street, and subsequently became a pupil in the Grammar School, Glasgow, under Mr.

* He was never known to be open to the charge of rashly or thoughtlessly exposing himself to draughts; and he was ever, summer and winter, scrupulously careful to avoid sitting in a room with an open window or even an open door; out of doors, an umbrella was invariably the symbol of his caution.

Gibson, in the class immediately succeeding that of which Lord Clyde, then Colin M'Liver, was a member.

When about eleven years old, he, and another boy four or five years his senior, were striving for the Greek prize. Other competitors had estimated their chances at zero, and the field was virtually left to these two. On the day for the distribution of prizes, a list, containing the number of times that the boys had been honourably mentioned, was put into the hands of David Thom, to be read aloud. He took it; but in reading, left out his own name each time that it occurred. This must have been suspected by the class, for, on their votes being taken, David Thom was almost unanimously chosen as worthy of the prize. Eleven-year-old voted for his competitor, but fifteen-year-old voted for himself. The censure of the master for the suppression when reading the list, was afterwards fully justified by the prizeman, who condemned himself in the strongest terms, for allowing a feeling of false pride rather than a sense of duty to actuate him in his procedure.

At this period his uncle, Mr. Falconer, was leaving Glasgow to pursue his commercial undertakings in Holland. He had decided to take his son, William, with him, there to conduct his education under his own eye; and, deeply interested in David Thom, and anxious to retain his companionship for his boy, he took steps to effect this object. A liberal education and eventual establishment in a good mercantile position, constituted a temptation against which his less wealthy brother-in-law, David's father, could hardly oppose a successful resistance. But, while acknowledging Mr. Falconer's generosity, parental affection and an honest pride asserted yet more urgent claims: his consent was withheld, and David and William were parted.

David Thom continued to pursue his studies in Glasgow; and in November, 1806, was matriculated in its university. He passed through his arts career, which lasted till 1812, under Professors Richardson, Young, Jardine, Milne, and Meikleham, with the celebrated linguist, John Reikie, as private tutor. In the Greek class of his year he was one of the *Optimates juniores*.

The choice of a Profession, at length, devolved upon him. His original destination was the Scottish Bar. The ambition of his youthful mind pointed to a judgeship. Two years were devoted to the study of Scotch law. But his father's health declining, he was deterred by circumstances from prosecuting his legal studies. With deep regret his original plans were abandoned. "God, however," he writes, "had ordered matters otherwise. Piously brought up, and piously inclined, loving the gospel of Christ so far as I knew it, I entered myself as a Student of Divinity under Professor Findlay, then 93 years of age,—Session 1812-13."

The clearness with which, at this period, it was his privilege to apprehend the nature of the gospel, and his own personal interest in it, is recorded by himself in connection with his public profession of his Christian faith. With his father, he took delight in the pulpit ministrations of Robert Balfour, D.D., an eloquent and impressive preacher, to whose public instructions as well as private friendship he ever regarded himself as lying under lasting obligations. Let David Thom tell us, in his own earnest way, the words which passed between his pastor and himself at the outset of that career which was destined to test, with unusual severity, the value of his Christian *profession*.

Balfour. "So, David, you propose taking your seat at the communion table. May I ask what is your reason for doing so? What do you believe? What is your view of Christ, and the ground of your hope towards God?"

David. "I believe that I am a sinful creature and that Jesus Christ came into the world to save sinners—even the chief. I have nothing more to say. This truth satisfies me, and speaks peace to my guilty conscience."

Balfour. "Enough. It satisfies me, too. I have no hesitation in admitting you. Upon application to ———, you will get your token."

On occasions of Dr. Balfour's absence from home, David would accompany his unsectarian father to the meetings of other religious bodies in the town, no matter how conspicuous or how obscure; and he thus became early acquainted with the views and modes of worship of a variety of sects, including Roman Catholics, Congregationalists, Baptists, Bereans, Sandemanians, and Universalists. He listened to the discourses of John Walker of Dublin, Neil Douglas, Ralph Wardlaw, and other celebrated preachers of the day.

With some uneasiness, David observed a growing partiality on the part of his father, during the last two years of his life, for Neil Douglas and his theology. His father's unhesitating avowal of the doctrine of Universal Salvation on principles similar to those advocated by Neil Douglas, (to use his own words) "sadly annoyed" him: and he adds, "I was then and for many years afterwards continued to be, a most determined opponent of this truly scriptural and spiritual doctrine." His father's end drew near. The visits of Dr. Balfour were highly valued, and the intercourse with this Christian pastor was most edifying to both father and son. We cannot do better than avail ourselves of the "Biography of John Thom" for what follows:

"Not less gratifying to my father, at this period of his life, when the shadows of evening were falling thick and deep upon him, were the frequent, sympathizing and most edifying visits of Mr. Douglas. I almost fancy that I yet behold the mild, amiable, benevolent, venerable, and Christian countenance of that most apostolic and devoted man. How shrewd and intelligent, too, the expression of his features! Disliking his leading doctrine as I did, at the time, thoroughly and conscientiously, his kind attentions to my **father were to me very annoying**......But how distressing to me to think, as I then did, that having erred from the faith himself, he was drawing my **beloved parent along with him**. No one can form any conception of the **uneasiness and anxiety of mind**, on my father's account, which **at that period of** my life I experienced. I could not but see that Mr. Thom's mind was relieved, and comforted........Strong and decided, certainly, were then my antipathies to Universalist doctrine (The Lord has forgiven me, for in ignorance they were cherished and exhibited. 1 Tim. i. 13). What so likely to arrest attention and impress, as an exhibition of marked and superior godliness, on the part of one holding and avowing **a doctrine so obnoxious to my views and feelings?** At the time, however, irritation and increased dislike, not acquiescence, was the result."......"Sunday, Oct. 16, 1814. I spent in a great measure at home in my father's company. A presentiment of his approaching dissolution I knew had for some days prior to this occupied my mother's mind, and an idea that his time on earth was not destined to be very long was, I have strong reason to suspect, not altogether a stranger to his own.......An air of peculiar solemnity seemed to all of us to hang over that Lord's day.......Besides reading several chapters of the Inspired Volume, and receiving from my father many valuable and spiritual suggestions, as to their meaning and bearing, I brought under his notice two works, with the study of which I was then occupying myself. These were Hervey's *Dialogues of Theron and Aspasio*, and Jonathan Edwards' treatise on *Original Sin*.......Briefly but very kindly, as knowing my then strong **prejudices on the subject**, he touched on the harsh and repulsive character **of some** parts of Edwards' theology, hinting at his complete inability to reconcile them with the **inspired declarations of God's Word**, considered as a whole.......The following morning, Oct. 17, an apoplectic fit, was followed by two hours of unconsciousness......." Death was in the cup. By 11 o'clock, a.m, the spirit had returned **to God who gave it**.......Such were the circumstances attending the **death of one of the most Christianly-thinking, amd Christianly-living men, whom** it has been my lot in passing through life **to know**."

 Terrible must have been felt the blow which separated John Thom from those whom he had guided by his wisdom, protected by his care, and nourished by his affection; and to none more terrible than to David, who, but for those truths which shed a radiance around the dying bed of his Christian father, would have sorrowed as those who have no hope. A hope, however, both sure and steadfast, we have seen him already rejoicing in: and, penetrating through the dim shadows of mortality and death, its object stood revealed in brighter glory.

 David was the eldest of a family of nine children.* Seven survived their father's death. Upon the eldest son devolved the

---

* David—William, **who** died a medical student, March, 1813—Jane Campbell, who fell a victim to consumption, May 23, 1822—John, **who** died in Jamaica after a residence of 34 years in that island—Margaret Corse, married to George Charles, Esq.—Christina Stewart, who died in infancy, 1805—James, whose brief but interesting career terminated at Kingston, Jamaica, May, 1824—Robert, the eminent Chinese scholar who after having rendered very considerable services to his country during our recent hostilities with the "Celestial Empire," was appointed Consul at Ningpo, March, 1844, and died there Sep. 14, 1846—and Janet Falconer, who expired at Rothesay, Isle **of Bute, Sep. 15, 1828.**

superintendence and education of the younger members of his family. This responsibility he carefully undertook; and he further charged himself with the bringing forward of his three brothers, for whom, either at home or abroad, he found situations, and in whose prosperity he never ceased to take the warmest interest, an interest which was affectionately and gratefully reciprocated by all of them.

The affectionate and reverential respect he cherished for Dr. Balfour, was the reflection of the Doctor's devoted attachment to this Christian youth. Balfour was pleased, in most kind and flattering terms, to speak of the benefit likely to accrue to the Church of Christ, from his devoting himself to the ministry.

In October, 1818, while Mr. Thom was residing with a relation* in Perthshire, his mother waited on Dr. Balfour with the view of engaging his attentions on behalf of her son. His kind remark was, "Mrs. Thom, give yourself no concern about David. It is long since I took the bringing of him forward on my own shoulders." Alluding to this circumstance, many year afterwards, Mr. Thom writes:

"The Lord, however, had determined otherwise. That very day, putting my papers in his pocket, he walked towards the College, to see my friends, Professor M'Gill, &c. Apoplexy seized him by the way in George's St. The following day he was in eternity. Need I tell you how I felt when informed of the event? I loved, I admired, I almost adored Balfour.......He knew that through my mother's ancestors, I was descended from a line of pious persons reaching back to the period of the Reformation. He knew that ancestors of my father's, had suffered for their attachment to the cause of religion, in the persecuting days of Charles and James II. (See Burns' edition of Wodrow's History, Vol. iii. concerning Robert Thom.) Circumstances like these,† drew Balfour's notice to me. And much did I profit by it. His last words to me before I went to Perthshire, still ring in my ears: "Now, David, see that you set God before you, in all your ways. I never again saw him."

We find him engaged, with unabated zeal, during the sessions 1816-17, 1817-18, 1818-19, as a student under Dr. M'Gill, in the Divinity Hall, Glasgow. His theological career was finished by his enrolling himself, (session 1819-20) in the University of Edinburgh, under Professors Ritchie and Meiklejohn.

At this period, Mr. Thom was tutor in the family of the Earl of Hopetoun. Nothing could exceed the distinguished courtesy and kindness with which he was treated. However noble the guests at Hopetoun House, the family tutor's place at table was held sacred. On one occasion, he had the honour of sharing the hospitalities of

* W. Stewart, Esq., of Ardvorlich, concerning whose family the reader may be referred for information to Sir W. Scott's *Legend of Montrose*, "Allan M'Aulay" is the pseudonym.

† Is not the perfect obliviousness of any personal attractions, by which the good Balfour's attentions might also have been won, worth a passing remark?

the noble Earl, with the present King of the Belgians; at that time, Prince Leopold.

But he was looking forward to the Christian ministry as the future and permanent sphere of his life's labours; and, dreading the effect upon his habits of his present luxurious mode of life and its incompatibility with the self-denying activities of a Christian pastor, he retired from this position after occupying it for nearly two years.

He was licensed by the Presbytery of Glasgow, July 5, 1820, and on the Lord's day following preached his first sermon for Dr. Clason, at Carmunnock. As assistant-minister (=curate in the episcopal church) several offers were made to him: that of the Rev. Robert Clason, of Logie, near Stirling, was accepted, in January, 1821, with whom he officiated in this capacity till March, 1823. Logie is one of the parishes in the Presbytery of Dunblane, and Mr. Thom was admitted Probationer or Licentiate within that Presbytery, in 1822. He was there rendered familiar with the vicinity of Dunblane, and in the church (formerly cathedral) whose walls had resounded with the voice of Archbishop Leighton, he officiated more than once for the late Dr. Grierson.

Ordination, at the hands of the Presbytery of Glasgow, he received on Wednesday, May 7, 1823; and he preached his first sermon, after the ceremony, on the following Sunday, at Ardoch, in the Presbytery of Auchterarder, when he also, for the first time, administered the rite of baptism. On Tuesday, the 13th, he attended the Presbytery of Auchterarder, by whom he was very kindly received, and a call to Ardoch was put into his hands. A month earlier, however, he had received another call.

In the early part of the year 1823, Mr. Thom was a candidate for the Oldham-street Kirk, Liverpool. The right of election was vested in the proprietors, and not in the congregation, of whom five-sixths were anxious to secure his ministrations, as successor to Dr. Barr, who had removed to Port-Glasgow. A bare majority of the thirteen proprietors, overruled the wishes of the people, by the election of another candidate. And it was the provocation given to the congregation by this act, that led to the withdrawal of a large portion of their number, and to their constituting themselves a new society, over which Mr. Thom was subsequently invited to preside. The call was given and accepted.

To a mind constituted like that of David Thom, Liverpool must have presented special attractions. Here the sphere of his usefulness would be most ample. The pulse of its general activity seemed to beat responsively to his own restless energy. Forty years ago, the town, like himself, might be said to have attained its majority, and to have further so far developed its resources, as to prove its capabilities and justify the largest expectations. As regards the town and port of Liverpool, the largest anticipations have been more than realized. Of David Thom, no mean estimate was formed, by those who had invited him to settle among them; and, by his adherents, bright and important results to the Church of God were predicted of the career upon which he was now entering. The natural susceptibility of his warm affections, vibrated in free and generous reciprocity to the thoroughly hearty invitations of the young Christian community; and among them, as the flock over whom he was to watch, his love was without dissimulation.

From the Music Hall, Bold Street, then temporarily occupied for worship, the congregation looked forward to the erection of a kirk, which, while worthily representing the Church of Scotland in Liverpool, should also express their confidence in and attachment to their newly-elected minister, and their conviction of the growing requirements of their fellowship under his ministrations. The fulfilment or frustration of their sanguine anticipations, will be decided, at the present day, according to the point of view from which their minister's career is regarded. The signal failure of David Thom's master, was obvious enough to the rulers of the Jews, when, before the door of his sepulchre, they had rolled their obstructive stone and set their watch,—the consummation and crowning act of their triumphant opposition; and even the hasty and desponding conclusion of his grieving and bewildered disciples found utterance in the exclamation: "we trusted that this had been He which should have redeemed Israel," &c. Enough is it that the servant should be as his lord. Outward and visible success, is not exactly conclusive evidence of the progress of a kingdom which cometh not with observation; and, to adopt the tone of orthodox uncertainty, we will only say, *it may be* that the thoughts upon which he lived, and to the defence of which he devoted his powers, though apparently dead and buried, will rise again and live for ever.

Of this there can be no question, that the purpose with which, at the age of twenty-eight years, he commenced his career in Liverpool, was to spend and be spent in the service of him, in whose cross he gloried and to whose claims he yielded supreme allegiance; satisfied that, whatever the course of his personal history might be, God would be glorified.

Little, doubtless, did he or others conceive the way in which this was to be accomplished! He duly entered upon the discharge of his ministerial functions, according to the rites and usages of the Church of Scotland, March 23rd, 1823,* and assisted Rear-admiral Murray, in laying the foundation stone of Rodney-street Kirk, June 17th following,† as little conscious of any divergence in

---

* A paper contributed to the *Historic Society of Lancashire and Cheshire*, 1850, on the "Scotch Kirks and Congregations of Liverpool," and printed in their *Transactions*, contains a clear outline of his early connection with Liverpool, and the events to which we shall have occasion presently to allude.

† From the *Liverpool Saturday Advertiser* of June 21st, 1823, which contains an account of the ceremony, we get a glimpse of the young minister taking his part on the occasion. The reporter says, "with his gown on, I saw him descend

his doctrinal creed from the Confession of the Westminster Assembly, as at any former period of his theological course.

His custom was, and continued to be to the end of his ministry, to expound the psalms which were read and sung in the church. This somewhat unusual course, drew attention to the still more unusual principle of their interpretation. It was not long before the soundness of his comments on this portion of the Word of God, and the orthodoxy of other points of his theology, began to be called in question. Nothing, however, but the application to the whole of the Psalms and the Books of the Prophets, of the hint given by Christ himself in Luke xxiv. 44, and thorough out-and-out Calvinism, unflinchingly held, and boldly and consistently proclaimed, seem—strange to say—to have been the means of arousing this suspicion of heresy in the minds of certain individuals who were really much more open to the charge than himself. So far had "*modern* Calvinism" fallen from its early integrity!

A small party was formed, largely tinged with the proprietory leaven, whose object was, *per fas aut per nefas*, to eject the obnoxious minister from his office. The majority of the congregation acknowledged the profit they derived from the instructive ministry they enjoyed, and encouraged their pastor in his disregard of the unscrupulous means resorted to, to induce his early resignation.

We have neither space nor inclination to record all the petty artifices contrived to annoy, to irritate, and to render Mr Thom's position intolerable. These proceedings were adopted at the instigation, almost exclusively, of one individual, who was as importunate as any of Mr. Thom's warmest friends, in urging his decision in favour of Liverpool. Yet neither in his own apprehension, nor traceable in his preaching, was there up to this time any departure from those doctrines which, from the first, he had avowed.

At length, a scheme was devised and announced, and, during several months, was discussed, having for its *ostensible* object the entire cessation of hostility and the restoration of harmony; but which was really nothing more nor less than a piece of generalship we

into the fosse....I understood he was to address the people....He has certainly high oratorical talent, and a ready command of language; but what I most admired was his ardent and impassioned manner. Feeling strongly himself, he impresses strongly all who hear him, and carries them with him like an overflowing torrent. I noticed a servant maid, on the opposite side of the street, busy rubbing the glass of a window. As the speaker proceeded, she gradually rubbed slower and slower, till at length her hand fell by her side, and she seemed absorbed in attention. This is, after all, the chief excellence of oratory.... Mr. Thom seems diffuse, however, but it may not be fair to criticise in this case too strictly, as I was told he declared it was entirely extempore: but certainly the principal fault of all the Scottish clergy that I have heard is want of condensation. I was pleased to see the attention with which he was heard by the crowd around, though composed of all ranks and ages. The prayer with which the ceremony closed was admirable, and came evidently from the heart of the speaker...His features are very flexible and assume those indications of the internal and passing feelings, which, however natural, do not appear to me sufficiently solemn, when we address the Almighty; at least to think it so, we would require to be more habituated to it."

do not wish to characterize. While his opponents proposed the obtrusion, upon the minister and congregation, of an "assistant" (!) pastor, *by way of compromise and for the sake of peace*,—an arrangement to which Mr. Thom was induced to become a consenting party,—they were, all the while, secretly in active communication with the Solicitor General, prosecuting their determined purpose to eject their minister from his position. It was soon seen that this assistant-minister scheme—this olive-branch of peace, was really intended to be employed as a wedge to be driven in, so as to widen the split to the full extent of entire separation!

During the progress of the negociation which resulted in the adoption of this arrangement, the building of the new Rodney-street Kirk approached completion, and it was finally decided that its opening should be simultaneous with the induction of the second minister.

"On Sunday, the 5th day of December, 1824, two days subsequent to the formal opening of the Kirk, three discourses were delivered within its walls. One by Edward Irving in the forenoon; one by the writer [Mr Thom] in the afternoon,* and one by Mr Wilson [the colleague] in the evening. The writer was at the time, regarded by many in the light of a heretic. Placed, therefore, he was, to use Lord Ellenborough's well-known simile, 'like a wild elephant between two tame ones.'"†

Much ill-feeling, and many grievous words, doubtless, grew out of this unhappy state of things; and strong views were taken and strong language was employed, on either side. A considerable amount of correspondence, documents, pamphlets, as well as petition and counter-petition, were published at the time; and to these we must refer the reader who wishes to see a fuller account of the dispute.

Where *truth* was concerned Mr. Thom evinced no disposition to adopt a temporizing policy. Indicated, by his conceding the appointment of a second minister, might the *sauviter in modo*, on his part, be; but equally established in the minds of all who heard him maintain his characteristic doctrines, was the *fortiter in re* a decidedly-prominent trait.

The seeds of discontent, which had been sown broadcast, had sprung up; and, had so far arrived at maturity, in the spring time of the year 1825, as to blossom forth in not fewer than nine charges of heresy! These were preferred before the Presbytery of Glasgow. In addition, his opponents had published appeals against their minister, intended to bias the minds of the public and of the Presbytery. Long had Mr. Thom refrained from any public and direct allusion to these proceedings, and any motive but the true one was assigned to his silence. At length a pamphlet of sixty-

* "His text on the occasion was Acts vii. 48—Howbeit the most High dwelleth not in temples made with hands."

† *On the Scotch Kirks and Congregations of Liverpool.* By David Thom, D.D., Ph.D.

two pages* shews that he thinks "there is a time to speak." In this *brochure* he reviews the field of the controversy generally, detects and exposes the character of his opponents, and examines, *seriatim*, their nine charges.

Our space is perplexingly narrow: yet we feel compelled, by the importance of this crisis in Mr. Thom's history, to give the charges *entire*; and although to his perspicuous and condensed reply, justice can scarcely be done without also embodying it *in extenso* enough, we hope, is here extracted to make intelligible to the reader the position assumed by the accused with reference to the charges of his accusers.

ACCUSER.

I.—"That the ordinary means of grace, such as prayer, attending on the public or private worship of God, and the other ordinances of our blessed religion, are of no manner of use to the unconverted; but that on the contrary, God not being found of those who seek him, but of those who seek him not; attending on such means of grace, with a view to benefit in religion, is worse than useless to the sinner; and that it will be to the condemnation of men, that they attempt to work out their own salvation, or to strive to enter into the kingdom of Heaven."

II.—"That assurance is of the essence of faith; or, that no one can by any possibility possess faith, in any degree, without also possessing a full and complete assurance; and that whosoever is not thus perfectly certain of salvation, has the best possible evidence that he is not at all converted to the faith of the Gospel."

III.—"That there are two natures in the believer: one of which (which he calls the old or natural man) makes no progress whatever in divine life, but remains till death in original corruption; while the other, (or the new man, as he denominates it,) being implanted by Christ, and continuing united to him, advances to glory in the heavenly kingdom, in constant opposition, however, to, and in contention with, the old man, until dissolution: but that in the unbeliever there is only one nature; to wit, the old or natural man."

ACCUSED.

I.—Charge divided into three parts. First and third—"Gross falsehoods." Of the second, "preventing or irresistible grace," he says, "I am happy to think that I coincide with the Westminster Confession of Faith and every other Calvinistic system of divinity yet published... It is not by the use of these Means of Grace, but by the atonement of Christ, revealed in and applied by them, that the sinner is saved. Scriptures *passim*. Conf. of Faith, chap. xvi. sec. 5.

II.—"A misrepresentation of my views on the subject.... All faith is in itself simply the assent of the understanding made known upon testimony." "Divine faith is assent upon a divine testimony... Wherever this faith exists the individual is conscious of it:" yet "not conscious of it when the object is not present to the mind. Though I admit all this—not so ignorant of the first principles of metaphysics as to maintain that faith in a testimony and the speculations of our minds upon that faith, are one and the same thing."

III.—"I am inclined to admit this charge almost in the very words in which it is stated... It is an accusation that I preach the doctrines and even the very words of Scripture. Rom. vii. 25, Gal. v. 17. Conf. of Faith, chap. vi. 4. 5... I also hold and preach, that that old nature is more and more controlled, mortified, and crucified, by the means of increasing strength, and larger measures of grace, imparted to the believer. Of the benefit of this latter view it is evidently the intention of my adversaries to deprive me, from the ambiguous language which they employ, about the beginning of the charge."

* *Remarks by the Rev. David Thom, Minister of the Scotch Church, Rodney Street, Liverpool, on a series of charges recently preferred against him before the Reverend the Presbytery of Glasgow, by certain individuals connected with the management of the said Church.* Liverpool, 1825.

IV.—"That no evil done in the body, however enormous in its nature, can in any way affect the salvation of him who believes; and that nothing in the life or conversation of men, is any evidence of the divine life within."

IV.—"The former part of this charge is neither more nor less than a distorted view of the doctrine of the Perseverance of the Saints, which along with the Church of Scotland I hold. Confession of Faith, chap. v. §5, is quoted. No sin from the commission of which the Christian is secured without watchfulness and prayer; no sin whatever under the dominion of which he can be brought. The old nature which he carries about with him exposes him to sin, the new nature abiding in him 'prevents his becoming its slave." Latter part of this charge—"a gross falsehood. I know no other proof of the reality or sincerity of a man's faith but the fruits which it produces. At the same time, having discovered from Scripture that there is all the difference in the world between the *works of the flesh*, and *the fruit of the Spirit*, I believe and preach, nay, I will continue to preach, that the former, however much they may be disguised, and however much in that state they may pass current with *certain professors*, as the genuine results of faith, are in truth no evidence at all of a man's Christianity. Herein, I suspect, consists the head and front of my offending.

V.—"That the epistles of the New Testament are addressed to the elect or invisible Church only, and that none other can consider himself as having anything to do with them."

V.—Indebted "for this view of the subject to one of the most eminent divines of our National Church, the late Dr. Erskine, of Edinburgh...Confirmed in this opinion by observing titles, and considering subject matter, of the epistles themselves. Conf. of Faith not dogmatic but favours the idea."

VI.—"That the invitations of the Gospel are not addressed to all men, but to the elect only; and that others have not the Gospel addressed to them in any other sense, than as hearing it preached to the elect; and, that the Gospel itself is not the cause of making men Christians, but that they being made so from all eternity, the Gospel manifests and brings them forth from the world."

VI.—"That none have been, are, or shall be called to the knowledge and belief of the truth except the elect, I do confess and maintain. But if, as I conceive it to be, it is the intention of the framers of this charge to represent me as denying, that all to whose ears the gospel comes are commanded to believe it, and that those who reject it do so to their more aggravated condemnation, then I beg leave to state, that their insinuation is grossly and notoriously false."

VII.—"That the fact of opposition and division prevailing in congregations and families, is the best proof that the Gospel is making progress among a people."

VII.—"That I have made an observation similar to that contained in this charge, and founded upon passages similar to Matthew x. 34, I at once freely admit. But what I have to complain of is the abominable want of candour displayed in the manner of stating this charge ... I never meant to represent dissentions and strifes as matters in themselves desirable, which is evidently here insinuated, but on the contrary have uniformly characterised them as being among the worst fruits of the flesh, and as being dispositions

VIII.—"That no preparation whatever is necessary in the believer, towards worthily partaking of the Lord's supper."

IX.—"That the Psalms are all of them addressed either by the Saviour for himself, or by him for and with or in the name of his Church, to his and their heavenly Father, or by the Church to the Saviour himself; and, by consequence, that when the speaker is represented as praying to be kept from secret sins, from presumptuous sins, from the sins of his youth, it is Christ and the invisible Church who are thus petitioning God; and that when the speaker says, he was conceived in sin and shapen in iniquity, it is Christ who describes himself thus, with the imputed sins of the elect laid to his charge."

cherished and exhibited, not by believers towards their unbelieving friends and connections, but by their unbelieving friends and connections towards them."

VIII.—"This charge as it stands is flatly denied. That I consider certain legal and self-righteous observances frequently represented as suitable preparations for the Lord's supper, not to be so, is granted, but surely there is a vast difference between such a view of matters, and the uncandid sweeping assertion upon which I am now commenting." This is followed by an examination of 1 Cor. xi. 28.

IX.—"That I regard the Saviour as the chief, although not the exclusive speaker in the Psalms, or rather, that I consider the inspired writer, in that interesting portion of scripture, to treat principally of *the sufferings of Christ, and of the glory that should follow,*[*] is if matter of accusation, one that I admit, and triumph in. Convinced as I am, *that the testimony of Jesus is the spirit of prophecy,*[†] and that to him and his glorious work of mediation the psalms, especially, bear witness; I should ill satisfy my own conscience, and ill discharge my duty to my people, were I to keep back from them any part, and especially so important a part as this, of the *counsel of God*... But lest I should be mistaken, let me observe, that the ninth charge is, as it stands, to a certain degree a misrepresentation of my sentiments on the point in question, and that although I hold the general principle of Christ being the chief personage treated of, exhibited, and speaking in the Psalms, it never was my intention to separate him for a single moment from his people, who constitute one mystical body with him,[‡] and who, being possessed of and united to him by his spirit, can, in a subordinate sense, in certain respects, use his language and lay claim to his experience;—nor to justify every expression or every idea which I may have employed in illustrating this portion of Scripture."

Fragmentary the quotations we have made from the replies of the accused necessarily are; enough, perhaps, is adduced to indicate the theological phasis of his mind at this period. That there was no special pleading,—no idea of quibbling, on his part, let the following extract from a letter to a friend bear witness:

"My dear M——," "July 26, 1824."

"I rejoice to think that my intentions, in regard to my opponents,

"[*] 1 Pet. i. 11. [†] Rev. xix. 10. [‡] See 1 Cor. xii. 12, downwards."

meet with your approbation.—Indeed, the conviction of the propriety of the step is growing more and more upon me. I see it to be a glorious opportunity, put into my power, of contending for the faith once delivered to the saints, and that, as you properly and scripturally remark, in the *spirit of meekness*. Indeed my intention is to make my answer, as little as possible a personal matter; and principally to take the objections of my adversaries, as occasions of stating, and enforcing the opposite truths. Never was a work of this kind, *so much called for*, as at the present day, when mixtures of the Gospel, and poisonous untruths, are dealt out largely from our pulpits—under the influence of some of which you yourself are evidently labouring; and although feeble the instrument employed for this purpose, the consolation and ground of support is, that the work is the Lord's,—that it is *not by power, nor by might, but by His Spirit, as the Lord of Hosts hath said*. I know well I shall have your prayers, and the prayers of many of God's people for a blessing upon the undertaking. It is growing I find upon my hands; for I must not content myself with refuting untruths, the opposite truths must be *clearly* and *scripturally* stated and enforced."

"I regret much, that you should have suffered so on my account. Do leave me to fight my own way in future, or rather leave the Lord to fight for me. He is doing so wondrously. It is his own cause that I am engaged in, and I therefore throw myself upon him to rescue me from the assults of all my enemies—professing and profane,—and to make all their assaults work together for my good, and for his glory. If I were not assailed in this way, where were the proof of my preaching the same truths which my dear redeemer and his apostles did?"

"Oh! my dear M—, learn more and more to think for yourself, to see with your own eyes, and judge with your own mind. A deference to the opinions of those who have obtained a name in what is called the Religious World, is one of the grand errors of this professing age.—I mean, such a deference in religious matters, as almost entirely excludes the exercise of our own judgment. To the law and to the testimony with all these. The Bible, and not human opinions, is to be the guide of my conduct, and rule of my opinions, both with regard to doctrines and professors."

"My mode of preaching, with however many defects it may be attended, is, I know, doing good. The man who, from the pulpit, proclaims a lie—that the death of Christ is a sufficient atonement for all—need not be surprised if the great bulk of his audience are lulled into carnal security, or turn out notorious hypocrites. But when I proclaim what is the truth—that our blessed Lord laid down his life only for his own people—how often has this been blessed, not merely to the awakening of the careless, but to plant a dart in the breast of the formal professor. Alarm is excited; Am I, or am I not, one of the goodly number of the redeemed?—is the question, which many a soul, alarmed, is induced to put to itself. Many pious ministers complain that this is a day of small things. But why is it so? Why, because they keep back part of the counsel of God. They prudently, (as if forsooth they could be wiser than God), suppress the doctrine of election, although running through the Bible, and do not inform their hearers of the distinction between the *old* and *new natures*, nor the operations of both, although distress of mind and hypocrisy must be the result of not knowing this, and yet they cry out, that souls are not——! Fie upon this kind of work! Ignorant they are that the fruit produced is the natural result of the seed sown. Of course all natural characters, and carnal and inexperienced professors will be against me

in this opinion, although that is to me but one confirmation of its truth. Their praise would make me suspect the truth even of my present sentiments. *The natural man receiveth not*, etc.—you know the rest."
"I am, Yours, etc."
"D. THOM."

The following, also, to the same friend, from a characteristic and suggestive letter, written a few days earlier, discloses the principle of his action towards offenders:

"You do not consider my Protest written in altogether a Christian temper and spirit. Perhaps not. But alas, how difficult, amidst the goadings of the ungodly, to act up to our profession, and how much better, with that candour, which is essential to the Christian character, to stigmatise villainy by its right name, at the same time that we forgive the man who is chargeable with it, than in the spirit of the world, too much copied by professors, to affect a calmness, and express an esteem, to which the heart is a stranger. I certainly have no wish to extenuate what is wrong. May my Divine Master vouchsafe to me more and more of His Spirit and enable me to contend for the faith once delivered to the saints, in a manner more and more becoming the meekness and mildness of the Christian character. At the present day many professors seem to consider, that no believer is to show that he regards himself as ill-used; most cheerfully would I subscribe to this maxim, could a sense of ill-usage likewise be banished from the mind; but I would rather charge the transgressor with his crime, forgive him, and pray for him, than under the externals of forgiveness, cherish a rancorous hatred towards him."
"I am, My dear M——, Yours, etc."
"D. THOM."

Obvious is it, to all who are acquainted with the progress of his mind, that the changes which subsequently took place, were substantially, rather of the nature of *development* than of *contradiction*. He did not lay one system of theology aside to take up another. If we find certain views superseded, it is only because others have been superinduced. Trace backward from any ulterior position attained, through any intermediate stage, to the earliest postulates of his faith, and, though the road seems to grow *narrower* it is not found to be *tortuous*: by-ways attempted and forsaken do not perplex your explorations, but you proceed in a straight line to those initial and essential truths which lay deep in the foundations of his theology. The kind of change which his mind underwent was, therefore, most properly regarded by himself, and by those who could fairly estimate his character, as of the nature of *expansion* and *enlargement*. What he relinquished as untrue, was *negative*; what he adopted by successive accretions, was *positive* in its nature.

But to resume our narrative. Early in June, 1825, Mr. Thom appeared at the bar of the Presbytery of Glasgow, when a Commission was appointed to sit in Liverpool, to take evidence. The examination of witnesses occupied several weeks. The evidence was published by Mr. Gillies. The *Memorial submitted by the Rev. David Thom to the Presbytery of Glasgow*, first published in August, passed through two editions. This consists of a series of theses on, 1, The Means of Grace; 2, Faith; 3, Repentance; 4, The Two Natures; 5, The Perseverance of the Saints; 6, The Evidence of of Faith: and extends to 29 pages, in which more formally and fully than in the former pamphlet, these theological questions are discussed.

The case was heard in the Tron Church, Glasgow. Advocates: for the accusers, Sir James Moncrieff; and, for the accused, Mr. John Jardine. The proceedings of this day extended, without intermission, over eight hours. The following is from a letter written in the evening of the same day, immediately after adjournment from the church:

"Mr. Moncrieff opened the business, and made a speech from three to four hours length; it was in my opinion as poor as the case deserved. Mr. Jardine then made a powerful and eloquent appeal before he went over the evidence, which was no easy task, but done very well. Mr. Moncrieff replied, and then Mr. Thom, fifteen minutes before seven, was allowed to speak. Upwards of 1000 persons must have been present, and I never saw such anxiety and attention manifested as when Mr. Thom rose. Of course I am a partial witness in the case, but I must say, that such an appeal, so powerfully made, so impressively and so beautifully delivered, was, even to me, who am not blind to Mr. Thom's talents, quite unexpected'

The Sentence was followed by an "Admonition of the Presbytery, through their Moderator, the Rev. James Marshall," in which the condemned heretic is, with a kindness which is quite cutting, thus addressed: "some members [of the Presbytery] whose theological attainments are of a very high order, and who *were decidedly partial towards you*, characterized these heresies as damnable." And the immoderate assumption, the arrogance, the implied infallibility of the anathematizing moderator,—all unconsciously to himself, perhaps,—consigning this "teacher of erroneous opinions," and those who listen to him, to "death and everlasting destruction," will be, hereafter, one of the many historical curiosities of the Church of Scotland in the nineteenth century.

Thus writes Mr. Thom, in review of the Sentence of the Presbytery, some years after the event (1842), in the appendix to his *Divine Inversion:*

"Sentence was pronounced at Glasgow, on the 22d. day of September, 1825. On the afternoon of that day, the great majority of my judges, the members of Presbytery, after having walked in procession to the spot, assisted at the laying of the foundation-stone of a monument to John Knox, the Scottish Reformer. In so doing, they professed in the afternoon their wish to heap honours upon the memory of a man, some of the most precious divine truths proclaimed and contended for by whom,— divine truths which God had seen meet eminently to bless,—they had in the morning, in my person, been engaged in condemning! It having happened further, curiously enough, that the man whom they were thus assembled to honour had been the subject of condemnation by the hierarchy of his time! Having addressed the Presbytery, after sentence had been pronounced by their moderator,—himself, by the way, now separated from the Scottish establishment,—I could not help alluding to the striking coincidence between the procedure of my ecclesiastical judges, in condemning in me what they professed to approve of in Knox, and that of the Pharisees, the pious portion of the Jewish people, in *building the tombs of the prophets, and garnishing the sepulchres of the righteous,* whom their fathers had persecuted and slain, while they were themselves ready to imbrue their hands in the blood of the Lord of Glory and his followers, for maintaining nothing else but what Moses in the law, and the very prophets whom they professed to honour, had written. Matt. xxiii. 29—32. See also, Acts vii. 51—53."

"The Presbytery of Glasgow, in 1825, saw meet to condemn the following among other divine doctrines held by me: (their condemnation of myself personally as a heretic was a matter of little consequence, and one which scarcely gave me a moment's concern)—1st. The perfect unconditionality of eternal life. Rom. vi. 23.—2dly. The sovereignty of Jehovah in the choice of the members of his church, and in the use of the means of conferring the knowledge of himself upon them; or rather, that it is as used by him, not by creatures, that prayer, reading the scriptures, attending on ordinances, &c., become means of salvation. Rom. ix. 15. 16.—3dly. The certainty of eternal life being involved in faith, and being the privilege of all members of the church. Gal. iv. 6.—4thly. The Christian's love to God not being in any respect the cause of God's love to him, but being always and necessarily an effect of the knowledge of the love borne by God eternally towards him. 1 John iv. 19.—5thly. The enmity essentially subsisting between human nature and the divine nature. Matt. x. 34. Gal. v. 17.—6thly. The fact of Jesus being the subject-matter of prophecy, Rev. xix. 10, especially of the book of Psalms. Luke xxiv. 44."

And now, happily released from the fetters of a "worldly establishment," and from the unedifying struggle and turmoil of Rodney-street kirk, we by no means find him looking like an outcast, or as one defeated. On Sunday, Oct. 2nd, 1825, (a few days only after the sentence of condemnation), he lifts up his voice again in the Music Hall, Bold street, his countenance wearing even more than its wonted animation; and his preaching of Christ, no longer stamped with the dignity of ecclesiastical sanctions, lacks none of its wonted power, *for he still speaks as one having authority and not as the scribes.* Whether the restraints and temptations which "subscription" imposes on the clerical mind would have operated to any great extent in retarding his growing perception and acknowledgment of divine truth, we are not called upon to determine; certain it is, however, that what God, in the course of his good providence, now did for him, through the instrumentality of the heads of a "worldly establishment," subserved the highest purposes in connection with his spiritual progress. The eaglet must be stirred and turned out of the nest, ere it discover the freedom of its nature, the range of its penetrating eye, and the heavenward destiny of its pinions. Once out of the eyrie, it must fly or fall! That the bird is on the wing, the following extract from a letter will show:

"My dear M——,"   "Nov. 2nd, 1825."

"The Lord has for some time past been opening up my mind most wonderfully to the reception of divine truth, and even within the last fortnight many points have been cleared up to me which were formerly dark and obscure. I am now particularly satisfied that I erred when I supposed with Calvinists that Christ only died for the sins of his own chosen people, and that on the contrary, he actually died, as the apostle John expresses it, for the sins of the whole world. I do not mean to say that he died to bring the whole world to glory, for the Scripture nowhere says so; but that he died to sweep away all the transgressions of the first covenant, or those committed against the law of "do and live," and that now, under the second covenant, salvation is connected with the belief of this truth, and damnation with the unbelief of it. Hebrews ix. 15, completely expresses my meaning on the subject. There is no sin under the present, or second covenant, unatoned for, but unbelief. The penalty of the first covenant, I see to have been temporal death, which, as a divine threatening, of course has been, and will be, fully executed; as the penalty of the second covenant I see to be eternal death, or an eternal exclusion from the presence and favour of God, and I see that this will be executed upon all who die ignorant and unbelieving. No man, at the last day, I perceive, will be acquitted for his good deeds, or condemned for his evil deeds; but at the same time every man shall be tried and judged according to his works. The righteous shall be acquitted on the ground of faith, the wicked condemned on the ground of unbelief; and yet the good works of the one shall be brought forward as the evidence of their faith, and the evil works of the other as the evidence of their unbelief."

"What do you think of this view? I bless the Lord for having brought me to see more of his truth. Never shall I forget the ecstasy with which I went to bed after having had the fact of the complete atonement for sin through Christ, revealed to me. Bless the Lord, oh, my soul! I am not now puzzled by the Sandemanians, those devilishly acute men, who used to enquire, how is it that your believing makes that true which was not true before? How is it that Christ comes to have died for your sins when you believe, and not before? I now perceive that when I come to believe the atonement, I believe that which was true, whether I believed it or not."   "I am, &c. D. Thom."

Deeply solicitous to let slip no opportunity which presented itself for the exhibition of those truths which were either denied or perverted by the professing Church, we find him, in June, 1827, in a pamphlet of 64 pages, entitled "A letter to the Rev. Richard Pope adverting to some important mistakes committed by him, in his recent Controversy with the Rev. Thomas Maguire,"—pointing out the weak because false position constantly assumed by Protestants in the Romish controversy. He maintains, by most lucid statements, 1. "*The Infallibility of the Church,*" as the result of *divine* teaching, against Mr. Pope's concessions,—concessions which amount to an admission, on the part of all Protestants who make them, of the essential infidelity of their minds. 2. "*The sufficiency of Scripture,*" as against the protestant Mr. Pope's advocacy of "notes and comments," and the implied necessity of proofs by human testimony of that Revelation of God, which, as divine, neither requires nor admits of them. And, 3. "*The Unity of the Church*," based upon the fact embodied in the simple confession of St. Peter, and "not in a *partial agreement* as to a number of *debated* and *debatable points*," oddly enough christened by Churches —"*creeds*." The direct, succinct, and lucid statements of this letter, lose none of their force through their connection with the particular occasion which called it forth, and will amply repay perusal.

In April, 1828, a new and commodious chapel was opened in Bold street, to which, with their minister, the congregation removed from the Music Hall, till this time temporarily occupied for worship.

Between 1826 and March, 1828, when Mr. Thom published the first edition of his "*Three Questions proposed and answered*," the thoroughly unscriptural character of all visible churches since the days of the apostles had attracted his attention. The *Three Questions* discovers the extent to which his mind had opened on several other most important points.

"The forfeiture of the paradisiacal state of Adam leading not to its restoration through Christ but to the introduction and establishment of a state of things infinitely superior—the immortality of man, not as a being descended from Adam, but as one with him who is *the Lord from heaven*—and everlasting punishment as consisting not in the everlasting perpetuation of sin or death, according to the respective theories of everlasting torments or annihilation, but in the complete and everlasting supersession of sinful and dying human nature, through the death and resurrection of Christ by the righteous and ever-living nature of God, are the grand, all-important, self-consistent, and scripturally-revealed doctrines which constitute the staple of this work; and are, from the beginning to the end of it, with such ability as God hath seen meet to bestow, strenuously and uncompromisingly insisted on and maintained."*

The book had not been out many days before Mr. Thom was honoured with the following letter from the Moderator of the Presbytery of Glasgow.

"SIR,—A pamphlet being circulated in this city bearing as its title 'Three Questions Proposed and Answered, concerning The Life Forfeited by Adam, The Resurrection of the Dead, and Eternal Punishment,' to which your name is attached as author of said pamphlet,—I am appointed by a committee specially appointed for considering the measures which ought to be adopted by the Presbytery, in relation to the tenets avowed in the answers attached to the above questions, to request you to say whether you avow yourself to be the author, as stated in the title.

"I write this accordingly in their name, expecting your answer."

"Glasgow, 14th April, 1828."

Mr. Thom replies. He points out the unconstitutional form in

---

* See "advertisement" to third edition of the "Three Questions," which, although published twenty years after the first, is, in the fundamental doctrines maintained, essentially the same work.

which the demand is made, but waiving all his claims founded upon Scottish jurisprudence, he says:

"I beg leave to observe, that I except to your authority and decline your jurisdiction upon much higher and far different principles. Do not misunderstand me. I am not going to annoy you with the 'thrice-told tale' of independency, or to read you a lecture upon what appear to me various unscriptural modes of Church Government, ranking yours, of course, among the number. I have just to say, that I object to all and every species of Church Government (as it is called) whatever, because I regard all believers of the Gospel as standing upon a footing of perfect equality and independency, in their character of *kings and priests unto God*, and consequently to inform the Presbytery, that I view them in no other light than as an assembly of respectable and learned individuals, whom the laws of the country have invested with certain secular privileges and immunities. You will have the goodness, therefore, to excuse me if I decline answering your question, lest by so doing I should even appear to acknowledge your authority, but as it is not by fear, contempt, or any other unworthy motive that I am actuated in this refusal, I beg leave to add, that if you or any other member of the Presbytery, shall feel inclined to address to me a letter written in your private and individual capacity, and reiterating the question contained in your official one, you may reckon upon a direct, immediate, and satisfactory answer."

He then proceeds, in his characteristically-vigorous style, to discuss those higher grounds upon which he acts.

Having hinted at the persecution to which he had been subjected, and from the charge of which he by no means relieves the learned Presbytery, he concludes his letter thus:

"As a small testimony of my respect for many of the individuals composing your body, as well as a proof that my views, in regard to the glorious doctrine of *the assurance of faith* remain unchanged, I intend soon, God willing, dedicating to you a little treatise on that subject."

"And now, Gentlemen, in sorrow, not in anger, I take my leave of you. May the Lord enable you to receive in good part, and profit by the hints which I have given you. You will of course understand, that the import of this letter is to intimate to you, that my connection with you *as a body* is henceforward at an end."

"Requesting you to accept personally of the assurance of my high and undiminished respect," "I am, SIR, Your most obedient servant,"
To the Rev. *John Lockhart, D.D.*, "D. THOM."
Moderator of the Presbytery of Glasgow.

The case was now referred by the Presbytery to the General Assembly of the Church of Scotland, before whom he was required to make his appearance. Having already duly and respectfully intimated his withdrawal from all connection with the Scotch established church, he, of course, took no notice of the Presbytery's reference.

"The second sentence was, therefore, pronounced in absence [June 2nd 1828]. 'John Lee,' who subscribes it, is the present [1842] able and learned Principal of the University of Edinburgh. To what precedes, it may be added, that, in both cases, on doctrinal grounds alone was the author assailed; and that, as, in the former case, his *status* as a minister and preacher of the Scottish Establishment, was not meddled with at all; so, in the latter, he was not formally deposed from office of the ministry, but only subjected to suspension, *sine die*, from the exercise of its functions, in connection with the body. Under the same sentence, for the same reason, namely, of alleged contumacy, every Free-kirk minister labours."

The conclusion at which, from the study of the sacred writings, he had now arrived was such, as, while leaving quite untouched the leading doctrines for which he had hitherto contended, rendered possible one of two fates to the bulk of the human race. Of these destinies, the truth of neither one nor the other had as yet presented itself with any conclusive evidence to his apprehension. "I am very far from pretending," he says,† "to understand every part of the sacred writings or to be able to explain all their difficulties. Indeed, the utmost length to which, in many cases, I can go, is to perceive what a text does not signify, without being able to see clearly and positively what its signification really is." With reference to the momentous and profoundly-interesting question now introduced to our notice, the doctrine of creature immortality and the dependant dogma of eternal torments were abandoned by Mr. Thom, and he frankly acknowledges his want of satisfaction on these points in the following passage:

"In regard, then, to the subject of the resurrection and immortality of unbelievers in a future state of existence, I desire to imitate the conduct of the inspired writers, in the silence which they have seen meet to observe. Of *this* I am satisfied, that all to whom the divine character is manifested here, live eternally hereafter, for *the knowledge of God, and of Jesus Christ whom he has sent, is eternal life,* John xvii. 3, 1 John v. 20. That I may not, however, expose myself to the charge of exhibiting any want of candour, I allow that one of two consequences, obviously and necessarily results from the views maintained in this work, either that the unbelieving have no interest at all in the resurrection and enjoyment of immortality, or that they rise again and inherit eternal life, in virtue of power received from the Lord Jesus, and as possessed of his nature, on the same footing with the righteous. Which of these two consequences is correct, I again repeat, I know not, but in whatever way the matter may be decided, I cannot perceive that it has the slightest tendency to affect the strength and solidity of the preceding arguments."

While thus committed to neither conclusion, and on the assumption that the scriptures were silent, Mr. Thom was content to postpone any attempt at a solution of the problem to the disclosures of eternity. As a coadjutor, the advocates of two systems— respectively denominated Annihilationists and Universalists—were disposed to claim him.

It was not long before certain religious bodies in the United States were aroused to inquiry respecting a work so startling to the orthodoxy of all sections of the religious community in Britain. The first American notice appeared in the *Trumpet*, (Boston, U.S.) edited by Whittemore, the following year, 1829. Subsequent

† *Three Questions*, FIRST Edit. p. 84. 1828.

notices and criticisms of the author and his works, by American reviews, were frequent and sometimes of considerable length. They appeared chiefly in the Universalist papers, but several were from the Unitarians, some of them long, searching, and valuable, and not a few from the "*Tribune*," New York, and other influential periodicals.

Continuing his regular pulpit ministrations, Sunday after Sunday, and the assiduous discharge of the laborious functions of an earnest and conscientious Christian pastor, and engaged in an ever-increasing correspondence, arising, to a great extent, out of the publication of his religious views,* Mr. Thom might be supposed to have little leisure for any thing else; but during this period, and prior to 1833, we find him "devoting much time," as he says in a recent letter to a friend,

"to an examination of the two following topics; viz. 'the difference between the soulical nature of Adam and the spiritual nature of Christ,' and the doctrine of 'the atonement:' the former having been suggested by views which presented themselves originally from the scriptures about ten years before, and had afterwards been enlarged by a perusal of Riccaltoun's works, and the latter having sprung out of my reading Edward Irving's treatise of Christ's *human nature*, Marcus Dod's work on the *Incarnation*, W. M'Gill's notorious essay on the *Divinity and Satisfactions of Christ*, and various other books. These inquiries resulted in the composition of rough drafts of two long and elaborate MSS. extending to several hundred pages each, entitled, the one, "*Soul and Spirit*," and the other "*On the Atonement*," which I cannot help thinking contain remarks which, besides being scriptural, are in many respects original and useful. But as I never could be persuaded to revise, abridge and polish them, they are not destined to see the light."

Not only was the year 1832, marked by its abundant "labour,"—for it brought him again before the public as an author, in a pamphlet entitled, *The Miracles of the Irving School shewn to be unworthy of serious examination*†—but it bore to him the cup of "sorrow." The object of his early and tender attachment was removed from his eyes. Consumption deprived him of his first wife. To one so affectionate, and fervent, the loss must have been felt with extraordinary acuteness.

His ministerial avocations, his voluminous correspondence, the interviews he encountered, his much reading, and the "two large MSS. never destined to see the light," during these four or five years, were enough to save any moderately-long life from the charge of idleness. And yet this was far from being all that he accomplished; for, during this period, he was also preparing to fulfil his pledge, to the Presbytery of Glasgow, publicly made in 1828, of "dedicating a little treatise on the 'assurance of faith,'

---

* With American Colleges, Libraries, Public Institutions, and public and private individuals, both abroad and at home.

† Some reader of Mrs. Oliphant's recently-published and most interesting Life of Edward Irving might be pleased with a sight of this pamphlet.

as a small testimony of respect for many of the individuals composing that body." The year 1833 witnessed the redemption of his pledge in the publication of *The Assurance of Faith, or Calvinism identified with Universalism*, in 2 vols. 8vo, consisting of nearly 1000 pages! *Perhaps* some of the members of the Presbytery did read it. It certainly *was* "in his power to congratulate" one of them, if not more, "on having ceased like himself, to belong to a worldly establishment,"—the measure they had meted having been measured to them again.

An analysis of this elaborate and carefully-written treatise is here out of the question. We curb our inclination to proclaim and praise its conspicuous excellencies; suffice it to say that it discloses, on the part of the author, great metaphysical subtlety and close and vigorous logic. An impetuous earnestness evidently carries him along from the dedication to the close of the work. Not the least important disclosure as to the progress of his mind in the knowledge of divine truth, is the clearing up which the question of the future fate of the unregenerate and unbelieving had received in the interval between the publication of the *Three Questions* and of this work. "Universalism" would not have appeared upon the title-page, had it been written and sent forth in 1828. In 1829 it might have been a question with him, for it was in the spring of that year that views of the doctrine of Universal Salvation were first suggested to him from the sacred Scriptures. We are aware of his early-cherished prejudices against this glorious doctrine when it was brought under his notice by his father. Nor were these removed when, subsequently, he gave it his careful consideration in the theories of Winchester, Murray, White, Chauncy and others. And, had nothing more scriptural ever presented itself—nothing more in harmony with his decided views of human nature, in its essential opposition to the divine and the utter impossibility of its ever rising above itself, we much doubt whether his prejudices would have been overcome. His perception of its truth was the result of divine teaching directly through the Scriptures: and, as the complement of other not less scriptural truths, he had become satisfied that it was part of *the whole counsel of God*. Moreover, it was not by arguments ordinarily propounded that he then could, or ever afterwards did maintain the truth of the salvation of all men,—a doctrine which our author found, in opposition to all classes of "Restorationists," *necessarily* to involve the eternal punishment, by everlasting destruction, of man's sinful nature. An extract from the preface to this work* will shew, in a few words, the relations of other theological systems to that which had now matured itself in his own mind.

"With the Calvinists he contends, that God, of His sovereign good

---

* The work which most nearly resembled it in some of its principles was published posthumously in 1795, entitled *Calvinism improved* by Dr. Huntingdon, of Connecticut.

pleasure chose in Christ before the foundation of the world, a certain number of the human race, that *they might be holy, and without blame before him in love:* Eph. i. 4; Rom. viii. 29, 30; xi. 7;—with the Arminians, that Christ died for all; having been *a propitiation, not for the sins of believers only, but also for the sins of the whole world:* 1 John ii. 2; Heb. ii. 9:—and with the Universalists, that Christ ultimately saves all; it having been the express purpose of his coming into the world, *that the world through him might be saved.* John iii. 16, 27; Rom. viii. 20, 21; 1 Tim. ii. 4, 6; James i. 18. And yet, with popular religionists of all descriptions, the author agrees in maintaining, that *the wicked shall be eternally punished.* Matt. xxv. 46; 2 Thess. i. 9; Rev. xxi. 8. With all deserving the Christian name, he strenuously contends for the supreme Deity of the Lord Jesus."

"The Universalism of the author will be found to differ from every other system hitherto propounded, in these respects : that it does not require him, with Tillotson, to suppose God untrue; with Winchester, that the punishment of the wicked is limited; or, with Ballou and Balfour, that the distinctive privileges of believers are confined to this present life: on the contrary, according to the system maintained by him, every divine threatening denounced against man is executed to the uttermost; the wicked are punished, not for a time, but everlastingly; and believers, having imparted to them upon earth the life-giving spirit of Christ Jesus, so far from dying as to their minds, are privileged at the moment of their departure from this world to enter into Paradise, and in due time to sit down with their Head upon his throne. If consistency with the declarations of scripture be the proper test of any system of theology being true, what system can be produced better able to abide this test than that of the author?"

The basis of "The Assurance of Faith" is laid in the deity of Christ, the atoning efficacy of his sacrifice and the vivifying power of his resurrection. The "Introduction" (chap. i.) gives the author's definition of the term "assurance of faith," and the treatment of the doctrine by the Church of Rome, and modern Protestant Churches, both Calvinistic and Arminian. He then states the object of his undertaking in the following terms:

"The present work has for its object to vindicate the grand scriptural and protestant doctrine of *the assurance of faith* against all classes and descriptions of opponents. But it will be found more particularly to have a reference to the sentiments of those who, under pretence of favouring and supporting the doctrine, are at bottom its bitterest and deadliest foes. I intend shewing that *the absolute and infallible certainty of God's love to ourselves personally, and of our own personal enjoyment of everlasting life,* is not merely a privilege which, as believers of the gospel and justified persons, *we may enjoy,* but that it is a privilege which as believers of the gospel and justified persons, *we all of us actually do enjoy.* As necessarily implied in this, it will be shewn that *every one who labours under doubts and fears concerning God's love to himself personally does not believe the gospel and is not justified.* One subject intimately connected with the doctrine of *the assurance of faith* will likewise be treated of. I mean *the fate of the family of man considered as a whole.* Concerning scarcely any other topic do the minds of such even as are Christians appear to be less informed than this, and therefore concerning scarcely any other topic do they appear more decidedly to stand in need of scriptural instruction. The fact is, that in regard to this topic the minds of Protestants *now*, are not one whit more advanced than the minds of their forefathers were *at the period of the reformation*. Besides, although, as shall afterwards be shewn, a man may believe the gospel, and thereby have the certain knowledge of what he himself personally and his fellow believers afterwards shall be, while his views concerning the ultimate fate of mankind in general may be exceedingly vague, obscure, and unsatisfactory; yet, as shall be shewn likewise, it is only by understanding upon scriptural principles what shall be the fate of all, that his privileges as a believer, and the value of *the assurance of faith* as a means to an end, can by him be thoroughly appreciated. A man may be a Christian who knows not distinctly what shall be the ultimate destiny of all—but no man can possess enlarged and enlightened views of Christianity—no man can understand the scriptures as a whole—by whom the paradox of the human race being *everlastingly punished*, and yet being through Christ Jesus *raised to the enjoyment of everlasting life*, is not comprehended."

Chap. ii. is headed, "The Infallibility of Consciousness:" and a masterly metaphysical essay is wound up with a statement, supported by argument, of the miserable consequences, which a denial of this infallibility entails. Thus:

"1. To maintain that *consciousness may deceive us* is to ren'er our own conviction of the existence of a divine revelation *a matter of uncertainty*. 2. A denial of the *infallibility of consciousness* is subversive of the inspiration and consequently of the divine authority of the scriptures; and 3. Lands us in absolute scepticism."

The following chapters treat of God's unconditional gift of eternal life.—The self-inconsistency of Calvinism in dealing with this fact.—Its certain knowledge and enjoyment as the present privilege of believers. The second volume opens with an exposition and defence of the ultimate investiture of every child of Adam with the blessings of eternal life. This is followed by a discussion of the *means* by which this magnificent consummation is to be effected. The compatibility of eternal life with eternal punishment is fully explained and illustrated, and every conceivable objection is brought forward and answered. The doctrine of the atonement—its nature and its application in connection with the grand scheme of Christian providence—is strikingly vindicated, and contrasted with the crude and unsatisfactory, misty and inconsistent dogmas of popular creeds.

As a specimen of the colloquial style in which he sometimes indulged, and which he adopted entirely in the construction of one of his works, we give the following from "The Assurance of Faith."

"The Christian regarding the final attainment of the heavenly glory by himself personally as *conditional*, of course regards it likewise as *uncertain*, and consequently finds himself unable to say with perfect confidence that he shall be either happy or miserable hereafter! Such is the representation of Christianity given us even by the disciples of Calvin, and by the numerous sects who, with various modifications, have adopted his sentiments. The religion of Jesus is, according to them, unable to inspire a man with *absolute* and *infallible certainty* respecting his own future and final destiny! Can such persons be aware, that by representing the personal hope of the believer of the gospel as *conditional* and therefore *uncertain*, they represent him as sharing a sceptical frame of mind with the open and avowed infidel? Just let them conceive of one of *their Christians* brought into contact with a shrewd and talented follower of Carlile and Taylor, and being thus interrogated by him. "INFIDEL. So you think my situation a dangerous one, do you? CALVINIST. I certainly do so and pray God to bring you out of it. INFIDEL. Well, I acknowledge, that I know nothing about what is to befal me hereafter. I may be happy,—I may be miserable,—I may be neither; futurity to me indeed is a matter of doubt, and uncertainty. CALVINIST. I pity you from the bottom of my heart. INFIDEL Your state of mind, no doubt, is a comfortable and an enviable one. You, no doubt, are triumphing in the prospect of the felicity which awaits you, when you leave this world. CALVINIST. Why, I hope I have a good hope through grace. I trust I shall be happy hereafter. INFIDEL. Surely my ears deceive me, or there is a something in your language, which justifies me in suspecting, that you are not so very confident after all respecting your own future prospects. Do you mean to say that you are *absolutely certain* of being happy hereafter? or is it your intention to intimate that you have some doubts upon the subject? CALVINIST. Why, I think that I have a well grounded hope. I think that I have observed in myself the work of the Spirit. Only one would not like to be presumptuous. It becomes a Christian to speak diffidently in regard to a point of so much importance as this. INFIDEL. Please come to the point at once. Are you *certain* that you shall be happy hereafter? or are there *some doubts* in in your mind respecting the matter? CALVINIST. Truly, I cannot say that I am *absolutely certain*. I am satisfied of this that *if* I persevere I shall get to heaven. INFIDEL. Come give me your hand, friend. Brother sceptic, I should rather say. Allow me to congratulate you on your truly philosophical confession Why, henceforward, should you and I quarrel about our respective sentiments? From the admission which you have just made, as to the nature of your hopes of future happiness, it appears plainly, that the difference between us is exceedingly slender—that it is, in fact, merely verbal. For, while I, *without any religion at all*, confess that I am *uncertain about futurity* it appears that *your religion* has left you *as uncertain about it* as I myself am. Surely, men who are thus both *confessedly sceptical* respecting a point of so much importance as their own future destiny, can have very little, in reality, to object to in one another."

It is in this work, the author writes,

"Understanding the grand feature of the Baconian system of philosophy to be, that nature is to be constantly searched and scrutinized; and that new principles are by the inductive process to be derived from her, regardless of the interference of these with inveterate maxims, or rashly concocted theories; the author conceived, that he could only make progress in his researches after divine truth, by dealing with the word of God, as Bacon, with a view to advancement in physical science, recommended his disciples to deal with nature. As *a discovery* in nature is, in the school of Bacon, held paramount to *every mere principle* by whomsoever adopted, and however long established; so *a discovery* in God's word, the author resolved, should to his mind carry greater weight, than *principles*, in theology resting on the authority, and established by the *dicta*, of names however celebrated. And this, because what *external nature*, with its store of facts, is to the true philosopher; *the word of God*, with its store of facts, is to the true theologian."

With a feeling very much akin to his whose method he felt to be equally applicable to the field of "revelation" as to that of "nature," Mr. Thom more than suspected the want of maturity on the part of the Church,—as Bacon did that of the scientific world—for both his method and the results of its application. If it was Bacon's misfortune to belong to an age whose generations were not yet born,—a misfortune, as he seems to have thought it, when in his will, he touchingly "bequeaths his name to posterity, after some time be past over;" so says David Thom,—" it is enough for him, if, ages after he and his work shall have been forgotten, the system itself shall be found silently making progress, and surmounting every difficulty, in virtue of its own inherent evidences of divine origin."

The Universalists of America constitute a considerable section of the professing church. None deplored more than Mr. Thom the low views entertained among them of the person and work of our Lord Jesus Christ. Yet he did not allow this important difference to stand as an insuperable barrier to every kind of intercourse with them. He was pleased to accept the appointment in 1830 of " Corresponding Secretary for England to the American Universalist Historical Society." This appointment was renewed annually for more than twenty years, and was the cause of his transmitting a number of communitions to the society. That he might lead them to truer and purer views of Christianity, he was not neglectful to keep up a courteous and friendly acquaintance with them; and not unfrequently opportunities occurred, and often he took occasion to administer a little wholesome chastisement, and a little faithful warning of the tendencies of their system.

With the name of John Barclay, A.M., every reader of Mr. Thom's writings must be familiar. To no human authority, perhaps, did he conceive himself as lying under deeper obligations. In spite of his *apparently* unamiable and vituperative style, Barclay's *Without Faith without God*, was highly esteemed, and was edited by Mr. Thom with an explanatory preface in 1835. In the same year, too, Mr. Thom brought out his pamphlet *Why is Popery progressing?* which reappeared in 1851.

The demand for the *Three Questions* continuing undiminished, and the first edition being exhausted, a second edition was published in 1836; this, as well as the first, drew forth reviews of considerable length.

With correspondents on the Continent as well as in the United States he was now frequently communicating; and with his youngest brother, Robert Thom, Esq., then H.B.M's Consul at Ningpo, to whom he was most devotedly attached, he was continually exchanging letters. To his congregation, twice every Lord's day, he continued to preach, with scarcely any assistance.

In 1838 appeared the first edition of his *Dialogues on Universal Salvation and Topics connected therewith*. As it is not out of print and difficult to procure, like his *Assurance of Faith*, we all the more readily waive our inclination to attempt an analysis of its contents. Suffice it to say that it affords indications of a considerable amount of *filling up* in our author's theological system. In the *Assurance of Faith* his primary object is the illustration of divine *principles*; in the "*Dialogues*" attention is more particularly directed to their historical development. The relations of Adam and of Abraham—the one to the whole, the other to a special portion of the human family; and the typical character of both respectively of the twofold relation of Christ to the race and to the elect—as spiritual Adam as well as spiritual Abraham, and the dispensational character of the divine administration as involving progressive manifestation, come in for a large share of original and scriptural treatment.

We cannot persuade ourselves to pass over, *sub silentio*, one of Mr. Thom's most interesting and most valued friendships, which commenced a few months after, and as the result of the publication of the *Dialogues*, in 1838. We allude to the late Mrs. M. M. Sherwood. For some years previously the so-called "evangelical" system had proved "a broken reed, and oft a spear," and views more in harmony with the love and life of God as revealed in Jesus Christ, had dawned upon her. These were indicated in works published by her in 1837. The *Dialogues on Universal Salvation* proved to be confirmatory of her faith, and, as we observed, resulted in an intimacy which subsisted unbroken to the day of that lady's death, in 1851. Deep must have been the influence of this religious intercourse on an individual who was pleased to avow that, although many years his senior, she regarded Mr. Thom as her spiritual father. Among his much-prized literary treasures were the letters addressed to him by this gifted lady; and shortly after her decease, he contributed an interesting little memoir of her to the *Universalist* (Dec. 1851).

Mr. Thom was married to his second wife, Euphemia Gardener, in January 1834. Around him a young family had sprung up, appealing to, and calling forth, his paternal affection and solicitude. We do not think that Mr. Thom had a *pet* among his children; at all events, if he had, the fact dwelt in his own bosom, a profound secret. The *minimum* of his abounding love for all of them, must have been so much in excess of the *maximum* of his partiality for any one in particular, that, even if it existed, its detection would have been impossible. Another progeny, however, was also on the increase—the offspring of his brain; and to this family was added a new member in 1842, an addition which we know, on his own authority, was his early and his latest *favourite*. Nor will we allow that this preference was the result of weakness or caprice. We confess to a participation in the partiality: and, if there were any possibility of adopting the entire family, we should decidedly enact the part of the patriarch by investing our darling with the many-coloured coat of our special commendation. Nor should we discover our preference with any apprehensions of jealousy on the part of other members of the family. It is not the youngest child. In age it comes about midway between the first-born and the last of the group. It appears to promote not only a good understanding among its seniors with itself, but, among them, a better understanding with each other; and, with profound intelligence and grace, introduces to the circle of its acquaintance, its juniors who, following their more conspicuous relative, evidently move more freely and unconstrained. Many of our readers will understand us as referring to *Divine Inversion: or a view of the character of God as in all respects opposed to the character of man*,—a work upon which the author was engaged from 1838 to the time of its publication, 1842. It proceeds on a principle known to the church in all ages, but which had never been before stated with the same clearness, variety of illustration, and range of application. We feel it to be almost a reproach, that it has been long, as it is now, out of print and not easily accessible.

Interesting is the progress of Mr. Thom's mind as recorded in the preface to this work. As early as 1829, Heb. xi. 3, appears to have afforded the earliest ray of that *principle* which was afterwards to bathe with its light the entire field of his spiritual vision. "About three years afterwards," a further illustration of the doctrine, during the perusal of Rom. viii. 10, 11, was brought under his notice. "Still," he says, "I had no idea of any general principle being involved in the discovery. It was not until the end of the year 1835, or the beginning of 1836, that I was enabled to generalize to a certain degree the views contained in these pages." The progress of his mind, under divine teaching, is further narrated,—and at length, the fact of a *general principle* was fully established. Still more recently (about 1839) *divine inversion*, seen heretofore as a principle concerned in the *divine order* or *succession* of things, was discovered to him as not less completely embracing their *divine constitution*—a far more important aspect of the principle in question.

At the time of the publication of this work, Mr. Thom was able to form, by a review of the treatment of himself and his former productions at the hands of the religious public, something more than a vague anticipation of the reception that awaited it. In his preface he indulges in a somewhat prophetic strain, and in reply to a question he imagines opponents addressing to him, as to what sort of treatment he considered himself as having a right to expect, he replies: "certainly no other but what I have already experienced, and what, of course, I am prepared still to experience : see Matt. xxi. 45, 46." We need hardly say, he was not much disappointed; and yet to some extent the prophecy was falsified by a considerable demand for the work. Among many instances of its usefulness, under God's blessing, a singular result of its perusal was communicated to Mr. Thom, by a clergyman of Liverpool, to the effect that it had been the means of preventing a duel in a case where one of the parties was a nobleman.

Both as to arrangement and style the *Divine Inversion* bears marks of special care. The principle is perspicuously stated and copiously illustrated from Scripture. The explication it affords of the deep problems of good and evil, life and death, time and eternity, God and man, is pointed out with much clearness. Our own opinion of the profound nature and far-reaching bearings of this great principle, has, we believe, been anticipated by such men as George Gilfillan and Philip James Bailey, and others who rank high among the celebrities of the day; and we claim for him no more than is due to the memory of the revered author of *Divine Inversion*, the honour of having been the first to point out and illustrate this grand Scripture principle.* Thus he writes of this book only a few months ago to a clerical friend, "This is the only one of my books in which I take any particular interest, and the only one of them about the existence and notice of which, until superseded by something better on the same subject, I feel any way solicitous."†

During the year 1844 Mr. Thom was carrying on that close and constant epistolary intercourse with M. Stanislas Julien, of the Paris Institute, which had been begun for the sake of his brother Robert, and to whose memory one of the works of this celebrated Chinese professor is dedicated. The long, interesting and instructive letters (from 30 to 40 in number) of M. Julien, were preserved by Mr. Thom with the greatest care.

Released from pulpit ministrations for a few weeks' relaxation

---

* The principle of *Divine Inversion* would not, perhaps, be despised, if understood, by such metaphysico-theological writers as the justly-celebrated editor of Sir W. Hamilton (the Rev. B. Mansel, D.D.). The purely negative results to which, by his conscientious and fearless logic, he is conducted, must create a powerful reaction in favour of the necessity of that *divine revelation* to which *human reason* stands opposed. On the other hand, science, with its ever-widening horizon, dealing with the phenomena only of both mind and matter,—finding itself thoroughly baffled in its attempt to make out the actual being and reality of things, (see Herbert Spencer's *First Principles*) grows humble, and may ere long be disposed to take a hint from the book entitled "*Divine Inversion*."

† It will be gratifying to those who have felt an interest in the perusal of the *Divine Inversion*, to know that very recently has appeared a work bearing the title of "Man and his Dwelling-place," in which a remarkable identity of subject, with some variety of treatment is traceable. We need offer no apology for thus introducing James Hinton, Esq. (its talented and amiable author), to the friends of the late Dr. Thom. With an undoubting reverence for the Sacred Scriptures, by means of scientific investigation, for which his order of mind and attainments particularly well qualify him, Mr. Hinton appears to have been forced to the conclusion of the absolute necessity of this doctrine to explain the otherwise inexplicable universe, a doctrine which he found already unmistakably implied in the Scriptures throughout. The fact that, till some time after the publication of his work, Mr. Hinton remained in complete ignorance of the existence of our author's "*Divine Inversion*," by no means detracts from the interest arising out of the remarkable coincidence we have ventured to point out.

every summer, wisely did Mr. Thom shut up his books and close his correspondence, that he might rest awhile from his arduous labours. Surrounded by his own family circle, these seasons were sometimes spent at Rhyl, then a quiet seaside place on the coast of Denbighshire. On other occasions he would go futher from home. In 1843 he visited France, Belgium and Holland spending some hours on the field of Waterloo, and going north as far as Amsterdam. During the summer of 1844 he made the tour of Ireland, having previously inspected many localities of interest in England and Scotland; and in the three following summers, among other important localities, he visited the cathedral cities. Well do we remember our astonishment when spending with us the evening of the day of his visit to St. Paul's and Westminster abbey, he took us as it were by the hand, and pointed out in *consecutive order*, as smoothly and unhesitatingly, as if he were reading from a book, first the company of the illustrious dead, under the dome of St. Paul's, and then the tombs of kings (noticing parenthetically the break in the chronological order created by the honours claimed by Windsor) and poets and other of our great ones interred in the Abbey. Perfect plans of these edifices appeared to have been engraved upon his brain from which he was able to read off the minutest details. From the English Universities we may be sure he could not hurry away; and *battle-fields*, we are told, he would not miss a sight of without regret.

With unabated activity and zeal his literary projects were still prosecuted. Towards the close of 1845, appeared a large and elaborate work of 558 pages, entitled, *Three Grand Exhibitions of Man's Enmity to God*. While the purpose of the author in his *Divine Inversion* was to point out the essential opposition of the natures of God and man respectively, his object in this work is to trace the progressive development of that opposition. The object of the Divine Being—always the manifestation of Himself as what He really is,—is effected by degrees, and by means of "experiments," upon human nature—the theatre of his own operations, that thereby his creatures having discovered to them what they are, or rather what they are not, may be prepared for that manifestation of the *divine* nature, which, when actually known, becomes the superseding power of fleshly principle, and involves the grand consummation contemplated as the final result of the three grand experiments, which, in their totality, comprise all the direct dealings of God the Creator with man his creature.

Mr. Thom's purpose, in the composition of this work, is expressed in the following brief extract from its *preface*:

"This work, which is one of a series of treatises, is subservient to what has been for years the leading and favourite object of my life,—to bring under the notice of the Church, upon true and Scriptual principles, the freedom, the certainty and the universality of the love borne by God to man"

Of all his productions it most abounds in repetitions of facts and re-statements of arguments. This was necessary, partly from the nature of the subject and its very methodical mode of treatment, and partly from a conviction that, in order to be understood, the author could not express himself too distinctly or with too great a variety of illustration. His previous works had not unfrequently been read 'upside down' and reviewers had combated their own shadows instead of the positions assumed and maintained by the writer. Besides a discussion of some length devoted to the *Divine Inversion* by a seceded clergyman of the Church of England,* who afterwards became a Universalist preacher in the United States, Mr. Thom was honoured with a criticism in a pamplet devoted exclusively to its discussion, by a respected fellow townsman.† The unintentional misapprehensions of his learned and friendly critics, naturally excited a strong wish on the part of our author to write with all possible explicitness. Any pains he would take, any seeming prolixity he would indulge, if thereby he might guard his readers against mistakes.

The "Three Grand Exhibitions" will ever remain pre-eminent as a striking example of its author's *order* and *constructiveness*. In *form*, it is less controversial and more expository than most of his other writings; and in it we have the completion of the outline of his theological system.‡ Here is a bit of self-reviewing a few months after the publication had taken place.

"No defect, dear friend, do I see in the *grand principle* maintained in my *Three Grand Exhibitions*. Manner, mode of getting it up, is where I see great defects. My title (the third grand exhibition) '*denial of divinely-revealed fact*,' is perfectly correct, understanding thereby, that every one, who, in so many words, or impliedly, makes his salvation *conditional*, which is the human idea, is denying the divinely-revealed fact of *his being really saved*. Still, perhaps, it would have borne a more popular aspect, and been better understood, while the idea would have been the same, had I said;—'*Gospel converted by man into law*.' He who does so makes the Gospel, not *the revelation of a fact*, but of something which we by our faith or otherwise *are to render or to strive to render a fact* That is, whenever Gospel is addressed as law, the fact of our *being saved*, which God reveals, is denied."

* *The Second Advent a past event*, by Robert Townly, M.A.
† *The Theory of Divine Inversion Examined*, by Thos. Wetherill, M.D. Liverpool. 1843.
‡ A careful appreciation and analysis of the *Three Grand Exhibitions* appeared in the pages of the *Universalist*, whose author's name we are restrained from the gratification of mentioning by the extreme modesty of the writer. Long, and in many respects, approving notices of this work appeared in the Reviews. We remember being struck at the time with the unintended compliment of the *British Quarterly*, which says, "No one can read the book which Mr. Thom has published without great respect for the manifest sincerity, and the grave religious feelings of the writer. But his plan is too symmetrical, compact, and perfect, and in too great a degree a personal discovery, to be wholly trustworthy. Divine truth is, no doubt, harmonious and perfect, but we are not more sure that the relations of truth must be of that nature, than that it is not given to mortal to trace out these relations, and to comprehend the whole in the manner attempted by Mr. Thom. (See *British Quarterly Review*, May, 1846.)

Ardent was the attachment which subsisted between Mr. Thom and Robert, his youngest brother; and deep was the wound inflicted by the tidings of Mr. Robert Thom's death, which reached Liverpool at the close of the year 1846. The second edition of the *Dialogues*, which was published the following year, contains an "Introductory Notice" of this individual, who was made an interlocutor in that work, and whose distinguished career was terminated, at the age of thirty-nine, at Ningpo, in September, 1846. In the following year, the shafts of "the insatiate archer" deprived him of his much-loved and venerated mother, at the advanced age of eighty. The sweet submission with which he bore these afflictive bereavements, was matter of admiring and grateful observation among his friends, who well knew how much the fibre of his strong human affections was lacerated and torn by these severe trials. In these as well as in other afflictions which fell to his lot, his doctrine was found to be no mere figment of the human brain, nor his faith an idle, vain and presumptuous boast.

In revising the *Dialogues* for a second edition, February, 1847, he writes:—

"Do you know that, with the exception of some little apparent inconsistency about one law and two laws to man, I am astonished to find after the lapse of eight or nine years, with much divine teaching in the interim, how little I have to alter or even comment on. Surely none teacheth like God! My chief blunder, I observe, is that corrected in the *Divine Inversion*, pp. 82-86. God's sovereignty forming God's nature and not *vice versa*, the opposite idea being the heathenish one of binding Jove by fate."

The following is from a communication of the same date:—

"I had a most glorious divine discovery made to me last week, which I gave to my friends last Lord's day evening. You know that I oppose ordinary Millenarianism. It has long appeared to me inconsistent and absurd, as well as unscriptural. Indeed, I never could exactly grasp it. Grossly proclaimed in the pages of Elhanan Winchester (see his four volumes of Discourses, preached in Glass-house Yard, Borough, in 1789), and in those of Pirie of Newburgh, and somewhat more refinedly in the pages of more modern writers, I have found it a shadow always eluding my embrace (see appendix to "Divine Inversion," letter D). Its grand absurdity is, however, that, like the restoration of Adam's state, it carries back instead of leading forward. Circumstances like these had made me neglect the subject of Judaism, for some time, in a great measure if not altogether. Some things, however, continued opening in my mind from time to time. At last the truth has disclosed itself. I now understand Romans xi. and Judaism past and future. I find that, in the main, I am right. No going back. No restorations of earthly Canaans. What I am now delighted to see is *the double typical character of the Jews*. Types of the true Church of God in their Old Testament state; types of the unregenerate world in their New Testament state. It is from this last quarter that light has burst in upon my mind. I have got an additional and glorious view of Universal Salvation, totally unexpected, and, I suspect, entirely new."

In 1846, short crops and potato-blight created great uneasiness throughout the country, and occasioned that deep distress which decimated the population of Ireland, during this period. A proclamation from the throne set apart March 24th as a day of fasting. How Mr. Thom regarded such days may be learnt from the following:

"Yesterday, we had service in the forenoon; and, in the evening I could not get my mind settled to anything.—So I crossed the water, and had a walk with my wife and little boy.—The Service was held by me *with reluctance*.—I dislike these days of 'fasting and humiliation,' as they are called, prodigiously. And this, for various reasons :—In *principle*, they are bad; as proceeding *a non habente potestatem*, the Queen not possessing the powers of an Israelitish Monarch, under a divinely-constituted system, and the assertion of the power, proceeding on the Establishment principle; besides involving the existence of external churches, &c. &c. ; (do they not justly excite the scoffs of infidelishly-inclined, shrewd, fleshly minds?) They are wrong also in *practice*.—Who, almost, thinks of fasting? Am I to be told seriously, that excellent fish and egg sauce, is a fast? Again: what become of the wages for the day, of the poor industrious mechanic, striving hard to rear a family? Are these wages paid to them,—I do not say, by their masters, for that perhaps were unreasonable,—but by those who ordain the fast? Are bishops, &c, mulcted in a day's salary; or do they pay it? Will not the wages of another day ['Good Friday'] go next week? To days of recreation, for the artisan, I have, abstractly speaking, no aversion. I could go, and would go, cheerfully, with Lord John Manners and others, not in making *religious* days of recreation, but in *having* days of recreation, were our state of society different from what it is,—were not one man treading on the heels of another,—or even if matters continued the same, were the dropped wages of the poor paid by public authority.—But to serve God for naught—to profess a fast, in which no self-denial is exercised—to overlook the beautiful principle embodied in the story of David and Araunah!—(All this taking them up on their own principles.) Faugh!—The thing is rank. It stinks in one's nostrils.—I say I spoke with reluctance. (I never keep 'Good Friday', or 'Christmas'.) To Naboth's vineyard, I drew their attention; then to Isaiah lviii. 1—7. (The "Times" of yesterday, I see, quotes verses 6 and 7. These clearly refer to the work of our blessed Lord, Jesus Christ. He was the true faster. He was the true self-denied one. Read, my friend, the verses carefully; and then see how, in verse 8, the blessings connected with his resurrection are set before us. Read Rom. xv.) I then spoke from James i. 27.—The 'religion' *practical*, not disjoined from principle, but derived from it: for it is believers the apostle is speaking of. 'Religion', that 'which is pleasing to God,' as lexicographers derive the word.—To 'visit'—the Greek word is the same as that from which bishop is derived. 'To oversee,'—not *passively* to wait till brought—but, *actively*, to look after.—1. Personal purity. 2. Benevolence to others.—These, not bringing out divine truth in reality, but only in so far as the world can see it, and in so far as believers, by practice, may be edified. We must take care that the truth of God be not, through our misconduct, blasphemed. We must be of service, indirectly and negatively, in commending the gospel to the notice of an unbelieving world. This is only to be done, by avoiding what is wrong, and by acting in such a way as *they* can understand. See 1 John. iii. 1. *end.*"

With America, in spite of unconquerable aversion to the Unitarian tendencies of his Universalist friends, he still kept up a large epistolary and personal intercourse; and many were the visits he received from, and many were the kind attentions he shewed to Universalist and other clergymen while on their "European tour." Sep. 30th, 1847, he writes:

"To-day I have had a long and most interesting conversation with Alex. Campbell, of Bethany, Virginia, the antagonist, in 1829, of Owen, and in 1837, of Bp. Purcell, at Cincinnati. To my astonishment and delight, I find that, although then unknown to each other, we were both in the Greek class, session 1807-8, at Glasgow, only he, *inter seniores*, and I, *inter juniores*. We both had the honour to carry off prizes that year. I, not much more than 13, he 18 or 19. He is now the head of a large sect of Baptists in America."

Early in 1847 we find him seeking as much as possible to withdraw himself into the retirement of his study, warning friends not to expect much of his society, or to see many of his letters. "I am going to sit down doggedly to my 'Numbers and Names of the Apocalyptic Beasts.' I must get this off my hands, and while engaged in it, I want to be distracted by nothing else. Two months of close attention will, I think, complete….I must fulfil my promises."*

Beautifully printed, "The Number and Names of the Apocalyptic Beasts: with an explanation and application, Part I.—The Number and Names," made its appearance before Midsummer, 1848. It is so well known, as well as readily accessible, that it would be superfluous to attempt a description of a work which, on all hands, is readily acknowledged to have entitled its author to take his place in the foremost rank of *learned* theologians. The collection and digestion of the materials, of which the bulk of the volume is composed, must have been the labour of years. A few months sufficed, as we have seen, to prepare it for and pass it through the press: and "the true solutions," following a long procession, in which some three or four look *very like* the creatures suggested in *the Book*, while other wild beasts look very unlike indeed, bring up the rear. The long procession has been driven over the precipice of "conjecture," and has disappeared: and standing alone before us are the two veritable beasts. There they are,—staring at the reader, and he at them! A few words only of introduction are offered, and the erudite author retires, leaving us to scrutinize the creatures at our leisure. Some of

---

* Such was the intimation received by us. We could patiently afford to wait his re-appearance after a couple or any number of months required for the completion of a Work to which we had long been looking forward. We wrote him to this effect, assuring him of our cheerful acquiescence in his proposed self-exclusion, and wishing him a speedy and happy deliverance! If we had murmured a little, and complained of the hardness of our lot, we might have heard no more; but gratitude in a day or two broke silence and diffused itself over four large sheets of paper, much to our pleasant dismay!

the reviewers could "make neither head nor tail of them;" others, as if the mirror were being held up to nature, growled or roared. A nonconformist might have thought it worth while to shew a little kindly treatment; for, without much coaxing, it was obvious that they could be driven through the strongholds of an "Establishment." One reviewer points at the egotism of some remarks in the preface. "They *may be* egotistical; they *are* inconsistent with the oily and humble style of shrewd human nature. This I confess,"—is D. T's comment. Another reviewer, either very stupid or very ———, ascribed to the author quite another species of beast for those which he claimed as his own discovery!

The condensed view of what had been written regarding the numbers 616 and 666, the classification adopted, the valuable references to other works, the careful and honest avowal of literary obligations, the original sources of information sought and obtained,—these, among other characteristics of this work, approve the learning, the research, the candour, and the painstaking of the author and justify the meed of praise which *some* honest reviewers bestowed upon it.

"Part II." which was to contain the "Application," was never published. Those who owned but a slender acquaintance with the author's system, knew something of *the creatures*, although they might not have had the wisdom to discover *their names*: and, probably, many of them have come to a conclusion similar to our own, viz: that "Part II." is already written, *fragmentarily*—but with considerable perspicuity, in the former works of Mr. Thom. It has also been written,—is still being written, alas! how clearly! in the pages of ecclesiastical history. The true solutions, "Η Φρην", and "Εκκλεσιαι Σαρκικαι," are ever finding their verification, in both the rationalistic and religious developments of Christendom.* But Part II. was not destined to be written according to the original design of the author. The design *was* conceived, but its gigantic proportions must almost have appalled his own mind: particularly when he felt, as we too soon find him confessing, the *tædium scribendi* creeping upon him. "The plan of the second part of my *Number and Names* is getting more and more digested in my mind," he says, in January, 1849; but, towards the end of the year, he writes,—"My Second Part of the *Number and Names* is up for the present. Two attempts have I made to begin, one extending to 40 pp. But it will not do. The disquisitions, necessary to illustrate my principles, will require a volume of themselves. This, therefore, I resolved yesterday to accomplish. Humanly speaking, I can do, and satisfactorily do it.

* The following explanation is by its author. "The two beasts stand to each other in the relation of 1. Principle or vital energy: 2. Embodiment of principle. That is, the two beasts are to each other, what soul and body are to each other. Soul and body form one compound person; so do the two beasts form one compound beast. This is the reason of the injunction (ver. 18) being, 'let him count the *number of the beast.*' See the beginning of ch. ii. Introduction. See ch. iii."

Seven short essays, on 'Sin and Death,' 'the Work of Christ,' 'New Creation,' 'Man like God,' 'the Origin of Evil,' 'Indefinite and Infinite,' and 'Jehovah and God,' will, if spared, be the appropriate and absolutely necessary introduction to my Second Part. I care nothing about taunts or delay. I must satisfy my own conscience. With much pleasure I have written a great part of the first essay to-day.

The vastness of the plan seems to have defied its accomplishment. Yet we doubt if the leaving of his learned work formally incomplete occasioned him much uneasiness; and, that the hand of Providence was writing it for him, he must have been convinced.

It will be obvious to any one who consults "Division III." of the *Number and Names*, that solutions have been found and might still be found, "which, if not *the truth* at all events, may have some connection with it." And it is equally obvious from what follows, that Mr. Thom, in the solutions submitted in his work, did not shut himself up from further suggestions. This observation is confirmed by the following extract, which we give not only for the sake of the matter of which it treats, but as disclosing the peculiar working of this extraordinary mind.

"Nov. 13th, 1848."

"Last Friday night I found myself sleepless. Unable to employ my mind better, I began to think over a truth, first suggested by 2 Thess. ii. 1—11, and afterwards brought out in my 'Three Grand Exhibitions,' &c. especially pp. 247-282. Sin, namely, in connection with this present time (the third era), and with the first beast, is seen in its strength. Not as, first, violating divine prohibition, or 2, Disobeying divine law; but 3. Presuming to act as God, and to issue laws as if they were divine. Thinking over the matter, I tried first ἁμαρτία which I found to be 453. Then it was suggested to me to try, ἁμαρτίας the genitive. This is 653. My curiosity was now aroused. Being in regimen, what is the noun governing? Before I slept I had settled, 1st, that the letters must amount to 13; 2nd. That it must be some word expressive of 'strength' or 'power.' On Saturday morning, βία, signifying strength, vigour, &c. was suggested. And it is a good Greek word, the Doric form of the Ionic βίη. See Hom. Il. iii. 45. (Δυναμις is used 1 Cor. xv. 55.) '*The strength of sin.*' Is not this as curious as it is an unexpected confirmation of my view?"

β	2		α	13
ι	10		μ	40
α	1		α	1
	—		ρ	100
	13		τ	300
			ι	10
			α	1
			ς	200
				—
				666

xxxix

But we are speaking of Mr. Thom, after Heidelberg has done him as well as itself an honour, by conferring upon him, by diploma, the degrees of Ph. D. and M.A., March 6th, 1848; and we may here record the fact that, by a similar diploma on the part of the University of Jena, he was created D.D., April 18th, 1849. The very high terms, in which the latter University, somewhat out of their usual course, were pleased to express their admiration and appreciation of his theological learning and attainments, afforded him a gratification he did not affect to despise.

"Have I not some reason to be pleased with their introduction of the 'probatus' after the 'propter', as well as with the manner in which they announced their having conferred the degree? 'Unanimously,' and not merely on the ground of many things complimentarily said, but of 'the genuineness and openness' with which I had acted? This was in their English letter. I repeat that I told them of my trials, convictions and condemnations, and of my having been turned out of the Scotch Established Church. The degree has been conferred and conferred with their own approbation—in the teeth of the knowledge of these facts. Have I not reason to be satisfied with this?..... The Church of Scotland's and England's practice of putting human compositions so far upon a level with God's word, as to make them *authoritative expositors* must be taken notice of [this in view of a new edition of the *Three Questions*]. Besides, their condemnation and the D.D. came into amusing contact. Neither condemnation nor D.D. degree possessed of the slightest value or authority in the decision of divine truth. Both *human*. A sort of neutralizing effect, like that of acids and alkalis, their only result. Besides, I have *always* acted on the principle of making my own views, **as mine**, of no value, and of giving full force to man's condemnation **of me**. Such force I mean as it deserves. I fear it not. Its assistance **I count** not. **Its** utmost force I brave. My views, as so far divine and **true**, shall **make** their way in spite and in the teeth of it. Pardon this **apparent** egotism. It is more properly defiance of human religion."

In corresponding with him on this occasion, his friend, George Gilfillan, writes: "I congratulate you cordially **on** your degree of D.D. It strikes **me as** such a rich idea, that **of a** condemned heretic receiving a D.D. which many will interpret 'Devil's doctrine.' Honour to Jena, **a** victory has been gained where formerly **a** battle was lost."

In 1848 appeared 'Jane Eyre', and we find this devourer of books yielding to the fascinating charms of Currer Bell. He had soon detected the sex of the author, and was tolerably well satisfied of her North-of-England residence. An interesting correspondence with the talented sister of Charlotte Brontë (Acton Bell) subsequently took place on the subject of Universalism.

Aug. 5, 1848, he writes:

"To-day I have just finished, with great care, another perusal of David Hume's 'Natural History of Religion.' How true many of his conclusions! And yet, knowing, as I do, the gospel, with what ease, upon *true* scriptural principles, I can explain and reconcile every phenomenon. It is a sad delusion to take religion of every descrip..."

"Tennymann's *Manual of Philosophy* I am going through with great care.—An admirable condensation and book of reference. How worthless the efforts of man's mind, in the regions of Philosophy, apart from Scripture!"

The "advertisement" to the third edition of the *Three Questions*, published in 1849 informs the reader that "the principal truths for which, during a period varying from 20 to 25 years, the author has been honoured to contend, are here presented unchanged." Not only had the Scriptures, and the works of writers advocating the doctrine of Universal Salvation—one of the topics discussed in the volume—in the interval between the publication of this and the former edition, been largely consulted, but every species of opposition had been courted, and every work of merit designed to overturn it had been studied, including Hamilton's "Revealed Doctrine of Rewards and Punishments," Brandon's "Everlasting Fire no Fancy;" and Edwards' "Salvation of all men strictly examined." Edwards' work was esteemed as "incomparably the ablest ever produced, against the doctrine of the unboundedness of God's love to the human family."

A tour northwards, in the autumn of the same year seems to have given him less relaxation and repose than fatigue and exhaustion. On Tuesday, Sep. 11th, he reached Edinburgh, where, till the 14th, he was renewing agreeable intercourse with many friends, including the Rev. Patrick Clason, Mr. Moncrieff, Rev. G. Smith, Jas. Simpson, Esq., R. Hamilton, Esq., Miss Margaret Miller, (governess of Sir W. Scott's daughters,) and her aged mother, the widow of James Donaldson the Berean pastor, Mr. James Brown, (afterwards of Glasgow), Miss King, Rev. Mr. Fairley, &c. &c.

"At Glasgow, Friday evening. Visited Paisley, (the seat of my ancestors, the Corses and Loves for 350 years)—Visited my great grand-mother's house, Canseyside (from 1766 till 1803), and sat in the room where I had not been since 1798. Remembered perfectly (3 years and 10 months). Visited old lady's grave in chancel, Abbey Church, where I deposited her body, April 24, 1806. Met, on the grave of our common ancestor, my cousin Mr. Campbell King, to our mutual surprise,—he not knowing that I was in Scotland. Went on to Johnstone, saw dear John Fraser. Did what I could to induce him to come forward, and resume, his former practice of addressing the Universalists of Johnstone. Pleasing interview. Do not despair of success. Returned to Glasgow in the evening. Made arrangements to preach for Universalists and Bereans the following day. Would allow no public announcement to be made. Sunday 16th,—spoke in the morning. Spent a quiet hour at the Temperance hotel. Evening —a crowded auditory. Representatives of all religious sects in Glasgow present. Two clergymen of the Established Church, John Dunmore Lang [an old and attached friend] also. Spoke easily. Christ's death and resurrection, as taking away sin and putting forth new-creation efficacy, with our personal interest, was the theme. Most attentive, and let me hope, edified. Terribly tired. Monday—got through business which principally took me to Scotland. Visited my father's grave in crypt of Cathedral (brother William and three sisters interred there), over which the queen had recently trod. Beautifully repaired. There met and had some conversation with my old friend, the Rev. John Macleod Campbell, formerly of Row. Saw several friends, and dined at Hollybank with my cousin in the evening. To Girvan on Tuesday, where I met with Mr. P. Hately Waddell and Dr. Aspinall. Pleasing interview with Corson, the parish minister.

"Returning on Wednesday, spent the evening pleasantly and I hope edifyingly with Mr. James Thomson and Christian party in Glasgow. Thursday—a most laborious day: called on parties innumerable yet saw not a third of those I intended to see. W. Wardlaw, jun. an old and intimate friend; Andrew Woodrow: W. Davey, Esq. Town Clerk, a most affectionate interview; John Strang, L.L.D., City Chamberlain, from whom I was inoculated; W. Steel, Esq., 'writer,'[*] one of my relations; John Thomson, Esq. Ed. of 'Glasgow Chronicle': John Poynter, Esq; Rev. John Bonar, leading Free-Kirk Minister, an old and intimate friend of mine, &c. &c. Spent three hours conversing with fourteen Universalist friends, on religion, most useful. Evening, at Mr. Steel's with pleasant party. Tired. Friday—saw Mr. Sutherland, Mr. Mitchell, whom I had seen several times. My cousins Falconer and King. Mr. H. Cogan: affectionate interview, came up to me on the street and took my hand. Some years ago, although one of the chief causes of my being in Liverpool, shied me. What a change! Met Mr. Thos. Muirhead, also Mr. T. Samuel,—did not know him,—had not seen him since 1823. Also others—most kindly received by all. With my old friend, Byers, minister of Bathgate, had a long conversation on Sunday evening, 16th. Friday saw me off;—glad to escape from kindness and labour. At Carlisle, night. There and then, and following morning, a most extraordinary conversation with a *talented* clergyman of a *certain* Church. Gave me his name. Avowed Universalism. Home. Well, except my eldest daughter,—now, blessed be God, better. Hard labour answering letters; a great number waiting."

The above small portion of a letter to a friend, is a specimen of the elliptical sort of style in which, when hurried, he would often write. It speaks for itself as to the warm and genial disposition of the writer, and records one of the very rare occasions on which he ever spoke in public away from Liverpool. That Sunday's gathering has not been effaced from the memory of many at Glasgow who will see his face no more.

With the commencement of the year 1850, a periodical was started under the editorship of the late Richard Roe, Esq. B.A., a gentleman who, for conscience'-sake, had many years previously quitted the Established Church; and for whom Dr. Thom cherished, on the score of his Christian character, advanced knowledge of Scripture truth, and literary attainments, marked respect and strong attachment. The idea of starting a periodical, having for its object the promulgation of doctrines, which "the world," both "professing" and "profane," would trample under their feet, was almost too bold for the Christian daring of David Thom; and, at its first suggestion, he actually recoiled. From an enterprise, which, for want of adequate support, might prematurely fall to the ground, he adopted a tone of dissuasion. Believers in the divine sovereignty and the univer-

[*] Afterwards *Sheriff*.

sality of God's love, were few and scattered; and of these still fewer were addicted to literary pursuits. Could a sufficiently-numerous staff of contributors, or anything like a paying circulation, be calculated upon? On the other hand, he saw the advantage of a medium of intercommunication between Christian brethren holding fundamentally the same faith, and how such a periodical might subserve the purpose of mutual edification. He felt strongly the importance and desirableness of making known the essential difference existing between the doctrines of Scripture and those doctrines of men, which, though assuming the same name, were by no means identical, and, though wearing a dress which had some appearance of being genuine, were found to be wrought entirely of a different stuff. Not lightly would he throw away an opportunity of repudiating fellowship with the advocates of an Universalism which made light of Revelation, or treated with contempt the fundamental doctrines of the Gospel. Not to be despised was the providential opening which this project seemed to afford for shewing American Universalists how great was their defection since the glorious gospel was first made known among them through the preaching of John Murray, and for pointing them once more to the more excellent way. Finally— he acceded to the proposition;—and in doing so, set to work with the vigour that never failed him in any enterprise in which he embarked. He pleaded for literary contributions and support in all directions. Unfettered by editorial responsibility he could use his liberty without restraint, and he appeared before the public merely as a *contributor*: yet it is well known that, but for *his* encouragement, the periodical would never have been started, and that, without his zealous and active support, it could never have been sustained. If not exactly his own offspring, he was ever the life of it, from beginning to end, and what he wrote on its behalf, in the way of correspondence, bore no inconsiderable proportion to the articles he contributed to its pages. The first number contained from his pen "*a brief sketch of the recent progress of Universalism.*" With a modesty one cannot now mark without emotion, he alludes, in this article, in the slightest possible way, to his own connection with the subject. His contributions to this periodical were continued from month to month. Many of them were of great length. The disappointment occasioned by the silence of some, upon whose co-operation he had reasonably counted, only impelled him to ply his pen with greater perseverance. How kind and encouraging he was to his less-gifted fellow-labourers, many of them could testify! He chose more frequently to take the reviewer's chair: that, in this capacity, he might shew his superiority?—display his critical acumen?—pour forth his resources of classical lore?—cope with intellectual giants of the day?—or range at large, with equal familiarity with the great ones of former times, through the labyrinths of ecclesiastical history, and theology?—and thereby enlarge his reputation, and bring himself into wider intercourse with the notabilities of literature? *Not so.* Christian friends whose modesty would have been shocked at literary fame, whose simple love of the gospel, backed frequently by the very slenderest pretentions to literature, impelled them to record their thoughts in a pamphlet of but a few pages, were the men and women he delighted to honour. *Their* friendship was more precious to him than worldly alliances, however distinguished. His love of Christ, in this way made itself known as love for the brethren. His reviews were the warm expression of kindness and fellow-feeling. Conscience, was, however, by no means repulsed, nor its place usurped by blind partiality and indiscriminate praise. Honest and candid criticism, always exercised in the same spirit of truth and love as that which dictated the praise, he brought to his delicate task, hoping thereby to benefit the reader of the review as well as the author he was reviewing. We have always been deeply impressed with the fact of his devoting his time to so great an extent to this kind of work,—as affording a striking evidence of his unobtrusive modesty, and his preference, even, for a certain kind of obscurity. Constitutionally shy, perhaps, would not his views of human nature, in the light of the Cross, rather foster than weaken this preference?

Only once or twice did he step beyond the usual limits within which he wielded his critical pen. Professor Newman's "Soul," at this period, was attracting unusual notice. This gentleman's personal history was not entirely unknown to Dr Thom. He felt interested in the crisis of religious thought and feeling, of which, in some of its aspects, this work was the exponent. To give it a sifting he resolved. One short paragraph of thirteen lines, and a quotation at the end of the review contain all the wheat, and that not of the finest, he could save from the heap of human chaff, which, with scriptural logic and Christian zeal, he proceeds to burn up with the consuming fire of divine truth, through an article extending to nearly thirty closely-printed pages. Its classical style, and its mythological allusions, though among its subordinate charms, evince the scholarship of the writer; and shew that, in dealing with the *Professor*, Dr. Thom conceived that there was a legitimate use of the heathen Pantheon, in the illustration and defence of the truth.

The Memoir of his father, which Dr. Thom wrote for the *Universalist*, and to which we have already adverted, has furnished us with some hints as to the early history of the son. In its delineation of the character and disposition of the father, have not its readers traced many of the lineaments of David Thom? Of this life of his father he writes, "I have not exaggerated. Indeed, I have, to use a painter's phrase, *toned down*. He was actually the most perfect man I have ever seen or known." The Memoir of John Thom could not be got into the periodical without adding to the number of its pages, and Dr. Thom, who was fully justified in claiming the insertion of the life of an Universalist who had so eminently and practically adorned the doctrine of God, his Saviour, would only consent to do so on the condition that the entire expense incurred should be charged to his account. In reference to this matter, we transcribe the following characteristic and, in some respects, suggestive paragraph, from a letter:

"Thanks for the account. Far less than I anticipated. No matter though it were ten, or fifteen, or even twenty pounds. I would have paid it cheerfully, and would have begged, borrowed, or *stolen* (?) the money, if necessary, in order to have paid it. Nothing too great—no expense grudged—which respects the memory of my father. And such a father! Careful am I in my personal and even house expenses. Having no vicious indulgences, attending no theatres, clothing my family plainly, &c., I do not throw much money away in *these various ways*. But where my father, or my dear brothers and sisters are concerned, I care not, *if possessed of the means*, as to the expense. *Here*, indeed 'the fool and his money are soon parted'. How many the projects as to my much-loved relations, which for years I have cherished, alas! never to be realized. They depend upon my becoming rich, and rich in this world's goods I shall never be. My heavenly Father hath seen meet that it shall be so. Faith acquiesces in this as good. Well, it is of no consequence. My projects can dwell in my own bosom: and they can die with me.'

"I am in many respects a strange creature. Perfectly capable of keeping my own secret. Perfectly capable of cherishing purposes for twenty, twenty-five, or thirty years; and then, when the suitable opportunity occurs, of carrying them into effect. The world gives me no credit for these things. No matter. The world and I are quits. Human society has always been with me so secondary a matter that I can do without it: I like it, and yet, with true Falconer feeling, I nauseate it. All the kicking, turning me out of Establishments, turning of cold shoulder to me, &c., have made no impression on me. I jog on. A kindly word affects me......Observe, purposes that are yet *in nubibus*, and may never be realized, I say nothing about. I have no right to trouble others with them. They exist in my breast, with fixed *contingent* resolve, notwithstanding. They interfere not with my present duty. That is done. When inconvenient, or improper to detail every motive or principle of conduct, I keep to myself what should be kept. The rest may be told. But the actions shall speak."

Perhaps the above will be found a help to the understanding of some traits of his private character.

Occupied in the spring of 1850, with an Introduction to *The Restoration of all things*, by Jeremiah White, which he was then editing for publication, Dr. Thom writes:

"The Lord enable me to write it with an eye to His glory. O, I loathe 'Heroes and Hero-worship.' And yet may I speak the truth in love. The Lord guide me. I shall soon have returned to dust. My trifles may follow me. Should they, or any of them survive, may love to God, through Christ Jesus, a rejoicing in the righteousness and life of Christ alone, and a pointing of others to the same, be seen to be their characteristics. *No self.* Self sunk in Christ!—This be my motto. Gal. ii. 20."

During the preparation of a new edition of *Why is Popery*

Progressing? in the autumn of 1850, he was overtaken and prostrated by a serious illness. The unmerciful way in which he worked himself, in spite of suffering and exhaustion, is painfully apparent in the following: "To day at great risk of a relapse, for I am reduced to the lowest degree of weakness, I have, with the assistance of my wife, gone through the proofs, and am now, with my daughter's assistance, addressing you. I am still confined to bed."

Here are his own remarks on *Why is Popery Progressing?*

"My tract is plainly and unpretendingly written. Not startling enough to draw the attention of the man of genius; indeed, intentionally avoiding the startling. Trying to keep down to the sober reality of facts. Combining the statement of truths the most important, with cautious argumentation, and expressing the whole in popular diction. Condensing much, and yet trying to do it without the appearing to condense. (To squeeze, rather.) It gratifies me to find that, while the fastidious have not found fault with my progressive statement of facts, the nature of my argumentation and my diction, I have been, on the whole, well understood, by the weak and the illiterate. *Upon such*, in several cases, an impression has been made."

The republication of the pamphlet during the agitation of the "papal aggression," brought him a mass of correspondence including the Bishops of Exeter and Durham; a most respectful and flattering letter from the Bp. of Hereford, Bp. of St. David's; Bp. of Cashel,—a most Christian letter in which he styles himself a fellow servant; the Earl of Winchelsea, the Earl of Roden, besides several M.P.s., including his highly-esteemed friend, Sir George Staunton.

To the correspondence in which, at this time, he was engaged with Lord Palmerston, respecting the affairs of his late brother Robert, he alludes in the following:

"By the communications of noblemen, &c. I set no great store. Many of them I have. But I do attach value to even these few autograph lines of Lord Palmerston. That a man with the weightiest affairs of Europe and the world now pressing on his shoulders and who generally replies to *public* communications by his secretary, should have found time to write these few friendly lines, I feel to be a high honour. I had, once before, a *longer* autograph communication from him, respecting my dear brother."

The autumn of 1851 brought with it another attack of bronchitis, from which, however, God was pleased, once more, to restore him to health. Hardly, however, could he have regained his former vigour. The respectful and affectionate watchfulness of his congregation appreciated the position of the individual who had ministered to them, Sunday after Sunday, with little intermission, since 1828, in Bold-street Chapel. Anxious were they that some provision should be made for the Dr. and his family. Ευπορια was not the beast he worshipped; nor did it ever constitute, even subordinately, the object of his pursuit. To *give* and not to *get*, was an instinct of his impulsive human nature, and the mighty self-crucifying action of the life and mind of Jesus, made generosity, in all possible forms of its manifestation, a central law of his spiritual being. By no *contract* were his friends held to support him for a single year. The tenure of his position at Liverpool involved no claims of commercial bargain. From a lower point of view, therefore, the future affected him in no ordinary degree, as uncertain and dark.

"My destiny, humanly speaking," he would say, "I do not know. My friends may detain me. They wish to do so. Let the Lord lead. I do not wish to originate my own motions. I may stay where I am. If not: London? America? New Holland? New Zealand?—I know not. A very dark cloud overhangs the future."

The kindness of his friends was, to him, an intimation of Providence. This kindness now manifested itself in the building of a new chapel, with contiguous property, which was appropriated as a mark of their high esteem for the Dr. and as a provision for his numerous family.

The æsthetics of the new chapel, in Crown Street, required no elaborate architectural display. Worshipping the one God and Father of all, through the one mediator between God and man, *the* man Christ Jesus, the preacher regarded himself as on precisely the same level as the humblest member of that family for whom that mediator gave himself a ransom. Over those who met with him for mutual edification he was neither king nor priest,—neither prophet nor professor. In the place of a pulpit, therefore, for convenience of speaking, was a platform, but slightly raised above the general level. Here he requested others to occupy a place as well as himself. He was as willing to learn as to teach.

The mission of the American Universalists to this country, in 1852, was carried into execution by the arrival of the Rev. Abel C. Thomas. Unable to offer any sympathy of a religious nature, indeed, giving a decided refusal of the slightest countenance or support, Dr. Thom paid the most polite and friendly attentions to Mr. and Mrs Thomas, and went so far as to offer advice, as to the best mode of prosecuting the object of his mission. His natural allies in this country were the Unitarians, and we suspect that the very slight impression made by this gentleman, in his missionary labours, may be mainly accounted for by the absorption of his efforts and their results by that body. Query, could Dr. Thom's neither supporting, nor publicly opposing him, have disarranged his plans?

Deeply was Dr. Thom affected by the loss of his old and intimate friend, Samuel M'Culloch, Esq. Surgeon, in the beginning of 1853. Notwithstanding the little Memoir in which he recorded his appreciation of his friend's general character and worth, we may be permitted to quote the following, from a letter written at the time:

"This has been a stunning blow to me, and to others, because unexpected. Thirty years close and uninterrupted friendship, broken off almost in a moment! O I feel it—feel it keenly! I cannot think of the affection,—the intense overwhelming affection, which he shewed me on his dying-bed, without shedding tears. But it is the Lord. I bow submissive to His blessed will. What a triumphant, what a glorious death was M'Culloch's. *No Universalism.* No *ism* of any other kind. The simple, true Word of God which had got hold of his conscience, enabled him positively to rejoice calmly, but decidedly, in the revealed divine righteousness of Jesus Christ. It was a sight for Deists and Unitarians to behold. Certain (*evangelical* (?) opposers of Scriptural Universalism were somewhat astonished, if not confounded and abashed, I ween. Even you, dear friend, will be astonished, if ever I have occasion to relate the particulars. Ten hours with him in his dying moments, enable me to do so. How his dying testimony reconciles me to the distressing event! Yesterday I assisted in committing his honored remains to the grave....Owing to his high standing, long practice, and established reputation, as well as the attachment cherished towards him by all, crowds awaited the arrival of the corpse. It was carried into Rodney-Street Kirk. I officiated. Every sect, in Liverpool sent forth its representatives. I addressed, in the old place of worship, capable of holding 1800 persons, from which I was ignominiously thrust out for conscience'-sake, nearly thirty years ago,—Unitarians Swedenborgians, Sandemanians, and even Jews. O, I trembled before I entered that desk. But I looked to my Heavenly Father. Blessed be His name, He sustained me......Contrary to my own anticipations I was enabled to speak with calmness, deliberation, dignity, perfect mastery of myself, and, I felt, with power. Good, I trust, was done. O God, bless Thy word! I had no abuse of persons. No Universalism. No glorification of the creature. I disclaimed eulogy of man. (That I left for the columns of a newspaper.) I tried to glorify God in Christ, and trust that I was not altogether unsuccessful. Sentiments were uttered by me, which evangelical men, if true to their profession, could not gainsay. And they felt it. They seemed astonished at my forbearance. No *remedial* scheme ('repairing the ruins of the fall') did I proclaim. To God be the glory. Christ's perfections I magnified. Dr. Raffles was one of my auditors. He had been invited as a friend of the deceased, and we rode down from Edge Hill together. Owing to some of Mr M'Culloch's family sitting under him, I asked him to take the closing prayer. He complied."

Stealthily, and yet not without frequent warnings, was that calamity advancing upon him which was eventually to hem him in, in "a land of darkness." We have now before us a letter of 50 pages of note paper, the concluding paragraph of which discloses the special motive which stimulated the writer—the conviction that it might not be long before his right hand must forget its cunning, since those that look out at the windows were darkening. He says, "*Perhaps*, you may keep it. It is, from the state of my eyesight, the last long letter which you will ever receive from me. Hence I have indulged and *palavered* a great deal."

He was now supplying articles on the "Churches and Chapels of Liverpool," and on its "Scotch Kirks," for the Historic Society of Lancashire and Cheshire—the largest, wealthiest, and most influential literary and antiquarian institution in the two Counties. Having assisted at its formation in 1848, and being one of the members of its Council till 1851, he was, from this period till 1856, when blindness and infirm health induced him to retire from its management, one of its Vice Presidents.*

Before the close of the year 1853, Dr. Thom had suffered that alarming attack of illness, which threatened to deprive his friends and his family of that presence which had become, to so great an extent, the centre of their social, intellectual and religious life. He tells us of his sufferings, Sep. 28th, 1853,

"It has pleased our Heavenly Father that recently I should be much out of sorts. Nervous complaints have assailed me. As the result, I have been unable to officiate for some Lord's days (three). God's hand has been laid very gently and graciously upon me. How sweet His Fatherly chastisement. Truly, truly can I say that, in this my hour of affliction, I have been given to experience personally,—the value of divine facts, divinely revealed, through divine testimony,—the value of Christ as my righteousness and life.—No human reasonings. Divine testimony imparts life to the conscience, and is productive of other divine effects. Blessed, blessed be God, for His most precious Word."

Still deeper were the sufferings he was yet to endure; and intense was the anxiety with which his friends watched the progress of his malady, which for four months deprived his congregation of his ministrations. We avail ourselves of the kindness of his early and latest and much-endeared friend, and medical adviser, Dr. MacIntyre, who, in describing this crisis, says:

"That he built up a very beautiful system on what he believed to be a scriptural foundation I am fully aware. But I know too well that in doing so, he spent years and years of his life in intellectual labour of the most exhausting kind;—and that this labour, having been carried on in opposition to the natural laws of health and life, at last produced its inevitable fruit—complete prostration of both body and mind. Of course, this state of things required and obtained the greatest care and consideration. For a good while the issue was very doubtful. But as the bodily strength was slowly restored the despondency of his mind gradually gave way. Now here you see, what I have often seen in men of great intellect, when they have over-worked themselves, caring neither for sleep nor sustenance, until nature can no longer hold out. But it pleased God that it should be otherwise with our friend, and I was enabled, I believe, under the divine blessing, to be in some degree, the means gradually of restoring him to that healthy state of mind in which he continued to rejoice, as a child of God, to the day of his death."

* On his retirement from the Chair of the Society, its members deemed, and unanimously voted, the services rendered by Dr. Thom as worthy of a special mark of recognition. A meeting was held in December 1856, at which a diploma of life membership (the first that the Society had ever conferred) was presented through their Hon. Sec., the Rev. Dr. Hume. Through the kindness of Joseph Mayer, Esq. F.A.S., the Hon. Curator of the Society, the diploma had been got up in a style of unusual elegance. An appropriate inscription was signed by the Hon. Secretary and Hon. Curator, as well as by Sir Edward Cust, the President, who was specially present on the occasion to subscribe his name to the diploma. The testimonial was presented with every mark of esteem, and acknowledged in a speech which was not only appropriate but affecting. In proof of the lively interest he took in the Society, and of his desire to promote its objects, he referred in this speech to several projected papers, for one of which he had collected valuable materials, and to which he thus alluded on this occasion: "What has pained me more than anything else, was my inability to

From November, 1853, until early in March, 1854, Dr. Thom was completely laid aside. Up to the time of this illness, he had preached twice every Lord's day; but from March, 1854, till April, 1860, he officiated only in the forenoon. At the latter period, a second attack, which brought with it excruciating and protracted pain in the eyes, compelled him to abandon public speaking altogether. His faithful Liverpool friends evinced their sympathizing regard by a continuance of their *undiminished* support; and, on his final retirement from the pulpit, in addition to the permanent provision they had already made (in 1851), they further expressed their affectionate and reverential attachment, by presenting him with a sum of money, amounting to nearly £1200.

The loss of sight, to a man who spent more than half his life in writing and reading, must have been felt as an extraordinary privation. While the calamity was impending, no effort was spared to avert it. In 1854 he consulted Dr. Mackenzie, at Glasgow, and paid him a second visit in June, 1855. And in 1857, when his sight was so far impaired as to permit him barely to discriminate light from darkness, he undertook the journey to Graefrath, near Elberfeldt, that he might have the advice of the renowned ophthalmist, the Hofrath, Dr. De Leuw. With scarcely a ray of hope that his sight would ever be recovered, he returned to England. His cheerful contentment—the result of an assured and happy persuasion that divine wisdom and love determined even the *minutiæ* of his life—inspired his friends with admiration; "and they glorified God in him." He wished to make neither much nor little of his blindness. From the platform of Spirit, to him the darkness and the light were both alike. With the eye of sense we see things but as they *seem*. Another visual faculty he had long enjoyed, with which he had a glimpse of things as they *really are*: he still lived, "as seeing Him"—and all else as in Him —"who is invisible."

Thus on one occasion (May 7th 1858), he adverts to his loss of sight:

"The compensations of the Almighty, in this life, when he withholds and when, after having vouchsafed for a time, he removes any of our faculties, are oftentimes truly astonishing. Particularly with the loss of outward, he may be pleased to give an increase of inward light, and thereby more than make up for the external night in which it may be his good pleasure that we should spend the remainder of our years upon earth. Nay, when completely deprived of eye-sight, and thereby, to appearance, reduced to a state of extremity as to the means of earning a livelihood, he can and may raise up friends in the most unexpected quarters, and render what would have been one of the greatest of earthly calamities, a source of the greatest of earthly advantages. Even should it not be so,— should the words of Habakkuk, so expressive of utter destitution, in

bring before your notice the celebrated Dr. Balcanqual, a man of historic fame, who occupied a conspicuous place in the history of the Civil Wars, and who is buried at no great distance from this place."

our case be fulfilled,—should the fruit of the olive fail, and should there be no grapes on the vine,—should we be thereby constrained more closely to cling to the Lord, and to rejoice in Him who is the God of our salvation, are we not, after all, gainers by the cruel disaster? Is it not the highest of blessings to have our faith in Christ strengthened and enlarged, and our affections towards Him drawn forth with increased intensity even amidst the wreck of all our worldly hopes?"

To some little extent, even the material resource was restored to him. There were those around him who were ready to pluck out their own eyes, and cut off their own right hand, that he might yet satisfy his voracity for books and keep up the pleasure of epistolary intercourse, and he was thus as much an Argus and a Briareus as they could make him.* It is more than probable, that these acts of self-denial are reckoned, by those who had the opportunity of performing them, among their happiest privileges and highest honours. But to dash off half a dozen long letters in a morning, as he used to do, *currente calamo*, as hard as he could drive, was not to be accomplished by other hands than his own, nor was he now physically equal to the exertion of dictating very much to others.—This he felt deeply, when he said, "May I hope that dear and respected friends will understand my silence to be no proof of want of esteem, or of diminished affection? The fact is, I have not time. I have not inclination. I have not eyes to write with. Can my friends yet trust me? Dear Waddell, (nearly a twelvemonth): dear P. J. Bailey (months): dear W. Rushton (months), &c. &c. O, I long to answer!"

To his dear old friend, the late Richard Roe, Esq. B.A., he addressed a long, most sympathizing and suitable letter, Nov. 23, 1854. Mr. Roe, with the weight of nearly 100 years upon him, was at this time suffering great prostration. We make no apology for an extract of some length from this letter, because it not only throws light upon Dr. Thom's religious views at this time, but supplies a key, by which his comparative reticence on the doctrine of Universalism, during the last few years, is explained.

"I am a Universalist, because God's word expressly declares that Christ, the living God, is the Saviour of all men, 1 Tim. iv. 10; and that unto God, through Christ, every knee shall bow, Isai. xlv. Phil. ii. 1—9; but my Universalism has long taken a subordinate, I think proper, place in my religious creed, and has no perceptible influence, that I am aware of, on my personal hope towards God. What I have said in regard to it in different parts of my works, especially in "Dialogue" 1st, still appears to be in the main true to my mind. Consisting, however, in some measure in inferences derived from Revealed Truth, and being as stated by me, the offspring of my own brain, were I to be influenced personally, as in the presence of God, by any thing which has emanated

---

* There is one lady, out of the Dr.'s own family, whose intelligent and devoted friendship we may here be permitted to mention. We allude to Miss Day, who was pleased for many hours every week to read with him, and whose thorough appreciation of the Dr.'s system stamped her services with a high value.

from my own pen, however apparently consistent and true, I should dread coming under the rebuke pronounced by the Holy Spirit, by the mouth of Isaiah, upon those carpenters who, having procured a piece of suitable wood, convert part of it into an idol which they worship, while they seek to warm themseves with the remainder. No, no, my dear friend. It is the simple and unadulterated word of God alone which, from first to last, speaks peace to our guilty consciences, shews us our possession of newness of life in the risen Messiah, fills us with joy and peace in believing, and carries us through every danger and obstacle safely and triumphantly unto the Heavenly Kingdom. To mix up any human views, whether those of ourselves or others, with what God himself has revealed, is not merely to mar its simplicity and beauty, but materially to interfere with and disturb its direct and immediate divine influence upon our own minds. It is the dead fly in the apothecaries' ointment. It is to suppose that, by the glowworm effulgence of our own paltry intellects, we can increase the lustre of that Sun of Righteousness—that uncreated and heavenly light—who alone speaking in his word,—is a light to our feet, and a lamp to our path."

The following extract from a letter to ourselves, June 7th, 1859, four years later, indicates the permanence of the convictions expressed in the above extract, and the growing absorption of his thoughts, his affections, and his aspirations, in the complete and full realization of his personal relationship to that Saviour into whose more immediate presence, it was his calm and holy conviction that, no longer separated by the veil of flesh, he was in a short time to receive a joyful and an abundant entrance.

" Your allusion to Peter's sheet is *apropos* and interesting. Undoubtedly my conscientious feelings and convictions are, and have always been, as my various works shew, chiefly with the Bereans. Christ and his Church, as one, constitute the grand topics of the Old and New Testament Scriptures. That Jesus is also Spiritual Adam, and that as such, in Him "*all are made alive*," is also Scripturally true; but it is a truth with which I find myself and other members of the Church to have no *immediate* concern, as it remains to be developed, not in the present but in the future state of things. 1 Tim. ii. 6, and iv. 10. The second glorious appearing of our Divine Head, is what interests us, his members. Heb. ix. 28."

To the same effect he expresses himself in his correspondence with the Rev. J. B. Marsden, author of the *Dictionary of Christian Sects and Churches*,* published in 1856. And to us he writes:

"Considering the position and sentiments of Mr. Marsden, his article on 'Universalism' appears to me to be a remarkably clear, fair, and well-written one. It presents an admirably-condensed view of the history of the doctrine from the earliest ages of Christianity until now. I particularly like its succinctness and inpartiality. The design to be brief has, however, betrayed him into some mistakes respecting the discussions which are now going on in America."

* "The principles maintained by the Liverpool Society are thus briefly stated by Dr. Thom, (to whose courtesy we are indebted for much valuable information on the subject of this article) in a private communication to the Editor. ' We love the leading doctrines of the Gospel, not as they appear in popular creeds, but as they are laid down in the Scriptures themselves. We know no

The autumn of 1855 found him, for the second time during this year, at Glasgow. With his brother-in-law (Mr. Charles), he attended the meetings of the "British Association." But beyond receiving his ticket as an old life-member of eighteen years standing, and attending several general and sectional meetings, he took no part whatever in the proceedings. On this occasion, with Col. Fawcett, then Mayor of Brighton; his friend and relative, Sheriff Steele; his old friend David Stow, Esq., of Normal School notoriety, and others, he renewed pleasurable intercourse.

Not less unexpected and affecting than the removal of his friend, Mr. M'Culloch, was the loss he was called to sustain, in the death of his eldest daughter (Mrs. Stewart), March, 1859. Thus he acquaints us with the event, which must have been the cause of grief the most poignant.

"March 16, 1859.—God, in the course of his adorable providence, hath been pleased most graciously and lovingly to remove from her husband and from me my eldest-born, my beloved daughter, Mrs. Stewart. An announcement to this effect would, I presume, reach you this morning. The wound is at present too fresh to permit my handling it. Yet last Lord's day our Heavenly Father was pleased to support me in addressing my friends. Oh, this has been a dreadful blow; but it is the stroke of Him who IS love."

"March 22. Jane was no ordinary wife, as she was no ordinary child. Amiable, tender, generous, disposed to take the best view of everything and everybody, she combined with such dispositions, what is not always found in connection with them, intellectual qualities and attainments of a superior order. She was peculiarly qualified to be the solace of a husband's heart, and a comfort and a counsellor to him amidst the disquietude of human life. Devoted to her husband, she was also deeply attached to her old blind father. And then, she loved, under divine teaching, the everlasting gospel. Well, she is gone; she well not return to us; but we shall go to her.....The Lord vouchsafes to me, and has, ever since the calamity overtook me, vouchsafed a strength and consolation which previously I could not have anticipated. Blessed be His name. Lord's day week I was enabled to speak in public; and last Lord's day, I was so supported and strengthened, as to address my friends (who turned out in considerable numbers, and showed the greatest sympathy and respect), from Isaiah xxxv. 10, *And the ransomed of the Lord*, &c. But I must dismiss this subject; as I find that, if persevered in, it would be apt to overcome me."*

---

teacher of Divine truth but the Holy Ghost Himself, speaking to us and teaching us in and through the Holy Scriptures. Nevertheless we can love and admire the statements of divine truth which are to be found in the Thirty-nine Articles of the Church of England, and in other publications, the leading views of which rest upon evangelical principles. To us Universalism is a truth, because God Himself reveals it; but it is not to us the main truth. Hence we very seldom speak of it. Regeneration by the Spirit of Christ-Jesus, admission into the knowledge and enjoyment of his love, and the fruits and effects which spring from the influence and operation of the truth, are our constant, as they are our Scriptural themes.'—See Marsden's *Dictionary of Christian Churches and Sects*, 1st Edit. vol. ii. pp. 358-369.

* Mrs. Stewart left behind her a little boy, who still survives. Bearing the

In the autumn, with Mrs. Thom, he visited Ross, and other places in Hereford and Gloucester. The charming scenery around Ross, the pleasant and intelligent acquaintances there formed, and the genial climate of the vicinity, were found most refreshing, and wonderfully promoted his health and enjoyment. The Rev. W. F. Buck, Independent minister of Ross, was at this time suffering deep domestic affliction. Notwithstanding important differences on some theological subjects, Mr. Buck, and some of his friends, asked the Dr. to take a Service for him. He acceded to the request. Will Mr. Buck pardon us for transcribing a portion of a letter in which reference is made to this unusual event?

"He very kindly complied with the request in the morning of Sept. 11th. His text from Isaiah xxvi. 19, was viewed in immediate connection with the resurrection, as described in 1 Cor. xv. I heard the discourse with much pleasure and profit, as did the people of my charge. It displayed both beauty and strength, and was delivered with much holy animation. I saw him more than once afterwards, and was greatly delighted with his tenderness and the kindness which he displayed. His heart appeared to be overflowing with love to all, but especially so to all the disciples of Christ. I shall ever bear him in recollection with much affection."

In the autumn of 1860, he gratified a long-cherished wish to visit Stonehenge. Accompanied by his wife, he made a four weeks' tour, taking in Clifton, Salisbury, Southampton, Walton Abbey, Warminster, Worcester, Bath, Birmingham, &c. It was astonishing how much he had to say of these towns, although he had had no ocular testimony concerning them. The attentions he invariably met with from strangers, while prosecuting these little excursions, gratified him exceedingly.

The comparative seclusion of the last two years of his life, was peaceful and happy. Quietness and rest he had well earned, by years of unremitting and arduous toil. A life-long active service, with many a hard-fought battle, entitled him to honourable retirement. Yet was his repose accepted as a kind and wise dispensation of Heaven, rather than sought as an object of desire. The faith that fought the fight, acquiesced in, rather than rejoiced at the putting off of the armour, and the sheathing of the sword. Nor did the faith, which unintermittingly sustained him in the field, now forsake him. May we not, without presumption, point to this grand reality of his life,—this living, glowing, active faith,—as identifying him with that great cloud of witnesses, still testifying to the presence of Jesus in the Church, and still testifying against that *wavering* which constitutes the chief characteristic of a "faith" no more built upon the true foundation than are the waves of the sea built upon the bottom of the ocean? We may truly say that the

honoured name of *David Thom*, earnestly pray his father and his friends that he may largely inherit the excellences of both his mother and his grand-father, and early acquire a knowledge and a love for the truths contended for in the following Sermons.

third and most convincing volume of his *Assurance of Faith*, was written in his life,—a life of holy, pure, and self-crucifying faith

He well knew the healthfulness of varied occupation. Much walking exercise was he in the habit of taking. The rust of disuse he shrank from. Only a few weeks before his last illness he was refreshing his Greek by committing to memory the *Odes of Anacreon*. Three of these he mastered, notwithstanding his failing health.

His reading, latterly, embraced History, Philosophy, Poetry, &c. Like an old soldier, he was, by engaging in religious controversy, aroused to a pitch of excitement which was apt to be too much for his nervous system. Theology was, indeed, judiciously forbidden by his physician.

Among recent books, *The Friendly Disputants*, by Miss Irvine, much interested him, and by the logical power it displayed, he was greatly struck. Much delight and edification did he express in perusing the late Rev. Mr. Head's *Proximate and Ultimate Results of Redemption*, assenting very cordially to its statements almost *in toto*.

"Bailey I thanked some time ago for his present of that extraordinary book the 'Mystic'—a work which I have heard read with great care and interest, and which in spite of anything that has been said, and can be said against it, is a most perfect production of its kind. The most finished poem it is that its author ever wrote."

Daily, the book which was always first read to him was the Word of God. With him, this was the book of books: its perusal was no matter of mere routine. To him it was the record of facts which were to be gathered from no other source. On its truths he loved to linger at the social meal. The breakfast was generally prolonged by a passage from Virgil, Tacitus, or some other classical author. Then came the Glasgow papers, &c. It was a special treat to get the New Testament in the original read to him on Sundays. No Concordance was necessary with the Doctor. Let a passage be quoted, and he would give the chapter and verse. It was only to mention chapter and verse, and he was ready to recite the passage. Subsequently to his loss of sight, the proceedings of the Synod of Dordt were read to him, by his daughters, in Latin, every sentence of which he translated to them, first literally, then freely. Sir W. Hamilton's *Discussions* had been gone through, years ago. The book was taken up again latterly only to be laid down, since, although he could follow the writer perfectly well, the tax upon his brain made the reading more laborious than pleasurable. To specify only one more: his friend, W. Atherstone's poem, *Israel in Egypt*, afforded him great delight.

The afternoon he would pass in calling on friends, visiting the sick, and, as far as lay in his power, relieving distress.

The lively interest which he ever took, in what was transpiring, both at home and abroad, and the way in which he would regard all events in the light of a true, because Christian philosophy, is transparent in the following extract from a letter to a Christian friend, dated January 2nd, 1860.

"That some great change is on the eve of taking place in Italy seems to me very manifest. What, however, that change is destined to be, events alone can declare. Probably the temporal sovereignty of the Pope may come to an end; but it is equally probable that the opposition of Austria and of the whole Ultramontane party in Great Britain, as well as on the Continent, may serve to stave off this result for a time. Italy is evidently at present in a state of great ferment, but I fear that the excitement there prevailing, is more of a political, than of a religious nature. Nevertheless, good, to many, through the spread of the Scriptures, the exposure of Popery, and the reception of the everlasting Gospel, will, I trust, be the consequence. In Ranke's *History of the Popes*, will be found some very curious particulars respecting a Society having a reforming tendency, which existed in Rome and other parts of the Peninsula, as early as 1525, or 1530. Cardinals Sandoleto, Pole, and others, are said to have been members of it. I confess that I am not very hopeful about this fine country."

"Not having regarded for many years the Pope as Antichrist,—or the Church of Rome as Babylon,—it would be to me of little importance, as to the destruction of these two powers, that even the Church of Rome herself were soon to be overthrown. Taught by Rev. xi. 8, followed up by xii. 7 to 9, and other passages of that wonderful Book, I have long perceived that the Harlot, Babylon, Sodom, Egypt, &c. of prophecy, is the *Jewish* or *Old-Testament Church* fallen, or cast out of Heaven, and the kings of the earth, with whom she had committed fornication, are *believers of the truth. They shall reign on the earth.* S.S. *passim.*"

"From this adulterous connection, has sprung a whole brood or spawn of Fleshly Churches. See Rev. xiii. 18, and Rev. xvii. throughout. As to the first, you may consult my solution of the *number of the beast*, and contrast what is said of it at the close of Rev. xiii, with the one true Spiritual Church, at the beginning of the Chap. xiv. In Chap. xvii. you have the filthy mother, the fallen Jewish Church, with her filthy brood of apostate Fleshly Churches, falsely called 'Christian,' placed before you. Of these harlot daughters, unquestionably the Church of Rome is first and foremost, inheriting all the vices, impurities and abominations of her harlot mother."

"In the entirety of these Fleshly Churches, established and dissenting, among whom there are, it is to be hoped, many righteous Lots, who are earnestly enjoined to come out of them, you have presented to you Antichrist, as a whole; understanding, of course, that antichrist first shewed himself in the opposing Jewish Church. See 2 Thess. ii. 1; 1 John iv."

How sweet and Christianly simple, the following passage from the same letter: some of its strains are like the plaintive and subdued notes of the home-bird's evening song.

"You enquire as to what literary labour I am now engaged in. Alas! the days of my intellectual working for the press are over. The consequences of the attack which I had in 1853, are now fearfully telling upon me. I dare not now, considering the shattered nature of my whole nervous system, tax or excite my brain by much mental effort. As a writer on the most interesting of all topics, I am now laid aside. Sleepless nights and great prostration of physical energy (rendering, as last Lord's day, a public address to my friends impossible), warn me to be on my guard, and are, perhaps, sent to me as a sweet but silent intimation from my dear and glorified Head that the time of my departure hence may not be far distant. Human nature, of course, dislikes this state of things, —recoils from it and would fain that it were otherwise. I feel particularly, my inability to employ my pen, in behalf of God's simple scriptural truth. But faith, or rather the Holy Spirit through faith, is triumphing in me over such feelings; and knowing that 'all things work together for good to them that love God, to them that are the called according to his purpose,' I desire to be found acting as one of God's redeemed creatures and dear children, until He shall be pleased to take me home to Himself, and bring me into the full enjoyment of Heavenly felicity. I suspect that this is the last long letter, it may be, should my state of exhaustion continue and increase, the last letter you may receive from me. Considering the degree to which my brain has been excited for the last three or four weeks by the dictating of letters on what appeared to be necessary topics, I may perhaps be chargeable with imprudence in having thus replied at such length to your much-esteemed letter. Indeed, long letters and protracted mental labour of any kind, have been expressly prohibited by medical and other friends: but I have once more broken through."

Have we not in this letter a striking and practical illustration of the doctrine of the "two natures"—so strangely shocking to his early opponents,—so full of mischief in the eyes of the anathematizing Presbytery and General Assembly of 1825, but not less delightful in the calm triumph of the one, over the subjugation and captivity of the other?

To his correspondence with the Rev. Mr. Nisbett we have already alluded. Carried on with the understanding that it was to constitute the basis of a sketch of his life for the Cyclopædia to which we have already referred, we cannot be wrong in attaching to it the greatest importance, in so far as it relates to his theology. How touching the modest adoption of the *past tense*, in speaking of his religious views, as he appears to glance back upon them, through the shadows of approaching dissolution, and the undisguised consciousness of decaying power, as expressed in the opening paragraph of this, the last letter of the series:

"'Death's shafts,' to use Blair's phrase, have been 'flying thick' of late among the small number of my much-endeared and highly-esteemed friends. Four of them, three of between 35 and 26 years standing, and two of them large and generous subscribers to my chapel fund, have been removed from time, since I went to Pen-y-sarn on the 25th of June last. This is a sad inroad upon the small number of my attached supporters, and has been productive in my mind of feelings of deep sorrow. Since writing to you last, I have had occasion to dictate five letters of condolence, all of them long, and all of them in no small degree taxing my powers of thought, as well as affection. These, besides communications on other topics. There was a time when I should scarcely have considered such efforts as worthy of having a thought bestowed on them; but alas! now, blind, and with impaired health and strength, I find that comparatively little matters are becoming great and important to me. *The grasshopper shall be a burden.* Eccles. xii."

" In answer to your kind inquiries, I should observe:—"

" 1. That the name of my former place of worship, from 1828 till 1851, was ' Bold-st. Chapel': and that of the latter, from 1851 till 1860, was ' Crown-st. Chapel.' We were known, popularly, as ' Berean Universalists,' which name appears in Gage's Map of Liverpool for 1835, and will be found occasionally in the Directories."

" 2. As to what have been my religious sentiments latterly, I have already made a reference to them in my second letter, when speaking of the publication of my *Assurance of Faith*, 1833. Lest, however, there should be any mistake, I may add:—These have always been, essentially and fundamentally, Calvinistic. Taken as a whole, with some slight objections to their sublapsarian character and tendencies, and a decided protest against the puritanical attempt to do away with the conviction of our personal interest in Christ's death and resurrection as essential to the faith of the gospel, I could almost yet subscribe the decrees of the Synod of Dordt, and the Confession of Faith of the Westminster Assembly. No doubt, with the late Edward Irving, I prefer the first, that is, Knox's Scottish Confession of Faith, 1560. If less logical and profound, this document is, to me, far more simple and scriptural than the Confession at present in use. Consistently with the views of Luther, and I may add, even of Calvin, it ignores 'the doubtsome faith of the Papists,' as Craig expressed it. I have all along contended for the special election and call of the Church, in the strictest Calvinistic sense. Abhorrent to my views and feelings has ever been the idea of any unbelieving unrighteous man inheriting the Kingdom of Christ and of God. From that Kingdom I believe the unrighteous to be everlastingly excluded, their new-creation in Christ taking place through the medium of that Kingdom being brought to an end. Sin and sinners I believe to be punished everlastingly, in the fullest extent of the term; but this, not by the everlasting perpetuation of sin, as popular, but Manichean, theories suppose, but by the complete and everlasting destruction of sin and man's sinful nature, through the death and resurrection of Him who was God manifest in flesh. For a fuller development of what have been my views on the subject, see several portions of the 5th Chapter, with what follows, of my 'Assurance of Faith,' my 2nd and 3rd 'Dialogues,' 'Divine Inversion,' 4th, 5th and 6th Sections, and my 'Introduction' to White's 'Restoration of all Things.'"

On the 12th of February, (1862), contrary to the urgent entreaties of his family, (for he had a cold, and the weather was foggy), he persisted in his determination to go out on business of some importance, which he conceived could not be done by proxy. This was the last day he crossed his own threshold. The affection of his chest increased. Strength diminished. He continued, however, to take his place at the family table, in spite of the paroxysm of cough and difficult breathing, induced by his ascending and descending the stairs. Strength failed. On the 22nd. he was persuaded to remain in the library, which was on the same floor as his bedroom. There (26th), he was sitting in the evening preceding his departure. At a late hour, and with the assistance of four of his family, he *walked* to his bedroom, and it was then that, for the first time, he began to imagine he might not recover. With the administration of an opiate, only an hour or two's sleep had, for some nights, been procured. On this occasion, his faculties continued perfectly clear, and he was remarkably cheerful.

But wakefulness gave way to drowsiness, and he expressed his surprise, to his wife, at his sleepy tendencies. After a short interval, addressing her by name he said, "Can this be death?" "If so, it could not be calmer or easier," was her reply. He rejoined, "No: all is loving, all is right." Presently, to Mrs. Thom, he again remarked his drowsiness. One of his family reminded him that it was nearly one o'clock, A.M., and that they were all sleepy. He raised his head, and with his own sweet smile, responded in some familiar words, indicative of

> "A heart at leisure from itself,
> To soothe and sympathize."

To his children, he spoke cheerfully after this, and bade them all good night.

"In the morning," writes one of his daughters, "when I went to his room to see him, he was speechless; and his hand, when I took it in mine, was cold and clammy. Even after I had held it for a long time, it would not grow warm, and never having seen death take place before, it was perfect agony to me. At ten minutes past nine, we assembled to see our beloved parent breathe his last. Mama is wonderfully supported, she has not yet had time to feel her full loss. Having been papa's loving and devoted nurse for the last five or six years at least, you can imagine what a blank must be made in her existence."

* * * * *

Once more was the name of David Thom to vibrate within the walls of Rodney-street Kirk. Nearly forty years had passed since he was cast out, as an unfaithful and unworthy son of the church to which he had given his earliest and most self-denying energies. Blessed be God! there is, then, something in Liverpool, stronger than ecclesiastical anathema, or theological dogma. For, now, our grief is soothed by words of admiration, respect, and sympathy. Thus spoke the present Incumbent of the Kirk, the Rev. John Orr (and to his honour we record it), at the close of his discourse on the morning of the Sunday immediately succeeding the death of our revered friend.

"I cannot bring these remarks to a close, without a passing tribute to the memory of one who has recently passed from the communion of saints on earth to the communion of the heavenly in eternity. I refer to the first minister of this church, for whom this church was built—the personal friend of many of us here, and venerated and esteemed by all. And although that ministry was associated with some measure of controversy, and, although decided controversial feeling was expressed by various parties, yet every one esteemed the Rev. Dr. Thom as a highly-gifted, truly-good, and faithful minister of the Lord Jesus Christ. Most sincerely would I endorse that opinion. And with a knowledge of the sentiments that he conscientiously entertained in contradistinction from others, I rejoice to say, in the face of these sentiments, that no one could have more firmly held evangelical truth in its great and essential characteristics. The fatherhood of God in Christ was his great theme of religious conversation. He gloried in the cross of Christ, and in comparison with other knowledge, was determined to know nothing, save Jesus Christ and him crucified. With a memory rarely equalled in any man, and a force of mind and power of expression truly wonderful, it was indeed no ordinary privilege to listen to his remembrances of the great departed, who had been foremost in ecclesiastical or literary efforts, with whom he had associated, and whose tastes were congenial with his own. Not unfrequently triumph in death, as well as greatness in life, formed the subject of his conversation; then, truly, his words had a pathos and power, touched as if with a live coal from off the altar of heaven. The mind of Dr. Thom was original, powerful, and stored to a remarkable degree with valuable information. He had, too, a heart deeply imbued with the milder graces of the Christian; and his disposition was affectionate, generous, and magnanimous. Friends collected on all sides around him, animated by his presence and joyous in the light of his conversation. His departure is a great and solemn loss to a large circle of friends; and especially is it so to his own family circle, where he was a most attached and exemplary husband and father. May the bereaved be consoled and be comforted in the knowledge that what is loss to them is gain unspeakable to him."

And we will venture to add, that this generous, affectionate and Christian expression of the minister, met with a general though silent response, on the part of his attentive congregation.

We abbreviate from the *Liverpool Courier* of March 5th, 1862, the following account of the *funeral*.

"The high regard in which the Rev. Dr. Thom was held by a large number of people in this town was amply testified yesterday by the procession which followed his mortal remains to the grave. The deceased minister was highly esteemed for his eminent Christian virtues; and amidst his varied scenes of labour, his amiability and kindness secured the regard of those from whom he differed in theological opinions. Whatever might be thought of his peculiar doctrinal views, he was esteemed by all who knew him as a thoroughly-conscientious minister, an amiable and pains-taking friend, and a man of rare learning. This feeling of universal respect was strikingly evidenced at the last rites of the departed; for yesterday, men who differed from Dr. Thom in his system of religious teaching willingly paid homage to his great Christian virtues; and perhaps no stronger proof could be afforded of the reverence in which he was held than by the numerous and influential procession which followed his remains to the grave. The friends and relatives of the deceased assembled at Dr. Thom's residence, 23, Erskine-street, and soon after ten o'clock in the morning the funeral procession was formed. The hearse was followed by mourning coaches containing relatives and friends of the deceased, next came a considerable number of private carriages. A large procession on foot, of upwards of two hundred gentlemen formed the rear of the mournful *cortege*. The cavalcade proceeded slowly to the Necropolis, Low-hill, in which Cemetery is the family vault. A considerable number of other friends had congregated at this place; and in all 350 persons, at least, were present to pay the last tribute of respect to their friend."

"The chapel of the Necropolis was crowded by the mourners. The services were read by the Rev. T. Dawson, minister of the Soho-street Chapel and Chaplain of the Cemetery. After reading various appropriate passages from Scripture, Mr. Dawson, in a brief address, referred to the Christian character of the departed, described the zeal and devotedness with which he had performed his ministerial functions, and the pathos and ability with which he had expounded some of the most touching passages of Scripture. The body was then borne to the grave at the upper part of the Necropolis, where the religious exercises were continued and concluded by Mr. Dawson, and the gentlemen soon afterwards dispersed."*

A blank, indeed, has been created, and will long be felt, beyond the limits of his own hearth. Many a social gathering will miss that extraordinary gift of conversation which rivetted attention as by a charm,—through which, too, with marvellous skill, and yet with perfect simplicity and ease, he managed to put each on good terms with everybody else, winning, withal, the kindliest and profoundest respect towards himself. The topic, whatever it might be, that interested you, he discovered himself as possessed of the rare capacity of being interested in also: he was equally ready with information on almost any subject that was worthy of the attention of a human being. His intellectual range sought expansion to the utmost limits of human knowledge. The *physical* possessed subordinate attractions to those of the *mental* sciences. Sir W. Hamilton's motto sums up his favorite investigation: "On earth there is nothing great but man: in man there is nothing great but mind." Subsidiary to the study of human nature, he had surveyed the fields of Ethnology and Philology, brought under his notice in the elaborate works of Prichard and other authors, whom he had studied with great care. Phrenology and Physiognomy had yielded to him what they could tell him by the mouth of Spurzheim (to whose lectures he had listened at Liverpool), and, Lavater, through whose voluminous work he had waded. As willing was he to learn what could be told him by an Owen or a Taylor or a Carlyle, with each of whom he had had correspondence, on the genesis and exodus of the human animal. We cannot pass from this topic, without introducing the following, from a letter written in 1847.

"I am a Phrenologist. I am not one.—I am. Until 1829, I had paid no

---

* In a codicil to his Will, made in August, 1857, Dr. Thom says, "I could have wished, had circumstances permitted, to be buried with my father and his four children, in that portion of the area of the crypt of the Cathedral of Glasgow, which he bought from the heritors of the Barony Parish, and where he himself is buried." Otherwise, he requests, that his remains may be deposited with those of his mother or former wife. The address which Dr. Thom delivered at the grave of the partner of his early joys and sorrows (whose maiden name was Margaret Steele), and which our limited space precludes our giving in this brief sketch of his Life, is an extraordinary exhibition of the wonderful superiority of the Christian faith, by which he was actuated, to the grief of his early bereavement. In this grave, over which nearly thirty years ago he proclaimed his victory through our Lord Jesus Christ, his own remains were interred. The same codicil contains these words, "Let any inscription over my body be brief, simple, and unflattering. Christ is my only and my certain hope towards God—my all in all."

attention to the subject. Then I attended Dr. Spurzheim's twelve lectures; and, what was more, I obtained his notice and friendship. The Dr. satisfied me that Phrenology has a basis of truth. In the brain we have the organ of all mental manifestations. Its conformation, taken along with the temperaments, gives us an approximation to personal character. I shall never forget how struck and amused I was, when, professing to do it from my head, he read me most accurately my personal character, and gave me, in a manner the most affectionate, a few cautions. 'I thought, at first, you had been of pure Scandinavian extract,' said he; 'but I observe decided traces of Celtic lineage, also, in the form of the cranium.' The fact is, both my grandfathers, Thom and Falconer, were of Scandinavian (Danish), and both my grandmothers, Stewart and Campbell, of Celtic origin. Never shall I forget the six hours which he spent at my table, in company with my old friend, James Sheridan Knowles, John M'Grigor, of the Board of Trade, &c. &c. His information as to races which I drew out, was rich, varied, and most instructive. Since then I have read, as well as heard, George Combe. Also other works, such as Scott's, &c., have been perused by me. My original impressions have been deepened."

"I am not a Phrenologist. To me, Phrenology is only one of three modes of looking at mind. And of these three, it is the *lowest*; as well as dependent, for its proper exercise, upon the other two."

"Mind may be looked at, 1. From below. That is phrenologically, or through cerebral manifestations. In this way, however, we can never come to *unity* of mind, having merely *a fasciculus* of faculties; and it can be of no assistance to us spiritually. Indeed, looked at by itself, Phrenology has a tendency, obviously, to *materialism*. This, the 'Zooist' people shew."

"2. Mind may be looked at on its own level, or introspectively. This is the ordinary plan of metaphysicians, and the only way in which fleshly-minded men can become accurately and satisfactorily acquainted with intellect and intellectual operations.—Indeed, upon this way of viewing mind, Phrenology itself is dependent."

"3. Mind may be looked down upon from above; or, from the level of the knowledge of God, and the divine nature. This is peculiar to the Church of God. And this mode of looking at it requires some practice; and can only grow, as our knowledge of the distinction between soul and spirit, and our ability to separate between the one and the other, grows. Heb. iv. 12."

"Looking down on soul from spirit, we see soul reflecting spirit, or resembling spirit, continually. We learn the origin of man's unity (individuality), conscience, &c. &c."

"Man is, although the highest of animals, yet one of their number; to Christ Jesus, and the conferring of the divine nature on him through his exalted Head,—not to anything natural, does he owe his immortality."

Thus he looked at human nature. God had testified of it that it was "vanity". History was the echo of His voice. "Of the earth," and admirably adapted to the stage on which it was to display itself, its possessors, in every age, have been found to be "earthy,"—in their possibilities, conceptions, and aims. Among projected essays was, "The impossibility of any creature's rising in the scale of Creation," an essay which might have been found suggestive, in the discussion recently raised by the ingenious author of the "Origin of Species;" nor less remarkable, as anticipating, on the authority of Scripture itself, the cautious scientific deductions of a Huxley as to "Man's place in Nature."

Personal rights and obligations, social and political relations and responsibilities, had their proper share of his consideration and due respect. His political convictions, though liberal, found no genial expression in "radicalism," and were never obtruded on others, but were held somewhat in reserve. From the animosities of *party* he instinctively shrank.

Warm and faithful in his friendships, he was sensitively alive to unkindness or unfaithfulness in others; and so abhorrent, to his generous and confiding disposition, were hypocrisy and treachery, that a place of repentance might, sometimes, be sought for in vain. Not that he cherished unforgiving or vindictive feelings. Far from it. But he could not *trust* the deceiver.

The dignity and courteousness of his manners were the natural expression of the nobility of his heart. Meanness and littleness were at his antipodes. David Thom,—the man—regarded every fellow man, whatever he might be socially,—whatever the accidental circumstances of his birth or position,—as on a level which entitled him to, and commanded, his respect and honour. Cherishing his own self-respect, he ever aimed to inspire others with the same moral quality.

"I am not conscious of assuming superiority over any one" (he writes many years ago): "I should be ashamed of myself if I did. Perhaps in many cases I am the superior, in certain respects, of those with whom I am brought into contact. But in how many other, and more valuable respects, are they *my* superiors! Never do I meet with one, almost, but he makes me conscious of my inferiority, by more than counterbalancing some trifling adventitious advantages which I may possess, by qualities to which I cannot make the shadow of a pretension........I cannot cringe to others; none, no, not even the beggar, is permitted by me to cringe to me........The only superiority ———— would find asserted by me—alas! I cannot help it!—is that of 52 over 31 years of age. He mistakes, in supposing that controversy would be the result of our meeting. He judges me, I suspect, from my writings. True, I have indulged in controversy. True, my *bumps*, probably, shew me to be polemically inclined. And true, when necessary, and when I cannot help it, I dispute for truth against error. But I appeal to all who know me, if controversy be an element of my every day life? Are any, unless they absolutely force me to it, and not always even then, troubled or bothered with poking questions? No, no. Far more afraid am I, lest, on minuter acquaintance, he should discover that I am a tremendous gossip. Fond of talking *de omnibus rebus et quibusdam aliis*. Glad to talk over any subject that turns up, and equally glad to dismiss it for some other. Horace says, *sapientis est desipere in loco*. I am afraid that my tendencies (not to loose conversation, for, as I never indulge in it myself so, I never allow others to indulge in it with me), but to gossip are so great and so inveterate, as vastly to exceed the bounds which Horace would have deemed allowable in his "*sapiens*."—Enough of this, however.—I am not, habitually or by preference, a controversialist."

His politeness made it sometimes a rather tedious matter to get along the street; for his greeting was cordial, but never with a *gloved* hand, and, as he passed through the town, he was sure to encounter a large number of acquaintances. The true *gentleman* shone, through the *sick* man, to the very last. In spite of their injunctions to the contrary, he *would* rise from his chair every time his medical attendants entered the room.

What he was as an Author, we have not space to discuss. Nor is it necessary. He was by no means careless about the graces of composition.* That he was conscientious, let the following from his own pen, testify. It may be of service to some of our readers.

" Alas! none but he who has to write upon divine truth,—to keep it pure—to state it accurately—to distinguish it from spurious resemblances—to do justice to an opponent—and above all, to be intelligible,—can form any conception of the difficulty of writing conscientiously on scriptural principles. To write a novel,—to treat on any mere human subject, is a trifle as compared with it. Brief I might have been. But could I have been understood? *Brevis esse labore, obscurus fio:* how applicable to the truth of God."

David Thom's *religious* life, embodied all the *essential* elements of his exalted conceptions of Christianity. His theological system was the intellectual representation of his religious life. Though chiselled into beautiful and harmonious symmetry, as by the hand of a skilful sculptor, his theory has none of the coldness of the marble; for it has *lived*, and is but the formal outgrowth of his Christian consciousness. It has throbbed, as vital principle and force, in the warm pulses of his own spiritual being.

We are expressing ourselves in terms neither of exaggeration nor praise; we testify to simple matter of fact *as those who know him most, know best*. Eulogy, so far from being necessary, we feel would be here out of place. Shining more and more unto perfect day, the path of the just, needs no flickering sickly light of our poor human commendation. "The actions shall speak." By the grace of God he was what he was. And if his system had not the coldness of the sculptured stone during its embodiment in his life, neither has it the coldness of a corpse though its principles are no longer illustrated in his holy life among us. As based upon divine facts, his theological system is no *mummy*, which, on exposure to the breath of heaven, will presently crumble away and be resolved into the earthly elements, of which human "bodies of divinity" are composed.

---

* Though a rapid writer, he was, on principle, scrupulous to the jot and tittle of literary composition. The following is interesting. "The repetition of the word 'and' page 1—is intentional. I wanted first to give a sort of aspect of colloquialism to the composition; and, secondly, I fancy that a grammatical solecism, like a discord in music, may *sometimes* (very rarely I am aware and with great caution) be introduced."

Not in a flood of sentiment could his generosity exhaust itself, nor could it spend itself in mere words of sympathy. Narrow pecuniary resources made him feel, and feel keenly, the restraint it became him to impose upon benevolent impulse. Visiting the abodes of penury and destitution, might almost sometimes have incited to covetousness, but only that he might have to give to him that needed—to him that had no helper. Scrupulously careful was he to avoid pecuniary obligation which he had not the means of duly discharging. This consideration was *sacred*. But subject to it, and often almost trenching upon it, was the beneficence of his open but unostentatious hand. Before us lies a dingy, torn scrap of paper, (accidentally turned up a few days ago among some old documents), evidently preserved as an acknowledgment for the payment of a debt. On one side we read:

"Sir,—Having been given to understand that you are proprietor, or agent for the proprietor of some houses in ——— Street, and farther, that a Mrs. G——— is owing, or supposed to be owing you some money for rent, as I do not wish the poor dying woman disturbed, I may say that, if she be owing you rent to the amount of £2. or forty shillings sterling, I will see you paid to that amount.—Yours, &c. D. Thom."

On the other side of the paper is the receipt of the landlord for the amount.

We are not surprised at "fleshly-minded men" misunderstanding and mistaking him. Even to more enlightened individuals, he might sometimes have appeared somewhat inconsistent, from their failing to perceive, in every case, the principle and temper according to which he acted. To such, perhaps, what follows may help to render him more intelligible.

"To aim low in life, has been my constant object; to keep as much as possible in the shade, my practice. If I have thereby missed *some*—and these not unimportant earthly advantages—I have saved myself thereby an immense deal of personal annoyance. Such has been my humour. I have estimated my powers low. (This was my brother's turn of mind, too). The result is that, *now and then*, we have found ourselves capable of things, which previously had appeared to us beyond our reach. Still, it has been our practice to pitch low. Even my bold and impudent language, at the end of the 'Introduction' to my '*Number and Names*,' is not inconsistent with this. And thus we have not been *much* annoyed by neglect or contempt. I was amused at ——— once, in a "critique" of his, expressing his surprise at my assumption of acquaintance with divine truth superior to his, as inconsistent with all that he had observed in me and knew of my character........A— and B— and C— belong, I am well aware, to the number of the illustrious unknown. But like, they say, draws like. A strange morbid pleasure one has in being in the company of one's equals and associates. The "unknown" are mine. I really wanted, just by way of opposition to common usage, to try what one could make of them. I happen to love some of them. In certain respects I am conscious of their superiority to me."

Could he appear otherwise than *bigoted*, to the humanly liberal? He hears the whisper, and speaks out:

"'*Thom bigoted*'.—Yes. Aye, and more so than —— is aware of. Bigoted as Noah was, when he stood out for 120 years against the sneers and gibes of the Antedeluvian world. Bigoted as Abraham was, when he preferred, on a bare promise of good to his remote posterity, to quit his comfortable home, and become a wanderer in countries where personally he did not possess an inch of ground. Bigoted as Moses was, when he preferred the reproach of Christ to all the treasures of Egypt. Lord, in such bigotry, cause me more and more to grow! Thy revealed Godhead, thy revealed death and resurrection, constitute all my hope. —— poor fellow, has no conception of the depth of this bigotry of mine. Yet in his mouth the word sounds oddly. Are not he, and many others, bigots to their larger brethren? Are they not so, especially, to Theodore Parker and his party? However, I pass this by. I am content, in his estimation, to be a bigot of the first water. Would to God that, under the influence of faith, I were more so."

"'*Stands in his own light*.'—What? Has he so little knowledge of the objects at which I have aimed, and am aiming? If I wanted popularity I should not go to —— to ask him to assist me in procuring it. He aims at an earthly spread of his doctrine. I am content that the truth of God shall be known by the very few to whom it is his purpose to make it known. 'When the Son of man cometh, shall he find faith on the earth'? I understand my friend—know him enough to dismiss him, with a kindly feeling towards himself and admiration for his talents.'

"I could, if I had so pleased, have been ten times more notorious than I am. But I shrink from unnecessary display. Seldom, if ever, am I found at a public meeting. I associate with no political or religious parties. It is true that I do desire to be notorious. But it is for a given object. To secure public notice to what I know—and rejoice to know to be the truth, there is no kind of notoriety which I am not desirous to obtain. I will struggle for it, even. But not one whit further than is subservient to my purpose. Except as proclaiming a finished salvation through Jesus Christ, and as desiring to spread this every where, I positively shrink into myself; I dislike, I shun the public gaze. You may or you may not believe me: but what I say is fact, nevertheless."

"'*Makes enemies*.' How pleasing to acquire a title and a just one to amiability, by never assailing or condemning the religious views of our fellow men; however much these may assail Christ, and trample under foot that worthy name by which we are called,—but always looking on with complacency while the truth is stabbed. Not so Christ Jesus. See Matt. xvi. 23. The most amiable natural feelings of Peter, were by him stigmatized as Satan; and Peter's wish that he might live on earth, was seen by him to have involved *murder*,—the everlasting death of all mankind. Lord preserve me from seeking human applause. —— seems struck by my 'coherency and consistency.' There may, no doubt, be *some* coherency and consistency without truth; but there can be no truth without coherency and consistency. I am coherent and consistent, solely because, so far as I know it, divine truth is so. No thanks to me. God forbid that I should causelessly hurt the feelings of any man; but the deity of the Lord Jesus and his atonement by sacrifice—(the destruction of human nature how little known by our evangelicals!)—I must maintain. My salvation, my new-creation, in Christ glorified, I cannot give up into the hands of infidels, or semi-infidels. What is Christianity to me, apart from the divine righteousness and the divine life of Christ as mine?"

As further illustrating his own tender and affectionate disposition, and as conveying his views of some of the more amiable as well as of some of the more repulsive phases of human nature, we avail ourselves of the following extract from his correspondence.

"Laying religion, even the Christian religion, for the moment out of the question, I would rather, a hundred times over, enjoy the sweets of domestic life, and be surrounded by my wife and children, conversing freely with the one, and listening to the innocent—say nonsensical—prattle of the others, than be raised to the most exalted rank in society, or be overwhelmed with the voice of fame. I speak as a man. Affection has always, in my apprehension, surpassed intellect. It appeals to my heart. It tells on it. Christianity has made me acquainted with something higher and nobler, than even the domestic affections. And it tends, in so far as divine things are concerned, to their crucifixion. But it leaves my judgment, as to the superiority of affection over intellect, untouched, viewing matters relatively. And it shews me the typical character of even the domestic relations and affections themselves. Is not the Church Christ's spouse? Is he not at once our father and elder brother? And is not the love of the creature, although opposed to, yet also the shadow of, the love of the Creator? I need not prosecute these subjects."

"Laughter is sadly connected with malice in the human mind. Deep thinkers have always known this. See those beautiful creations of Shakspeare's fancy, in his *Midsummer Night's Dream*; and consider the common notions respecting fairies. The Word of God, a higher authority than even Shakspeare, speaks of 'foolish jestings which are not convenient.' This I require to have constantly before my mind. I am not, perhaps, what would be denominated a malicious character. And yet I have detected the working of malice in my mind, in connection with fun and merriment. Prone, sadly prone as a youth was I to humour. Kindly it may be. Still, occasionally, merriment delighted me. Not, perhaps, so much as my father or my brother Robert. But, when I knew my company and felt my spirits high, I have given loose a little to what I have deemed innocent frolic and merriment. I am not aware of having consciously intended to hurt the feelings of others. But sometimes two or three days of vexation have followed the indulgence of humour. And I have both had my own feelings hurt, and I have seen the feelings of others hurt, too, by the sallies of those who are called, and who perhaps consider themselves 'funny dogs.' Therefore, for years, my turn for humour has been under severe controul. It may break out sometimes. I may find nature, now and then, too strong for all the precautions taken, and the guards which I put upon myself. But never is the exercise or play of the domestic affections with me a subject of ridicule. On the contrary I have more than once felt a tear of sympathy stealing into my eye, when I have observed them. They claim, they have, my tenderest sympathy. Pretension of every kind, I may even now,—I have formerly—treated as a fit subject for ridicule. About this, however, I am getting chary. The light of the glory of Christ is disclosing so much evil,—so much pretension in myself that ridicule I feel it now difficult to use. It is apt to recoil. One feels conscience saying, *et tu quoque*, when one would laugh at a pretender. This checks. Lord! what is man? Blessed be God for a free, full, and everlasting salvation."

To epitomize the leading facts of his career,—to trace, only in outline, the growth of his spiritual life,—and to illustrate his human and his Christian character, from materials which lay immediately at hand,—was all that could be here attempted. In subserviency to this purpose, our selections from Dr. Thom's correspondence have been made; and these are so considerable, that our pages, to a great extent, assume the form of "auto-biography." A review of his theological system as a whole, a critical appreciation of its doctrines in relation to the theological and philosophical aspects of the age, as well as an estimate of the influence it is likely to exert upon the future of the Christian Faith, and the development of Christian Society, have yet to be accomplished. May we be allowed to cherish the hope that, with a fuller Memoir, including a selection from the rich store of his epistolary correspondence, now treasured up by a host of faithful friends, this may yet, at no distant period, be achieved?

*　　　*　　　*　　　*　　　*

February 27th, 1863.

A year has passed, since his dying testimony to his Heavenly Father's rectitude and love, fell, like a still small voice, upon the storm of our grief. More audible, in the now quieter air of acquiescent and grateful faith, his last words—"All is loving: all is right"—are full of heavenly music, to our sorrowing hearts. The sentiment they breathe is just that to which David Thom gave utterance, in many a dark hour during his life of faith on earth: they are thus, not only the concluding strain, but the sweet echo of his "song in the house of his pilgrimage."

> "Through the vista of life's hist'ry,
>   Now I trace my Heav'nly Guide;
> Earth is less and less a myst'ry,
>   As our hearts in Heaven abide:
> Thence the words I now indite—
> All is loving: all is right.
>
> Early blossom strewn by storm-wind,
>   Heat and burden of life's day; –
> Dreams and visions bright, determin'd
>   In most unexpected way:
> Toilsome day, or darksome night –
> All is loving: all is right.
>
> When *they* spurn'd who once caress'd me—
>   Wounded me with treach'ry's dart;
> When afflictions' weight oppress'd me, –
>   When deep sorrows whelm'd my heart;—
> Sigh'd I;—yet from Heaven's height,
> All is loving: all is right.

Did not sorrow near Him bring me
  Who the Man of Sorrows was?
And desertion seem to wing me
  All the swifter in His cause,
To whose joy I sped my flight?—
All is loving: all is right.

Foes I see no longer, plotting
  Heresy's disgraceful fall;
Had I always through church windows
  Look'd, had I seen truth at all?
'Gainst man's wrath why should I fight?—
All is loving: all is right.

Dark is earth; or, when 'tis lightest,
  Blank is the world-studded sky;
Worlds not seen, are worlds that brightest
  Shine, when here God blinds the eye.
Faith sees not in Earth's gross light—
All is loving: all is right.

All is loving: Death, by-standing,
  Pales, as startled by strange words;
All is right: 'tis God's commanding;
  Faith her firm 'amen' records.
Earth's receding: Heaven's in sight:
All is loving: all is right.

See! the light of Heaven is breaking!
  Hark! the music of the Skies,
(To my spirit—earth forsaking—)
  Swells in sweetest symphonies!
Dawn bright day without a night!—
All is loving: all is right."

SERMONS, &c.

SERVICE I.

PSALM.

ALL Scripture is given by inspiration of God, and is, therefore, profitable for our instruction and edification. Again and again have I had occasion to impress on your minds that there is no portion of the Word of God more sweet and precious—none in which the character of the Lord Jesus Christ is more clearly and powerfully displayed, than in the Book of Psalms. We have, in this portion of the Holy Scriptures, the inspired language of the Holy Ghost, concerning the future Messiah, just as in the New Testament Scriptures we have the inspired interpretation of the same. In this same precious book are contained portions of divine truth, adapted to the varied circumstances of the family of God. Sometimes our blessed Lord is presented to us in the character of a superior—sometimes as an intercessor—sometimes as speaking triumphantly and rejoicing in his Church as the grand trophy of his victorious grace—sometimes he describes the Church itself, and the privileges it enjoys in virtue of its union to, and communion with him. The psalm I shall ask you to join with me in singing, or rather a portion of it, is the 48th:—

> "Great is the Lord, and greatly he
> Is to be praised still,
> Within the city of our God,
> Upon His Holy hill."

Now the greatness of God, hundreds and thousands will profess in words, who have no scriptural idea of that wherein His greatness consists. We are taught by the word of God, that He is great; great in His existence, for He is the self-existent one—great in His manifestations of Himself, which are infinite—great in His goodness—great in His love—great in His power—great in His justice—great in every point of view. And, as He is thus great, so He is greatly to be praised. He is the subject of the praises of His Church now, and will be of all the redeemed throughout everlasting ages. In the 5th chapter of the Book of Revelations, we have specimens of the purity, tone, and nature of the praises to which I allude. Their praises are "to him that sitteth upon the throne, and unto the Lamb for ever and ever." They ascribe unto God and to the Lamb all blessing, and honour, and glory, and riches, and power, and strength, as the Creator to whom all pertaineth, and from whom all proceedeth. Then there is a very beautiful observation, or rather a hint given, as to the parties by whom His greatness is understood, and from whom His praises proceed,—

" Within the city of our God
Upon His holy hill."

The world knows nothing of the character of God; to know His character pertains to His Church. Therefore observe, the praises were not in one sense from all beings—although all things praise the Lord—but positively and directly, only from those who are priests unto the living God, constituted as such by their separation from the world and from their being brought to the enjoyment of God's glorious character. Therefore as He is, His greatness, and the greatness of His praises can only be understood by, and can only ascend from, the New Jerusalem — the city which cometh down from above—the city in which God dwelleth. From thence alone can His praises ascend for ever:—

" Mount Zion stands most beautiful,
The joy of all the land :
The city of the mighty King
On her north side doth stand."

Mount Zion lay, as those who have a map of Palestine, or have read of it, can testify, on the northern part of the city of Jerusalem, or rather to the north-east ; and it was on this Mount Zion that God specially dwelt, in Old Testament times, with His earthly Church, and where David, as his anointed King, dwelt. It was here the temple of the living God stood. "This city was most beautiful, and it was the joy of all the land"—the joy of the tribes of the Lord, and thither they were appointed to repair thrice a year. It was faith that incited those who were enlightened, and who rejoiced when it was said, "Let us go up to Jerusalem, the city of the living God." But we know that this city was the type of a higher Zion that cometh down from above— the Zion in which God Himself dwelleth, and the Zion in which all His purposes are unfolded and displayed. Of it, it may indeed be said—

> "It stands most beautiful
> The joy of the whole land."

It is "the city of the mighty King," the city of that great King, of whom we have heard, in whom we believe, and whose praises the Church rejoices to proclaim. It stands "on the north side." It stands opposed to that point from whence light proceeds, and in itself is *dark*, for you know that the south side is the side of meridian light and splendour, inasmuch as the eastern side is that from whence light arises, and the western where light sets; so the Church of God, standing on the north side, is dark in itself; but, although dark in itself—just as the slope on the north is exposed to the action of meridian light, so the Church of God is exposed to the meridian light of Christ Jesus. Such is the situation of the city of the great King—it needs neither the light of the sun, nor of the moon, for God and the Lamb constitute the everlasting light thereof. Therefore where all is darkness naturally, in Christ Jesus there is light.

Now, passing on to the end of the psalm, in the last two stanzas we find the words—

> "Walk about Zion, and go round;
> The high towers thereof tell:
> Consider ye her palaces,
> And mark her bulwarks well;
> That ye may tell posterity.
> For this God doth abide
> Our God for evermore: he will
> Ev'n unto death us guide."

We have been told where Zion is, and we have been told of her beauty and attractiveness to all who understand the character of God; we are now desired, as members of the Church, to go round, to examine, and to inquire concerning her. For Mount Zion is not only great and beautifully situated, but the more it is examined, the more its strength, as well as its beauty, presents itself to view. It is found to be exceedingly strong, having for its towers the divine protection which surrounds it. But, as it is well protected, so it has its palaces wherein God dwells—that is, believers themselves—for "know ye not that ye are the temple of God, and that the spirit of God dwelleth in you." Then, mark its towers, mark its bulwarks, consider its defences, for it is under divine protection. And this is not merely to be told for our own comfort and consolation, but

> "That ye may tell posterity.
> For this God doth abide
> Our God for evermore ; he will
> Ev'n unto death us guide."

Understand here, that by "posterity" is meant the "New Testament Church." These comforting truths were not to be restricted to the Jews, but must be handed down and transmitted to another generation—to that generation of individuals who are to know God as revealed in the person of his Son. This is one grand reason why the Church is called upon to engage in praises—or, I should rather say, the grand reason is, because "God doth abide her God for ever and ever." It is the character of God that He is unchangeable, "I am the Lord, I change not, therefore ye sons of Jacob are not consumed." Our safety consists not on anything in ourselves—not in the unchangeableness of anything else,—it rests upon the unchangeableness of God's character—the unchangeableness of His purposes—upon the fact that He *is* God—a character which implies that He is the portion not of the dead but of the living, and, therefore, as He will guide us unto death, so will He guide us through death into the regions of life everlasting, for He Himself is "the life," as well as "the way and the truth." I will only ask you, then, to sing these two portions of this very sweet, instructive, and valuable psalm. Of course I cannot go over it again ; but I ask you to sing the two first and the two last stanzas,—Herein the greatness of God—the magnitude of His praises—the beauty and strength of Zion—her true position, the security of the Church under the Lord's protection —the unchangeable relationship which He sustains towards her, and the relationship which she sustains towards Him— her safety in time, and her safety throughout eternity ; these, with many other truths, are set forth in this beautiful psalm for our edification.

THE PRAYER.

Let us give thanks ! We desire at this time, Heavenly Father, to consider in our meditations and in our approaches to Thee, that we are the subjects at once of Thy sovereignty and of Thy love. We would not separate what Thou hast put together, and we would desire not only to consider Thine attributes in their reference and relation one to another—in their agreement to all that is revealed concerning Thee in the Old and New Testament Scriptures, but also in their agreement with the whole of Thy revealed character. We would ever bear in mind Thy sovereignty, although it is exceedingly difficult—nay, impossible, for creature minds like ours, thoroughly and scripturally to grasp it. We are ourselves beings of limited power—we see around us nothing but exhibitions of limited power, and we find, that if left to ourselves, and to the conceptions of our own minds, that power, limited in one way or another, is all we can conceive of. It is not until we have been led to Thy word, and to the understanding of Thy character, as revealed in Christ Jesus, that we understand Thee as possessed of unlimited sovereignty both by the work of creation, and by the still greater and mightier work of grace. When we consider that Thou didst call all things into existence out of nothing in the space of six days, and didst pronounce them to be very good, when we consider Thy providential dealings with the children of men in every age, when we look at the way in which Thou hast punished them for their misdoings, by the flood, by fire, by the sea, and otherwise, in all these things we certainly behold mighty exhibitions of Thy power; and we especially see it in the fact that all things still continue, on the whole, as they were, since the beginning of the creation. The sun and moon still going through their regular courses—the stars of heaven still appearing according to Thy will—the seasons still duly succeeding each other as prescribed—all keeping their proper situations, and executing their proper purposes. All these exhibitions of Thy greatness far transcend *our* limited power. Yet the New Testament Scriptures show us, that even these things are but faint exhibitions of what Thou art, and what Thou canst do, as compared with what Thou hast accomplished in the still more glorious work of man's redemption. Sin had entered into the world, and death by sin, in consequence of which, generations of the children of men had been swept away, and in spite of all that man could do, by investigation or by his own efforts, to resist this course of events, it went on and must have continued to go on without any possibility of its being stayed or overcome by any efforts of our own. Here, however, *Thou* didst step in, saying, "I have found a ransom," therefore, save him—save man—from going down to the pit. Thou didst then begin to exhibit and develop a scheme of wonder and of glory which the created mind never could have conceived or anticipated—which created power could still less have executed—a system in which, through the medium of apparent weakness, the greatest power is exhibited—in which through the medium of the entrance of sin, divine righteousness is manifested—in which through the medium of death stepping in and sweeping away myriads of earth's inhabitants, life is made to achieve its greatest triumphs and exhibit its glories for evermore. How wondrous to think that by the appearance of the babe of Bethlehem—that by Jesus being made for a little time lower than the angels—that by the fact of God being manifest in the flesh—and despised and rejected of men in that capacity—rejected even by those to whom he came—that by means of apparent weakness, through a life of suffering, God both achieved a conquest which transcends infinitely all created perfections—and which is calculated to fill the sons and daughters of humanity with endless joy. Oh! how extraordinary to think that by thus sinking lower and lower in the estimation of his fellow-man—that by being brought to the bar of his own creatures—that by being nailed to the accursed tree, and by giving up his spirit into Thy hands, he has triumphed over sin by bringing in everlasting righteousness—that he has swallowed up sin in righteousness, and that by his resurrection from the dead, and his subsequent ascension to thy right hand, he has swallowed up death itself in victory—exchanged the temporary reign of sin, for the everlasting reign of righteousness; exchanged the temporary reign of death, for the everlasting reign of life; and all in virtue of his desire to exhibit *Thy* character, and show forth *Thy* love. Well may we feel astonished, well might heaven and earth be called upon to be amazed at the transcendent work of human redemption. This is, indeed, what finite man could not have anticipated—and is something which the creature mind cannot understand or realize. But when a mind is given to comprehend divine principles, and divine acts, and divine revelations are made to be apprehended, then do we discover in the mystery of godliness what no human mind could of itself have found out—exhibitions of Thy power, and wisdom, and grace, which overwhelm us with absolute astonishment. We find that all is done for Thy glory, and according to Thine own purposes, given in Christ Jesus before the world began, and that in no case hath the creature been

Thy counsellor—that the whole work is Thine, both in the conception and execution thereof, and to Thee most deservedly redounds all the glory. But how sweet, how delightful to recognize in connection with Thy sovereignty, the sovereignty that worketh all things after the counsel of its own will, to which all the armies of heaven, as well as the inhabitants of the earth are subservient—how delightful to recognize in *this*, an exhibition of Thy love as unbounded as Thy sovereignty—that as Thou art sovereign, so Thou art *love* also. Thy sovereignty is not that of demons—it is not that of a being whom we can only approach with terror and alarm. It is that of our Father, revealed to us as such in the face of, and through the work of Thy Son. Thou hast made Thy creature what he is, and destined him for that glory which eye hath not seen, nor ear heard, and which it hath not entered into the heart of man to conceive. And all this, as springing from thine own love—transcendent—infinite—everlasting love. And blessed be thy name in revealing Thyself to us, in the fact of having sent Thy Son to save us—in the fact of his having saved us with an everlasting salvation, by shedding his precious blood in our behalf, and rising again to Thy right hand—in the fact of revealing Thyself to us through Thy Spirit, in drawing us with the cords of love, as with the bands of a man, and shedding Thy love abroad in our hearts—thus making us to feel irresistibly that power which Thou puttest forth—a power that aims at our good, and only rests satisfied with accomplishing our good—a power shown in raising Christ from the dead, and shown in raising us likewise to life here, and to the fulness of life hereafter. Thy love is as transcendent as Thy power. We cannot fathom the depths of it. It is but a slight idea of its greatness and sweetness and attractiveness that we can form. But, as Thou art love, so he that dwelleth in love dwelleth in Thee, and we find it is by having Thy love shed abroad in our hearts, that our opposition is overcome—our feelings of attachment to Thee are drawn forth, and our affections are raised to things above, so that we are made one with Thy children in glory, clothed upon with Thy divine nature, and made to enjoy Thy glorious presence. Lord, we desire to dwell upon Christ in our thoughts, and meditations—Christ, the lovely one, in whom every grace is exhibited, and every perfection displayed. We desire to dwell upon him who shrunk not from death, that through it he might destroy death, and him that had the power of death—who shrunk not from the shame, that he might rise to the glory prepared for him—who so loved the world that he gave himself a ransom for it, setting his people an example of that love which they should manifest towards others. But, Heavenly Father, in every age, men have striven to better themselves, and to make themselves more acceptable to Thee—or have been careless concerning Thee—not discerning Thy true revealed character; but, where Thy power and the sovereignty of Thy love is displayed, there is found both a righteousness which they never could have wrought out, and a life which they never could have conferred upon themselves—indifference is exchanged for interest—they who were formerly afar off, are now brought nigh, and brought under the power of Thy love, and they bring forth fruits to Thy praise and glory—thus giving themselves as a living sacrifice to him who died for their sins, and rose again for their justification. Heavenly Father, teach us more and more (not by our own imaginations—not by leaving us to the vain surmises of men—but by Thy Spirit and Thy word) of Thy sovereignty as revealed in Christ Jesus. May we find more and more that the knowledge of this, imparted by the Holy Ghost, exercises a practical influence on our lives and conversation. The more it dwells in us by the power of Thy Spirit, the more it brings us out from the world; for as Christ separated himself from the world, so are we also separated in him. But how delightful the consideration that as in the first Adam we have sinned, so in the second Adam we have righteousness, that as the knowledge of the first brings death, the knowledge of the second shows us that we have life in Christ Jesus—and in him have perfect freedom, a freedom to live, not unto ourselves, but to him who died for us and rose again. Lord, in passing through this present world may the power and influence of the truth be exemplified in our lives and conversation. May it be exemplified in circumstances of comfort, as well as in circumstances of difficulty. May we remember the declaration made by Thee to Joshua, and repeated by the Apostle, as applicable to the New Testament Church, "I will never leave thee, nor forsake thee." God having guided His own Son through his own arduous undertaking—having brought him to the holy hill of Zion, in spite of every difficulty. Oh! how strong is the security we have in Him, the munition of rocks—our everlasting refuge. In Him no ill can betide us, for "God being for us, who can be against us." It is true Thou hast not promised that we shall be free from difficulties, dangers, and trials—on the contrary, Thy word and the experience of human life, as shown in thy Apostles and others, manifest to us that we shall have trials within, and trials without. But it is also shown us that in every difficulty Thou openest a way of escape—or givest us grace to enable us to bear our trials patiently—Thou upholdest us with Thy strength—Thy rod, and Thy staff, they comfort us. When the creature fails, Thou, the Creator, dost step in, accomplishing that for which in vain we might have looked to flesh and blood, to ourselves or creatures like ourselves. But, Lord, amidst all the situations of human life, enable us to set Thee always before us, being constantly strengthened by Thy revealed perfections, and preserved from falling into temptation and evil, by Thy mighty power. Let us not forget that it is not in us to direct our steps aright, but that Thou hast undertaken for us, and wilt perfect that which concerneth us, to work in us all the good pleasure of Thy will, and the work of faith with power. Whenever any of us are doubtful as to what is the path of duty, and are surrounded by darkness which we cannot penetrate—whenever any of us have been disappointed in our expectations, or discouraged in the performance of what we deem to be right, then, Lord, throw light on the path of righteousness through Thy word. And do Thou show us more and more when the purposes for which these trials have been sent are accomplished, that Thy hand is not shortened, that it cannot save, or Thy ear heavy that it cannot hear. "Art Thou not He who of old smote Rahab, and slew the Dragon?" What Thou hast done in times past, Thou canst do still, and Thou hast supported and wilt still support the hearts of Thy people in every age, by the knowledge of what Thou art—and by the experience of the fact that Thy strength is made perfect in their weakness. Bless all the denominations of Thy people, under whatever name they may be known. May grace, mercy, and peace be their abundant portion. Direct them in all their works, preserve them from all evil, and supply all their wants. Our desire is that Thou wouldst bring Thy Church to a more intimate knowledge of Thy revealed character than she has hitherto shown. But when we look at the number of fleshly churches, which are the spawn of old Babylon—when we see man, looking to man, and not entirely to Thee—when we look at the corruptions which have ever prevailed, we are satisfied that Thy people cannot see Thee, as it is desirable they should see Thee—or enjoy Thee, as it is desirable they should enjoy Thee. We would have them set aside all the traditions and commandments of men, to look unto Jesus alone, as the author and finisher of their faith. By the testimony of the inspired prophets and apostles, we are led to look for the "cunning craftiness of those who lie in wait to deceive," but we are also taught by Thy word, that it is Thy will that those who recognize the spiritual and internal character of Thy Church, should be brought out from anti-Christian connections, to all the freedom of Mount Zion. It is this we look for, and we pray that Thou wouldst hasten the arrival of the period when this shall take place, so that Thy people may be increased in all the principles of heavenly truth and love—and kept free from those corruptions which they would never have been subject to had they not mixed themselves up with Babylon, and been made partakers of her plagues. Oh, give us to know the evil of our own hearts—for Thy word declares, "That the heart is deceitful above all things, and desperately wicked." Whilst Thou teachest us our own depravity, teach us also Thy glory—make us to feel that our safety is in the Almighty alone. Thus carry us from grace to grace, and strength to strength, till we appear in Zion. Keep us in Christ Jesus from having any confidence in the flesh. Lord! direct us in our various exercises. Enable the speaker to point the hearers not to himself, but to lead them to look to Jesus. Lead them to understand that it is because men have looked too much to their fellow-men, that they have shown so little of the mind, temper, and spirit of Jesus. Oh! that all might be led to delight in Jesus more—in the light of his heavenly testimony more—and that this might be made apparent in the fruits, heavenly, spiritual, and divine, which they bring forth. Hear, now (we beseech Thee), *our* supplications, and the supplications of him who is our great intercessor before Thy throne, and, through him, do for us above and beyond all we can ask or think, and what we ask is for Christ's sake.—Amen.

THE SERMON.

The passage of Scripture, from which I would address you this morning, is contained in the 10th chapter of the Second Epistle to the Corinthians. I shall speak this morning chiefly—if God enable me—from the end of the fourth, with some general allusions to the fifth verse; but, in order to have a clear conception of the tenor and connection of the whole subject, you may take in the third, fourth, and fifth verses. Being unable, very clearly, to see them, I shall try to repeat them as well as I can :—

"For, though we walk in the flesh, we do not war after the flesh (for the weapons of our warfare are not carnal, but mighty through God to the pulling down of strongholds). Casting down imaginations and every high thing that exalteth itself against the knowledge of God, and bringing into captivity every thought to the obedience of Christ."

With but a brief allusion to the observations last Lord's day submitted to your notice, I shall proceed to the consideration of the topic which this morning demands our attention. After shewing that the apostles, like all believers who have appeared upon earth, were for a time in the flesh, we contrasted this very natural and human condition with the fact, that the warfare in which they were engaged, and which, during the whole of the period they were in the flesh, and under the influence of the knowledge of the truth they maintained, was not a warfare after the creature or the flesh—but was a warfare springing from spiritual principles—from the mind of Christ Jesus imparted to them—and was a warfare conducted and waged on their part against natural principles of every description,—a warfare against the pride of the Jews, and a warfare against the contempt and opposition given to the Gospel by the Gentiles. Now, this warfare of theirs, which was not after the flesh, is explained in the 4th verse, the former part of which attracted our attention on a previous occasion.

As you will observe, the 4th verse begins with the word "For," a word which, I have often observed, assigns a cause or reason for what goes before. I remarked, therefore, that, as it was properly the apostles who were referred to as waging this warfare—spoken of in the 3rd and 4th verses (although not exclusively so, for all believers, loving the same truth, and possessing the same mind, necessarily wage the same warfare as the apostles),—we must not throw out of view their peculiar position—whilst we must bear in mind also that, in a subordinate degree, they spoke for the Church of God in all ages. Then, bearing in mind that the apostle is speaking primarily of himself and the other apostles, and, in a subordinate sense, of true believers in all ages; we understand that "the weapons of our warfare are not carnal." If our warfare were conducted according to the flesh, we should clothe ourselves with fleshly armour, both offensive and defensive, or if it consisted in intellectual strife, we should furnish ourselves with the arguments of metaphysicians and philosophers, in order to overturn the views of our opponents —but the weapons of our warfare, either as apostles or believers—are not carnal—on the other hand, they are of a spiritual description. We showed you last Lord's day that we are not left at any loss to know what these weapons are, for, we have a brief but emphatic catalogue of these weapons, offensive and defensive, given in the 6th chapter of the Epistle to the Ephesians. There is the sword of the spirit, put into his hand, by which the believer is enabled to make assaults successfully upon his, and upon Christ's enemies— the sword of the spirit being the Word of God—and as he is exposed to assaults at all points, so he is furnished with proper and appropriate defences. He has for his head the helmet of salvation, he bears upon his left arm, as a defence for his own person, a shield—the shield of faith. And he has his members and his life protected from enemies, numerous and mighty, by various kinds of armour, all furnished him by the author of his salvation. These weapons, therefore, both offensive and defensive, are found in the armoury of God, are taken out of it and belong to it. These weapons enabled the apostles to conduct a life-long warfare against Jews and Gentiles—and still enable all who have the spirit of the apostles—or I would rather say—the spirit of one higher than the apostles—the divine spirit of Christ Jesus—to conduct a life-long warfare against sin—against themselves and against the world. I have no intention to occupy your time longer with any preliminary observations, or recapitulation of what has been already said.

I now, therefore, proceed to the consideration of what remains before us, namely, the latter part of the 4th verse, which seems to me to receive illustration from the whole of the 5th verse.

"The weapons of our warfare," says the apostle, in his own name and in the name of his brother apostles, as well as in the name of the members of the Church, "are not carnal," or fleshly; they are weapons of a heavenly description, and are "mighty through God to the pulling down of strongholds." In every age this statement has met with the ridicule of men of the world. "Mighty," say they, "mighty!" why they are the poorest and the most paltry weapons imaginable. So poor and paltry, that if you will but consider those who have made use of them, they have ever sunk beneath the opposition of their enemies. The head even of those using these weapons was not able to defend himself against the assaults of Jews and Gentiles, but perished on the cross. His leading supporters in New Testament times, and those who prophesied of him in times that went before, were also sufferers at the hands of men, and could not shield themselves from their revilers. We are told that some of them perished in dungeons; others were burnt at the stake; others were sawn asunder; some wandered about in sheepskins and goatskins, being destitute, afflicted, tormented; and we have reason to believe that the Apostle of the Gentiles was decapitated. Some were crucified, some exposed to wild beasts, others had trial of cruel mockings and scourgings, and many wandered in deserts and in mountains, and in dens and caves of the earth. Thus the weakness of their defences was made manifest to the world. What reason, then, have you for boasting of them? Yes, we do boast of them; we glory in them, and are satisfied of their might—of their everlasting, aye, and even of their temporary, might and efficacy, let the world sneer as it may.

We perceive their might illustrated in the case of the Church's head. We see a poor child, born at Bethlehem, of poor parents, whose life was sought after from his earliest infancy, and which was only saved through divine intervention, and by the flight of his parents into Egypt. We see this poor infant returning with his parents, on the death of his enemy, into a quiet town in Galilee. We see this poor child, who never knew letters, and was, therefore, held in contempt by the better taught classes of his countrymen, astonishing the Jewish doctors in early life with his questions and answers. We perceive this poor child, brought up in industry, for he seems to have wrought at his father's trade as a carpenter. We perceive this poor child arriving at manhood, and at last making his appearance on the banks of Jordan, where hundreds were assembled to receive the baptism of repentance, at the hands of John. We see him demanding to be baptized himself, in order to fulfil all righteousness, and, notwithstanding John's remonstrances, having his wish conceded to him. We see him afterwards appearing in Judea, in Galilee, and in Jerusalem, going about healing all manner of sickness and diseases amongst the people. We see him, not selecting as his companions and followers the great, the high, and the illustrious, but a few poor fishermen of Galilee. We find him going about in no ostentatious manner—not causing his voice to be heard in the streets, but we find him going about to do good, to illustrate his Heavenly Father's character, to make known the Old Testament Scriptures, and to show the nature of the kingdom he came to set up. We find him going about, notwithstanding the unkind treatment he received at the hands of those among whom he came—preaching the gospel of the Heavenly Kingdom,—and we find him going about doing good continually. In spite of all opposition, both from Jews and Gentiles, he went on, regardless of their enmity, fearing not the cross, but despising the shame; and, although they nailed him to the accursed tree, and imbued their hands in his blood, the same heavenly spirit, which had guided him through the whole of his earthly career, breathed forth in his expiring language: "Father, forgive them, for they know not what they do." Oh, how did this poor, despised, feeble, persecuted one achieve his triumph? We have shown that it was not by human learning; we have shown that it was not by human station; we have proved that it was not by means of associating with the great and the wealthy. How, then, were his triumphs achieved? for that he did triumph, it is the object of the New Testament Scriptures to inform us. How, then, did he triumph? How was it that he disregarded the cross and despised the shame? How was he enabled to exhibit that love which he did towards those who were his murderers? The Scriptures show us. It was by the use of the very weapons which are here spoken of. His stay upon earth was a continual warfare against the flesh, a warfare against sin, a warfare against his own countrymen, the Jews, and against the Gentiles, a warfare against the world, a warfare against the devil, and a warfare against all his own and his Father's enemies. Yet he never had recourse to earthly weapons in order to carry on this warfare.

When he came among us, he was the word made flesh. The spirit of the Old Testament Scriptures begat him, and the spirit of the Old Testament Scriptures was embodied in him. He was the word made flesh,—not only the Eternal word, abstractedly considered, but that word embodied as it was in the Old Testament Scriptures. As the word was, in him, embodied, so that word, in him, was the principle of every thought which he realized, of every word which he uttered, and of every action which he performed. Faith in that word dictated all his glorious proceedings. Thus he said, before he came in the flesh, in one of the Psalms, "I believe, therefore have I spoken" (116 Ps., 10). He acted under the influence of that belief. He met Satan on his own ground, as related in the 4th chapter of St. Matthew, and by the use of that word foiled him on three several occasions. Satan made use of God's own word in the attempt to foil the son of God, as his choicest weapons; but with those weapons he was defeated. As Christ foiled Satan in the wilderness, so did he foil him on every other occasion in his subsequent career. It was through faith in God's testimony, unlimited and uncontrolled; it was through the hope set before him, it was through the influence of the love of God, constituting the grand motive of his conduct,—*that* love which was in his heart,—it was under the influence of heavenly principles,—it was through using the heavenly weapons to which I have alluded, that the poor man of Nazareth, the despised and rejected of men, was content to be treated as the offscouring of all things,—was content to be treated as a worm and no man. It was under the influence of these heavenly principles, and by the use of these heavenly weapons, that he gave himself to be a sacrifice, without blemish and without spot, unto God—ultimately triumphed over all enemies—ascended to God's right hand—received a name which is above every name—and, having all things made subject to his sway, occupies the throne of his glory until all his enemies shall be made his footstool. Here, then, is the might of these weapons displayed. We have heard of the title of a play "She Stoops to Conquer." What is implied in these words was exemplified in the person of Jesus, who thought it not robbery to be equal with God, yet took on him the form of a servant, was found in fashion as a man, and humbled himself even unto death, not despising the death of the cross. Having accomplished the work which the Father gave him to do, having become a curse for us, having put away sin by destroying it,—swallowing it up in his own righteousness,— and having destroyed death by swallowing it up in victory, he rose to his Father's right hand, leading captivity captive, and receiving gifts for men; and thus in heaven he is enabled to shower down blessings on the rebellious, and confer everlasting benefits on the children of his love. Here, then, you have a proof that the weapons in question are mighty to overcome all that opposition before which the mightiest of men have necessarily fallen prostrate. When I see the mightiest of men, —not merely the leaders of armies, but the mightiest of men in point of intellect,— those whose understanding and conceptions have been most enlarged,—those whose acquirements in literature have been most extensive,—I find that they never achieved conquests such as these. I find that they chiefly aimed at the gratification of selfish principles; but Jesus triumphed through love and overcame by faith, showing us what the use of these scriptural weapons is capable of accomplishing, even when wielded by the hands of others than himself.

What he did, his apostles did also. Do you ask how the poor fishermen of Galilee were enabled, in spite of all their privations, temptations, and trials, to stand their ground, and to fear not the threats held out to them of punishment by violent death, not to speak of the tortures inflicted upon them from time to time? Why did they go forward, in spite of all opposition, to proclaim the truth as it is in Jesus, and to do good to those by whom they were proscribed? How was this? Why, the weapons of their warfare were mighty through God, which carried them through every difficulty, which enabled them to triumph over every danger, which made them more than conquerors, through him that loved them, and washed them from their sins in his most precious blood. And are they not mighty still? Yes; eighteen hundred years have passed away since the personal mission of the Son of God; yet these weapons still exhibit and show forth their might in the belief of the testimony which is found in the inspired record concerning God in Christ Jesus. If I look to what is probable, I perceive that there is a might in them to overcome strongholds: if I look to what is proved, I see the same manifestation. But, perhaps, some may say, "You have omitted to speak to us on the phrase 'Mighty through God.'" Well, let me do so before I proceed. Mighty or powerful signifies clearly that which is superior, in point of strength, to something else. There needs no metaphysical acuteness in order to understand this. If a man stand before me, and, by the power of his arm, throws me down, in spite of my opposition, I can at once perceive that the man has far more muscular power than myself. Again, if in the course of argument between two men, I perceive that the feebleness of one man's mental power and intellectual acquirements does not enable him to combat with the other, the strength of the other is evinced in point of intellectual power. This is illustrated in various passages of Scripture. For instance, Our Lord has given us a beautiful illustration when he says, "When a strong man, armed, keepeth his palace, his goods are in peace; but when a stronger than he shall come upon him, and overcome him, he taketh from him all his armour wherein he trusted, and divides his spoil." (Luke xi, 21, 22).

The same thing is beautifully brought before us in the 15th chapter of the First Corinthians, in that part of it which is read in our burial service, where it is said the soulical body is sown in weakness, and the spiritual body is raised in power. Now the weakness of the soulical body is manifest in that it is subject to the process of decay, subject to the elements, and subject to death; powers which are stronger than ourselves; and death being the strongest of all, by it we are all ultimately overcome. But, on the contrary, when I rise to glory, to see my Divine Head as He is,—when my body is raised,—it is raised in power, because in rising it overcomes the process of decay and dissolution. Thus the weakness of the elements and the weakness of death are made manifest in being overcome by something stronger. Thus we recognize the same idea in the words of my text, "Mighty through God to the pulling down of strongholds." The strength of these weapons is shown to be mighty through God, inasmuch as they are found "overcoming, casting down, and destroying."

A little reflection may show us that "Mighty through God," like many other passages found in the Scriptures, is most rich in suggestion. There seem to me to be three things implied in "mighty through God"—mighty through God's testimony—or mighty through God by His spirit accompanying it,—not as if there were any might employed by the creature, but rather by the Creator. "Mighty through God" implies that there is a divine efficacy in the weapons themselves—they are not creaturely weapons, but weapons that are Divine; the word of the Old Testament Scriptures issued from the living God, not from man. All the weapons used by the apostles, not forgetting the weapons of prayer and the weapons of miracles, were, in their very nature divine. As our Lord said to Nicodemus, "That which is born of the flesh is flesh, and that which is born of the spirit is spirit." Because they are divine, these weapons overcome, or "are mighty to the pulling down of strongholds." To the flesh they may appear to be weak, to be unable to withstand human arguments, but they are mighty notwithstanding, and so mighty, that wherever the divine nature takes effect in the heart and conscience of any individual, there is a process of overcoming carried on within, which there is no possibility of resisting. "Mighty through God,"—God's people are mighty through God's assistance—mighty through their own divine nature. But the phrase has, in my apprehension, a still deeper meaning.

Who was Jesus Christ? Was he the creature or the creator? Was he a being like ourselves, or the mighty God manifest in the flesh? Unquestionably he was Emanuel—God with us—for so the name signifies. The apostle declares him to be "God over all blessed for ever." Still, although this was the case, we have seen that he employed the Old Testament Scriptures as his weapons in personal action and personal conflict. Were they not mighty in him, and through his use of them? By using them, what has he not done? Why, he has put away sin by the sacrifice of himself—brought in everlasting righteousness, and swallowed up death in victory. Ah, then, the employment of these weapons gave Christ Jesus power to triumph over sin and Satan, the flesh, the world, and death; and, as being mighty in him, they are therefore mighty in us. Through their employment, the work given him to do was accomplished, and the truth is made manifest, that he hath wrought out for us a full and free salvation, to which you and I are not asked to contribute one iota. We cannot improve his work—it is rather given us to recognize the might which God in flesh hath put forth—which the holy spirit—the spirit of the Lord Jesus—revealing to us, the accomplished might of the Son of God becomes power and strength in us also. Therefore these weapons are mighty and powerful through God's working with them—they are the weapons with which Christ achieved his triumphs; and they are mighty in us, as revealing his triumphant, perfect, and finished work.

They are "mighty to the pulling down of strongholds." Ah! the siege of Sebastopol has given us an idea of what an earthly stronghold is. Many cities, fortified according to the best principles, have fallen. Many citadels which have been deemed impregnable have been taken; but Sebastopol, although we may hope that it will be taken, still holds out, resisting all the skill and ingenuity of the allied armies, and the power brought to bear against it. Well, then, here *is* a stronghold. I need not go into any further explanation, as it is a topic with which you are all conversant. Now, the strongholds alluded to by the apostle, are internal strongholds—strongholds existing in the human mind itself. These are the most impregnable strongholds, and the most difficult to be overcome; but there is a power that can overcome them—that is the power here referred to—the power of spiritual weapons—the power of faith, hope, love, and every other grace—the power of the apostolic testimony, carried home to the conscience by the Holy Ghost—this is the power that overcomes the strongholds of the human mind, let the resistance be ever so long continued or determined. What are these strongholds? I might have contented myself by saying, that they are the strongholds of "law, sin, and death," and might have shewn you from the Scriptures, if time had permitted, how strong these holds are in the minds of each of us. So powerful is law, that there is in every human breast, naturally, a strong suspicion that the law of God must be fulfilled by every one, before he can obtain salvation; and men are continually manifesting this fact by endeavouring to fulfil law, and to work out their own righteousness. It is only when divine revelation is made known to us through him, by whom the whole law of God has been magnified and made honourable, and everlasting righteousness brought in, that we learn that this stronghold must be stormed.

It is only when the knowledge of sin, as coming down to us from Adam, is brought home to our hearts and consciences, that we gain strength to eject the notion of working out our own righteousness, and learn to apply some better unction to our souls. Even then, circumstances may occur and feelings may arise in the mind, leading us to suppose that the stronghold remains as impregnable as ever—but they are stormed by the blood which cleanses from all sin—and whenever it is given us to know that Jesus shed his blood for us—and that that precious blood cleanses us from all sin—then the strongholds of law and sin are stormed—and we are set free. But there remains the stronghold of death—the weapon of sin—and this is stormed again, by the manifestation to us of Christ as our life, as having swallowed up death in victory—and that we live in him for ever. "The wages of sin is death, but the gift of God is eternal life through our Lord Jesus Christ." In him the stronghold of death is stormed, and we rejoice that in him we live for evermore. I have no occasion to dwell upon these strongholds, for you have some of them pointed out in the following verse: "Casting down imaginations and every high thing that exalteth itself against the knowledge of God." I do not like this translation. It appears to me that the word intended is "reasonings," not "imaginations,"—casting down *reasonings*—the reasonings of the Jewish mind, and still more of the learned and scientific Grecian mind. Any of us, who have had the slightest acquaintance with arguments of this description, know well that these vain reasonings are set up and opposed to the Gospel, and that nothing short of the truth itself can storm them. It is by the revelation of divine facts—the revelation of God's love to me in Christ Jesus—the revelation of my salvation as accomplished, not by works of righteousness which I have done, but according to his love and mercy. By this revelation the reasonings of my own mind are stormed—and fall before the divine fact, and Jesus enters triumphantly into the citadel of my conscience, which no longer reasons against him, but delights to own his sway.

Again there is another fact that strikes us, in the examination of the Old Testament Scriptures, and that is, that Judaism was set upon a mountain, as compared to the rest of the world. God chose the seed of Jacob to be a peculiar people to himself. This fact influenced them—it was one of their strongholds, and the majority refused to come down and take lower ground—or at least, as the apostle shews us in the Epistle to the Hebrews, they tried to combine Christianity with Judaism, in order to satisfy human pride, by causing Christianity to stand, as they thought, on high ground. This stronghold was stormed. It was shewn to Paul that Christianity was the fulfilment of Judaism, and he, therefore, found, to his astonishment, that he was a blasphemer, a persecutor, and injurious, in opposing Christ Jesus. The stronghold of Judaism which, in his mind, had opposed itself to the knowledge of God, was cast down. So not only in Judaism, but in every case, if there is any species of pride in ourselves, to make us think highly of ourselves, more highly than we ought to think, or to make us boast of our fancied superiority to our fellow-men, then that citadel is stormed, and we are made to see and feel, that in the matter of salvation we stand on the same footing with others, and we learn that God resisteth the proud, but giveth grace to the humble. God places the Jew and the Gentile, in the matter of salvation, on one common level—and through the *same* medium, we have access unto the Father. Thus then, high Judaism and everything else, is cast down—stormed by the weapons we use—which are not carnal, but spiritual, mighty through God, to the pulling down of strongholds.

Lastly. Thus brought into subjection, to the obedience of Christ—we are taken captive by him—to serve and obey him. Whenever a conquering hero meets with an enemy, he does not destroy him, but takes him captive, in order that he may be his servant. We are all naturally disobedient to God—we are selfish and high-minded—and what we do has a tendency to glorify self. But when we are led to a proper understanding of revealed truth, we are carried captive, and bound to the chariot wheels of Christ Jesus. He who formerly had his thoughts occupied on the world and the things of the world, has them now brought into subjection by these mighty weapons—those glorious truths which, in the word of God, are made known to the believer by the Holy Ghost, and are brought home with power to his heart and conscience. I had a great deal more to say, but I cannot further trespass upon your time. May the Lord open up to you His word, and give you by experience to know more and more of the truth, as expressed in this passage, and made known in our Lord Jesus Christ.

May the Lord bless His word, and the exercises of this morning so far as agreeable to His mind and will, and to His name be praise for evermore.—Amen.

SERVICE II.

PSALM.

Allow me to ask you to sing with me a part of a Psalm which I have frequently brought under your notice, with which, and with the terms in which I am accustomed to speak of it, you must be perfectly familiar. It happens to be connected with the subject on which I intend this morning to address you—God willing. Hence, I conceive, its appropriateness to our opening service. The Psalm I allude to is the 19th, which, from the beginning to the end, has a spiritual import, however much it may have been misapprehended, and however much men of infidel sentiments may have attempted to extract from it a meaning which, in the light of the New Testament Scriptures, it never can bear. The 19th Psalm has had God's interpretation put upon it in the 10th chapter of the Epistle to the Romans, and guided by the hint which is there given, as well as by the analogy of faith, we can have no hesitation whatever in assigning to it its legitimate, that is, its scriptural meaning. The 19th Psalm at the beginning :—

> "The heavens God's glory do declare,
> The skies His hand-works preach;
> Day utters speech to day, and night
> To night doth knowledge teach."

Now, it is unquestionable, that in these words there is a reference to the natural heavens—to the sun, and moon, and stars, which adorn the firmament, and to the natural light which they are constantly shedding upon our earth and upon the universe with which we are connected. The meaning which the infidel mind attempts to extract from them is, "that by means of looking upon them—by means of their natural light—by means of the natural information which they convey, we may attain to the knowledge of God, become acquainted with our duty, and even with the means of salvation. It is however very true—it cannot be denied—neither do we attempt to deny it, that in the light of Scripture the natural universe is made to teach a lesson. In the light of Scripture, we know, that the natural universe took its origin from God's hands—that by Him it is sustained, and in consequence of God's mighty power put forth, it fulfils all the purposes for which He destined it; all this is perfectly true—but then, we do not know these things by what the natural heavens, and what the skies and firmament of themselves teach. They might have existed until now—the revolution of day and night—the revolution of the seasons might have gone on until the present time, but unless God Himself had been pleased to teach us His character, we might have seen everything that is glorious and beautiful in nature, without having had suggested to us the Being from whom they took their origin. But God hath seen fit to tell us that all things were created by Him, and are sustained by Him; He hath shewn us through Christ Jesus, that everything that exists has been called into being by Himself, and, having learned this from His word—that word which He hath magnified above *all His name*—we know now, not by our own investigation, but by His teaching, what the natural heavens are, why they were created, and what purposes they are intended to subserve. The fact is, the New Testament Scriptures shew us, that the natural skies and the natural light which they give, are emblems and symbols of something infinitely higher. What the natural heavens are to the natural earth—namely, the source of heat and light, the word of God is to us—both Jews and Gentiles—the spiritual firmament, in which God hath placed His spiritual luminaries, from which they shed down light, and from which they send forth every kindly influence into the hearts and consciences of God's people. Now, looking at the matter in this light, then, the heavens, that is God's word—the Old and New Testaments in which His glory alone is declared—the heavens shew forth God's glory—the skies set forth His handiwork—that is, the skies, as constituting the spiritual heavens in Old Testament times—the Mosaic institutions were part of the heavens, and were so constituted by God, the very sacrifices of the law being part of the light by which God shewed forth His character and glory—and it is through them, day unto day uttereth speech, and so on; it was through the medium of these Scriptures that in the former period God taught the Old Testament Church, even in times of comparative darkness—and thus through them, under the light of the New Testament dispensation He is teaching us—giving us a clear understanding and knowledge of Himself. Now, that this is the meaning intended is shewn by the second verse:—

> " There is no speech nor tongue to which
> Their voice doth not extend,
> Their line is gone through all the earth,
> Their words to the world's end."

Now, a person may say, "Do not you see clearly here, that this points to the universality of the natural heavens, the sun is seen everywhere, even in most northern and southern parts during certain times of the year, and in all other parts daily, and the moon, every month sheds forth her mild effulgent beams, and the stars also, make a display of themselves, giving their influence to the earth and conveying it to the children of men! Well, I do not dispute the fact. There is universality connected with these lines; but what I dispute is, that this is spiritually what the Holy Ghost meant; and, I affirm, that He intended to make use of these, as so many emblems or symbols of something infinitely higher, and infinitely more glorious. He intended to make use of them as emblems and symbols of holy Scripture, and, in accordance with this, the preaching of the apostle and prophets has been heard in every tongue, and has been listened to by men speaking every variety of language. It seems to me to refer to the fact that in consequence of the miraculous gift of tongues bestowed upon the apostles and through them, upon the various congregations, that they in many places gathered, that through this instrumentality, men in every country and out of every nation, should hear in their own tongue the wonderful works of God. Now this becomes plain from the following verse:—

> " Their line is gone through all the earth,
> Their words to the world's end."

Here, again, it might be said, it is still of the sun, moon, and stars—it is still of the natural heavens he is speaking. If however, you will turn to the 10th chapter of the Epistle to the Romans, you will find that this passage is expressly quoted by the apostle Paul, as applying to the doctrine of the apostles, and the universality of their teaching, to the fact that they had gone to every inhabited part of the globe, proclaiming the unsearchable riches of Christ, in the various tongues of the children of men. Just, as in this way, the apostles preached the gospel—so, they became the antitype of the heavenly bodies in the firmament, and shine forth as stars in that firmament, through the inspired writings of the New Testament which, through the industry of learned men have been translated into every known language. As the natural luminaries are seen in every part of the world, so the Scriptures alone constitute God's heavens, constitute God's spiritual luminaries; as such, are listened to, and the things they contain are made known to men in every part of the world. Now, when the Holy Ghost himself has, in the 10th chapter of Romans, put an inspired interpretation on these words, and given us a clue to their true meaning, it would argue the utmost arrogance on our part to attach a different meaning to them, to that put upon them by infallibility. But

> " In them he set the sun a tent
> Who bridegroom-like, forth goes
> From 's chamber, as a strong man doth
> To run his race rejoice."

Now, that tent, we know, was the body—the personal appearance of the Lord Jesus Christ. Well, here, Jesus Christ, the true Sun of Righteousness, the centre of this heavenly system, has appeared in this earthly tent—has appeared in the character of a bridegroom to his church—to take that church to himself as his everlasting spouse, and he goeth forth like a bridegroom, in all the strength and majesty of his character, overcoming sin and overcoming death, and bringing his heavenly spouse out of all the dangers in which she is enveloped, and the difficulties by which she is surrounded—bringing her home to himself in glory, giving her to sit down with him on his throne, and so enjoy him for ever. Then, the psalm goes on still further to point out other characters connected with this heavenly light—connected with the spiritual heavens—characters which you will find spoken of in the 4th and other stanzas—all not only being capable of interpretation—but which are interpreted on the same principle, all pointing to what is spiritual, and emblems of what is heavenly; all pointing to Christ Jesus, and his glorious Gospel; the universality of the divine proclamation; the light it conveys to the understanding, the heat it conveys to the heart, and the warmth it conveys to the affections—even heavenly love circling from one end of the earth to the other, until God at last appears through Christ Jesus—(this heavenly Sun, this centre of the whole heavenly system)—

until God at last appears as all and in all. I ask you to sing from the beginning of this 19th Psalm, a psalm apparently pointing, and in reality pointing to the natural heavens, but through them as symbols pointing to Christ, to the apostles, as well as the whole body of believers; to the light they shew forth, and the effulgence which by them is extended to the whole globe; pointing also to the apostles addressing nations in their several tongues—pointing to the writings which they left on record, and their being translated into all languages, and made accessible to every people, name, kingdom, kindred, tribe, and nation.

THE PRAYER.

Let us give thanks. Heavenly Father! Thou conductest Thy heavenly administration over Thy Church and people, in a manner totally different from that by which earthly monarchies and republics are established and carried on. All earthly governments, require either expressly or impliedly, to be maintained by force, and without ultimate appeals to force (which every human being knows will take place, on human authority being resisted), laws would be set at nought and human society brought into a state of anarchy and confusion. Therefore, we perceive, that all civil governments are supported by civil officers, and when necessary, even by such as are military, the servants of such governments fighting when occasion for fighting occurs—and, thus, the whole of that authority is maintained, either expressly, but, in general impliedly, by the recourse to force, upon which it is known ultimately to rest. But blessed be Thy name, Thy Government begins—Thy Government is carried on, upon principles totally opposed to those which are known, and recognized, among the children of men as inhabitants of this present world. The head of Thy Government is a king, but, he is not a man, he is the Lord of Glory! He is the king, who condescended to become a subject, the king who condescended to be treated with scorn and contumely, and at last to be nailed to the accursed tree—by those to whom he came; he is the king who after having encountered, and baffled, and overcome sin and death, and after having burst asunder those terrific bonds by which for a time he had been held—rose from the dead, swallowed up death in victory, and triumphantly ascended to God's right hand—sitting down upon the throne prepared for him of old, and who is destined there to sit until all his people shall be brought home to himself, and until all his enemies shall be made his footstool. We rejoice to know, that his authority begins not by force, but by love, that he manifests himself to his subjects as having loved them before time began—as loving them until time shall be no more—shows himself as having loved them without any ground for love in themselves; for they were black, polluted, defiled; they were his enemies, and had been consigned to death—but he loved them because he had chosen in his sovereignty to set his love upon them—and because in the exercise of this love, he hath chosen to bring them unto himself here, and the enjoyment of himself hereafter. We rejoice to think that, if thou thus manifestest thyself to the conscience of any one individual in that day of thy heavenly, sovereign power, the understanding of that individual is enlightened—his ignorance being overcome and driven away, the flame of love is imparted to his heart, the previous enmity being subdued and destroyed, he is brought under the dominion of him, who is King in Zion, becomes his subject, attains what are the privileges of a friend, nay, becomes related to him as his property—as his alone—becomes, connected with him, in every possible—every conceivable endearing relation, and, thus, rejoices in having been brought out of the kingdom of darkness into the kingdom of God's dear Son; being so completely secured in that kingdom, and so completely secured in alliance to its head, that, henceforth he feels drawn by the heavenly cords of love not only here, but throughout everlasting ages; rejoices in being devoted to him who died for him and rose again; rejoices in serving him, who by his power is able, as by his love, he is willing, to rescue him from the position in which he is naturally, to raise him from being the servant of sin here to righteousness and life everlasting. Oh, how sweet are the cords by which we are drawn towards and chained to the chariot wheels of the Heavenly Monarch, they are indeed cords of love, they are stronger than death, they have a power commensurate with eternity itself. Oh, how delightful it is for us who have been bond slaves of sin and Satan, to have experienced the freedom wherewith alone the Son of man can make free—freedom from this evil world; freedom from sin and death; freedom from ourselves. For, oh, how great the blessedness of this freedom, in that we are taken out of the state in which we are naturally and brought into a state which is heavenly and divine, a state which is secured to us, not because of any distinction between ourselves and others, but secured to us by the good pleasure of him whose purpose it was from everlasting that we should know his truth, that that truth should make us free, that we should become his willing subjects, and rejoice in, and enjoy him for ever. O, Heavenly Father, we now see that instead of fear influencing us, we are influenced by joy—the joy of the Lord, which is our strength—and if we fear Thee (and blessed is the man that feareth Thee), we fear Thee because we love Thee; we know that Thou art our Father, that Thou art invested with all the privileges and authority of a Father; we know that Thy love to us is too strong, Thy regard to us too great to permit us to go astray without being checked and chastised. We know that if Thy children forsake Thy laws and keep not Thy commandments, then Thou dost visit their transgression with the rod, and their iniquity with stripes. We know that these hearts of ours are deceitful above all things, and desperately wicked, and living in a world that lieth in wickedness, the temptations to go astray are constant and powerful. Therefore it becomes us to fear—becomes us to fear Thee with that fear which every affectionate child cherishes towards a loving, tender, and affectionate parent. That it is not the fear of bondage, it is not the fear that makes us dread Thee, and makes us crouch like slaves in Thy presence—but it is the fear of love—it is a fear which springs from the knowledge of our relationship to Thee—the knowledge that Thou hadst set Thy love upon us before time began—it is the knowledge of our being Thine—Thine, because Thou hast chosen to make us Thine; Thine, because Christ's precious blood was shed for us; Thine, because he rose on our behalf, leading captivity captive, and receiving gifts for men—bringing us out of the hole of the pit into which we had fallen, and releasing us from the rock unto which we had been bound. We know it, because Thou hast shewn us that salvation is freely bestowed, seeing that it is recorded that Thou hast given us eternal life, and that this life is in Thy Son—and because Thou hast given us to see that it is not by works of righteousness which we have done, but according to Thy mercy that Thou hast saved us. Thou hast spoken peace to our guilty consciences by shewing us sin washed away—all sin expiated by the atoning blood of Thy well-beloved Son. Thou hast inspired us with joy in the prospect of getting rid of this world, of getting rid of this evil nature of ours—of being conformed to our blessed Head, and of seeing him in all the fulness of glory at his second appearing. O, how sweet then is this joy. It is a joy which springs from a knowledge of what Thou art, as revealed in the light, and work, and character of Thy Son. But how different is the true joy of Thy people compared with the joy which is like unto the crackling of thorns under a pot, which lasts but for a moment, and is then gone for ever; how different, too, from the joy of the hypocrite, which perisheth—a joy which is derived from the supposition that he differs in some respects from his fellow-men, and is superior in some respects to them, —a joy which rests itself upon what he is, and not upon what God is. O, blessed be Thy name, in drawing our attention to this awful tendency of our minds, to endeavour, like the silkworm, or at least like the spider, to extract a ground of hope out of ourselves, to find something of our own by which we may weave a garment which, thrown around our bodies, shall protect us from being exposed and naked before Thee; but Thou hast given us to see that all such clothing resembles the fig leaves in which our first parents attempted to clothe themselves after having offended Thee. Blessed be Thy name, that as Thou didst clothe them in the skins of slain beasts, which typified the sacrifice, and work of Jesus, so Thou hast given us to be clothed in Christ's righteousness, and in the garments of his salvation, and thus we appear before Thee in his wedding garments, rejoicing not in that which we supply ourselves, but in that which Thou hast given us. We appear before Thee, accepted in the beloved, one with him in his righteousness and life, Thou thereby passing over the mountains of our transgressions, and casting our iniquities into the depths of the sea. We know that it is all for Christ's sake—that in him we appear beautiful, but in ourselves are ungraceful and unlovely—we appear clothed upon with his righteousness, and invested with his salvation. O, Heavenly Father, give us more and more of this joy—joy arising from increased discoveries of what Thou art, increased delight in Thy divine perfections, increased clinging to Thy heavenly testimony, preferring Thee and what Thou hast revealed Thyself to be above all things beside—finding in Christ an anchor of hope, both sure and steadfast—finding in him all our salvation and all our desire. O, Lord, we find indeed that we are strong in the Lord, and in the power of his might; while we are weak—while all humanity is weak—while no real assistance can be afforded to us, amidst all the dangers and difficulties of this world, while we are ready to halt when left to ourselves—we find that whenever Thy character is revealed, whenever Thou takest possession of our hearts and consciences—whenever the glory of Christ shines in upon us, in all its fulness, then do we glory in him, and having nothing corresponding in ourselves, Christ is, indeed, to us all and in all. And it is our desire that Thou, through Thy word, and the light thrown upon it by Thy Spirit, mayest dwell in us increasingly in spiritual understanding, so manifesting Thyself unto us, as Thou dost not unto the world, strengthening us with might in the inner man, carrying us on from grace to grace, and from strength to strength, lifting us above ourselves unto Christ, and out of ourselves into Christ, to see more and more our human nature nailed by Christ to his cross, to see that we are raised with him in his resurrection, experiencing its power, and rejoicing in the ultimate fruits of its operation. O, Lord, may the fruits of Thy word, operating upon us, become increasingly apparent in our lives and conversations—may they appear in the fact of crucifying the flesh, with its affections and lusts; that we may appear not living to ourselves, but to him that died for us and rose again; in our having our affections set on things above, and not on things of the earth, in our endeavouring to live, and so to act, and so to walk, as that we may glorify him in our bodies and in our spirits, which are his. For we desire ever to bear in mind that we are his, not merely by nature, as being his creatures, but his by grace, as being his redeemed creatures, seeing he hath raised us out of our natural enmity—brought us into a large and wealthy place, and even now given us an earnest of what afterwards remains for us, and in due time will bring us into his own immediate presence, that where he is, there we may be also. O, what manner of love hath the Father bestowed upon us, that we should be called the sons of God. It is true that it doth not yet appear to the eye of sense, nor can it be understood by the mind of flesh, what we shall be, but this we know, by the eye and mind of faith, that when he shall appear we shall be like him, and see him as he is. Then shall that earnest of heavenly light and love which hath already been imparted to us, according to his good pleasure, that earnest of heavenly light and love which enables us to know what he is, enables us to know the greatness of the love which he hath borne towards us, and draws our hearts in corresponding affection to him—be consummated in knowing what Thou hast in store for us in all its fulness, in all its glory, and in all its blessedness for ever. Lord, we ask Thee to give us to see, that in passing through this present world, we are found acting continually as it becomes the followers, and friends, and children of the Lord Jesus. May we turn our backs upon the world, having our faces turned Zionward; may we turn neither to the right hand, or to the left, but go straight forward in the way everlasting, finding in Christ that we hear the voice saying, "This is the way, walk ye in it." Christ himself having declared, I am the way, as well as the truth and the life. And, Lord, walking in Christ the way, may we be preserved from ourselves, preserved from an evil world, and preserved from all things that are continually drawing our affections from him. And whether we are engaged in business or professions, or whatever may be our employment, or whether maintaining ourselves by manual industry—may we in all respects, set Thee before us continually, aiming at Thy glory, and whatever we do may we so live and so die as unto the Lord. Our wish is to show that we have been separated from the world—not by anything human, or any distinction from our fellow-men, but by that word of Thine which is truth, working in our hearts the work of faith with power. Prepare us for whatsoever in the course of Thy providence Thou hast prepared for us, enabling us to bear with patience Thy afflicting hand. But Lord, while we believe that poverty is an awful snare, we believe that riches are an awful snare also. We are desirous if Thou dost make our possessions more abundant, that it may be given to us to devote them to Thy service. Enable us to consider ourselves stewards of the Lord, and dispensers of his bounty. If we are rich in this world, may we walk humbly before Thee, remembering that riches frequently take to themselves wings and flee away. If our circumstances are moderate, enable us to bless Thee for these moderate circumstances, remembering that having food and raiment we should be therewith content, and that having brought nothing into the world, we shall most certainly carry nothing out of it. O, how sweet the consideration that salvation is confined to no class of men, that Jew and Greek, Barbarian and Scythian, bond and free, male and female, rich and poor, slave and freeman, all are *one* in Christ Jesus—all are made partakers of his glory—all enjoy its blessings here, and shall be brought into the full enjoyment of its blessings hereafter. We rejoice that salvation is by grace alone, through the righteousness of the Lord Jesus Christ, and we desire, under the influence of this blessed and heavenly truth, to live continually. Lord prepare as for whatever trials may await us—trials in our families, or trials that may await us in our own bodies. Lord, we are in the body, and when trials come, may we welcome them as from Thy hand recognizing them as the portion of Thy children—and may we rejoice that in Christ Jesus we have one who sympathises with us, and will never leave or forsake us. May we bow submissively to Thy rod, and be humbled under Thy Fatherly hand. Lord we desire to bring before Thee, all Thy people in all the various circumstances of their earthly condition. We would ever think of them as being Thy specially redeemed people—redeemed by the blood of Thy Son. We would think of them abroad and at home, on land and sea, and we would entreat on their behalf Thy favourable protection. Wherever they may be, keep them in Thy freedom, supply them with all the good things of which they stand in need, and bring them in due time to glory. If any are under Thy afflicting hand—and some now may be so—O draw near to them in the hour of nature's trial, and make them to feel even, that when passing through the waters, Thou art with them, as with Israel of old, when passing through the Red Sea; and that as Thou wast with the three children in the heat of the fiery furnace, so Thou the son of man art with them, and Thou wilt make them triumph over every difficulty and every species of suffering, and over every foe, and ultimately bring them to glory. Lord, in old age, be with Thy people, and make them feel that as Thou hast sustained them in times past, so Thy everlasting arm is round them still. Lord be with the young—be with them whilst passing through this world—enable them to overcome its temptations, and conduct them safely to the end of their journey. Be with the middle-aged, and make them feel that Thou art the God who wilt protect Thy people, even unto old age. Lord, be with us this morning, and enable us to speak and hear as becomes the word spoken—not the word of the creature, but the word of the Creator. Whatever may be spoken that is not according to Thy word, forgive—or whatever may be spoken that proceeds merely from the speaker's own lips; but we know that what is Thine Thou wilt bless, and that Thy word shall not return unto Thee void, but shall accomplish that which Thou pleasest, and prosper in the thing whereunto Thou hast sent it. Be it done unto us, according to Thy testimony, and not to us only, but to all the sons and daughters of salvation scattered throughout the globe. May it be felt by them universally, that the heavenly influences of the Sun of Righteousness is confined to no clime or class. And wherever Thy people are, keep them in Thy love—that love which is simply an earnest of what shall be realized hereafter, and in due time usher them into Thy glorious presence. Hear, we beseech Thee, our supplications, and accept our thanksgivings, and do for us above and beyond what we can either ask or think, and what we ask is for Christ's sake.

THE SERMON.

The passage of Scripture from which I would address you this morning, is contained in the 52nd chapter of the prophecies of Isaiah, and at the 7th verse. "How beautiful upon the mountains are the feet of him that bringeth good tidings, that publisheth peace; that bringeth good tidings of good, that publisheth salvation; that saith unto Zion, 'Thy God reigneth.'"

Imagine to yourselves, my Christian brethren, a nation, or a portion of a nation, which has rebelled against a great and powerful monarch; which, after having waged war with him for many years, has been driven into a corner, having been defeated at every point, and is expecting to suffer the utmost weight of his justly-inflamed vengeance. Imagine such a people, and under such circumstances, confined to and living within the limits of some small valley, and so encompassed on every hand, that they find it difficult to maintain or provide themselves with sustenance or support. Imagine them sending to their outraged monarch a message soliciting peace and reconciliation, and offering their submission. But we may suppose otherwise. Suppose that nation is so conscious of its guilt, and so overwhelmed by fear, that it *dare* not send any message to the monarch against whom it has warred so unjustly, and so unsuccessfully. Suppose it to be waiting with the most anxious expectation for the arrival of the period when, upon the surrounding mountains, it shall see the executioners of his vengeance making their appearance, or, that armies are anticipated, hurrying and plunging down into the valley to execute upon them their due punishment. Suppose this state of things continuing for days, and weeks, and perhaps years; that this anxious expectation is cherished, and above all, that no hope is entertained of being rescued from their miserable condition. Suppose, as their eyes are set upon the top of the mountains, from which they anticipate the appearance of the executioners, or the appearance of the multitude by whom they are to be decimated, or entirely destroyed—suppose there appear a few individuals in the attitude of messengers, dressed in simple raiment, with sandals on their feet, and those feet soiled and dirtied, as if they had come on a long journey; these men, not looking like executioners, but wearing smiling and benignant countenances; not carrying in their hands the sword of vengeance, but a banner upon which the words "peace and comfort," "peace and joy," are inscribed; and suppose, in addition to the display of the banner in question, their voices are heard from the top of the mountains, saying, " Be calm, be comforted; rejoice; your king is not only at peace with you, and will not wreak upon you the vengeance which you anticipate, and have deserved, but, he hath sent us to tell you, that he will take you out of this bounded valley, where you have scarcely any sustenance, where you are straitened on every side, and where water and provisions are failing you; and will bring you unto some large and wealthy place, and introduce you to a flourishing situation, and will there heap upon you comforts and enjoyments of every kind, and make you just as safe, and much happier than you ever were before." Conceive of this intimation, conceive of the joy, which, if believed in, it would inspire within the breasts of these wretched individuals; conceive of the fact, that however poor these messengers—however soiled their garments—however much soiled or dirtied their feet by the length of their previous journey—all these will appear to be beautiful, and they will be even looked upon with admiration and pleasure. Conceive of all this, and it strikes me, you may have, if not in its fullest meaning, at all events some sort of idea of the sense of what the Holy Ghost intended to convey in the words of my text—and which, in a much higher point of view, in Christ Jesus, is fully, perfectly, and everlastingly realized. The fact is, the passage which constitutes the words of our text, is taken from a portion of the prophecies of Isaiah; and is one of the sweetest, and at the same time one of the most pathetic passages contained in that sweetest and most pathetic, as well as most edifying of all the divine productions. It occurs in that part where Christ is immediately introduced to our notice, as the " Man of sorrow, and acquainted with grief"—and then as a mighty conqueror. And occurring as it does, it is plain even before we proceed to any minute examination of it, that it must have some reference to him, and the character which he sustained on earth; some reference to the blessings which he came to bestow; some reference to the glad tidings which, through him, in every age have been proclaimed, and by the guilty children of men have been welcomed and triumphed in. We have no occasion, however, to draw this conclusion on the subject. We have no occasion even to strive to investigate the relation which the words contained in this verse may bear to those which go before and those which follow; for the Holy Ghost himself, in the 10th chapter of the Epistle to the Romans, has epitomised the language of my text, and has shewn that the words therein contained refer to the apostles of Jesus Christ, and refer to the glorious message of peace and salvation which they were commissioned to announce, first to the Jew, and then to the Gentile. In that most instructive and condensed chapter, to which I have just referred, the apostle had been shewing the Jews rejection of God's righteousness, as fulfilled by and revealed in Jesus Christ; he had been shewing the medium through which that righteousness is bestowed, he had been shewing that it came not by the works of the law, but by the hearing of faith; that it was not by saying in the heart, "Who shall ascend into heaven," for that would be bringing Christ down from above—or "Who shall descend into the deep," for that would be bringing up Christ again from the dead—but he had been shewing that the word was nigh them —even in their mouth and in their heart—and that was the word of faith which he and his brother apostles preached, and wherever there was believing with the heart unto righteousness, and confession with the mouth unto salvation, there were the blessings of the Gospel realized, and the individual believer introduced into the Church of God here, in preparation for his being introduced into the realms of bliss hereafter. After having illustrated his premises by one or two most appropriate Scripture citations, he goes on to put a series of questions such as, "How shall they believe in Him of whom they have not heard, and how shall they hear without a preacher?" And having brought the matter to that point, he then gives the quotation—or an epitome of the quotation of this verse, "As it is written, How beautiful upon the mountains are the feet of them"—for the words are there in the plural number—"that preach the Gospel of peace, and bring glad tidings of good things." Then it follows that these words taken in connection with what goes before, and what follows, are predicated of the apostles. But you are aware, that in modern times, men calling themselves preachers of the Gospel, and assuming the character of priests and ministers of God, have endeavoured to apply these words to themselves.

I am aware that if any private individual is made the instrument of bringing me to Christ Jesus, or leading me into the knowledge of the truth of God, through the word of God, that individual is to me a messenger bringing good tidings, publishing peace and salvation from the mountains. I do not say that individuals who have been brought to the understanding of God's revealed character through the belief of God's truth, and who, while proclaiming these good tidings, find their testimony brought home to the hearts and consciences of others, are not messengers of good. I do not dispute that individuals occupying such a position, and proclaiming things concerning God, concerning Christ, and concerning the salvation which is in Christ, and God blessing what is thus said to the understanding of the hearers; I do not dispute that in that case, this language may be applied to them in a subordinate sense, and in thus speaking from the pulpit, or elsewhere, men may be messengers of glad tidings to parties benefited by their statements; but I cannot permit myself so to regard these words of holy Scripture, as to understand their having reference to ordinary and uninspired human beings—that is, a reference directly and properly—but I can understand them having reference to the apostles, through the 10th chapter of the Epistle to the Romans throwing light upon them, inasmuch as they were the inspired messengers of the Lord Jesus Christ, and in this sense I do understand them; I understand that the apostles were the parties who first came upon the mountains proclaiming around the glad tidings which they themselves had learnt. And as the time at last came when they were to quit this present world—when the earthly house of this tabernacle was to be dissolved, the same glad tidings which before had been proclaimed by the apostles with their own lips, were left upon record for the use and benefit of succeeding generations of the Church; so that being dead, like Abel of old, speaking by his blood, they now speak unto us by their writings. Well then, the advantages I have in referring to the 10th chapter of the Romans are, that I get an inspired interpretation of the words and meaning of my text;

such an interpretation as saves me from the necessity of having recourse to any mere conjectures of men; and not only do I find that the apostles are involved in the meaning of my text, but that the words having a direct reference to one, have an indirect reference to many; and I am led also to the discovery of the nature of the messages which these messengers proclaimed. Now, passing by the epitomised explanation—for you will observe it is epitomised—I go back to the words of my text itself, and shall endeavour, as the Lord may enable me, to shew in the light of the New Testament Scriptures how beautifully they epitomise the whole Gospel itself, and how gloriously they come home to the conscience of each one of us, giving us a ground of hope towards God, and of joy and gladness everlasting. Observe, "How beautiful upon the mountains are the feet of them that bring good tidings." I have already hinted and have just now added, in a sort of preliminary way, that the feet of an individual who is traveling over great deserts, especially in a warm climate, and where the ground is sandy and marshy, cannot be very pleasant to look upon, and that his garments will necessarily have a soiled and dirty appearance. But if that individual be a messenger of good —if he brings tidings of the utmost importance—if he announces to us that blessings of the highest description belong to us, then the sight of his dirty feet and soiled garments will be overlooked, and we shall behold in him only that which is beautiful and attractive; his message throws a lustre around him, which causes to disappear all external pollution and defilement; and we shall be almost ready to hug him to our bosoms as being the messenger who brings such glad tidings as the text speaks of and announces.

But I may observe further, that by the mountains here spoken of, I understand the Mosaic dispensation. As mountains are elevations upon the surface of our globe—as they are points which give to him that stands upon them a much greater range of view than those who are in the valley—so in the Old Testament dispensation there were mountains— that is, the kingdoms of Israel and Judah, which rose above all nations of the earth. God did not dwell with every nation. He chose Israel to be His peculiar people, above all peoples of the earth; and as the apostles were all Jews they stood upon these mountains—they stood upon the heights of Judaism, and from these heights announced the glad tidings which they were commissioned to proclaim. It is true these mountains were not to last for ever. It is true God had declared that in New Testament times "every valley should be exalted, and every mountain and hill made low," but not until the destruction of Jerusalem was this accomplished, and until the Old Testament dispensation passed away the apostles stood upon these mountains, and from them proclaimed their glorious message; and when that message had been proclaimed the mountains passed away, and the children of God in New Testament times stood then upon the same level, whether previously Jews or previously Gentiles.

Well, but what did they proclaim? It appears to me that these messengers, these apostles, coming upon the mountains of Judaism, with all the advantages derived from their position as descendants of Abraham according to the flesh, and the superior advantages derived from being children of faithful Abraham, I say they proclaimed three things in their character of ambassadors. In the first place they were messengers of good tidings, publishing peace. In the second place they brought good tidings of good, publishing salvation; and in the third place, they proclaimed unto Zion, "Thy God reigneth." But before I advance into the subject, and attempt to make it as plain as I can from the Scriptures, I must not lose sight of, or omit to call your attention to, the order in which these proclamations are given. Peace is the lowest announcement—salvation is still higher, and "Thy God reigneth" is the highest announcement of all. The proclamations rise from a lower to a higher blessing until they reach the climax, which stands at the head and top of all the proclamations, "Thy God reigneth."

Well, then, in the first place, these messengers or apostles bring good tidings—namely, they publish peace. Now, this expression in a moment testifies to you and me the condition of the parties to whom the message was addressed; they were exactly in the state and condition which at the commencement of my discourse I endeavoured to portray to you; they were a body of rebels against the Most High; they had in the person of Adam revolted from Him who was their Creator; they had revolted from Him who had placed their ancestor in the Garden of Eden, and had surrounded him with every blessing; they had promulgated the act of their progenitor by rebelling against God and against His authority; they had conducted themselves in a manner which was derogatory to the Most High and His heavenly prerogatives, and provoked God, as did their fathers of old, when He swept away all the human race, except a few individuals, from the earth, by the flood; brought down fire and brimstone from heaven on the guilty cities of the plain; destroyed the inhabitants of Canaan before the Israelites, and in various ways testified His displeasure to the Gentile world as the main body of Adam's descendants; and not only so, but God having elected a body of individuals to understand His name, to possess His peculiar institutions, and to be brought into the promised land—(this body having been the descendants of Abraham according to the flesh)—we find that they, instead of being guided by a different spirit from that of the Gentile world around them, had actually copied their example, had plunged into idolatry, had been guilty of every species of abomination, had trampled under foot the authority of their Benefactor, had caused Him to declare, as in the Book of Isaiah, that they were as a filthy body, without soundness, from the sole of the foot to the crown of the head, and full of wounds and bruises, and putrifying sores. Well, then, both Jew and Gentile stood before God in the condition of rebels against His authority, exposed to His awful displeasure, and, if He pleased, the victims of His Almighty wrath. To these individuals so situated the messengers now spoken of came—not to conceal from them their condition, for if we look into the Acts of the Apostles we find that they were not backward to teach, and when we read the lessons taught by Christ himself, we find that neither was he backward to teach both Jews and Gentiles what their real condition before God was, and they proclaimed to them that all were by nature in a lost, guilty, undone condition. But they did not leave them there—they came to proclaim, and to proclaim in accents of love and mercy, that the Being against whom they had rebelled, whose authority they had trampled under foot, and at whose mercy they lay, that that Being had sent them, the apostles, with the message of His reconciliation to them, and that He had done so in virtue of what He had previously done, in sending His own Son into the world, and in virtue of what that Son had done and suffered, and the gifts which he had received for man—they came to proclaim that God had laid on him the iniquities of them all—even the sins of the unbelieving Jewish people, and that Christ had put away sin by the sacrifice of himself; they came to proclaim that Christ was their peace, God having put him forward as an offering for sin, and having made peace by the blood of his cross; they, the apostles, were now proclaiming that peace, so that they who were afar off might be brought nigh, proclaiming peace to the Jew and peace to the Gentile. Not proclaiming to them peace provided they made themselves worthy of it, but proclaiming peace to them unworthy as they were; for as Christ had died for them, not when they were friends, but when they were enemies, so, even if they still continued enemies, the message of peace and reconciliation was by the apostles proclaimed to them, "Peace on earth and good will towards men," was the substance of the precious message which they bore. And was not this good tidings to individuals who had been plunged in idolatry and every species of abomination, and had given up all idea of future bliss in despair; or to individuals, who, after trying all in their power to render themselves objects of the divine favour, and finding themselves unable to do so, were enveloped in unquestionable fear and trembling, as to what should become of them—was it not glad tidings to them to be told, "God is at peace with you—God sent us not to proclaim wrath, but mercy—God loves you—God intends kindness towards you here, and kindness towards you hereafter. Be therefore of good cheer." It is He who speaks, "Be not afraid." Let fear pass away, for your sins are all washed away in the blood of His own Son. He now beholds you accepted in Christ the beloved one. Here indeed was glad tidings—glorious tidings—tidings of good.

In the second place they brought good tidings of good, they published salvation. They came to individuals who had been cooped up in a narrow place, who, after being expelled from an earthly paradise, had been cast down to earth; to individuals who had been made to eat of the fruit of their own doings—individuals exposed to sufferings and sorrows of all descriptions, and finally to death itself. They came to individuals in such a state of existence to proclaim that he who was their peace, and had shed his blood to bring peace to the guilty conscience—that as he had quitted this world by his resurrection from the dead, as he had ascended to glory, as he had put aside entirely the condition of humanity, and had now taken possession of the throne prepared for him, so he had sent them to proclaim glad tidings of the highest description—even the glad tidings that Jesus Christ being the second man, the Lord from heaven, and having reascended to that heaven from which he had previously descended, having taken possession of the heavenly mansions—having done all this in behalf of, and for their sakes—that he had sent them, the apostles, to proclaim to them peace here; and that when life's fitful fever was over, and all their earthly sufferings and trials had passed away, Jesus would take them home to himself, take them into his Father's glorious presence, that where he was, there they might be also. They were therefore proclaimers of salvation—salvation and deliverance from this present evil world—not merely deliverance hereafter, but deliverance *here*. They came to proclaim deliverance to those who, through fear of death, had all their lifetime been subject to bondage—to proclaim that by the knowledge of Christ Jesus, they had even already life everlasting. And as there was to be communicated salvation even in the present world, so also in the heavenly world hereafter, throughout eternity. For as they had borne the image of the earthy, and as such were sinful, polluted, and dying, so they were to bear the image of the heavenly, and appear glorious and divine for evermore. They were to bear it in earnest here; for although the body while upon earth was dead because of sin, the spirit was life because of righteousness; the joy of the Lord was to constitute their strength; and, having entered into his courts on earth, they were to enter into the heavenly temple itself, there to see and enjoy him whom their hearts had previously loved. Therefore, if there were good tidings of peace proclaimed—so there was good tidings of good, even salvation proclaimed, not merely "The King is at peace with you, and has forgiven you your trespasses;" but there is nothing that you can conceive of, or ask for, that shall be for your good, but what you shall enjoy—not only what you would have enjoyed had Paradise not been lost to you, but he will cause blessings to descend upon you which it hath not entered into the heart of man to conceive of—blessings which he hath prepared for you from the foundation of the world. He hath prepared for you "salvation," deliverance from the present evil world—deliverance from the Adamic nature—deliverance from sin and death, and the enjoyment of life everlasting.

But this is not all. Not only are these glad tidings to be proclaimed, but there is a climax to the whole—the most important of all the messages which the messengers were chosen to proclaim, "Behold thy God reigneth." It may not, perhaps, at first sight appear that there is a climax here; but a little reflection, a very little understanding of the divine word, a very little love of it in your hearts will make you feel as well as see that there is here a most amazing announcement. I do not know whether I have sufficient time to dwell on the ground of the message which Christ gave his apostles and disciples to proclaim both in Judea and throughout the earth. You will remember that message was "The kingdom of heaven—or of God—is at hand." If you look in the Gospels you will find that "The Kingdom of God" was a subject on which they frequently spoke. Indeed, the moment these points come under your notice, you cannot fail to perceive the contrast between the kingdom of God and the kingdoms of men; not merely earthly kingdoms, in which human monarchs may display their earthly passions and feelings, but contrast such as is shewn in the 3rd chapter of Hebrews, between the kingdom of Moses, and the kingdom of Jesus Christ, the Lord of Moses, and Lord over the New Testament dispensation. It is as if God said, "For a time I have permitted men to rule over you; for a time you have been governed by men, although under my special protection; but the time shall come, when the Government shall be laid upon Christ's shoulders; when God, in Christ, shall reign directly over His Church; when the Church shall acknowledge His authority alone —when it shall throw aside that of the creature, and the Creator Himself shall reign directly over every heart, and over every conscience." Now, I understand then by the proclamation, "The kingdom of heaven—or the kingdom of God—is at hand," that the period was approaching when the interference of men in the earthly governments of the Church should be exchanged for the direct assumption of authority over it by the Lord of Glory Himself. Now here observe, a third fact is to be proclaimed, cry unto Zion—unto the Old Testament Church, and unto the New also, "Thy God reigneth." The very fact of proclaiming unto them, "Thy God reigneth," told them that a Being of infinite perfection now swayed the sceptre—and that he who now sat upon the throne was from everlasting to everlasting. It also told them that they were free from all partial or defective authority; men might err through ignorance, or through mistaken affection; but he who now occupied the throne, could commit no mistake, inasmuch as his knowledge was infinite, and his love as infinite as his knowledge; therefore all that he did would be right; all that he did would be just; all that he did would be thoroughly impartial. O, what peace —what a salvation to speak of to guilty rebels. What glorious tidings of good—to those who were looking for, and expecting nothing less than divine wrath, and the execution of the divine sentence.

But observe one little word here in this precious declaration. It is worth drawing your attention to, "Say unto Zion, *Thy*

God reigneth." It is not "God reigneth," but it is "*Thy God reigneth.*" He, who was the God of Israel in Old Testament times. He, who had selected Abraham from the other nations of the earth. He, who had put forth His Almighty arm as a shield—to interpose and save Israel from danger in former times. He, who had been unto Old Testament Israel as their God. He was the God who would now rule directly, and not through the interposition of earthly preachers, over His people. But there is more implied. When you and I look into the New Testament Scriptures, we find that God was made manifest in flesh. He, who had been the God of Israel, appeared in the form of a man—appeared in the form of a Jew—and was connected with the Jews, as their kinsman more particularly, but he was connected with the Gentiles also, inasmuch as he was the word made flesh, and dwelt among us, and was one with us. He passed through this world, obeyed God's law—through love—offered himself a sacrifice without spot to God—rose from the dead—rose to the power of an endless life—rose to occupy the throne prepared for him of old—rose to the heavens from which he had previously descended; and thus he, God, who was one with man, one with Jew and Gentile, bone of their bone, and flesh of their flesh, by partaking of their nature. He took his place upon his throne. He rose to glory, that he might bring many sons and daughters to glory likewise, so that they are not only under him whose reign is a reign of power and justice—but he, whose reign is the reign of a friend, the reign of a lover, the reign of a brother, the reign of a husband, the reign of one who stands in every endearing relation; the reign of one who ever stands on their side to overcome every enemy—to bring them, in spite of every obstacle, to glory—and who sits on his throne, that he might give each one of them, in due time, to sit down with himself, to see his face, and enjoy him for ever. Therefore if any doubt whatever might have existed with respect to the two other proclamations—those of peace and of salvation—if any should say this is too good news to be true, "Remember it is thy God who speaks, thy God who governs, thy God who sits upon the throne." There is no enemy there; there is no being of a debased character there; there is no being who wills thee evil there; on the contrary, he who sits there came to procure peace by his death, and by his resurrection from the dead, and ascension to God's right hand, and ever lives to carry into effect what he hath accomplished on earth, by dying and rising from the dead, and ascending up on high—his reign is a reign of love, and is exercised on your behalf, not only for time but for everlasting ages. Thus then observe the last proclamation, "*Thy* God reigneth." This proclamation is the groundwork of the other two. Proclaim good tidings, for the monarch who proclaims it is one with those to whom it is proclaimed. He hath died for them and risen in their behalf, and is by this proclamation carrying into effect what he died and rose again for. Therefore the very fact of his being called their God—and of the reign in question being ascribed to him—taken in connection with his power and justice, are to us so many pledges that he will carry into full effect the proclamations made by those who stood upon these divine—these glorious mountains.

May the Lord bless what has been spoken, so far as agreeable to His mind and will, and to His name be praise for evermore.—Amen.

SERVICE III.

December 3rd, 1854.

PSALM.

The 12th Psalm, at the beginning.

You may remember a very remarkable and instructive passage, contained in the second chapter of the Gospel according to St. John, where it is said, that Jesus did not commit himself to those who were his disciples, for he knew what was in man, and needed not that any should testify of man. One of the grand proofs of the intimate knowledge of the human heart—possessed by God, and possessed by the spirit of Christ—which speaks in the Old Testament Scriptures, is the minute and accurate representation of human motives and human aims, with which it abounds. You are struck to find that it searches the thoughts and intents of the heart,—laying them bare, and giving a hint as to the source of all the various actions, by which the human race, publicly and privately, has been and ever will be distinguished.

We have, for some time past, been speaking, more or less directly, of the principle of fancied self-independence, either possessed by man, or which he aims at possessing. The Book of Psalms, that sweet portion of the Old Testament Scriptures, lays bare this tendency or disposition of the human heart, and shews us that it was intimately known to him with whom we have to do, and is in his sight one of the most prominent characteristics of man's earthly and fallen nature.

At the beginning of the 12th Psalm we meet with the words:

"Help, Lord, because the godly man
Doth daily fade away."

We had occasion, lately, to bring this Psalm under your notice, and I then observed that the godly man, in the highest sense of the term, is Christ Jesus himself, who, while he was on earth, was the object of man's opposition, reproach and hatred, who, under the burden which he bore internally and externally, appeared to fade away; and who showed that the help he required could not come from the creature;—for the creature, as such, could not sympathize with him; but that help must come from the Creator, and from the Creator alone. And as it was with the Son of God, so has it been with the Church; its members have always been a small body, ever, apparently, on the eve of destruction; but, like the smoking flax, it has not been quenched, and like the bruised reed, it has not been broken. As it has ever been preserved, so, according to God's Word, it ever will be preserved. But it has not been by any internal power, possessed by the members of the Church themselves, that they have been preserved, but solely by the power of Him who calleth those things which are not as though they were, and with whom all things are possible; that God who, in every age, has thrown His arms around the members of His Church, preserving them from every evil and every danger, and from that greatest of all dangers, their own wicked hearts; that God who, in spite of the strong stream of selfishness, corruption, and depravity of the human heart, running its course in one direction, has kept them, by His mighty power, from sinking in that stream, until at last they are to see him and enjoy him in glory.

" And from among the sons of men,
The faithful do decay."

They pass away, their places scarcely seeming to be filled up; God has taken them to Himself, to bring them forward in due time, the destined heirs of salvation. The body of believers, viewed humanly, is fragile; each member being only maintained by a power infinitely greater than his own, and without which he could not be sustained.

I cannot say that I sympathize with the theology of Bunyan's "Pilgrim's Progress;" nevertheless, one of the prettiest incidents contained in that interesting, though human, production, is that which is represented as having taken place at the Interpreter's house, where the flame, always appearing ready to be extinguished, yet blazes up; and *Christian*, being admitted behind the wall, is shewed one, no doubt the Son of Man, who is engaged in feeding and preserving the flame, and protecting it from destruction, unseen by the eye of man, nevertheless in reality acting upon, sustaining and causing that flame so to burn, as to swallow up all opposition and to destroy every enemy.

" Unto his neighbour every one
Doth utter vanity."

It would be better if you were to read the first four stanzas of the psalm for yourselves, particularly that portion where it is said—

> "God shall cut off all flattering lips,
> Tongues that speak proudly thus;
> We'll with our tongues prevail, our lips
> Are ours: who's Lord o'er us?"

We have here human nature delineated and described in a manner at once pointed and characteristic; and that important subject to which I have frequently of late alluded is here strikingly brought before us—man's fancied self-independence, his pride, his disposition to set himself up as a being who is the rival and antagonist, if not the superior of God himself. We have here an exhibition of human nature in that vaunted character so proudly boasted of by the human race; in that character which has prompted many, in Germany and elsewhere, to trample under foot and treat with the utmost contempt the divine sovereignty, as set down in the 9th chapter of the Epistle to the Romans and elsewhere. "All they shall be cut down, for I the Lord alone will reign in that day." The Lord will permit no rivals, and He will make those who, in the pride of human nature, set themselves up in fancied independence of Him, to feel, to their confusion, that they are but His creatures—but as vessels in the hands of Him the potter, and that when He pleases, in spite of their opposition, and in spite of their mighty thoughts of themselves, He can, and will, dash them to pieces.

> "For poor, oppress'd, and for the sighs
> Of needy, rise will I,
> Saith God, and him in safety set
> From such as him defy."

Here we see God interposes. The creature may rage; the whole powers of earth and Satan may appear to be combined against His Son—His anointed Son, and against His Son's people; but greater is he that is for them than all those that are or can be against them. The arms of the Almighty are thrown around them, His mighty power is put forth in their behalf; and, therefore, their opponents, instead of succeeding, are made the subjects of His condign and everlasting vengeance.

The psalm, therefore, is of extreme importance to us, both from what it suggests and from its close agreement with the whole spirit of Scripture from first to last. You remember that in the first promise; God addressed the serpent: "I will put enmity between thy seed and her seed; it shall bruise thy head, and thou shalt bruise his heel;" and, to the members of the Church of God, this is a proof of the truth of God's word, for, down to the present day, that enmity exists and will continue to exist to the end of time. The seed of the serpent is, in the whole of the human race, opposed to the divine purposes; it is only when the spirit of Christ in the minds of believers takes effect, that they obtain grace in Christ Jesus, and the opposition of their natural minds to the seed of the woman is overcome; but the seed of the serpent, hating the seed of the woman, is opposed to the power and other perfections of God, and there is, of necessity, opposition between them: but the children of God exhibit a character which the world likes not, and which the world would fain stifle and destroy; and if the world does nominally pretend to respect Christ and his character, it is not that it may have an opportunity of establishing the work of Christ and his free salvation; for the grace and the salvation which the world would establish are in direct opposition to Christ and the salvation of God. In the work of salvation, which belongs to God alone, He is supreme: the salvation is His, and the glory redounds to Him. But in man's work of salvation the creature is set up: the creature and the works of the creature would fain be substituted for the works of the Creator. In other words, in the one case the pride of man is put down by the revelation of the glory of God, and in the other case the pride of man is stimulated, and his evil propensities are drawn out and strengthened, and a disposition is evinced directly in opposition to that which the word of God produces, and which the word of God displays in Christ.

PRAYER.

Let us pray.

Heavenly Father, we desire ever to bear in mind that there are but two classes of individuals existing and passing through this present world—those who know and love Thee, and those who know Thee not and love Thee not; and we remember that the distinction in question was first made known in the world when, proceeding to pass sentence upon man, Thou didst inform him that Thou wouldst put enmity between the seed of the woman and the seed of the serpent; that the seed of the serpent should be permitted to bruise the heel of the seed of the woman, but that the seed of the woman was destined to bruise, to crush, to destroy the serpent's head.

Ever since that memorable declaration was made, this enmity has appeared. It was shewn, immediately, in the opposition subsisting between Cain and Abel, between the faith of the latter and the want of faith on the part of the former; it was shewn in the fact that, when unaccepted by Thee, the murderous feelings of the human heart were aroused and excited in the breast of Cain, and that this issued in the shedding of his brother's blood.

We trace the same enmity in the opposition that subsisted on the part of Seth and his descendants to the descendants of Cain. And, we perceive that at last, matters were reduced to a narrow compass, when one individual, having built an ark in token of his faith in Thee, stood with his family opposed to the rest of the world; and when he in that ark of safety—the type of Christ—was saved with his little family from the wreck and destruction of the surrounding world.

And when we look at the human race, as renewed in the persons of Noah's descendants, we immediately discover the same opposition between the seed of the woman and the seed of the serpent making itself manifest. We trace it in the case of Abraham as opposed to the rest of the world: and when we see Thee separating the descendants of Abraham from the other nations of the earth, we see this enmity made distinctly apparent. Still more, when we look at the seed of Abraham itself,—his descendants according to the flesh, we perceive it existing even among them, for they were not all Israel who were of Israel, but in Isaac was thy seed blessed.

And we perceive, tracing matters down to the days of our Blessed Lord, a small number of individuals selected out of Israel itself to know Thy name and show forth Thy praise; and we see them the objects of opposition to their kinsmen and countrymen, and we see that, but for Thy protecting and fostering care, at the hands of their bitter opponents they would have met with destruction.

And when Thou drawest our attention to Christ, to the followers whom he had chosen, to the course of procedure which he engaged in, and to the usage which he met with at the hands of his own to whom he came, but who received him not, we perceive the same opposition made most distinctly manifest. And we perceive that the Son of God, in proportion as he evinced God's character and shewed himself to be possessed of God's mind, and in proportion as he aimed at the fulfilment of God's purposes, became more and more the object of hatred to the Jews. And, when his character came out in all its beauty, in all its divine loveliness, and in all the charms of its heavenly devotion, we perceive that, then, the hatred of man to him appeared, rose to its height, and issued in their nailing him to the accursed tree. And when he, having risen from the dead, and ascended to Thy right hand, had there taken possession of the Throne prepared for him of old, and when he had shed forth the Holy Spirit upon his apostles and disciples, and when by them the truth as it is in him had been proclaimed, first to Jews, and then to Gentiles, we find the same spirit of hatred and the same spirit of marked opposition, evincing itself on the part of those Jews and on the part of those Gentiles who believed not in Thy testimony. We find it evinced first in Jerusalem, in the treatment which Peter and John met with at the hands of their countrymen. We see it especially evinced in the martyrdom of Stephen, who died proclaiming that he saw Christ sitting at Thy right hand, and who, with the words of life everlasting and the expressions of intense love upon his lips, fell asleep in Christ Jesus. And we trace the same opposition at every stage of the apostles' progress throughout the Gentile world, in the evil treatment they met with at the hands of their unbelieving countrymen in the various towns to which they came, and where the Gospel by them was proclaimed. We trace it in the opposition of Gentiles, who set up to oppose and blaspheme the name by which Christ's disciples were called and known. We see the same opposition at the very close of the record Thou hast given concerning Thine apostle Paul; for when he had summoned the Jews together, when he laid bare the prophecies concerning the future Messiah, and when he had shown that they had received their fulfilment so far, in the mission, work, death, and resurrection of Thy Son, then we find that, while a few believed Thy testimony and rejoiced in the salvation Thou hadst wrought out, the majority contradicted and blasphemed it, and were dismissed by the apostle with an allusion to the ancient prophecy of Isaiah, who said that they should have eyes and see not, ears which should not hear, and minds which should not understand; that there should, in fact, be evinced in them that judicial blindness to Divine truth, which, when men are left entirely to themselves, uniformly makes its appearance.

But we desire to bear in mind that the opposition existing between God and man,—that the distinct opposition between the seed of the serpent and the seed of the woman, did not finish with New Testament history, but has come down through succeeding generations to our own time; that it exists even among ourselves. And we desire to bear in mind that as there is a woe pronounced upon him of whom all speak well, this woe is connected with the fact that if any one would live godly in Christ Jesus, he must suffer persecution. It is true that the laws of our country may, in some degree, protect us from violence, and, blessed be Thy name, we can express our thanksgiving to Thee for such a provision; but we know that the opposition of man to God will go as far as it can, and we know that as of old, Ishmael sneered and laughed at Isaac,—an instance of the seed of the serpent laughing at the seed of the woman,—so we know that, even now, people must have their opinions misrepresented, must have Christ and their views of him set at nought by reason of unbelief, and must be subjected, if they make a profession becoming the Gospel, to all the opposition of an unbelieving world, in so far as they come into contact with it, and are exposed to its censure and reproaches. But we desire to rejoice in every circumstance by which we are connected, even externally, with Christ Jesus the Lord. We desire to remember that if they have called the master of the house Beelzebub, they will apply a similar appellation to those who are his disciples. We desire to remember the blessed declaration of Thine apostle, that if we be persecuted for Christ's name, we are happy, for the spirit of grace and glory resteth on us; that while on their part he is evil spoken of, on our part he is glorified. And, oh, how blessed the declaration contained in Thy word, that if we suffer with Christ here, we shall reign with him hereafter. We desire at the same time ever to bear in mind that we are not permitted to defy the world; and to remember Christ's command to his disciples, that they brave not persecution, but that if persecuted in one city, they should flee to another. We remember the Apostle's language, in so far as it applies, that thus they should live peaceably with all men. Oh, may we recollect that if we manifest the mind of Christ and act consistently with our character, we cannot escape the censure and opposition of the world. We remember that it is our privilege to rejoice in this, that we are assimilated to our head here, and have the assurance of our being thoroughly assimilated to him hereafter.

Oh, Heavenly Father, blessed be Thy name, for all the mercies that belong to the life that now is. Oh, how sweet to think that we can bless Thee also for Christ Jesus, in whom all mercies, temporal and spiritual, are summed up; for Christ Jesus as our source and channel of life everlasting; for Christ Jesus in whom all things are treasured up, from whom they flow to us in earnest now, and in whom we shall enjoy them to their full extent in the heavenly glory hereafter.

Oh, we desire to have the eyes of our faith directed towards Christ Jesus, its author and finisher, knowing that, for the joy that was set before him, he endured the cross, despising the shame, and is now set down at Thy right hand. And knowing that wherever there is the possession of knowledge of Thee, there is the mind of Thee—a mind without which no man can belong to Thee. We rejoice to know that as Christ kept for us that word of promise continually in view, so the members of Christ's heavenly body—those constituting the Church, are keeping the promise of Thy second coming continually before their minds, and are rejoicing in hope of the glory of God.

Oh, heavenly Father, our desire is, that the various principles which are laid down in Thy word, and which are imparted to us successively, by the Holy Spirit taking of the things of Christ and applying them to us,—our desire is that they may operate more and more powerfully upon our understandings, and upon our hearts and consciences. May we be influenced more and more by the mind that was in Christ Jesus the Lord; and, under the influence of this mind, may we live, walk, and act. May we bring forth much fruit to Thy praise and glory, not acting in order to obtain it by our own merits, but because it is given freely in thy Son, secured to us in Thy heavenly declarations and promises, and because we know that heaven and earth may pass away, but that one jot or tittle of Thy word shall not pass away, until all shall be fulfilled.

Oh, how delightful the consideration that Thou art the God of truth, as well as the God of power and life, and that whatsoever Thou hast said shall not return unto Thee void, but shall accomplish all the purposes for which Thou hast sent it. Oh, how glorious to think that while Thou art true to all Thy people, and that while the wages of sin is known to be death to every human being, yet equally art Thou true to Thy blessed and sovereign promises, seeing that Thou gavest us eternal life, and that this is freely given to us in Thy Son; seeing that this is the promise which Thou hast promised us, even eternal life. Oh how glorious, while passing through this world, receiving its good things and receiving its evil things, to be enabled to sit loose to its precepts as well as to its threats. How delightful to pass through the world, having caught the spirit of our divine head, as strangers and pilgrims, receiving from Thy hand with thankfulness what Thou givest, but at the same time receiving it in the prospect of that ocean of bliss in which we are destined to exist hereafter, where no desire is ungratified, where all our wishes shall be satisfied to the uttermost, when Christ shall be enjoyed in a way, and to an extent of which we have now no conception, and where we shall partake of those rivers of pleasure and joy at Thy right hand for evermore.

Oh, Lord, influence us by Thy truth more and more, even by that word of Thine which is truth; and while we are guarding against the phantom of looking to the mere feelings of our minds, may we be constantly kept open by Thee, who alone can keep us open to all the heavenly influences of Thy word, and the operations of Thy spirit, and have our affections more and more fastened upon Thee, and ourselves more and more crucified unto the world with all its affections and lusts. Lord, work in us all the good pleasure of Thy goodness and the work of faith with mighty power; and while the world, lying in wickedness, sheweth opposition to our head and therefore to us, may we not retaliate, but pray in the words of him who said, " Father forgive them, for they know not what they do," and of him who said, " Lay not this sin to their charge." Under the influence of Thy heavenly love, which is God dwelling in us, for he that dwelleth in love dwelleth in God, and God in him,—under the influence of that heavenly love, may we not return evil for good, but good for evil. Lord, preserve us from all duplicity and hypocrisy: thou knowest that our hearts are desperately wicked, beyond what we can conceive; but, oh, cause Thy truth to search our inmost hearts, to pervade our inmost thoughts. Lord, give us to act with sincerity towards the children of men; not under the influence of human nature, for its principles are vile and deceitful; but with a godly sincerity, under the influence of the divine nature, which is truth itself.

Heavenly Father, give thy people to cultivate more and more all these heavenly affections which become the divine nature, and which become our holy profession: may we pass through the world blameless, and harmless, and without rebuke, shewing forth the praises of Him who hath called us out of darkness into His marvellous light. **Lord, do thou** suit the dispensations of Thy providence and the communications of Thy spirit to the various circumstances in which we are placed; and do Thou give us, if labouring under difficulties, to trust in Thee, the only living and true God, and to entreat at Thy hands the supply of those blessings of which we stand in need. And, Lord, if we are basking in the sunshine of worldly prosperity, may we give Thee the glory, remembering that Thou hast made us stewards so far as we possess prosperity, and that in proportion as our obligations to Thee become greater, so our responsibilities are greater also.

Oh, heavenly Father, preserve us from doing wrong in any respect whatever: keep us shunning the very appearance of evil, and enable us to desire in all respects to act so as to glorify Thee our Father which art in heaven; not under the influence of a slavish principle, and regarding Thee as a harsh God who reapest where Thou hast not sowed, and who gatherest where Thou hast not strewed, but as a God of beneficence, who art heaping mercies continually upon us, and to whom our deepest, our everlasting gratitude is therefore justly due. Oh may the free-born spirit of Christianity, that ingenuousness of Christianity, which is begotten in those who are the sons of God, influence us continually, and enable us to walk worthy of our high and heavenly vocation.

Do Thou this day bless the proclamation of Thy word, and its reading in every place where it may be found. Lord, pardon all our mistakes; pardon any that we may make this day. Oh, we have in all things sinned and come short of Thy glory.

Bless Thy holy word, and cause it to have free course, and be abundantly glorified. Ride forth this day, oh, thou Saviour of men, in the chariot of Thy salvation, conquering and to conquer, and may the result of Thy mighty power be that Thine arrows stick sharp in the hearts of Thine enemies, —arrows of conviction,—arrows communicating heavenly light and heavenly love. Bring Thine enemies to be thy friends, and bring many sons and daughters in Thy good time to glory.

Oh, be with us this forenoon for good. Be ever present with us to bless us with Thy peculiar blessing. Make Thy word more and more precious to us, and keep us from listening to the words of a human being as if they had any authority. May we be enabled to see more and more clearly the word of the living and true God, and to love it increasingly, and to feel its influence increasingly, to Thy praise and glory.

Hear, we entreat thee, our supplications, and do for us exceeding abundantly above all that we can ask or think, and what we ask is for Christ's sake. Amen.

SERMON.

The passage from which I purpose to address you this morning is contained in the First Epistle to the Corinthians, the 6th chapter and the 19th and 20th verses:—"Ye are not your own! For ye are bought with a price: therefore glorify God in your body, and in your spirit, which are God's."

Such of you as have been brought to know and rejoice in the truth as it is in Christ Jesus, can scarcely have heard me address you on the last three Lord's days, without perceiving that, connected with the various subjects of which I treated, I was aiming at some practical conclusion. The fact that Jesus Christ was the Eternal Word made flesh; that he was God manifest in flesh; that he was God with us: the fact that he came into our world to magnify the law and make it honourable; that he came into our world to offer himself a sacrifice without spot unto God, and to take away sin by the sacrifice of himself: the fact that, after having accomplished the work of salvation which had been assigned to him, he descended into the grave, and entered the regions of death; the fact that he rose from that temporary death; that he ascended to the right hand of the throne of the majesty on high; that he took his seat upon the throne which had been prepared for him of old, and again partook of the glory that he had with the Father before the foundation of the world: all these facts, it was perfectly obvious could not have been barren of results—results of the most important description.

Now, as the facts themselves, of which I have been speaking, are not the production of human fancy, but spring directly from God's own testimony: as they are facts which occurred, facts which are recorded, and facts which are communicated to us by God himself; so the results to which they lead, the practical consequences in which they issue, the everlasting glory with which they are connected, all are likewise, to us, matters of divine revelation, and which, when made known to us, bespeak the same divine glory which is manifested in the facts themselves.

Jesus is God. Jesus became incarnate: Jesus died and rose again: and Jesus did all this, not that matters might remain as they were, not that the earth's downward tendency should continue without stint and without interruption; but he did all this that an issue worthy of himself, and worthy of God, might be accomplished; an issue which, as it involves our everlasting happiness, should be the theme of the redeemed in heaven itself throughout everlasting ages. And in that most precious part of Scripture, the Book of Revelation, a book the full import of which is too bright, and the language of which is clothed with too great a lustre, for the present state of our faculties, in that book we find that, when the saints are assembled in heaven before the throne, and when they are contemplating the full blaze of the divine glory, it is not some paltry, earthly result; it is not some vague heavenly idea; it is a definite fact which they are contemplating and which is the source of their everlasting gratitude: it is the work that was finished on Calvary; it is the resurrection from the dead that followed; it is the result that was involved in that death and resurrection, that constitutes the subject matter of their thoughts, that constitutes the theme of their everlasting praises. Unto him that loved us, and hath washed us from our sins in his own blood; and hath made us kings and priests, unto his heavenly Father; unto him be praise, and glory, and dominion, and blessedness, and thanksgiving, for evermore.

Now it is to the result, the grand result of the interposition of God himself in man's behalf, that I this morning, and perhaps for one or two Lord's day mornings more, shall draw your attention.

"Ye are not your own, ye are bought with a price, therefore glorify God in your body and in your spirit, which are God's.

Now, in reflecting upon this subject, it has occurred to me that it might be proper to divide the words of our text, which are an abridgment of the whole scope of divine revelation, into two distinct heads, the consideration of one of which may fitly occupy our attention this morning, and the consideration of the other, may be deferred until another opportunity, if God, in the course of His providence, should spare us to carry out our intention.

Now, that head, which we will consider on the present occasion, consists of the words, "Ye are not your own, for ye are bought with a price." Even these words suggest to us a twofold aspect of the subject, and a twofold aspect which is to a certain degree of the nature of a climax.

In the first place, "Ye are not your own." Observe whom the apostle is addressing. He is addressing believers of the truth; he is addressing men who have a certain apprehension of what is implied in the manifestation of the character and work of Christ Jesus, and a certain apprehension not only of the relationship in which Christ stands to them, but also of the corresponding relationship in which they stand to him: "Ye are not your own."

I can conceive a great number of human beings, men of intellect and learning, perhaps, but men whose minds have never been enlightened by the truth as it is in Christ Jesus; men who may fancy that this is a subject too trite and too obvious to deserve any particular consideration. It is what every one knows, say they: We are not our own, we are God's creatures. Say you so, my friends? Well, the admission so far as it goes, is good; but know ye what is implied in that admission? Have you ever had your minds suitably, because thoroughly, directed towards the subject? and not only have you had your understandings engaged with it, but have you ever felt it occupying your hearts and asserting that supremacy over your thoughts and conduct to which it is entitled? It is one thing to say, "Lord, Lord," as our Saviour when on earth wisely observed on one occasion: it is another thing to do those things which he hath commanded us to do: it is one thing to say: Oh, we know that we are not our own; it is another thing to understand and to be influenced by the glorious fact, which, with their tongues, so many are ready to confess.

"Ye are not your own." Ah! Is this a matter which men are constantly confessing with their lips, and upon the understanding of which they are constantly acting in their lives and in their ordinary practice? Pardon me! A little consideration of the subject, will show that the knowledge that we are not our own and the practical effect of that knowledge, are not so generally diffused and not so generally acted on as is commonly, but erroneously, supposed. Are you aware that the history of man opens with a view of man's not acknowledging this apparently simple fact? Are you aware that the first transgression of Adam and Eve was connected with their rejection of it? God, the Creator of the heavens and the earth and the creator of man, and subsequently of woman, had declared to Adam that he might freely eat of the trees of the garden; that every production of nature was at his command and under his control, with one exception; that exception intimating that He who granted the permission was Lord of all, and had a right to limit His grant in the way and to the extent He pleased. But did man observe in this grant, and in the condition on which it was made, and in the penalty of disobedience, a second feature— a distinct proof that he was not his own by creation? No: so far from that, when Satan tempted Adam and Eve to eat of the forbidden tree, he intimated that God had prohibited them from doing so, because he knew that in the moment of their eating of it they would rise to the dignity of gods; and when he had thus held out the suitable temptation, the woman, and subsequently her husband, influenced by the sense of fancied self-independence, and influenced by that principle of ambition which dwells so deeply and is so extensively diffused in the human heart—I say the woman, and subsequently the man, influenced by this, ate; had their eyes opened, and found that they had acquired the knowledge of good and evil; but found that in doing so they had cut off the natural communion which they had previously possessed with their Creator and their God. In eating of the forbidden fruit they threw off His yoke; they practically disowned His authority; they said, "We are our own and we will shew that we are so." And, in this daring act, sin came out; man's eyes were fleshlily enlightened, and man, as to the flesh, sinned and died. The human race immediately began to exhibit the same characteristic: assuming to be their own, and acting as such; and the human race has continued to do so in all subsequent ages and generations. When Cain, in opposition to the divine command, ventured to present his offering of the fruit of the ground, and to fancy that he was honouring God by offering an unbloody sacrifice, he was acting as if he were his own and not God's; and, as the result, God rejected his sacrifice and condemned him.

As we travel down the stream of time, we find the whole of the idolatrous nations acting upon the principle that they were their own, in setting up various forms of religion, all opposed to God; all having the human mind for their origin, and the corruptions of the human heart for their fosterers and supporters: we find the practical import of all their conduct to be "We are our own."

We find the same principle evinced among the Jews themselves: we find it charged against them in that psalm, a portion of which we have been singing, "With our tongue will we prevail; our lips are our own: who is Lord over us?" We find it practically asserted in all the opposition given by the Israelites in the wilderness to the commands and injunctions of Jehovah: and it was because they fancied themselves their own, and that they had a right to dispose of their conduct, that He said, "This is a stiff-necked people." The same principle influenced them in their idolatrous practices after their settlement in the land of Canaan: the same principle was evinced by Jeroboam, when, with a view to prevent the ten tribes from going up to Jerusalem to worship, he set up calves in Dan and elsewhere, and represented them as the gods the people were to worship. "We are our own," was the practical language of this impious pretence of Jeroboam: and the same conduct evinced itself among the two remaining tribes, until at last they were sent into captivity.

We have reason to believe that, down to the time of the appearance of our blessed Lord, the same feeling, "We are our own," continued to prevail among the majority of the Jewish people, and stamped their character as identical with that of the Gentile nations by whom they were surrounded. When Christ made his appearance did he find faith upon the earth? Yes, but only among a very few: in a John the Baptist, in a Simon, in an Andrew, and in a few others; but he found the majority of those to whom he came steeped in hypocrisy, steeped in self-righteousness, steeped in the conviction that they were their own, and that they had a right to dispose of themselves, of their conduct, and of their worship, as they pleased. When Christ, in his own conduct, practically shewed that he was not his own, but God's; that he was devoted to the love and service of his heavenly Father; that he came not to do his own will, but the will of Him that sent him; and when he had influenced a few poor fishermen and tax-gatherers to believe in him as the Messiah and to be witnesses of his character and conduct and motives, the minds of men possessed of the feeling "We are our own," began to shew itself in their treatment of him, and subsequently in their treatment of his apostles; they crucified the Lord of Glory as an impostor; they persecuted his followers; they pleased not God, and were contrary to all men; and therefore the wrath of God came down upon them to the uttermost. The Gentiles, too, even those of them professing Christian love and gentleness, we find from the epistles, were, from time to time, evincing the same spirit, and required, in order to their embracing and holding fast Christian principles, the exercise of apostolic discipline.

With the close of the period of Christ and his apostles, did this spirit of self-independence on the part of man; did the feeling "We are our own," among professing Christians, pass away? No: it has come down to our own day as an heir-loom of human nature; it exists among ourselves in all its force and in all its intensity. The great mass of professing Christians are influenced by the feeling "We are our own;" and against it the people of God require continually to strive.

This disposition to act independently of God, this feeling "We are our own," is the grand enemy which the people of God require to crucify, or rather, I should say, which requires to be crucified by the mind of Christ Jesus given to them, and by the spirit of our God operating upon their hearts and consciences.

"We are our own." Oh, what a feeling on the part of man! Putting the whole history of Jesus Christ aside, and supposing the Redeemer had never appeared on the earth; and supposing, however, that we had been told upon God's authority that He was our Creator, and that He was sustaining us continually; that He was our bountiful benefactor; that it is to Him we owed our continued existence; and that from day to day he was loading us with his benefits; that from Him we received the food we eat, the water we drink, the raiment with which we are clothed, and all the other earthly advantages of which we are possessed: why, the knowledge of that alone, were the mind of man not perverted —were his mind not biassed and distorted, would satisfy him that he was not his own, but that all he had received was from his Creator, and that, when the purposes for which the temporary concession of life was made, are accomplished, he must return to the dust from which he was taken. How could a being, dependent upon God for life and breath and all things, be his own? Yet it is as our own that we are, by nature, continually acting: we act as our own, when we receive the blessings that God bestows upon us, as if we had a right to them; ay, and as if we had a right to much more, when we indulge in the spirit of murmuring, should those blessings be temporarily or entirely withdrawn; and when we act as if we had a right from our circumstances, as human beings, to claim at God's hands what we can only receive from Him as a favour, seeing that we are condemned and dying creatures.

All this intimates, practically, the feelings of our minds; for it is the language of depraved human beings to say, as it were, to God, "We are our own: we have a right to ourselves: we have a right to all we have, aye, and a right to much more than we have; and if Thou seest good to withhold it, why, then we turn upon Thee and tell Thee that Thou art a hard master, reaping where Thou hast not sown, and gathering where Thou hast not strewed." This is the feeling of human nature, and it appears in every individual who comes into the world. It is the principle upon which human society rests, and is the grand manifestation of human nature: aye, and in the people of God themselves, the principle naturally exists just as in other human beings: even they are manifesting it continually, and under the burden connected with this feeling they are made continually to groan; and it is in opposition to all this that the apostle says, in addressing the Corinthian church, "Ye are not your own;" remember the fact—who created you? remember the fact, who has given you these natural blessings? remember the fact, that you are subject to His control continually, and that when He pleases He can command the execution of the sentence upon you, "Dust thou art, and unto dust thou shalt return."

I said the subject was of the nature of a climax. Now, I have taken the very lowest view of the matter in supposing the address, as a general one, to rest upon the principle that God is our creator and sustainer, and that He it is in whom we live, and move, and have our being; that our existence is dependent upon Him alone. But even viewing the matter in that light, we are not our own, we are God's; and if the feeling of self-independence starts up in our minds, it is the parent of a lie—the lie by which man was first drawn aside, and the cause of the isolation in which man in every succeeding age has been living. But is this the only proof that we are not our own?—that God created us and providentially sustains us? No: we are bound to God by a double tie, by a deeper relation, by a far more important bond; and therefore the apostle says, "Ye are not your own." Practically as if he had said to us, ye are actually the property of another; ye are not your own; ye do not belong to yourselves; ye are not at your own disposal; and he adds, "For ye are bought with a price."

This, then, is the grand, the Christian manner of viewing

the subject; and all apostolic expositions of Divine views addressed to the Church of God suppose, and are founded on this principle, "Ye are bought," bought with a price. When we hear these words, perhaps from our previous acquaintance with the Christian system, or, perhaps from the education we originally and naturally received, we feel conscious of, and admit that this is very obvious. But does it influence us as it should do, namely, as a divine principle? Has it entered into our inmost hearts and souls? Has it become the pervading principle and influence of our lives and conversation? I trow, that just as unregenerate men, either think not at all, or think but little of the natural relationship in which they stand to God, and in which God stands to them, and are therefore scarcely, if at all, influenced, even slavishly, by the consideration that God is their creator and preserver, and that they belong to Him by nature; just so, the members of the Church of God, in respect to the influence it exercises and possesses over them, are too little influenced by the higher consideration that they are God's property, having been redeemed by the blood of God's own Son.

The words, "For ye are bought with a price," give the grand reason why, as Christians, we are not our own. The apostle is addressing Christians. If he had addressed them merely as human beings, then the consideration that they were bought would have been the grand point. But he does more, he addresses them as the redeemed of the Lord. Well then, the word "for" comes in; ye are not your own as Christians, *for*, here is the reason why ye are not your own, why ye belong to another; *for* ye are bought with a price paid by him who alone could pay it, and who, in consequence of having paid it, has made you his absolute and everlasting property.

Now there are two things declared in these words, "Ye are bought;" not bought nominally, not bought in the way of mere theory, not bought invisibly, but bought in reality; bought by the payment of an adequate and suitable price. Ye are bought. This implies that by nature we were the property of another; that other we know was Satan. We belonged to the prince of this world—the prince of the power of the air; and while we were the children of disobedience, we were shewing in our every thought and action that we were his property; that we were the bond-slaves of Satan. To use the language of the Apostle in the 7th of Romans, we were "sold under sin;" and from the state in which we were existing, we were not only unable to extricate ourselves, but we were unwilling to do so. We were unable, for that was the work not of a creature, but of the Creator. It was a thing impossible with man, although possible with God: it was God's work, not man's; and therefore from the thraldom in which we naturally were we could not have delivered ourselves, the pit into which we were fallen was too deep for us to extricate ourselves, the fetters by which we were held were too strong for us to break; it was God's prerogative to bring us out of the pit wherein there was no water, and to wrench asunder the chains of our captivity. But we ourselves had no inclination to be free. We hugged our chains; we delighted ourselves in the state of bondage in which we were. We, no doubt, found it irksome in various respects; we found our situations implied many miseries, and implied death as the issue of the whole: we knew all that, but still we knew no better; or if we thought of trying to extricate ourselves, if we had that kind of beneficence which characterizes a Robert Owen, which characterizes the Socialists and a great many of that class who respect the claims of human nature, we should try some mere expedient, for bettering the circumstances of man, and bringing a better state of things, to bear upon the interests of mankind; but we never could get higher than that.

In all such attempts what were we doing? Was this extricating us from the state of captivity in which we were held? Was this giving us true freedom? Was this elevating us above our present unhappy condition? No: it was merely varying, under certain aspects, the circumstances under which we were placed, if you can call it varying; it was like shifting the figures of a kaleidoscope; it was like altering the views presented by a magic lantern, or by some of those magnificent dioramas which, from time to time, have attracted our notice and captivated our minds; it was like shifting the scenery or changing the dresses—the actors were the same. It was not man rising out of the dungeon in which he was confined, and throwing off the yoke of the oppressor; it was the conduct of madmen confined in and belonging to a Bedlam, who conceiving that they must take things as they are, request their keepers to indulge them with a ball, or with a concert perhaps, and who adapt their circumstances and pleasures to the situation in which they are placed. It was the conduct of individuals endeavouring to make the best of what they were. This is human nature: men can neither rise above their lot, nor do they desire to do so, and therefore they would at the utmost make the best of the circumstances in which they are placed; but in trying to make the best of them they often make bad worse, for the efforts of Socialism and the efforts of those who would reduce human beings to one common level, and deprive men of the stimulus of human industry and the various blessings which flow from it; the efforts of all such individuals are to set up a state of things different from that which God has created—a state of things which, instead of bettering men, would throw them back centuries in their progress, and bring them back, if not to the state of savages, to one not much better.

We are bought. Christ comes and finds us in this state of captivity; he finds us willing it should be so; he extricates us from it by buying us. Buying us? Yes: redeeming you, if you prefer the word, because redeem is merely a Latin word having the same signification as buy; redeemed, that is, bought. Here comes, on the part of some, an exhibition of the depravity of the human heart. Bought us? What right had he to buy us? The best of all rights: you belonged to him before; you were his property; he could as your creator dispose of you as he liked; nay more, as the All-wise, he knew what was best for you, better than you did yourselves; he knew that the only way of benefiting you was by buying you from those who held you in thraldom. Ay, and God, whose very nature was love, has destined for you blessings of which you yourselves have no conception, and for which you had no desire. Talk of right: ah, he had a right, and, blessed be his name, he who had a right to dispose of you was love; but he was also a God of justice. He might, by an arbitrary act, have set you free, but justice had claims, and these claims required to be satisfied. Those who held you in thraldom, required to be satisfied; they required a very great price to be paid for you, and you could not be justly set free from the thraldom unless this was done; therefore the God of power, the God of wisdom, and the God of love, being also a God of justice, paid for you the required price, and thereby set you free—bought you—bought you with a price, and in buying you made you his own, that is, brought you into the best and highest circumstances into which you could be introduced; he bought you from the hands of the enemy, rescued you from the hands of the oppressor; and it is a delightful consideration, that in buying you—in satisfying those who held you in captivity, he actually destroyed their very existence; the satisfaction demanded was paid, but in receiving that satisfaction not only did their claims expire, but they themselves expired also; he satisfied their claims, and in satisfying their claims he destroyed them—destroyed sin by submitting to its temporary reign,—destroyed death when for a time he put himself under its power—destroyed both—leading captivity captive—and this because he had received gifts for men. He bought you, made you his own; he paid the price required, and you became thus his property at once, and for ever. You, who had been his by nature, became also his by grace; became his by passing into the best and sweetest and most glorious of all relationships; became his as his heavenly bride; became one with him in divine love for evermore.

Ye are bought with a price. This is a point often insisted on in the Holy Scriptures. The precious price, we are told in one passage, is not silver or gold or other perishable things; but the Lamb, without spot and without blemish; this was the price paid for your redemption—the price in virtue of which you are rescued from the thraldom of the oppressor; the price by which you have become his property in a new and in a higher sense, a sense higher and more glorious than that in which you are his by nature.

The price! Have you thought of it? Have you thought of God once appealing to men's moral understanding, and asking them if, for the redemption of the soul, Lebanon would be a sufficient burnt-offering? Extend the idea. Would the whole world be a sufficient price to bring about the result of our redemption? Would the sun whose light is now seen shining into this apartment, and the moon that removes to a certain degree the cheerlessness of the night—would those lights or those bodies from which light proceeds—would all the other orbs of heaven—would the whole of the glorious stars which adorn our firmament—would these be an adequate price for our redemption? No: Canaan and Lebanon and all these would fall far short of a sufficient offering. Extend the idea. Would the sacrifice of any number of human lives have been an adequate offering? No: God delighteth not in the death of a sinner. Would the sacrifice of angels and archangels have been sufficient? No: no creature could have satisfied the demand; no created sacrifice could satisfy the justice of the uncreated God; and the whole creation might have stood aghast if a mere creature price had been demanded, and if it had been paid the price would have been inadequate. Think of the price: think of what we have been bringing under your notice for the last three Lord's days: God was manifest in flesh; the eternal Word that was with God, and was God, became flesh; the man Christ Jesus was the man who was one with God: the life of Jesus in flesh was the life of God manifest in flesh. Think of that: Christ could say, "I and the father are one."

And what did Christ do? Why, after washing his hands in innocency—after exhibiting the most perfect purity of thought and conduct—after magnifying the law and making it honourable by exhibiting love to him who imposed it—delighting in the law, after its every requirement, and in the fulfilment of it, what did he finish with? He destroyed sin by sacrificing the life of God in flesh, the life of the man who was one with God, the second man, the Lord from heaven; for a life which had not been forfeited, a life over which no creature had power, a life which could only be forfeited by his own free will: he offered up through himself and through the eternal spirit, without spot or blemish, and in doing so paid the price of our redemption. He paid the price of his own most precious blood, and the price, the costliness of which was infinite, was the blood not of a creature, but of the Creator: a price that is in itself priceless, being infinite in its value. The price paid was accepted, for he rose from the dead by the power of the Father. God was justified by his dying and shewed that he was indeed his beloved and everlasting Son by enabling him to burst the bonds of death asunder and ascend to the glory prepared for him of old. The price was paid, the price was accepted, and having been paid and accepted—the price of the blood of God's own dear Son—you became his: bought by him, you became his property for evermore; and being his, being no longer your own, having no false right of self-independence, but belonging to the living and true God with his Son Jesus Christ, who, as one with you died, and who gives you, as one with him, to rise and live for ever; you, as one with him, have no right to dispose of yourself, of your thoughts, or your actions; you belong in all respects to him; your freedom consists in the Lord, in whose service there is true and perfect freedom, and just in proportion as you know his character and the value of the price paid for your redemption, in proportion as you are acquainted with the glories of redeeming love as evinced in the finished work of Christ Jesus, in the same proportion is the feeling that you are his property, made to exist in your hearts, influencing you to live not unto yourselves but unto Him who died for you and rose again.

This brings me to the second part of the subject, which,

however, I shall reserve to another opportunity. I have shown from the words, "Ye are not your own, for ye are bought with a price," that ye are God's property absolutely and for ever; but certain consequences follow, contained in the words, "Therefore glorify God in your body and in your spirit, which are his."

May the Lord bless what has been said, and to his name be praise for ever more.—Amen.

SERMON IV.

December 10th, 1854.

THE words from which I would address you this morning, are contained in the First Epistle to the Corinthians—a portion of the same passage from which I spoke last Lord's day forenoon—they occur in the 6th chapter, towards the close of the 20th verse:—"Therefore, glorify God in your body and in your spirit, which are God's."

I do not know whether I can read the passage at the beginning of the 17th chapter of St. John's Gospel, but I should like to do so, as it is the best comment upon, and explanation of my text that I can give you. "These words spake Jesus, and lifted up his eyes to heaven, and said, Father, the hour is come, glorify Thy Son that Thy Son may also glorify Thee: as Thou hast given him power over all flesh, that he should give eternal life to as many as Thou hast given him. And this is life eternal, that they might know Thee, the only true God, and Jesus Christ whom Thou hast sent. I have glorified Thee on earth, I have finished the work Thou gavest me to do. And now, O Father, glorify Thou me, with Thine own self, with the glory which I had with Thee before the world was." And so on. It would be extremely difficult for me to read the whole passage, but what I have read will be sufficient to lay the foundation of the remarks which I have to submit to you.

Suffice it to say with reference to the remarks submitted to you last Lord's day forenoon; that they were founded on the words "Ye are not your own, for ye are bought with a price." That is, the statment of a negative, followed by the statement of an affirmative. "Ye are not your own," that is, ye are not your own by nature, seeing that God is your Creator, and your bountiful preserver and benefactor; you owe to Him all you have, and all you can have at any future period; you owe to Him the life that now is, and still more you owe to Him life everlasting. You owe to Him all these things, not as ever disconnected from Him, but as living, moving, and having your being in Him; therefore, you are His necessarily and essentially by nature. But we observed that the inspired apostle, or rather the Holy Ghost speaking by the mouth of the apostle, does not confine the fact of our belonging to God to the circumstances of our creation and preservation by Him, but founds it upon a higher and much more distinct and definite principle; through the medium of a logical or causal statement, "Ye are bought with a price;" that is to say, ye were once in the hands of an enemy, strong and powerful, an enemy from whose grasp ye could not extricate yourselves, from whose power over you no creature and no mass of creatures, however numerous and mighty, could have extricated you; but an interposition has taken place in your behalf, by one, "mighty to save," even by the living and true God manifest in flesh; and he having paid an adequate price, even the price of his own most precious blood, having parted with his pure and holy earthly life on your behalf, has bought you, and has made you his property; therefore, not merely by the low right of creation, but by the higher, more special, and more powerfully operative right of redemption; he hath bought you with a price. He hath, therefore, brought you out of the power of the enemy; brought you into his own immediate presence; brought you into his own heavenly fold, and brought you under the influence of his own heavenly love.

I would now observe with reference to the words, "Ye are not your own, for ye are bought with a price," that they lay the foundation of the practical conclusion which we are this forenoon to enforce upon your attention; for observe, the language of our text begins with "Therefore." Now, having laid down the preceding premises, we intend to found on them a practical conclusion, and our practical conclusion is "Therefore, glorify God in your body and in your spirit, which are God's."

I have again and again had occasion to observe that men boast of their logical acumen and attainments—and a clear, accurate, and argumentative style of writing is greatly valued, and very properly so by all who are capable of thinking justly, soundly, and profoundly. Now, there is no book in which a logic stronger and more perfect in all its forms is to be found than in the book of the Scriptures of truth: At one time we find the causal form of reasoning as in the word "for"—that is, assigning a reason for some statement made or exhortation enforced. On the other hand we are sometimes treated to the syllogistic conclusion—"therefore". They are opposite modes of reasoning, but, as it can be clearly shewn, they are closely and inseparably connected.

In the one there is the making of a statement, and then assigning a reason for it; in the other there is the making of a statement, and then drawing a conclusion from it. My text, with its context, affords an instance of both the causal and the syllogistic forms of reasoning. Ye are not your own "for" ye are bought with a price. "Therefore" glorify God in your body and in your spirit, which are God's.

Having made these few remarks, without anything further in the way of preface, I now proceed to address you from the words of our text; and these words clearly divide themselves into three parts :—

In the first place, the exhortation, " glorify God ;"

In the second place, the medium through which this is to be done—" in your body and in your spirit ;"

And in the third place, the reason why this is to be done, " which are God's."

Glorify God. Divine truth assumes the form of command and exhortation; of command, not that in reality divine truth is carried into effect in this way, for the law of prohibitions and commands belongs properly to the Old Testament dispensation of Moses, a dispensation that has passed away. Christianity is properly a religion of privileges as we find it expressed in the 8th chapter of the Epistle to the Hebrews, quoting from the 31st chapter of Jeremiah. God no longer speaks to the children of Israel, that is, to his believing people, as in the days of old : he no longer addresses them in the language of prohibition and command, but he now acts after an opposite fashion, he puts his law in their minds, and writes it on their hearts; that is to say, he imparts to them principles of a Heavenly description, principles of light, principles of love, and under the influence of these heavenly principles they are constrained to act more or less as becomes their high and holy vocation. Still, though this is true, God is at times pleased to address the language of command, and when this language of command, by the teaching and influence of his spirit, is exchanged for the possession of principle, or rather, when it is made to be connected with the operation of principle, then the believer not only hears the command " glorify God," but there is established in him the principle of glorifying God. It becomes a law of principle implanted in his heart and conscience, and is more or less carried into effect continually. It is the law of the spirit of life in Christ Jesus, superseding the law of sin and death.

Glorify God. I have so often pointed out to you the

meaning of the word "glory," that by this time the explanation must be familiar to all of you. I have observed that "glory" signifies "manifestation:" therefore to glorify God is to manifest, to declare, to make God's character and perfections known. Instead then of dwelling upon what I have so often tried to explain, I would now observe, that the mere English reader may understand the meaning of the phraseology, without any etymological derivation, and without reference to the original language, by simply referring to various passages in the New Testament Scriptures. I regret the state of my sight prevents my going through them as I should have done had I been able; however, I have read one which is most fitting, proper, and suitable for the purpose—that contained in Our Lord's intercessory prayer as recorded in the 17th chapter of Saint John's gospel. Now, if you observe throughout the passage the word "glorify" is used interchangeably with the word "manifest." The mere English reader can see this without any enforcement of mine. In one place Christ says "I have glorified thee on earth;" elsewhere he says "I have manifested thy name unto men." The one expression is perfectly synonymous with the other: to manifest or to glorify on Christ's part, was to make God's character and perfections known.

Well, then, glorifying God is making God known, making his perfections manifest, shewing forth His praise. And this brings out by contrast, or rather by ellipse, as well as contrast, a fact which I have often tried to enforce upon your attention, and which cannot be too frequently or too decidedly kept in view, and that is, that there can only be two ends or objects set before us at which we can be aiming, and by which our character and conduct, can be known. One of these objects is magnifying man, and making self our end; the other is making God the end and aim of our lives and conduct. Now, you cannot find any other object in addition to these, or separate from them, by which we can be influenced: we are either glorifying ourselves, or we are glorifying God, in what we do and in what we aim at. I may observe that the selfish principle is that which alone exists in us as human beings, and with this selfish principle Adam was created; Adam was not a generous man, and he had not the capability of being generous. At his creation he loved God for the natural benefits which God had bestowed upon him, and this only to the extent to which he was capable of understanding God; he did not love God on the ground of God's power revealed and made known to him; for being possessed of mere fleshly mind he could not comprehend God as he is now spiritually revealed to us through His Son; He could only take natural views of the divine character; he could only be gratified upon natural grounds, and he could only exhibit the selfish principle pure and free. I admit that the selfish principle with which Adam was created pure, has been transmitted to us through our progenitors in an impure fleshly state; in the state of manifested enmity to God, in that state into which man fell when Adam and Eve transgressed. Adam was selfish and so are we. In him selfishness went forth in the shape of gratitude to God, so long as he was capable of understanding God as man's Creator and natural benefactor; but in us the principle of selfishness does not so come forth, and cannot so come forth, because the principle of selfishness in us has self alone, self ever, self exclusively for its object. This selfishness is shewn unquestionably in a great variety of forms. In gratifying earthly lust, in seeking after earthly pleasures, in getting rid of earthly trials and earthly sufferings, and in a great many other cases self is exclusively ur aim and object, and God is not in our thoughts at all. But when God is in our thoughts, or rather when what is said of Him enters our minds, and is considered from a mere natural point of view, self comes out in direct opposition to the principle of making God our aim and object.

The principle of self appears in the form of a desire to obtain human applause, to commend ourselves to the notice and to obtain the approbation of our fellow-men. I now appeal to my own conscience, and I appeal to the consciences of my believing friends, and to the consciences of all whose minds have been enlightened by the truth as it is in Christ Jesus, if I am not speaking what is exactly and literally true. Do you not fleshlily aim at obtaining human applause? Do you not aim at obtaining human approbation; at attracting the notice of your fellow men? I would ask you my friends, is God your aim naturally? Is it His glory you would promote? Is it His perfections you would shew forth naturally? Ah! my friends, when we do come to know what God is; when we do come to know how His glory is made manifest; when we do come, above all, to be acquainted with the way in which the Lord Jesus Christ from the hour of his birth until he presented himself as the sacrifice without spot to God was shewing forth God's glory, that he was never shewing forth his own, but always making God's glory his end and aim; I say, when we do come to know these things, then, there is such a flood of light shed into the "chambers of our *imagery*," such a view given us of ourselves, our principles, and our works, and such a view of human nature, in general, that we discover the carnal mind to be enmity against God, and that no man can naturally aim at shewing forth what God is, but that on the contrary, all men aim naturally at shewing forth themselves. Take any principle of human nature in illustration of this: say the principle of ambition. If my disposition is to rise to the heights of human society, and to obtain the power of governing my fellow-men, is it God I aim at? Is it his glory I would promote? No: I desire to be the observed of all observers. I want, perhaps, to become the prime minister of a monarchy; or I want, perhaps, as in the case of a Napoleon to occupy the throne myself; I want to take such a place among my fellow-men as shall attract their attention towards me, and make me not only in my own time, but through successive ages the object of the world's history, and the world's applause. I want to glorify myself when I am shewing forth the operation of the ambitious principle. And so, if I am an author and write a book, is it God I aim at glorifying naturally? Is it His perfections I want to shew forth? No: I want to become famous; I want men to read my work and to talk of its contents, and I hope that my name may be transmitted down to posterity with those who are great, and good, and mighty. Is that to manifest God's glory? No: it manifests my own disposition to be considered great by my fellow-men, and an exhibition of my desire to glorify self. And so we might go through the whole catalogue of human beings—of all ranks and grades—and our own consciences will tell us—mine tells me, and the conscience of every man and woman will respond to it—that it is not God's glory we aim at naturally, but the glorification of self. We want to show forth, in one way or another, our superiority over our fellow-men; we want to attract their notice and to obtain their applause, and to this end we often sacrifice health, and many of the comforts of this present life, and even life itself.

Well, seeing that men naturally aim at glorifying self by making themselves eminent if possible, not only in their own, but in succeeding ages—I say seeing this, what is the other principle, and how does it operate? If we desire to know this, we must go to the character of Christ Jesus. I know of none other who, without any doubt or hesitation, without human admixture of any kind, aimed at God's glory, shewed what it really was, and how that glory is or can be promoted. Jesus Christ came on earth, God with us, God manifest in flesh. From the earliest dawn of his mind, and through all the successive stages of his wondrous and holy earthly career, even when struggling with the anguish in the garden of Gethsemane and on the cross, no selfish thought ever entered into his mind, no selfish object was ever aimed at by him. When the first dawn of intellect took place, the glory of his heavenly Father was presented to his mind in all its beauty and perfection, and the Old Testament Scriptures disclosed to him the beauty and glory of the character of God, and these he aimed at shewing forth, and thought no other object worthy aiming at. As years advanced, and as he grew in wisdom as well as in stature, God's glory more decidedly occupied his mind; and, as his power strengthened, it still more decidedly shone forth as opportunities of exhibiting it increased. In the temple at Jerusalem, when reasoning with the doctors, and asking and answering questions, it was not in order to make his own superiority known, it was to make God known; it was to attract the attention of those Jewish doctors to what God is; it was to correct their erroneous and pharisaical notions of God, that he thus acted. And when at last he came forth to the performance of his public ministry; when at Canaan of Galilee he changed the water into wine; when on the banks of the lake of Gennesaret he caused the miraculous draught of fishes; when from a few loaves and fishes he produced sufficient for the maintenance of thousands; when on the lake of Galilee he rebuked the wind, and said unto the sea, "Peace, be still," and there was a calm; when he raised the dead to life; and when he performed any other great work, it was not the glorification of himself he aimed at; it was the manifestation of God's character and the promotion of God's glory. "I come," was his language, "not to do my own will, but the will of Him that sent me." His character is contrasted with man's in this, that while man seeks his own honour and the honour that comes from himself, Jesus sought God's honour and the honour that comes from God only; and therefore in circumstances in which his mighty power might have enabled him to occupy an earthly throne, and to see the nations of the earth bowing prostrate at his feet, and recognizing his sceptre, he put all those gaudy and attractive toys aside. He looked to the glory that awaited him at God's right hand, the only glory consistent with the manifestation of God's glory; and, therefore, instead of claiming an earthly throne, instead of claiming earthly superiority of any kind, for the joy that was set before him, he endured the cross despising the shame, and is now set down at God's right hand for evermore.

Now, Christ has revealed God, and no man can see God unless he hath seen Christ; "He that hath seen me hath seen the Father," was his own emphatic language. He hath made God known; made Him as thoroughly known as He can be known during our sojourn on earth. He has accomplished the object at which he aimed; and, while philosophers, of ancient as well as of modern times, have been obliged to confess themselves ignorant of God, and have abandoned the subject as a thing impossible to attain to, Jesus Christ, by his simple and divine manifestation—by his sufferings—by his death—by the light which he poured into the minds of the apostles and prophets—by the New Testament Scriptures illustrating the Old, has made God's character known, and has laid the foundation of that knowledge, that infinite knowledge of Him, which when we come to see Him as He is, shall be our glory and everlasting privilege.

My dear friends, you have here a specimen of what it is to glorify God, to make Him known, and to shew forth His perfections. And why is this so important? For the best and most obvious of all reasons. God can never aim at any object inferior to Himself. Can God make a creature His object? That would be to descend from the heights of His own infinite perfections. He cannot do so; He can only make Himself the end of His actions, and He has made His great end His own glory, that is, the manifestation of Himself, and in that manifestation you and I, as creatures, have most important, and infinite, and everlasting interests; for we know that this is life eternal, that is divine life, to know the true God through Jesus Christ, whom He hath sent; and in proportion as that knowledge is communicated to us, the principle of everlasting life, that is, the earnest of the divine nature, dwells in us.

In the case of our Blessed Lord, the shewing forth of his Father's glory or the making of his Father's perfections manifest was directly connected with his own glory, for he says, "I have glorified Thee, and now, O Father, glorify Thou me." That is, I have shewn forth Thy perfections, now shew forth mine. And so it is with the members of the Church of God; they are enabled to shew forth the divine perfections; they are made to aim not at manifesting themselves, but at manifesting what God is, and therefore whatever they do, whether they eat or drink, they do all to His glory, and in due time are glorified with their divine head.

Well, then, under the influence of faith and love, the members of the Church glorify God in their lives and conduct, and the selfish principle common to them, with all other human beings, is crucified. We have some remarkable instances of this, in the conduct of the apostles. Under the influence of the truth revealed to them, the flesh was crucified, natural selfishness was destroyed, and instead of aiming at the glory of self, they aimed at God's glory.

You remember the case of Peter, when he went to Cornelius, as recorded in the 10th chapter of the Acts of the Apostles, in which we are told that Cornelius met him, and fell down at his feet, and worshipped him. Did Peter accept of this? No. An earthly monarch might have done so; a man aspiring to earthly rank and dignity might have done so, but such was not the case with Peter. Stand up, he said to Cornelius, " I, myself, also am a man;" let thy worship be directed to Him who alone is worthy of it, I will not receive it. In Peter the selfish principle was crucified, it was God's glory he had come to shew to Cornelius and his company, and he was not going to contradict and stultify him who had sent him, or contradict his blessed and glorious message. Just so, we find that when the apostles, Paul and Barnabas, had been the means of curing the impotent man, when a besotted population conceived that some of the gods had come down among them, in the likeness of men, and when the priest of Jupiter brought oxen and garlands to the gates of the city, and would have done sacrifice with the people, thinking that Paul and Barnabas would be gratified with their homage. Did Paul and Barnabas suffer this? No! They rent their clothes, and ran in among the people, crying out, " Sirs, why do ye these things? We also are men of like passions with you. We come not to be worshipped, but we come to point your worship towards the living and true God, who made the heavens and the earth, and hath sent you rain and the return of fruitful seasons, filling your hearts with food and gladness."

I give you these as simple specimens of what I mean. But you may go through the whole of the apostolic writings, especially those of St. Paul, and you will find the spirit of self-denial exhibited, under the influence of the knowledge of God, and that a desire and disposition to glorify

Him, and shew forth His praise, was the prominent characteristic of their lives. And as it was with them, so will it be with us; in proportion as we are influenced by the truth as it is in Christ Jesus. All of us are selfish by nature, and cannot but be so, but when we come to know Christ, when we see him to be our righteousness and our life, then, and not until then, is the death-blow given to the principle of self in us. "I am crucified with Christ, nevertheless I live, yet not I, but Christ liveth in me." We find our life hid with Christ in God, who is our life, and with that knowledge, God and God's glory becomes our end and aim; and we rejoice to know that in Christ Jesus the selfish principle is swept away for ever, and is superseded by the divine principle of love, for he that loveth dwelleth in God, and God in him. The selfish principle is crucified, and the divine principle of love makes its appearance, and where this principle of love exists, even in the smallest degree, it is shewn in giving, not to God, for God can receive nothing at our hands, but in giving to others, in doing good to all men as we have opportunity, and in this way we realize the language of our Blessed Lord, "Let your light so shine before men that they may see your good works, and glorify your Father which is in heaven."

I had much more to say on this subject had time permitted, but I find it does not, and I must be very brief in my remarks on the remaining divisions of my text. The medium through which God is to be glorified, "In your body and in your spirit."

Glorify God in your body, by crucifying the flesh with its affections and lusts. Glorify God in your body, whether you travel abroad, or remain at home, in whatever place you are, or in whatever you are doing; and it is only by the deeds done in the body that your Christian character can become manifest to your fellow-men. Glorify God in your body by manifesting the divine perfections, by making your body not only an instrument of virtuous actions, but an instrument of godliness; instead of cursing with the tongue, bless with it; instead of using the bodily members for vile and unholy purposes, use them as instruments for shewing forth the praise, the purposes, and the glory of God. See how Christ glorified God in the body by making use of his body as the instrument of conveying blessings to mankind while on earth, so do you glorify God in the body by your virtuous life and conduct, and by doing good to your fellow-men as you have opportunity.

Glorify God in your spirit. You are renewed in the spirit of your minds, therefore glorify God in all your spiritual devotions. You are created anew through faith and love, and have the earnest of the divine nature dwelling in you; you not only inherit salvation in time, but as one with Christ Jesus you are made partakers of it throughout eternity.

The first man was a living soul; the second man, the Lord from heaven is a life-giving spirit; and as you are renewed in the spirit of your minds, and as such are possessed of the earnest of the heavenly mind, therefore let this heavenly mind, by its thoughts, and by the language and actions to which these thoughts give birth, I say, let this heavenly mind be exercised in shewing forth God's glory. The medium through which God is to be glorified, is the body, and the mind, or spirit.

Then remember the grand principle upon which the whole rests is, your body and spirit are God's. Why? Because God hath bought you. How? By paying for you the price of his own blood.

You are to glorify God, because God hath bought you, because Jesus Christ was God, and because you are, in the emphatic language of the apostle in his address to the elders of the Church of Ephesus, at Miletus, "The Church of God which he hath purchased with his own blood"— language which Arians and Unitarians so hate and have endeavoured to get rid of; but there the language is, "The Church of God which he hath purchased with his own blood."

The import of this language is, Christ and the Father are one, and very strong arguments may be, and very properly have been founded upon it, for the Deity of Christ; and the expression, "glorify God in your body and in your spirit, which are God's," confirms the argument. Why God's? Because God has bought you; because God in Christ has paid the required price for you; because he hath laid down his life for you, and has thus redeemed you from the land of slavery, and from the house of bondage.

I regret that time will not permit me to go further into the subject; it is perhaps sufficient, if by drawing your attention to Christ as having made God's glory incessantly his object; if by drawing your attention to the apostles and prophets as having in a great measure made God's glory their object, I have elucidated the language of our text, and have shewn that to glorify God is to shew forth His wisdom, His power, His love, and all His other perfections, as manifested in and through the finished work of man's salvation by Christ Jesus; and that these truths, when understood and believed in, have an influence upon our minds, and lives, and conversation, not merely in the crucifying of what is evil, but in causing us to have our affections set upon things above, not on things on the earth, and to act under the influence of heavenly motives, and to aim at heavenly ends.

May the Lord bless what has been spoken, and to His name be the glory for ever.—Amen.

SERMON V.

Sunday Morning, 17th December, 1854.

I am now about to draw your attention to some passages, contained in the Second Epistle of Paul to Timothy, the 2nd chapter, where, commencing at the 17th verse, we read these words:—

"And their word will eat, as doth a canker: of whom is Hymeneus and Philetus: who, concerning the truth have erred, saying that the resurrection is past already; and overthrow the faith of some. Nevertheless the foundation of God standeth sure, having this seal; The Lord knoweth them that are his; And, Let every one that nameth the name of Christ depart from iniquity."

Now the passage, from which I would address you, is the 19th verse of this chapter:—"Nevertheless the foundation of God standeth sure, having this seal; The Lord knoweth them that are his; And, Let every one that nameth the name of Christ depart from iniquity."

My reason for reading the context with the passage itself, has, no doubt, already become apparent to such of my hearers as are acquainted with God's Word, and take an interest in it. The word "nevertheless," exhibits forcibly and clearly a contrast between something going before, and that which immediately follows; and, in this 19th verse, most unquestionably such a contrast is drawn. After having, in the preceding part of this most instructive chapter, directed the attention of his readers to a variety of circumstances connected with Christian faith and virtue, as well as Christian practice; after having connected, in the case of believers, their peculiar sufferings with Christ here, with their peculiar reign with him hereafter; and after having laid down, as the grand foundation-truth of Christianity—that Jesus, as Christ, *had been* raised from the dead, according to the Apostle's Gospel, thereby shewing what I have tried to enforce upon your attention for several Lord's days past, that the Resurrection of Christ from the dead may, under certain aspects, be regarded as *the* grand event of Christianity: I say, after having drawn their attention to these various topics—and to several others, the Apostle proceeds, in the 17th and 18th verses, to point out the misconduct of a certain class of individuals, who had assumed the rank of Christian teachers; and to shew that not only had they misconducted *themselves*, but that they had been the means of drawing aside several others, along with them; and the Apostle, through the medium of pointing to them, gives a hint to the Church, that it must, in every age, be prrepared for the rising up of individuals of a similar description; for the propagation of errors such as these individuals sought to introduce; and for the fact of others being drawn aside by them, into erroneous doctrines and practices. Now, this part of the chapter, beginning at the 16th, and ending at the 18th verses, brings under our notice the changeful character of man; and that man is no fit subject of trust and confidence. Hymeneus and Philetus had, I presume, embraced Christianity: they had been received into the Christian Church; had there occupied, very probably, a prominent place; had there, perhaps, been teachers of doctrine; but, being unstable, and being left to themselves, they were captivated by a leading error, namely, that the Resurrection was past already; and, having adopted and been influenced by this error; and having led others into the belief of it, we find that they had been separated from the Church; that they had fallen from their Christian state, and had been severed from their Christian fellowship.

Now, to this, the Apostle alludes, not merely for the sake of conveying information to Timothy, and his immediate converts to Christianity; but, for the sake of conveying information to us; for the Scriptures are all written for the instruction, as well as for the comfort, direction, and admonition of believers, in every successive age.

Now, observe what is laid down in the passage I have quoted; the changeful character of man; man professing at one time what he ceases to profess at another time; and his standing in the Church even, being of itself no certain guarantee, that he shall continue in its communion: man having no standing in himself, and when left to himself, being constantly liable to fall away. What, then, is a suitable subject for contrast with this unsteadfastness; with this mutability of man?—The steadfastness and the immutability of God, to be sure!—And this constitutes the beautiful and glorious contrast which the 19th verse of this chapter brings before us—the passage from which more immediately I mean to address you,—which presents God himself, brought in and visibly and strikingly contrasted with man. Man *may* change and *does* change; man may profess at one time, what he may cease to profess at another time; but "God changeth not." And the fact of any individual, or any set of individuals, abandoning the profession of the Christian faith, does not prove that Christian faith is untrue: it merely proves, that there is something wrong in the profession of such individuals: it is a warning to him "That thinketh he standeth, to take heed lest he fall:" it merely tends to contrast with this misconduct of man, the fact that God hath foreknown His Church and people, as He had foreknown Christ; and that in him and not in themselves, do they stand secure and blessed for ever.

Well, then, throwing out of view, for a moment, the contrast which the passage presents; we are, in the words of the text, presented with the following topics for consideration,—When I can do so, I always, prefer treating of such subjects *textually*, that is, as the Word of God treats of them, to the coining of any artificial divisions of my own.

Now, in the passage before us, we find the fact declared that "The foundation of God standeth sure;" and then we have brought under notice, in connection with this, what is here stated as a seal,—that seal having on it the following inscriptions:—"The Lord knoweth them that are His," and "Let every one that nameth the name of Christ depart from iniquity." We find the latter division consisting, itself, of two subdivisions, to be separately and distinctly treated of.

Well, then, the very first thing that obtrudes itself upon our notice, in the passage which we have selected for present consideration—is the broad declaration, that "The foundation of God standeth sure."—You and I are not permitted to put an interpretation upon this word "foundation," any more than we are permitted to put an interpretation upon any phrase, or declaration, which occurs in God's Word. We are bound to compare spiritual things with spiritual; we are bound to seek the interpretation of Scripture, in Scripture itself; and to be guided by the decision of God, in preference to the suggestions of our own minds, or the determinations of the highest critical authority.

What then is here meant by the phrase, "The foundation

of God?" From many passages of Scripture, I should be inclined to draw the conclusion, that we are bound to confine the phrase to Christ himself,—under certain aspects at all events,—for we are told in the Old Testament Scriptures, as quoted by the Apostle Peter, in the 2nd chapter of his First Epistle, "Behold I lay in Zion a foundation-stone, elect, precious; and whosoever believeth on him shall not be confounded," or, "shall not be ashamed."—Now we have it explained to us, elsewhere, that this foundation-stone is Christ himself—" the stone which was rejected" by the Jewish rulers, who should have laid it, as "the corner stone" of the Spiritual Temple; but they having rejected it, God himself hath laid it, in the fact of raising His Son from the dead, to the power of an endless life. And, so important is this foundation, that the Apostle says, "other foundation can no man lay, than that is laid, which is Jesus Christ."—Here then, we have Scripture authority for the meaning of the phrase, "foundation of God." It is our blessed Lord himself, in his work of humiliation; but still more in his work of exaltation and glory; and in his Resurrection from the dead: and it would almost appear to me, that these facts were chiefly in the Apostle's view, when we read of the false notions adopted by Hymeneus and Philetus. From these glorious views concerning the Resurrection—the Resurrection of Christ and his Church; the Holy Ghost inspires the Apostle immediately, to proceed to Christ himself, in whose death and Resurrection from the dead, God hath laid the foundation of all our hopes here, and of all our blessedness hereafter.

If we were to enlarge upon this idea, we should find that it rises up into the perfections of God; that it speaks of Christ as in the form of man, but still Christ as one with God;—"He that hath sent me is with me. I and my father are one," is his own language. Therefore, when I say that the "foundation of God" may signify God's perfections, it is still to say, that it is significant of Christ, for all the perfections of God are made manifest in Christ Jesus; they shine forth in his blessed character, and still more in his mediatorial work. Do you speak of God's power? Where is the power of God evinced so mightily as in the conflict of Christ with principalities and powers, and in his overcoming them; in his leading captivity captive, by his resurrection from the dead, and in the Life Everlasting that he bestows upon the sons of men? His work in Creation—for He created all things—was great; but his work of Redeeming

Love is infinitely greater; and from these we acquire a still higher idea of what the "power" of God is.

And then again, if you speak of his "wisdom," it is still Christ—Christ is the "wisdom of God" as well as the "power of God"—and, in the whole plan of salvation, as it originally existed in the Divine mind, and as it was carried into effect, by each successive step, through Christ as our mediator: in all these we see the "wisdom of God" displayed; it is carried into effect through a series of manifestations and operations, all interlinked with each other and crossing each other; and yet running parallel with each other; all pointing to *one* result, and all moving on, in sweet and glorious harmony;—the "wisdom of God" is evinced in such a way, in the work of Christ, that no one step, as recorded, could have been omitted: all concurred to bring about the same glorious result; and though, as a whole, they bring out God's character entirely, yet the omission of one step would have been the means of presenting that character in a mutilated form. But the result of all the steps, in harmony, shews us the character of God as a whole, and as thoroughly and everlastingly consistent with the subject. And so we have evidently the "power of God" and the "wisdom of God" laid down as "foundations in Christ."

Why did Christ come into the world? Did he come merely to triumph over guilty and fallen humanity? Was his object to present his own character, in glorious contrast to that of man, in order that man might shrink from the perfect exhibition, in dismay? Certainly not! Christ no doubt came to evince a character, in all respects not only superior to, and in contrast with, that of man; but he came to exhibit it, that man might gaze upon the glorious exhibition with confidence, with admiration, and with love. Christ came, "not to condemn the world, but to save the world." He came amongst us, that in the exhibition of a character, that was Heavenly and Divine, we might find a foundation of hope and joy, which from ourselves, which from no mere *creature*, however exalted, could ever have sprung. Therefore, if I were to try to enlarge the idea, and merely to say, that the foundation, here spoken of, is the perfection of God, I am brought back to Christ again, because all the perfections of God are made manifest, and shewn forth in Christ alone.

But I might say, in the third place, the "foundation" is God himself. When you get to the ultimate (to use a phrase of the Swedenborgian), it is God. In reality there is no being but God; for nothing can have existence, apart from him, or separate from him; "in him we live, and move, and have our being." As, therefore, there can be no existence apart from God,—God is the ultimate foundation, upon which all things rest; as well as the ultimate source, from which all things spring.

And even here, again, Jesus comes into view, because Jesus is God: because Jesus is one with God; because as God, Jesus is he, in whom it is said, that "all things consist." Therefore, whether I make Christ the foundation; or the perfections of God the foundation; or God himself the foundation; in all such cases, I have equally, and decidedly, and evidently, Christ set before me, crucified and glorified.

Some, however, may say that the foundation of God—judging from the mottoes on the seal—does not mean Christ, but means the Church.

My dear friends, you may be easily satisfied, that the objection you raise, is perfectly reconcilable with what I have said. There is no foundation-stone alone; no foundation-stone, without other stones resting upon it; and hence it is, that in the Scriptures of Truth, Christ is never separated from his Church, and if he be the "foundation," there is a superstructure erected upon him: if he be the foundation-stone, there are living stones built upon him; until at last the whole being completed, it becomes a Temple of God, and a habitation of God, through the spirit. And while I speak of Christ and the perfections of God, in Christ; while I speak of Christ in God, and God in Christ, as the "foundation;" so far from excluding the goodly superstructure, reared thereon, I take it along with the foundation, and rejoice to know, that the one is inseparable from the other; that the foundation of God implies not only Christ in God, and God in Christ; but those also who rest in Christ, as the foundation;—those who are built up in him, he being the chief corner stone; and with him, constitute that Heavenly Temple, the dwelling-place of the Most High, for ever and ever. The language of our Redeemer is, "Lord, I have loved the habitation of Thy house and the place where Thine honour dwelleth." I am therefore willing to take, and do cheerfully take, the superstructure along with, and as inseparable from, the "foundation."

But what is said of Christ, I now proceed to shew, is said also of his Church; that "The foundation standeth sure." Oh! how beautiful and impressive, is the contrast between Christ with his Church, and such characters as those to whom the Apostle had just been alluding—Hymeneus and Philetus, and those whom *they* had deluded. They had passed away from, had quitted, the communion of the Church of the living God; they "had erred concerning the truth," having been left to themselves and to the exhibition of their own fleshly minds, and fleshly tendencies: and thus they had evinced what they were. Man is, in his best condition, altogether "vanity;" and vain, in a religious point of view, they had shewn themselves to be.

But is this the case with the Church of the living God? or, with the Head? No!—"I will never leave thee, nor forsake thee," said God to Joshua, of old; and in saying it to him, the Apostle, in the 13th chapter of Hebrews, instructs us, that it was said to a greater than Joshua; and said to those who have received the Spirit of that greater one. It was said to the Son of God himself; the true Jesus or Joshua, he who knew that God "would never leave him nor forsake him;" therefore he travelled through the work of his mediation, in the greatness of his strength; "Having his garments spotted with blood, like him that treadeth the wine vat." I say the Son of God went on, from beginning to end, in his mediatorial undertaking, in the strength of the Most High: and as it was with Our Blessed Lord; as he remembered, and acted upon, the words, "I will never leave thee nor forsake thee;—as he knew, that the everlasting arms of his Heavenly Father were thrown around him, to uphold him; so is it with his Church. They know, that as one with him, they are interested in all his privileges, and are partakers of his blessedness; and, therefore, says the Apostle, we may boldly say, "The Lord is our helper, we will not fear what man can do unto us;" and all this, knowing that he hath said, "I will never leave thee, nor forsake thee."

Now, all this is expressed in the simple language before us—"The foundation of God standeth sure." It is not, that as in the case of Hymeneus and Philetus,—beings have *themselves* come profanely forward; have *themselves* tried to lay the foundation of life everlasting, but have not succeeded in the attempt,—the foundation is laid by God himself, when it is laid at all. The foundation—Christ, was laid in Zion, by God, not by man. And as it was with Christ, so it is with us: God lays every stone of the spiritual temple: it is He who, according to his everlasting purposes, in due time enlightens the understanding, and operates upon the hearts of the destined heirs of salvation; it is He who brings them out of darkness, into his marvellous light; it is He who places them as living stones in His spiritual temple, each one in due order, and in its proper situation; and it is He who adorns these various stones, with beauty and glory: enabling them, each in his several place and sphere, to shew forth the praises of Him who hath called him out of darkness into marvellous light, and laid him as a living stone in His spiritual temple.

It is God who does all this; and, like all God's works, it is a perfect work; and God having done it, man cannot shake nor move it. If they had been stones, laid by the *creature*, the creature might have removed them; but they are laid by the Creator Himself, in virtue of His own everlasting purpose, and placed by Him in the situations exactly adapted for them; and He who lays them, keeps them there.

Being thus in the keeping of God; being a portion of God's building; being of God's husbandry; being watered by Him; being, every moment, kept under His own immediate eye; and being preserved by His own immediate care, they stand sure; their security is in His everlasting purpose, and in His continued manifestation of Light; their security is in His power; not in any purpose or illuminations or power of their own.

"The foundation standeth sure." Christ, the foundation, is a sure one; and not more sure is God himself, as the foundation and chief corner-stone, than is each one of the living stones, that are laid upon him: they have, each and all, God for their builder; and they belong, each and all, to one and the same structure. In the 7th chapter of St. Matthew's Gospel, we read of a distinction between men building on the sand, and men building on a rock. The house that is built upon the sand, cannot withstand the assaults of rain, and storm, and tempest; but is soon swept away as by an overflowing flood; but that which is built upon a rock, stands secure from every wind, and every storm, and every tempest, because it is built on a sure foundation. Thus it shews, that God is the layer of the foundation; that God is the placer, or raiser, of every stone contained in the structure; and that, as God hath taken the building of the edifice under His peculiar care, so will He complete it, in His own good time, in spite of every enemy, and in spite of all opposition.

It "standeth sure," because the Head himself, and all the members of the Church, are included in the same

Heavenly purpose; are embraced in the same Heavenly plan; and are parts of the same Heavenly scheme; no one part of which can be separated from another. They belong to one and the same whole; and, as parts of the whole, they shall all be found, in due time, in heaven itself; when God gives completion to the edifice; when "He shall bring forth the headstone thereof with shoutings, crying, grace, grace unto it."

Well, then, the grand topic here is, "the foundation of God." Christ, the Church built by Christ, "stands sure;" it cannot be moved in any way, or be shaken by every wind of doctrine, as Hymeneus and Philetus were; it cannot be moved, even by its own folly; it cannot be moved, even by its own incapability; it stands secure, in Christ. The members of the Church can say, the Wisdom of God is our wisdom, and we stand secure in Him, not in ourselves.

Not only is this stated in general, but a beautiful illustration of it is afforded us, in the second place, in the language that follows: "Nevertheless this foundation standeth sure." Having this seal: "The Lord knoweth them that are his, And, Let every one that nameth the name of Christ depart from iniquity."

As to the phraseology here employed, "having this seal," many observations have been made, by various commentators; and while I have no wish, merely to indulge a vain curiosity, I would observe, that at least *two* distinct ideas are presented to our minds by means of this language. The one idea is, that of a coin or medal, which has always two sides:—the other, that of a foundation-stone, impressed by a seal, having two inscriptions upon it.

In the former you have the idea of a coin, or medal, issued by God himself,—upon each side of which there is an inscription. On the one side—the obverse—there is the inscription, "The Lord knoweth them that are his;"—that is God's side. On the other—the reverse—there is the inscription, "Let every one that nameth the name of Christ, depart from iniquity;" that is man's side, of the coin, or medal.

On the other hand, although it is quite possible the inspired Apostle may have had in view, the fact of a coin having two sides and bearing two mottoes or inscriptions, yet I cannot but think, that the allusion here, is to a foundation-stone, upon which a seal is placed, having on it two inscriptions. You are aware, that at the present day, when the foundation-stone of any edifice of a remarkable kind is laid, there is generally deposited in a cavity of the stone,—previously prepared,—a few coins of the sovereign, in whose reign the ceremony is performed; and other objects of interest are enclosed in a bottle, or bottles, hermetically sealed; and upon this hollow in the stone, is generally placed a plate—made of copper or zinc—upon which some inscription is engraved; so that, in the event of the records of the building being lost, and the building should come to be taken down, by a reference to the inscription on the plate, and to the coins placed in the hollow of the stone, it may be known in what reign, at what time, and for what purpose, the building in question was erected. We know, that this is the practice at the present day, with regard to the laying of the foundation-stones of public buildings; but whether this practice obtained among the Greeks or Romans, there may be some difficulty in ascertaining; but supposing that this was the case, you have here an allusion to it; for here is the foundation-stone laid, along with the structure; and in reference to the foundation-stone and to the superstructure, there is a "seal" placed upon it, and that seal has two distinct inscriptions, each of which appears to be of the utmost importance; the one pointing to what is in God, and the other pointing to what, when the foundation and the superstructure are laid, will be evinced on the part of man;— the one inscription, "The Lord knoweth them that are his," bringing out God's character and power; and the other, "Let every one that nameth the name of Christ, depart from iniquity," pointing to what will be the line of procedure, adopted by those to whom God's mind is made known; and who have been chosen by Him to be placed,—as living stones, —upon Christ, the corner and foundation-stone.

It would be impossible for us, to take up both mottoes this morning; but at all events, we may briefly, and I hope edifyingly, consider the *first* of these inscriptions, placed upon the foundation-stone; or, the "seal" referring to the foundation-stone, taken along with the whole building.

The first inscription is, "The Lord knoweth them that are his."—Now this has, evidently, a reference to the case of Hymeneus and Philetus, as well as those who had been led astray by them. It may be said by some, "Oh then the Church of God is not secure: the members of the Church of God *may* fall short of the Heavenly glory: they may so err in point of doctrine, so deviate from a holy and pure practice, and become so alienated from the Church, as to shew themselves children of perdition." "No," says the Holy Ghost, "the foundation of God standeth sure;" and, along with that foundation, standeth sure the whole superstructure, reared upon it. Remember, that God is not only the layer of the foundation, but He is the sealer of it; and when He seals it, the import of his "seal," or of one part of his "seal" is, "The Lord knoweth them that are his."

"The Lord," observe, the Lord Jehovah,—the everlasting one, the Creator of the ends of the earth,—"He who fainteth not, neither is weary,"—against whom no potentate can rise up and conquer,—yes, "the Lord Jehovah" is the person who speaks here, or is spoken of in the first motto: and "the Lord" also means the Lord Jesus Christ; that is, the Lord Jehovah manifest,—for "I and the Father are one" is his own language, and all that is said of the Father, can equally be said, and is said, of His Son Jesus Christ.

Now, this supreme Jehovah, manifest in the Lord Jesus Christ; this supreme Jehovah, "knoweth them that are his." The word "knoweth" here, is a most emphatic word. It occurs in the Old Testament Scriptures, as well as in the New, in corresponding, or in somewhat corresponding passages; and of the import of the word, various views have been taken. One view, that has been entertained, has been arrived at, by understanding it as implying approbation; thus, "the Lord approveth them that are his;" and the passage in the 1st Psalm, and some other passages, have been pointed to, as corroborative of this. Now it cannot be denied, that "the Lord" does approve of them that are his; not for any merit in themselves; for in themselves they are vile, and sinful, and dying creatures; but as one with his own Son Jesus Christ; as clothed upon with his righteousness, the righteousness of Christ; as possessed of his spirit; and as his trees, bringing forth, more or less, the fruits of that Spirit. He approves of them, in that point of view: but I perceive that though an *approbation* of them is *not* to be excluded, from the meaning of the word, I cannot persuade myself that this is its *real*, or full import. I would rather take the word, as it stands before me, and understand it in its naked and heavenly simplicity—"the Lord knoweth."

In the 8th chapter of Romans, we are informed, that "Whom God did foreknow, he also did predestinate, to be conformed to the image of his Son," and so on. Here the foreknowledge of God is laid down as that upon which the ultimate glorification of his people is made to rest; but there is a still higher point of view, than even "foreknowledge," capable of being predicated of God. Often, from the press, and from this place, and elsewhere, have I tried to bring under your notice, and to shew you, the meaning of the phrase, "I AM;" that with Jehovah, as the "I AM," there is no change, no change in existence, no change in knowledge. God never acquired, and God never can acquire, a single *new* idea; with Him there is no succession of ideas, as there is with His creatures; with Him there is no succession of events as there is with His creatures;—what He knows, He knew *from* Everlasting, and will know *to* Everlasting. All the knowledge of God is, properly and distinctively, *present* knowledge—"The Lord knoweth." It is very true, that foreknowledge is predicated with regard to God, but it is so, with a view to meet the comprehension of our minds. We are so constituted that our minds are limited. We can think of the past, we can think of the future; but the present of one moment is to us the past of the next; but with God past, present, and future are all one everlasting now; and it is with reference to the constitution of our minds that God is pleased to speak of His foreknowledge. But when we look at the matter, in the light of His own Word, we discover, that even "foreknowledge" is *comparatively* but a low view of God; that the true view of God is absolute and present *knowledge*; that everything that has ever happened, or ever will happen is *present* with Him, with whom there is "no variableness, neither shadow of turning." Therefore the Lord knoweth them that are His; they are present to Him, because He has known them before ever time began, and will know them when time is no more: they are in His sight, as they ever have been, and always will be.

And what are they, in His sight; and what does He know them as? As His *property:* He knows them as His. "The Lord knoweth them that are His." He knoweth them that belong to Him.

You remember last Lord's day, and the Lord's day before, on which occasions we drew your attention to that beautiful passage in the 6th chapter of the First Epistle to the Corinthians, which occurs towards the close of the chapter, "Ye are not your own, for ye are bought with a price, therefore, glorify God in your body and in your spirit, which are God's." There, you are distinctly informed, that you are God's property; and you may remember, that we went into the subject at some length, and with some minuteness, shewing how and why, believers addressed by the Apostle personally, and believers addressed by him, in every age, through the medium of his writings — constituted God's property.

Now, here is the same idea — "The Lord knoweth them that are His;" knoweth them with a *present*, unchangeable *knowledge*; knoweth them that are His property — His peculiar property; for while it is true, that God is the Saviour of *all* men, that God, in Christ, hath redeemed humanity; yet it is true also, that, in a peculiar sense, He is the Saviour of them that believe — the peculiar Saviour of His Body, the Church, — the peculiar Saviour of those who are destined to reign with Him in His heavenly kingdom. They are not only His property in general — as all God's creatures are, for all creatures were brought into existence by Him, and are sustained by Him — but they are peculiarly His property, not only by "Redemption" — for Christ is the Saviour of *all* men — but they are *peculiarly* His property, as having been destined by Him to be, in *time*, "brought out of darkness into His marvellous light," to be made "partakers of the earnest of the Divine nature," and, in due time, to be introduced by Him, into the full enjoyment of His heavenly kingdom.

Now, *such* individuals are known by Him, as peculiarly His property; "they are heirs of God, and joint heirs with Christ Jesus;" and this, through the medium of "faith, that worketh by love." And as God knows them, so we discover that they know God; for when the light of the knowledge of the Glory of God, in the face of Jesus Christ, hath shined into their hearts; when the marvellous light of the everlasting Gospel brings them out of darkness, they discover the relationship, in which God stands to them, and in which they stand to God; and they cry, "Abba, Father," they cherish, towards God, the feelings of children :— they love Him, as having first loved them. And though they, as human beings, are sinning continually; "for if we say, we have no sin, we deceive ourselves, and the truth is not in us;" yet they are kept by the power of God, through faith unto salvation, "ready to be revealed in the last time." Although they, in all things, come short of the glory of God, yet are they kept always rejoicing, knowing that there is "a fountain opened to the house of David, for sin and for uncleanness," they find the blood shed on Calvary, continually washing their consciences from the stain of guilt; and they find also, that as Christ rose from the dead, they rose in him; and having risen in him, to newness of life they are kept, standing upon him as their foundation, and they rejoice in him, as their all in all. **They** are thus kept by God, through His mighty power; and it is, because He has taken them to Himself—drawn them to Him, with the "cords of love as with the bands of a man," and thrown His everlasting arms around them, and placed them in His Heavenly fold, and kept them there; it is because He does this, not because *they* do anything, that they are seen to be His, and are preserved "from the paths of the destroyer."

Hymeneus and Philetus,—and persons of a similar description,—may abnegate the truth which they once *professed* to believe;—men who stop short, and are bewitched by the principles of human intellect, *may* quit the cause that they once *professed* to love, and adhere to; but God's people are under a higher guidance—that of the divine nature, the faith that worketh by love. As God knows them, as His peculiar property; as His eye is upon them every moment; as He keeps them from themselves, as well as from others; they are kept through faith unto salvation. Therefore, this peculiar "seal,"—or, rather, this peculiar *motto* on the seal,—"The Lord knoweth them that are His," gives you the true reason why they cannot fall, like Hymeneus and Philetus; it gives you the true reason why the "falling away" of such men cannot mean the "falling away" of a single believer of the truth, as it is in Christ Jesus:—it gives you to understand, that while human nature is shewn, in the case of every recanting "mere professor;" the divine nature is that which preserves the Church of God, and *every* member of it. They are kept upon the "sure foundation" of Christ Jesus: they have an interest in God's everlasting purposes of grace and mercy towards them.

"The Lord knoweth them that are His." He has a present—an ever-present knowledge of what they are, and have been, and will be; and, as the objects of His knowledge, and, consequently, of His approval and love, they are safe in Him; they are safe from themselves; and they are safe from every enemy.

What is *also* connected with this peculiar privilege of the Church of God, we shall, if the Lord permit, consider in the next discourse, namely, "Let every one that nameth the name of Christ, depart from iniquity."

May the Lord bless what has been said, and to His name be the glory, for ever and ever.

SERMON VI.

Sunday Morning, December 21th, 1851.

I AGAIN draw your attention to a passage contained in the Second Epistle, or letter addressed, by Paul to Timothy, the 2nd chapter, at the 17th verse, where we read of certain individuals " whose word doth eat as doth a canker, of whom is Hymeneus and Philetus; who concerning the truth have erred, saying the Resurrection is past already, and overthrow the faith of some." Then the 19th verse is that from which we shall address you:—

"Nevertheless the foundation of God standeth sure, having this 'seal;' the Lord knoweth them that are his, and, let every one that nameth the name of Christ depart from iniquity."

Few words are required by way of preface. The passage which I have just read is one of practical import, and beautifully and powerfully illustrates the inseparable connection between the belief of the Truth of the Gospel, and the effects of that belief, in leading to a life and conversation becoming it. There is no such thing in Christianity as doctrine without practice; on the contrary, every divine doctrine contained in the Scriptures is calculated to have, and, when believed in, *will* have a powerfully spiritual influence upon the mind and conduct—divine is the principle and divine are the effects which flow therefrom.

Last Lord's day we drew your attention to the former part of this 19th verse. We spoke to you of the declaration first of all made, that "The foundation of God standeth sure;" the foundation of God—Christ who is laid as the foundation-stone by God himself; the foundation of God—the whole superstructure which is built upon, and connected with that foundation—namely, the Church of the Lord;—the foundation of God—God's purposes and God's promises:—and, above all, the foundation of God—that is, the foundation that is laid in God himself—not a human foundation—not a creaturely foundation—but God himself is the foundation,—and He is the foundation and everything connected therewith, being correspondingly firm and secure—this foundation of God standeth sure, is perfect, is incapable of being removed. Hymeneus and Philetus and others of the same class, after making a profession of the gospel, or of something like it, may abandon it; but Hymeneus and Philetus are mere creatures, and the conduct of the creature in no respect interferes with, or nullifies, the purposes and work of the Creator. The Creator himself stands firm, unchanged, and unchangeable; " the same yesterday, and to-day, and for ever." And as is the Creator, so is everything that is built up on Him and connected with Him.

Yes—the foundation of God, Christ the great foundation, in whom all God's purposes and promises are accomplished and fulfilled; this foundation of God hath a seal impressed upon it, and, after observing that we might conceive the apostle to have had in view the idea of a coin or medal, with an obverse and a reverse side, the obverse having a particular inscription, and the reverse having another inscription, we stated that we preferred the idea of a "seal" impressed on the foundation-stone; this seal having two mottoes, and the two mottoes being those which are here given. I will not recapitulate all that was said respecting the laying of foundation-stones and the customary ceremonies on such occasions, I merely notice the fact of the seal being impressed upon the foundation with two mottoes. *One* of these two mottoes occupied our attention last Lord's day. "The Lord knoweth them that are His." "The Lord"—Jehovah, Jehovah manifest in Christ Jesus, Christ Jesus himself, He knoweth,—not merely approveth of, not merely hath foreknowledge of, but knoweth from everlasting to everlasting them that are His. He hath a full, clear, infinite understanding ever present to His mind, of those who belong to Him, of those who are specially redeemed by Him, of those who are destined to know Him, not only here, but to know and enjoy Him hereafter throughout eternity. All these He knows; they never can fall away, for, being brought by Himself, by His own mighty power, to the knowledge of the Truth, according to His own everlasting purposes, they are kept by Him through faith unto salvation. They are not left to themselves; if left to themselves a single instant they would fall away,—for the creature hath no standing and no power in *himself*, but being upheld by Jehovah—having God's everlasting arms thrown around him; having God's everlasting purposes and promises for his protection, as well as for his foundation, no evil that is invented against him, or that can be brought to bear against him can prosper. Those who are known to the Lord as His, are preserved from the natural enmity of their own hearts; "He that trusteth in his own heart is a fool," for "the heart is deceitful above all things, and desperately wicked," but God overcometh the evil tendencies of our hearts as He continually overcometh the tendencies of a world that lieth in wickedness; not by means of any goodness or strength in ourselves, but solely in virtue of Himself having laid the foundation stone in Zion; solely in virtue of His everlasting purposes, and in virtue of the strength that He himself puts forth, and by which we are kept from the world and from ourselves, and are given in due time to appear before Him in the heavenly glory. He knoweth them that are His; no one therefore can take them out of his hands.

Our attention may now be drawn to the second motto upon the seal. This is not a counter-motto to the other, nor inconsistent with it; on the contrary, it is in perfect harmony with it, carrying out the truth of, and giving effect to, the first motto, so far as the children of God upon earth are concerned. Who are God's? Who belong to Him? Those that have been bought with a price, and consequently are not their own, but His by whom the price was paid, and to them only is the second motto applicable, "Let every one that nameth the name of Christ depart from iniquity."

This second motto evidently divides itself into two parts. An individual, or rather a class of individuals, is spoken of, "Every one that nameth the name of Christ." And then there is a course of conduct prescribed to them, or rather they are exhorted to pursue a certain course of conduct— "let every such individual depart from iniquity."

First of all, "Let every one that nameth the name of Christ." It may perhaps have appeared to you, my dear Christian friends, that I have been too anxious from time to time to point out the distinction between the Church and the world; that I have perhaps been over-solicitous in shewing that all the instructions, as well as all the exhortations of God's word, belong, not to the world, but to the Church: and yet in so far as my anxiety on this point is concerned, I cannot see that I am wrong. The word of God from first to last proceeds upon the principle that in the knowledge and enjoyment of its contents, the children of God alone are concerned; that to *them* its communications are made, and that upon them its injunctions are enforced. The father of a family has to do with the members of that family; to him God has committed their superintendence; he is to see that they are properly fed and clothed; that they are brought up and educated aright; he is to exercise proper discipline over them, and he is to watch over their morals and see that they do not go astray. But the father of a family has nothing to do, properly speaking, with any other family than his own: he has no right to enter into the family of another and to interfere with the arrangements of its head, or with the concerns of that family,—suffice it for him, if he attend to the instruction, and provide for the maintenance of his own. Just so do the Scriptures of truth instruct us; just so does the case stand with regard to God and his heavenly family. He is the father of them that are His, as spoken of in the preceding motto. He hath begotten them again by the knowledge of the truth, not with corruptible but with incorruptible seed. God hath thereby brought them into His heavenly family and household; He hath taken them under His special charge; He hath provided them with the spiritual food of which they stood in need; He hath exercised over them the chastisements which, from time to time, are required; but with the *world* he does not meddle after the same fashion. While to the Church He stands in the relationship of a father,—to the world He stands in that of a judge: and He hath so completely reserved judgment unto Himself in regard to unbelieving men, that He will not allow even His Church to exercise it over them. And, therefore, when the members of His Church are wronged, and when they find themselves unable to obtain redress by Christian means, they are not to have recourse to the practice of violence, they are not to regard themselves, because they are God's children, as having a right to avail themselves of violence or any other earthly expedient; but their business is come to Him who judgeth uprightly, and to leave the case with Him, remembering that He is the judge, and that what is right and proper in the case He will do. "Vengeance is mine, I will repay, saith the Lord."

The grand principle that the Church of God is God's family, that the Church of God receives instructions at His hands, is by Him protected from evil, and from time to time subjected to discipline. I say, this grand principle runs throughout the Scriptures. The Scriptures are addressed to the Church; the exhortations of the Scriptures are addressed by God in the capacity of their father to the members of the Church, "My little children keep yourselves from idols;" "I beseech you therefore, as dear children, that ye keep aloof from all that is evil," and so on. It is God, I say, who addresses His Church in the sacred volume from first to last, addresses that Church as constituting His family, as under His peculiar charge, and as destined to dwell with Him after a peculiar fashion in the heavenly world of glory.

Now, remembering this, you observe the expression is not *every man*, but "*every one that nameth the name of Christ.*" That is, every member of God's family; every one begotten from above; every one that is a partaker of the earnest of the Divine nature; every one that is brought out of darkness into God's marvellous light; every one who is enabled to cry "Abba Father," and who, regarding God in the light of a father, cherishes towards him filial sentiments of love. It is to all such, and to such only, that the words are addressed, "Let every one that nameth the name of Christ depart from iniquity."

The phrase—"nameth the name of Christ"—is perfectly intelligible from numerous passages of Scripture. Before the Lord Messiah, the Lord Christ, or the Lord the Anointed-one came; before that period there were in the world Gentiles and Jews, that is, there were nations of the earth who *knew not* God, and to whom, consequently, the Sacred volume was not sent, and who had no interest in the God of Israel. These were the Gentiles. And there were Jews who constituted God's family, for the time being, whom he had separated from the other nations of the earth, and towards whom he shewed peculiar favour; but when Christ came, when the Messiah had fulfilled the purposes of his Heavenly Father upon earth, in abstaining from all evil, in dying "the just for the unjust," in bringing in everlasting righteousness; when he had risen from the dead and had "ascended to God's right hand," then commenced a new phase of things. The distinction thenceforward was not to be between Gentile and Jew, but between him who did not name the name of Christ, and him who did; between him who knew not God and him who did know him, as He is revealed in the face of His own dear Son.

Now, all those who were brought to know Him, made a profession of naming Him. They named Jesus of Nazareth as the Christ or the Messiah; they acknowledged that the long-promised Messiah had made his appearance in His person; they acknowledged that in him the desire of all nations had been revealed; they named the name of Christ, and they were named by the name of Christ, and this, by a special divine interposition; for believers of the truth, were by God named followers of Christ or the anointed one, by a special revelation at Antioch, where the disciples of Christ were first called by the new name of Christians.

It is a very interesting circumstance, that, in some editions of the New Testament, there is another word employed here instead of *Christ*, and apparently upon very good authority. In the editions to which I refer it is rendered, "every one that nameth the name of *the Lord*." You are aware that our translators were guided by a considerable number of manuscripts, as well as by numerous versions, in the translation which they made of the Scriptures—and a most excellent translation it is, both as to the idiom employed, and the subject matter itself—but they were not in possession of numerous manuscripts, which have since been brought to light, and some of these of considerable value. Many men of critical skill have conceived that, according to some of the best manuscripts, the word "Lord" should be employed, and consequently, in some critical Greek versions you will find the word "Lord" used instead of "Christ".

If they be right, this still more strengthens what I have been saying, and brings to view more beautifully the connection between the two mottoes. The first motto, you observe, is "The Lord knoweth them that are His," and this is the aspect which God bears towards his people. Then, the second motto brings in the aspect which God's people bear towards Him—how appropriate the phrase, "let every one that nameth the name of the Lord," that is, every one that nameth the name of Him, who knoweth them that are His; every one that nameth the name of Him, who is not only the Christ, but the Lord. If you remember, in the 2nd chapter of the Acts, when the apostle Peter is addressing the assembled multitude, he shews that in the resurrection of our blessed Redeemer, God had shewed him to be both Lord and Christ: "Lord," that is, king, ruler, or governor; and "Christ" that is, the anointed one. He pointed him out both in his kingly and in his priestly capacity.

"Every one that nameth the name of the Lord." That is, every one that acknowledgeth that Jesus is Lord, and as such professes to be subject to his will—for let me bring under your notice this interesting fact, also brought before us in the New Testament Scriptures, that if we call Jesus, Lord, we bind ourselves thereby to do whatsoever things he hath commanded us; we profess, in other words, to be subject to his authority; we profess to acknowledge him as the Lord of our consciences, and we profess to be regulated by him at all times and in all respects; and therefore "every one that nameth the name of the Lord," is not only every one that believeth in Jesus as Lord as well as Christ; is not only every one that acknowledges that Christ hath come to fulfil the Old Testament Scriptures, that he was God manifest in flesh, and is God now reigning as the glorified mediator; but who also acknowledges the authority that Jesus hath over him, and that by his will as well as by his example his every thought and action should be regulated.

This leads me to the second head—"And let every one that nameth the name of Christ," that is, every one that acknowledges Jesus as the Messiah, and professes to be regulated by his authority, let every such person "depart from iniquity."

There is something most clear and emphatic in this. Christianity is decidedly a religion of consolation and joy; it speaks joy and hope through Christ, to the guilty conscience, and it has not a single word to say to any individual, until he hath been first brought out of darkness into God's marvellous light; until God's character in Christ has been revealed to him; and until the name of Christ, or the name of Him who is "Lord," has been named by him; but when brought into God's family; when introduced among the number of those whom God loves with especial love; when made to recognize God as his Father, revealed as such in Christ Jesus; when given to know that he is an heir of God and joint-heir with Jesus Christ,—then comes down upon him all the exhortations to purity of mind and to purity of external conduct; all the exhortations to a life and conversation becoming the Gospel, with which the word of God abounds.

The expression "let him depart from iniquity" brings under our notice two things, namely, what we are exhorted to do, and the ends or motives upon which the exhortation rests and by which it is enforced. In the first place, the exhortation itself "Let him depart from iniquity." You have, no doubt, all of you heard of the teachings of heathen antiquity in matters of religion; and you are aware that the better class of philosophers among the ancients, when speaking of the cardinal virtues, as they call them, generally arranged them under four heads, namely, *prudence, temperance, virtue,* and *justice.* I am not going to enforce heathen philosophy, but merely mention the fact, or rather call it to your remembrance, and I now remark that Christianity also has its divisions, in regard to Christian conduct, and these divisions are beautifully brought forward, not merely in various passages, both of the Old and New Testament Scriptures, but they are condensed in *one* passage of Scripture *so* strikingly, that I am not permitted to overlook it—it is that very remarkable passage in Titus, in which believers of the truth are exhorted to live soberly, righteously, and godly. Now these terms appear to exhaust all the scope of Christian duty; the passage appears to bring in, under these categories, everything which a Christian should do, everything he should aim at, all the points of conduct, by which he should be distinguished while passing through this present world. "Soberly," including every duty respecting himself; "righteously," including every duty as respects others; "godly," including every duty as respects his Heavenly Father. Hence, "sobriety" concerns himself, "righteousness" concerns others, "godliness" concerns God. These three categories seem to exhaust the whole sum of Christian duty.

It may be observed that in the words of our text, it would appear nominally as if only one of these three points is brought under our notice, "Let him depart from iniquity;" but it is clear that the second class of duties, to which I have just alluded, is strictly included, namely, duties of "righteousness," or those duties which respect our neighbours; let him depart from what is unjust, that is, from what in any degree would affect the character, person, or property of others. Let him guard against the want of due respect to parents, and to those who are in authority over him—let him guard against violence or unkindly feeling to others; let him guard against the violation of chastity, and against everything of the nature of theft and covetousness, which is in reality the germ of theft; let him guard against evil speaking, and so on. It is well-known that all these duties point to the second table of the Ten Commandments, comprising those, connected with the duties we owe to others; attention to which is connected with righteous conduct, and the violation of which is iniquity, that is, unjust conduct.

"Let him depart from iniquity;" let him depart from every species of conduct and conversation, by which his neighbour, and especially his Christian brethren, might in any respect be injured; and this without regard to the sentiments of *men* upon the subject. There is often a sort of conventional morality, by which the pure morality of God is set aside; this you have not to do with; your business as Christians is to see, that in no respect whatever your brother is injured; and not only your brother, but that your fellow-man, is in no respect injured. You are bound to act uprightly, not only towards those who are within, but also towards those who are without. Not only are you to depart from iniquity externally, but also *internally*. You are not to encourage a murderous, lustful, or covetous thought. The 5th chapter of Matthew is stern and express on this subject; all that is evil in thought, as well as evil in action, is to be avoided, for there is injustice or iniquity in the improper thought, as well as in the improper and unjust action.

Therefore, when we look at the words, " Let him depart from iniquity," it is properly the second category of Christian duty, or that which respects our duty towards our neighbour, towards those who believe the truth, and towards those who believe it not ; and throughout the whole of Scripture, this is enforced on the attention and on the consciences of believers. We cannot too often have precepts of this kind in mind, we cannot too much act upon them. I am aware that our human nature is prone to do what is unjust, when an advantage is likely to accrue to ourselves thereby—but here the crucifying influence of divine truth comes in. Are we tempted to do this or that, which is iniquitous or unjust, Christianity constrains us to pursue an opposite course of conduct; constrains us to feel that Christ died, not that we might live unto ourselves, by performing acts of injustice, which might happen to be of advantage to us ; Christianity constrains us not to act or live to ourselves in any respect whatever—but to live unto him, that died for us, and that rose again.

I understand, however, that this expression, " Depart from iniquity," is not confined to acts of injustice. It appears to me to be a brief form of expression, exhorting the attention of believers, to other classes of duties ; to the duty of sobriety, to the duty of temperance, to the duty of avoiding whatever might injure self, as well as others ; for by injuring self we bring reproach upon our Christian profession, as much as when we injure others; and the duty of believers is to abstain from doing that, by which the glorious character of God, in Christ, might be compromised. We are bound to abstain from every appearance of evil, both as respects our own personal conduct and welfare, the welfare of others, and in what respects God also; for a believer of the truth is bound to maintain towards his heavenly Father the conduct, thoughts, and feelings, that become a son or a daughter of the Lord Almighty.

I may speak of the conventional mode of shewing "godliness." There are Roman Catholics, who tell us, we can never live godlily except by attendance upon *mass*, and making confession to priests; and by attention to other superstitious practices in which the members of that Church indulge. And so the members of any particular Church might say to us, you cannot act godlily, except you practise the peculiar rites of that particular Church. This is not the way to act godlily. We act godlily when God is kept in view continually, and is made the end of our actions. We act godlily when we aim at the promotion of His glory; when His love is our influencing principle, and when that love carries us, in all our straits and difficulties, to His throne; when we are led by prayer, and supplication, and thanksgiving, to make our requests known to Him; when we are led to trust in Him for the life that now is, as well as for the life which is to come; when we are made to "Look up to Jesus as the author and finisher of our faith, who for the joy that was set before him, endured the cross, despising the shame, and is now set down at God's right hand."

Unless love to God be our actuating motive, we cannot act righteously and soberly, upon Christian principles; for, until the heart be purified, until faith, that worketh by *love*, enters into the mind; until we are brought out of darkness into marvellous light, by the manifestation of Christ as our Saviour, and God as our Father; until we know that we are "Heirs of God, and joint heirs with Christ;" until the influences of these holy and heavenly principles come to be felt by us, it is impossible for us to know how we should act towards our fellow-Christians and fellow-men, and how we should act in regard to ourselves.

It is the knowledge of Jesus as our Saviour and our God; the knowledge of Jesus as having died for us and risen again, as having washed us from sin in his own most precious blood, and given us life everlasting freely in himself; it is this knowledge, which forms in the mind the influential principle of living godlily, righteously, and soberly.

I cannot part with the subject without speaking of the motive from whence this is to spring—on the part of the Christian. It is not to qualify himself for the heavenly kingdom; for until we see that our qualifications are in Christ alone; until we see that he hath bought us with his own blood, that we are his property, that we rose with him, as we died in him; that it is in him, and him alone, that our salvation is realized; until we understand the import of the words uttered by him on the cross, "It is finished," and we perceive that the whole work of salvation being finished by him, no part is left to be finished by us; it is not until all this is seen, and the glorious truth has taken possession of our minds, as the principle of life everlasting; that the exhortation of my text, or any other exhortation, can come home to our minds in demonstration of the spirit and with power. But when God is recognized as what He is; when His love is shed abroad in our hearts; when we know ourselves to be members of God's family; and feel that He hath put His "honour," as it were, into our hands; that He calls upon us to take care, that that honour is not tarnished by our conduct; it is not until then that the exhortations come fully home, "Let every one that nameth the name of Christ depart from iniquity."

Thus we know that our object, in passing through this world, is not merely to *shew* the divine judgments; for I admit, that if we do evil, God's judgments *will* come down upon us, and why? Because we are His children, and just as a father chastiseth *his own* children when they are found doing wrong, not for his own pleasure, but for their good, so our heavenly Father chastiseth us "for our profit, that we might be partakers of His holiness." This, however, is but a very low principle on the part of the people of God. It is very useful as taking possession of the mind in the absence of other principles: but the grand principle of conduct is, love to God, as having first loved us; the knowledge that we are His; that in this world this knowledge begins, as the fulness of it is carried out in the eternal state; and being His, we are one with Him; being His, we are devoted to Him; being His, whatsoever is evil is hateful to us, as dishonouring to Him; being His, true love will shew itself, not in *word* merely, but in deed and in truth.

My dear Christian friends, it is love to God, then, as having first loved us; that is the motive and the only motive, under the influence of which, the words of my text can be carried into effect in our hearts, as well as in our lives and conversation.

There are various other matters I might notice, if time permitted, in the enforcement of the words of the text, but I see I have exhausted all the time I can occupy upon this occasion.

It will be enough for me if I have drawn attention to the importance of the two mottoes sealed upon this foundation-stone, the one motto having a reference to God, and the other motto having a reference to God's people. Men may at one time profess, and at another time may fall away; but no individual known of God hath ever fallen away or ever can fall away. Them that are His are always present, as members of God's family, to His sight—to the sight of Him who seeth things as they are, and not as man seeth them. The Lord hath purposed to bring them to the knowledge of Himself; and whom the Lord foreknew He also predestinated to be conformed to the image of His Son, that he might be the first-born among many brethren; moreover whom he predestinated, them He also called; and whom He called, them He also justified; and whom He justified, them He also glorified." There is no possibility of any one of them coming short of His glory, and why? because they are better than they who fall? No, but because they are under His special charge, and because they are the heirs of His everlasting and unchangeable purposes.

Then, as "the Lord knoweth them that are His," this rule of conduct follows—"Let every one that nameth the name of Christ depart from iniquity." This proves *negatively* that such an one is not a false professor. I do not mean to say that the peculiar effects of Christianity can ever be seen or acknowledged by the *world*. We know these peculiar effects which spring from the knowledge of the truth as it is in Christ Jesus, but these the *world* cannot recognize; they belong to the members of the Church alone; but the world *negatively* can perceive when a man stultifies his Christian profession by improper and inconsistent conduct. The *world* can see *negatively* when a man's conduct is morally pure. In this point of view the members of the Church are spoken of in reference to the glory of God, but their business is not to make the world understand what it never can understand—namely, the peculiar nature of Christian love; of "that faith which worketh by love;" the connection between the purification of the heart by faith, and the peculiar consequences flowing from it. But the world can understand any man, who professing the truth, does not stand aloof from every appearance of evil; and when he does not act a just and proper part, every such man brings a disgrace upon his fellow-men, and makes Christianity itself suspected; and every such man, being a child of God, lays himself open to the most awful and fearful chastisements at God's hand.

May the Lord bless what has been said, and to His name be the praise for evermore.

SERMON VII.

Sunday, October 8th, 1854.

Jeremiah, ch. xii.—Dr. Thom commenced reading the chapter from the beginning, but finding his sight almost entirely fail him, he merely read the first two or three verses, and then the text, which is the 5th verse, and is as follows :—

"If thou hast run with the footmen, and they have wearied thee, then how canst thou contend with horses? and *if* in the land of peace, *wherein* thou trustedst, *they wearied thee*, then how wilt thou do in the swelling of Jordan."

I should have liked to read the whole of the chapter in consequence of its connection with the text, but the state of my eyesight renders me totally unable to do so. The passage from which I have now to address you is the 5th verse, which I have just read. I need not tell you—in fact, your own eyes will shew you—that there have been some words introduced into the translation of the passage which I have selected as my text; the words in italics are those to which I allude. Perhaps, on the whole, a careful and very sound judgment has been exercised on what has been done, though it is evident that our translators have been greatly puzzled to understand the meaning of the sentence. I see that they have made of it a new paragraph; they cannot very well conceive how it comes in; they cannot well conceive what connection it has with what goes before or with what comes after it; and, therefore, after having translated it as well as it was in their power to do, they have left it as I have read it.

For many years this passage has been, from time to time, before my eyes, and I have been satisfied that it expresses a vast deal more than meets either the eye or the ear, and, in despair of ascertaining its meaning by the aid of commentators I have thrown them aside, and have striven to look up to God for that light and direction which He alone can give; to ascertain if, by a careful examination of the remainder of the chapter, and if, by light thrown upon the passage elsewhere, I might come to something like a scriptural understanding of it. It has appeared, within the last week or two, to me, that the meaning of the passage has become clearer, that it is no longer surrounded by the difficulties which formerly environed it, and that now, instead of being obscure, it shines forth with a glory, and is possessed of a sweetness and a power, with which all God's words are, and are felt to be possessed, when they are seen and rightly understood in their own light—the bright rays of Scripture.

Remember that these words occur in a book of prophecy; that they have no means of explaining themselves,—that is to say, of explaining their own spiritual meaning. Remember, that although there may be a sense in which the cotemporaries of Jeremiah might understand his lamentations, and a sense in which they might understand the sufferings undergone by him, and to which he here alludes, yet, that the language here employed had a reference to a higher than Jeremiah, and has received its accomplishment in Christ Jesus, is, I suspect, what the men of Jeremiah's time, had but faint means of ascertaining; and is what, I suspect, there are but few who meddle with the Scriptures, and profess to teach their meaning, have a correct understanding of, even at the present day.

Looking at this most wonderful and, when rightly understood, beautiful and delightful chapter, it is clear that a far greater than Jeremiah is here brought under our notice. We have here the pleadings of the Lord Jesus Christ himself, as he comes before his heavenly Father in the character of intercessor; as intercessor *for* his Church, but intercessor also, in certain respects, *against* it—against the Old Testament Church, against which he is forced to plead, and the judgment of which he is forced, as it were, to anticipate. This Old Testament Church he represents, under the symbol of his vine, as having been planted by himself, as having been his own peculiar heritage; and he represents those who are connected with it, as having dealt wickedly and even treacherously with him. And, in the verse which immediately follows the language of our text, we find this treachery of conduct represented as having been exhibited towards himself, and as having come from a quarter from which it might have been least expected.

Taking the chapter as a whole, there cannot be the shadow of a doubt, that the Lord Jesus Christ himself is here either speaking or spoken of; for, in certain passages there is, as it were, a break off from the immediate manner of expression—a break off from Christ himself speaking, to Christ himself addressing and pleading with his heavenly Father; and then such a break off as brings in himself as the person addressed, and brings under our observation in brief form, his own wondrous, sublime, and divine character.

Now, after all the consideration which I have been able to give to the subject, this fifth verse, notwithstanding the difficulties with which it may be clogged, appears to me to be an address to the Lord Jesus Christ—to the Lord Jesus Christ himself; and, as such, connected with the verse which follows; an address, however, which, when it comes to be examined, is found to be clear, simple, and consistent with New Testament truth, and one of the briefest, most condensed, and most powerful exhibitions of what Jesus Christ was, especially as a power of God, when he came on earth, to appear as our Saviour, and to accomplish the work of our salvation.

I need not observe to you that the language is clearly figurative. We have footmen; we have horses; we have a land of peace; and we have the swelling of Jordan. Now all these things naturally suggest to us such circumstances as the following:—The footmen and the horses bring under our notice something like conflict; or, at all events, a state of war. We have the footmen running, we have the horses running. Again, we have peace—a land in a state of comparative peace, brought under our notice. And then we have the river Jordan pourtrayed, which periodically, as we know, overflowed its banks; concerning which overflowings some interesting circumstances are recorded in the Old Testament Scriptures.

Now, if the Lord Jesus Christ be the subject-matter of this beautiful chapter in Jeremiah—a chapter which puzzled our translators, which has also puzzled commentators (more by the false theories they adopted than from any other cause —for unfortunately with not a few, both translators and commentators, the idea of Jeremiah, and David, and others, being the persons prominently speaking, has so occupied their minds, that they did not see that the Lord Jesus Christ is the great subject-matter of all prophecy)—it is no wonder if, in the course of its interpretation, they stumbled, and were often baffled. Let us, however, for once understand them to have been tolerably correct in the translation they have given us, and then let us see if, in the character of the Lord Jesus Christ, we do not find something which exactly corresponds with what is here suggested.

Now, recollect, before I proceed, that the Old Testament Scriptures are so constructed that, in the prophecies concerning Christ, they exhibit him and his future career under an amazing variety of forms. Sometimes he is simply prophesied of. He was to appear as the son of a woman. He was to appear as a conqueror, advancing from glory to glory. He was to appear as being wounded for our transgressions and bruised for our iniquities. Sometimes he is thus plainly set before us.—Sometimes he is set before us in the language of type. Sometimes Adam is represented as a type of him. Sometimes Abraham is a type of him, especially in his character of the father of the faithful. David is a type of him; Solomon also.—Again, he is often presented to us in language of exhortation. He is exhorted to do what only Christ did or could do; that is to say, the word of God comes forth to him directly in the form of a law—a law which he was destined, to the very uttermost, to fulfil. Few understand the meaning of, or reason for, that expression which Christ quoted in the 22nd of Matthew, "*Thou shalt love the Lord thy God with all thy heart.*" Few think that these words were addressed to Christ and were actually fulfilled by him. Few think that the words, "*Fret not thyself because of evil doers,*" were addressed to him, and were actually fulfilled by him. He did not fret himself because of evil doers. All these things, when you find them addressed to Christ, suggest that his character was to stand out differently from, and opposed to, that of ordinary human beings.

I understand the passage before me to be of this description: it is an intimation to us, through the medium of queries addressed to Christ in relation to us, that he should prosecute unweariedly his mediatorial career, overcoming every difficulty and every enemy; and that thus, by his own mighty power, as well as by his own divine wisdom, he should enter in due time into his glory. He should not only run with footmen without being wearied, but he should run with horses also without being wearied; and not only in the land of peace, to which he originally came, should he not be wearied or overcome by the treatment he should meet with, but, when at last he came to the swellings of Jordan, he should encounter them without alarm, and should triumph over them—passing through them to the other side.

Well, then, these words consist of two parts: a contrast between running with footmen and running with horses; a contrast between being wearied in a land of peace, and being brought to the swellings of Jordan, where a conflict of an extraordinary kind must be engaged in, in which victory must be the result.

Now, I have no hesitation as to the meaning of the first part of this passage. Our blessed Lord had two sets of enemies to encounter: *men* and *devils*. And I understand that the expressions here set down—footmen and horses—have reference to those two distinct classes of enemies whom our Lord was fated to encounter, and whom he was destined to overcome.

In the first place, *footmen*. Our Lord made his appearance in the flesh. For the first thirty years of his life he lived in comparative obscurity; yet even in that obscurity he was daily growing, not merely in stature but in wisdom; not merely in favour with men but in favour with God also. In that comparative obscurity he was meditating upon the law of God day and night, and the life of God in his heart was exhibiting itself more and more. It is true that, under the impression that God's word prohibited him from the assumption of the priestly office till thirty years of his life had expired, our Lord, as the great high priest of our profession, did not come forward until he had accomplished the thirtieth year of his age. But though he assumed no public character until then, still, beams of his greatness, still, outshinings of his heavenly glory, still, fruits of his Messiahship from time to time made their appearance; especially that great wonder recorded in the second chapter of Luke, in which we are told that, after his parents had anxiously sought him in the company returning to Galilee, they went back to Jerusalem, where they found him, after three days' search, in the temple, sitting in the midst of the doctors and astonishing all present by his understanding and his answers. Even at twelve years of age that Word of God which he himself was, embodied, that Word of God, dwelt in him so richly, and the power of it, in him, shone forth so efficiently, that he shewed himself wiser than his teachers. He could not only answer every question propounded to him by the doctors, but he could put questions to them which brought to view the shallowness of their minds, and the self-righteousness of their characters. He made them feel that in the boy who stood before them—in the stripling who was speaking and conversing with them—they were in the company of one of no ordinary mind; and though the pride of their hearts would not permit them to acknowledge, in this youth, their future Messiah, yet no doubt they felt abashed at many of the questions he put to them, at the searching inquiries he propounded to them, and at the shallowness of their acquaintance with divine truth, which he was the means of bringing to light. Still, the Son of God lived for thirty years in comparative obscurity; but, when the destined period had arrived, when the full time drew nigh that he was no longer to continue in Galilee, but was to make his appearance as the preacher of righteousness and the great high priest of our salvation, then commenced his running with the *footmen*. He came forth first in Galilee at the time when he converted the water into wine; at the time when, in the synagogue, he astonished those present by the comment which he made upon a portion of the sixty-first chapter of Isaiah. Then, he made his appearance in Jerusalem, where he performed miracles of the most extraordinary description, speaking as never *man* spoke, his words coming home to the consciences of those whom he addressed, and making his auditory feel that no ordinary individual had made his appearance amongst them. Thus he was running with the footmen, with the children of men, with his own brethren according to the flesh; and immediately that he commenced to run with them, they endeavoured to impede him in his career, to outstrip him in his efforts. But they were unsuccessful. He distanced these footmen; he made the Herodians to feel when they presented to him the tribute money, and tried him with a hypocritical question; that he knew what was in them; that he could go to the bottom of their hearts, and there read the inmost motives by which they were actuated. He made the Sadducees to feel that their reasoning, when brought to bear against the truth of God, was shallow, miserable, and paltry in the extreme, by shewing, from the language of a part of Scripture which they acknowledged to be divine, that God is not changeable as men are; that the state of the resurrection being a divine state, is not, like our earthly state, subject to change. He brought them so to feel, that they were abashed by his answers. He even provoked the praises and the approbation of the Pharisees themselves, who, when they rejoiced to find that he had silenced their hated antagonists, the Sadducees, expected a compliment at his hands; but by the question which he put to them, he made them also to feel that they had taken a false estimate of divine righteousness as well as of his character, by shewing them that, complete love to God accompanied by love to man, to the exclusion of all selfishness, were the grand characteristics of the law of God, and that their Phariseeism, so far from meeting and fulfilling the requirements of the Old Testament Scriptures, was the substitution of a low form of creature-righteousness, for the righteousness required by God. The footmen ran with him, but they were distanced: he outstripped them, when, not satisfied with tearing the mask from the hypocritical hearts of those with whom he had to deal, he propounded that single question in which the doctrine of Divine Inversion is involved, "What think ye of Christ, whose son is he?" and when they answered him "The Son of David," by the next question—the question resting upon it—"How then doth David in spirit call him Lord? if David call him Lord, how is he his Son?" he silenced all his antagonists for ever.

Thus, then, he shewed that the footmen in running with him had no chance, that instead of being wearied in the race and overcome in the conflict, he could go on unwearied to the close of his mediatorial career; and hence it was, that up to the period when accused, he stood at the bar of the Sanhedrim, at the bar of Herod, and before Pontius Pilate, he was running with the footmen, and shewing them, that they had no chance of obtaining the mastery when striving and straining with *him*. And in the same unweariedness of effort, the same desire to obtain the crown that was set before him, to promote the glory of his heavenly Father; the same disposition to endure the cross and despise the shame—in that unweariedness he went on, till upon Calvary He could say, "It is finished."

In this running with the footmen, that is, with mere human beings, with those parties who stood upon no higher platform than is furnished by human nature itself, he was unwearied; but he had yet horses also to contend with. The powers of hell were let loose upon him; Satan and his angels came into deadly conflict and deadly grip with the Son of God, and this especially towards the close of his mediatorial career upon earth. Even then, however, it was shewn, that he could be unwearied in the race which he ran with the footmen, and that, with equal unweariedness, he could enter upon a conflict and a race of a still higher description. Unwearied I say, for he was God with us; and when, therefore, Satan came in upon him with all his power;

when he endeavoured to shew him that sin was of such a deadly description, that it was impossible for even himself to put it away; and when he endeavoured by all the terrors of death to destroy in him the prospect of the joy that was set before him; when he endeavoured to impede him in his heavenward career, Satan found he had one to deal with who was his master. This was proved even at the commencement of Christ's career; for, when Satan, in the wilderness (after Jesus had been declared to be the Son of God, and this directly by a voice from heaven) when Satan in the wilderness tempted him, first, by means of calling in question his being the Son of God and saying, "If thou be the Son of God, command that these stones be made bread," not by directly saying that he was not the Son of God, but by trying to induce him to shew by this method that he was the Messiah—a temptation, compliance with which would have been the failure and destruction of his faith; for it would have been to make his confidence in God to rest, not upon God's testimony to that effect, but upon something done by the creature. After Satan had been foiled in this, by Christ's declaring that he was "not to live by bread alone, but by every word that proceedeth out of the mouth of God," Christ being God made flesh, and able to fast forty days upon his Father's word, when it was God's pleasure for him so to do, he tempted him to cast himself from the pinnacle of the temple. But Christ at once resisted the temptation by recalling the divine command, "Thou shalt not tempt the Lord thy God." And after Christ had in the last place refused the tempting offer of all the kingdoms of this world—every species of earthly sovereignty — upon the condition of worshipping Satan, after he had refused that offer and shewn, or rather complied with, the divine command, "Thou shalt worship the Lord thy God, and Him only shalt thou serve," Satan, who had been thus foiled, retired from the encounter for a time. He had tried to wrestle, he had tried to run with the Son of God, but he had found that that Son of God had the mastery over him. At various points in Christ's career, Satan from time to time interposed, and the Son of God on one occasion witnessed him as lightning falling down from heaven; it was found, however, that instead of Satan making head against him, the Son of God was making head against Satan and his kingdom. But it was not until he came to the garden of Gethsemane, not until he came to the cross, that Satan was let loose upon him with all his legions of apostate angels, and with all his hellish supporters; it was not until then, that the true conflict made its appearance—that the true race between the Son of God and his hellish opponents became apparent. Then it was, that he who had outwearied the footmen, he who had gone beyond the quickest, and the greatest, and the most noble, in the race with man, distanced even Satan himself, shewing that no mere creature, however vast his power, however deep his insight into human nature, and his power over human nature, that no mere creature in entering into a contest with the Son of God, has any chance whatever of succeeding, but that, on the contrary, the creature, however exalted he may be, must submit to the Creator, and be content to see him run before him in the race, achieve the victory, reach the goal, and possess all that mastery which the Son of God in perfection alone could possess, and which the Son of God did possess, and which he was destined to possess, by the mere effect of his power as the Son of God. Well, then, I understand these two words, footmen and horsemen, to refer to the fact that the Son of God, who was unwearied in his conflict with mere men—in his race with mere human beings, was equally unwearied in his conflict with Satan and devils,—that he distanced them both, obtained the mastery over both, reached the goal, and received the crown of everlasting life.

But there is another thing suggested, "If in the land of peace they have dealt treacherously with thee, how shalt thou do at the swelling of Jordan?" I forget the *exact* expression, "What wilt thou do at the swelling of Jordan?" This is just another view of the character of the Son of God during his abode in the flesh, and while accomplishing the work of our salvation. It brings under our notice two states of things in which he was to make his appearance. It suggests, in the first place, that he was to come unto his own. I do not speak of the fact that Israel—that the land of Judea—was in a state of peace naturally, when he made his appearance; that is true, and some think, and truly, that this is not to be kept out of view in our consideration of the passage, but that is not what I think is suggested by the words, "He came unto his own." He came unto that nation which he had selected for himself, at Mount Sinai, or rather selected in the person of Abraham his faithful progenitor. He came to that nation with whom he had especially connected Himself by being born of a Jewish family, and by possessing the seed of Abraham. I say that he came to that nation particularly, and when he first made his appearance he was received with apparent kindness by it. It is true, that at

Nazareth, the doctrine of Election being raised by him, so aroused the people of that city, that they were wishful to cast him down headlong; yet he was not so tried at Cana, where he converted the water into wine; when he fed the people with a few loaves and fishes, and when he performed many other wondrous works, the people of Galilee proclaimed his name abroad, spoke high things of him, commended his character, and recommended him to others; so that in Galilee, upon the whole, he may be said to have been in a land of peace. The same thing may be said of Samaria. We learn from the woman of Samaria, with whom he conversed upon religious matters, at Jacob's Well, and to whom he gave reason to believe one thing especially, that he was greater than ordinary men; we find that, in consequence of his sojourn there, this woman and many others were brought to believe on him as the long-promised Messiah. This, therefore, was to him, in certain respects, a land of peace. Still more was this the case with regard to Judea; for we know that when he made his appearance there, he was received with great kindness and marked approbation. We know that testimony was there given to the great miracles which he wrought, that approbation was expressed of the words that issued from his lips; and that upon his lips hung many of the followers of John the Baptist, as well as many others of the Jews. Thus, to him, that land was, to all appearance, a land of peace; and it continued to appear to be so till within a short period before his crucifixion; for we find him on the first day of the week, before he was crucified, entering into Jerusalem, riding on an ass, with palm branches strewed in the way, and we hear the song, "Hosanna to the Son of David, blessed is he that cometh in the name of the Lord, Hosanna in the highest," resounding from almost every tongue. You would have said under such circumstances as these that he had come to a land of peace—that he had come to his own—to those who were in truth his kinsmen according to the flesh. He was received, apparently, with so much kindness and approbation, that on one occasion a strong wish was expressed that he might become a king, and something like an offer of an earthly crown was made to him. But amidst all this apparent peacefulness of conduct and demeanour there lurked a secret hatred of his character. The more the character of God was manifested in him, the more obvious it became that his standard was totally opposed to the standard of men; that while almost all the Pharisees and others of that class were satisfied with mere professions,

Christ went to the bottom of their hearts. Christ could only be contented with such conduct as corresponded with true principles. Christ preferred the poor widow's last mite to the large and ostentatious offerings of rich men. He condemned the self-righteous Pharisee, and preferred to him the poor publican, who had no plea to offer at the bar of God but simply, "God be merciful to me, a sinner." Hatred to him grew, in proportion as the exhibition of the character of God in him became more and more apparent; and indeed, my dear friends, I scarcely know a more marked exhibition on the one hand, of the truth of the doctrine of Divine Inversion, or a view of what that doctrine is, than in the fact that, just in proportion as the character of God appeared in Jesus Christ manifested, just in proportion as gracious words flowed from his lips; in proportion as miraculous acts of love and mercy were performed by him; in proportion as the common people began to bear witness to his wondrous superiority of character; in that same proportion did human nature dislike him; in the same proportion did those holding the highest places in society shew themselves disposed to put him down and ensnare him; in the same proportion did he find that in a land of peace there was treacherous dealing towards him. This treachery was exhibited on the part of Herodians, Sadducees, and Pharisees. This treachery also was exhibited in the fact that they met from time to time to consider how they might seize him in the midst of his speech and put him to death. And at length it was consummated, in the high priest's sending his officers with staves and other weapons to apprehend him. But this treachery was in the highest degree insulting: one of his own disciples going to give information against him, and even descending to become the leader of those by whom he was apprehended. Thus, in a state of peace, in a land apparently of peace, there was hatred towards him, gradually increasing in proportion as the character of God in him was actually unfolding itself more and more; and this hatred was rapidly and awfully maturing in exhibitions of the most dreadful and atrocious treachery. But did Jesus readily shew a disposition to avoid it? No: he knew what was in the hearts of men, and contemplated his own crucifixion with calmness—with more than calmness — with pleasure, because he knew that it was for the salvation of his fellow-creatures. Hints of these coming events were given at Mount Tabor, by Moses and Elijah, when they entered into holy converse with him. He knew that an ignominious death was to be inflicted upon Him by those by whom he had been rejected. He knew all this, and therefore he went on in his career unwearied; he went on in his labours of love and mercy unwearied; he went about doing good continually, even to those who were his enemies, and by whom he was to be nailed to the accursed tree. He went on, I say, continually acting upon the principle of good-dealing towards them, not retaliating evil upon them, but, on the contrary, heaping coals of fire upon their heads by his very forbearance. Thus, in working out these acts of mercy, he was proclaiming the approach of his kingdom, and in every respect shewing himself to be the pure and holy, as also the beloved Son of God.

This was the case then with Jesus, so far as my understanding of the passage goes. But was this *all* that awaited him? Had he merely to encounter human and Satanic opposition under pretence of peace, under disguises of various kinds and degrees? Had he only *these* to encounter? No; a conflict of a far more awful description—the swellings of Jordan, awaited him; through Jordan he was to pass to God. Jordan was to him a wide river; it was not merely, as some suppose, the symbol of death, but it was the symbol of all the pangs and agonies that precede and accompany death—those pangs and agonies which, at the beginning of the sixty-ninth Psalm, are so graphically described. Jordan had swollen. He had not merely footmen to encounter; he had not merely horsemen to encounter; he had not merely devils to encounter; he had not merely to outrun devils as well as men, in order to obtain the mastery and reach the goal; but, after having encountered the opposition—the treacherous opposition of men, he had to encounter what was still more awful—the opposition and the open desertion of him by his fellow-labourers. It was this, it was the consequences involved in this desertion that constituted the swellings of Jordan, in which his pure, and holy, and righteous soul was tried to the very uttermost, but from which he emerged triumphant. God, in one sense, helped him. I say *in one sense* God helped him; for "God loved him with an everlasting love;" God loved him intensely as "his only begotten Son, in whom he was well pleased," long before Jesus had clothed himself with our flesh and blood, long before Jesus had appeared as our representative, long before Jesus had taken upon him all the wrath that was due to the sin of the world, and all the wrath that was due to the transgression of man, the fruits of which began to overflow in the garden of Gethsemane, and the anguish of which was inexpressible.

Jordan overflowed its banks. The terror, or rather the anguish, connected with our sin entered, to overflowing, into his pure and holy soul. The waters began "to go over His face," (an expression used at the beginning of the 69th Psalm) the agony was such, that "the sweat" at last became "as drops of blood falling to the ground." There appeared to him an angel strengthening him. And did he decline these swellings of Jordan? No: Jordan had to swell yet more; for besides the anguish of Gethsemane, there was yet the anguish of the cross to encounter; there was not only the darkness of the sun's eclipse, but all the darkness of man's guilt to come down upon his devoted head: and hence it was that, while in the garden of Gethsemane, he said, "Father, if it be possible, let this cup pass from me; nevertheless not my will but thine be done." And while he hung upon the cross, he gave forth that still more agonising cry, "My God, my God, why hast thou forsaken me?"

Here were the swellings of Jordan; here were the waters of Divine wrath let out upon the soul of the Son of God. This he was to bear; through this he was to pass; from this he was to emerge. Ah! blessed be God's name, he shrank not from the trial. He would return man's treachery shewn under the appearance of simulated peace, with kindness and acts of benevolence; he would meet wrath with heavenly, with increased love, because he knew that the wrath against man's sin was the expression of the divine wrath; he knew that if God had not loved him, that wrath would never have assailed him to the extent it did, and therefore he encountered the swellings of Jordan, and at the last went down under the waters, when he said, "Father, into thy hands I commend my spirit."

Here, then, I think, we have the text before us explained. We have the Son of God himself set before us; in the first place, meeting with mere human beings, with their opposition, or rather hatred, and with their attempt to outrun him in the race. We have him outrunning them all and distancing them in the race; and we have seen that all their efforts to overcome him, to outstrip him in the race, were futile *in the extreme*. We have him encountering devils (or horses), and we have him outstripping *them* also, putting them under his feet, and making them the objects of signal defeat. Still further, he came upon the earth, he came into a land that was apparently a land of peace, but under that disguise of peace there was hate, and hate increasing in proportion as the character of God increasingly appeared in him; this hatred took the form of treachery, and at last treachery does its work. Even here, the Son of God was fulfilling what was said of him in the rest of this chapter; he was performing acts of beneficence continually. He continued to perform those acts of beneficence and grace until the day when, in agony, he exclaimed, " Father, forgive them, for they know not what they do." The swellings of Jordan were encountered by him, and the swellings of Jordan were overcome by him. The wrath of God in all its fierceness he encountered, that wrath he bore, well knowing that the sin which he bore, deserved it; and he bore the wrath to the uttermost, till the sin and the wrath were both exhausted in his spotless and righteous death. The swellings of Jordan went over his head, but only for a time. On the third day he emerged. Jordan was under his feet, Jordan was drained up for ever.

It was my purpose to shew you that there is a sense in which the words of my text affect the consciences of men, but I will take some other opportunity of speaking of this. I have said enough to suggest that here Jesus Christ is not only spoken of, but that he is here also the *speaker;* speaking not only to the Jewish Church in particular, but also referring to his Church in general.

However, I must leave the matter in your hands; and may the blessing of God attend the reading of his Word.

SERMON VIII.

Sunday Morning, October 29th, 1854.

I AM now to—I scarcely dare say—direct your attention to a *single* text, because the text from which I am about to speak may be said to be scattered through the whole of the sacred volume. Let me take one specimen of it from the lips of the very highest authority, as given in the Gospel according to St. Matthew. I shall select the beginning of the 4th verse of the 4th chapter of the Gospel of St. Matthew.

"He" (that is, Jesus) "answered and said, it is written." I shall not go further, because this forms the subject-matter or basis of the observations which I am about to make.

"He" (that is, Jesus) "answered and said, It is written."

I am not going to deliver to you any metaphysically-constructed discourse. I am not going to enter upon this subject in a way calculated or likely to puzzle any of my friends. I shall try to treat of it simply and plainly, and, towards the close, with personal application to ourselves.

"It is written." This is a formula or mode of expression, with which every individual whom I now address, and who is conversant with the Scriptures, must be familiar. It occurs incessantly in the New Testament Scriptures, or, at any rate, language very similar to it is found there. It occurs continually, as uttered by the lips both of our blessed Lord and his apostles; that is, we find there, an incessant reference to what is written—an incessant reference to the language of the Old Testament Scriptures, as possessed of the highest of all authority, and as forming a conclusive statement as to all the disputes and questionings that may arise. That is to say: is anything doubtful to the mind of any one as to religion? "*It is written,*" silences the doubt. Is information as to any point of doctrine required? "*It is written,*" communicates the information wanted. Is anxiety as to a future state of existence felt? "*It is written,*" removes the anxiety, and fills the heart of him who was formerly troubled, with joy that is unspeakable and full of glory.

It is true, "It is written," is not uttered by every lip, and what has been written is not the authority that is to *every one* conclusive. I am not going to dwell upon the fact, that in former days, and also in our own times, there have existed individuals whose minds have been so debased, whose hearts have been in such kindred union wedded to the dust, that God Himself and religion in every form and shape, have been dismissed by them as subjects not merely incomprehensible, but also absurd.

I am not going to dwell upon the fact that, at the present day even, there exists an alliance in Germany, with ramifications in this country, and also in America; a society which puts God aside altogether, and tramples religion under foot; a society which pretends to have found a better morality than that which is contained in the Bible; a society which boasts of having found far more noble modes of action and thought, than even the word of God describes. I am not going to speak of persons and societies such as those to which I have alluded. These, of course, have nothing whatever to do with "It is written;" they dismiss, and despise, and trample under foot every such authority. "It is written," is to them simply and solely a matter of scorn.

No. I am not going to speak to you even of Deists—of a class of men who profess to believe in the existence of God, and who, like Lord Herbert of Cherbury, have had their ideas of faith and morals, and have pretended to draw up systems of religious government, independently of the word of God altogether. Of such individuals, professing to believe in the existence of a god or gods, but not such a God as that which the Scriptures reveal to us, I am not going to speak. They never say with reference to the Scriptures, "It is written," for the Scriptures of truth possess, to such men, no authority whatever.

I dismiss, therefore, the Atheist, and I dismiss the Deist, and indeed all such classes of men, as classes of men who very clearly and obviously have nothing whatever to do, even professedly, with the language of our text, or with any corresponding language.

I now, however, observe, and observe with pain as it is no new fact, that there exists now, and has existed in every age, a body of individuals, or rather bodies of individuals; who while they profess to recognize the Scriptures as either entirely of divine origin and authority, or for the most part so, yet nevertheless contrive to nullify their statements, and to shew the desperate infidelity of the human heart, by bringing in something along with God's word, as being co-ordinate with, or superior to, or as aiding and assisting it, in the communication of divine authority; for, as I shall observe afterwards, the word of God is such when rightly understood, and when looked at in its own light, as to reject not only all opposition, but all confirmation from the words of men.

God stands supreme and alone. He utters His word, He causes it to be recorded in writing; there it is, claiming an authority, peculiarly its own. "I, the Lord," constitutes the sanction by which it comes home to our understandings and our consciences.

Our Blessed Lord, while he was in the flesh, is reported to have said, speaking of John, "He was a burning and a shining light, and ye were willing for a season to rejoice in his light," but, he immediately adds, "I receive not testimony from man." That is to say, if I refer to John, it is not to derive testimony from the creature, but to carry home the conviction of divine truth to the mind of the creature. I speak alone; when I speak, I speak upon my own and upon my Father's authority; when I speak, I speak, not as do the Scribes, but with a power which equally scorns the opposition and the support of men. I receive not testimony from men.

Just so with regard to the Scriptures. They come forward authoritatively; not saying, ask so-and-so what *he* thinks, and you will find that he agrees with *us!* Ask the common-sense of mankind, what is the result of all its deliberations. It refers not to science, nor to literature, nor to works of nature. Even so the word of God comes forward speaking, because God utters it. The word of God speaks with authority, not as do the Scribes. The word of God comes forward with such a degree of certainty, as well as fulness, and with declarations of such authority, as entirely to supersede all that men may think or conceive, respecting the subject.

This is the case with respect to the word of God: but how much is it nullified by a number of individuals who profess, either in whole or in part, to believe it! Here we have, among the Roman Catholics, a whole body of individuals, calling themselves professors of the oldest form of Christianity in the world, and we have this body telling us, Ah! there is *tradition* as well as the written word of God. There have been portions of the language of the apostles: there have been various views, entertained by Christ and his followers and expressed by them, which do not stand recorded in this book, but which have been handed down to us from generation to generation, and which have been kept within the repositories of the Church, and for which the Church stands as sponsor and witness. And they have the impudence to tell us that this tradition—this unwritten word of God—is of equal authority and as worthy to be listened to by us, as the written testimony of Jehovah himself. This is setting the word of God aside; because whenever a point of difficulty arises, or a dispute comes to be settled or considered, they refer to their tradition, and thus make the traditions of their Church the explanation of the meaning of the words of divine testimony. They put their tradition above the word of God, and they tell us that theirs was the Church which informed us that the Scriptures came down from God, and it is on the authority of their Church alone that we can believe. Thus they set their tradition above the testimony of the written word of God, and, by giving it too important a place, in their explanations of what is contained in the Scriptures, they put it far above God's word. Thus is the written word of God nullified by them, as the written testimony, in the Old Testament, was nullified by the Jews, by means of *their* traditions.

Now, this is the way in which men who profess Christianity—men who profess to believe in the divine testimony, have contrived actually to set both Christianity and that divine testimony aside. But is it peculiar to the Roman Catholic Church to set, "It is written,"—to set the written testimony of God aside, and to trample it under foot by their traditions? No: I am sorry to say that very large masses of individuals calling themselves Protestants, and regarded as such by their neighbours, have been found concurring with the Roman Catholics—not certainly in setting up tradition, because Protestants agree in rejecting it—but in setting up what they call, "natural religion," along with revealed religion. They tell us it is a delightful thing to find, that natural religion suggests the same things, that revealed religion does; that it is delightful to have the testimony of the Scriptures so satisfactorily confirmed by the testimony of natural religion. Long since did Barclay, and even before his time did many others, possessed of, and influenced by, the same spirit, indicate and clearly shew the suicidal character of such a mode of statement. They have shown that, if God's Word can be corroborated by the testimony of men, it ceases to be the Word of God. The light of the sun surrounds us with a brightness that sets at nought every other light. All other lights are obscured by its bright meridian splendour. When we bask in the rays of the sun and are filled with delight, what would be thought of the folly of the man who would bring out a farthing candle, and by its feeble light pretend to prove to us that the sun is shining, when it is plain that the light of the glorious luminary of day is outshining every other light, and rendering every other light inefficacious, evanescent, and obscure? It would not be the luminary which we understand it to be if it required such a proof as this. Just so the word of God—the entrance of God's word—gives light, and such a light as when it shines into the heart and conscience of a man, sets all other lights at defiance; for when it shines there, it is in vain to bring any other light to shew that it is shining—in vain for any other real or pretended light to make manifest to the conscience the indications of that spiritual testimony there. The principal characteristic of light is that it makes manifest, and if the Word of God cannot make manifest—which we know it does, for it makes manifest the character of God by making manifest the character of Christ—I say, if the word of God could not make manifest, it would want the first characteristics of light. But it does make manifest, and by doing so it sets all other testimonies at defiance. It cares not for the pretended corroborations of other testimonies, but simply sets them aside; it shines into our minds and with authority, and it is given to us to receive it and to walk in it, and no other light do we either seek or require.

When men talk of natural religion, as walking hand in hand with the religion of God, as corroborating the religion of God, as lending its confirmation to the religion of God, we should turn a deaf ear to such; because if this were true the inspired testimony of God would cease to be light. It would shine in this case, not with unrivalled, but with a rivalled authority: it would not shine with a lustre that sets all other lustre at defiance; but it would shine, by consenting to borrow some aid from the paltry testimony of men. It is true that where the word of God shines, it brings to view what is obscure in human nature—facts and principles which in the light of human nature could never have been seen. It gives us a wondrous handle to the putting away of what is false, and finding out and embracing what is true. But it is certainly not the case, that the testimony of man has helped the testimony of God, but that the word of God has enabled us to understand many of the testimonies of men.

I might have gone on to show further, that neither science nor literature has, in the slightest degree, helped to throw light upon the testimony of God, but that, on the contrary, they have been darkening counsel by words without knowledge continually. Among human testimonies to this evil effect in our own times, the doctrines of La Place, one of the most distinguished astronomers of late years— and of many other men, of one of whom we have some traces in the "Vestiges of Creation," a work—and a very infidel work too—published some years ago, have, alas! assisted. And in geology, we have many doctrines propounded which have the tendency to darken, if not actually to set aside the word of God. That is, the persons who have constructed such theories have thought that the facts, as they call them, of science must be received gradually. I never dispute facts, except when they begin to be mixed up with speculative theories. So that, for instance, which, from certain appearances, argues the existence of the earth for many thousands of years before the Scripture testimony began, we turn a deaf ear, and say that the same God that made Adam and Eve *mature;* the same God that called every creature into maturity at once, called the world itself into existence; at once created the world, with the few exceptions to be found on its surface, which exceptions can be, without any great difficulty, explained—I say, that with a few exceptions, the same God created the world *as we find it,* with the various strata lying in their particular positions and order (of course we are obliged to geologists for telling us how these strata *are* placed),—the same God created the fossil fishes, shells, birds, and quadrupeds, deposited them in the earth, and left them there, in order to puzzle the wise of this world. Therefore certain things exist in nature to shew the non-dependence of the minds of such men upon God's testimony, and the impossibility of finding out God by human reasonings and by human theories, and they are led to adopt views, which contradict the truth of God's word, and looked at in the light of that word, altogether set aside Providence, as if it were undeserving the slightest notice.

Last Lord's day we spent a part of our time in endeavouring to shew, that all *false* religion may be summed up in the simple category of *independence of God;* while all *true* religion may be called a constant sense of dependence *upon*

God through our union with God, in Christ Jesus. This was the substance of my discourse. I pointed out the tendency, not only of Atheism and Deism, but the tendency of the Roman Catholic Church, to set up natural against revealed religion, and that all attempts to introduce this natural handmaid to religion, are so many attempts to bring in the creature at the expense of the Creator, to set up the creature as independent of the Creator, and to trample under foot God's word, and to put out, if it were possible, the light of God's word by what is dim and obscure, and by the awfully erring intellect of man.

Well, now, having mentioned these things, the text before me states that when the tempter came to Jesus and tried, in the very teeth of what had come down directly from heaven—the testimony, "This is my beloved Son, in whom I am well pleased"—to shake and subvert the faith of Jesus, by calling upon him to "command the stones that they may be made bread," as if he had said, Do not trust the testimony of God that you are the Son of God; if you are the Son of God, prove it to yourself. Well did the devil know, that if Jesus could have listened to his vile insinuations, his faith in God would have been gone; he would have ceased to be actuated by God's testimony, and would have begun to set up some testimony of his own—to set up in fact a God of his own, as the foundation of his belief that he was God's son, thereby destroying the divine testimony, as the sole foundation of his conviction of the fact. But Jesus was not thus to be overcome. Though in every age human beings have allowed their faith to be subverted by an inducement to seek for evidence in themselves, to prove the existence of God, and their relationship to Him, instead of being satisfied with His testimony to the fact, viz., "Whosoever believeth that Jesus is the Christ, is born of God," or with this testimony, "As Moses lifted up the serpent in the wilderness, even so must the son of man be lifted up, that whosoever believeth in him should not perish, but have eternal life." Instead of being satisfied with this fact, and knowing that we are the sons of God, through the medium of faith in what he hath done for us, and the hope of his future appearing, whenever they try to seek for something in themselves they come down from the high court of divine testimony, and to the Lord and His testimony they do not appeal.

Our Lord, when he was tempted thus, met the tempter by the language of our text, "It is written." To no other testimony than "It is written," did he appeal. "It is written," and because it is written, thus, what is written is conclusive. This answer sets aside all thy insinuations; it laughs to scorn all thy attempts.

It is an interesting fact to those who are well acquainted with the New Testament Scriptures, that this expression, "It is written," or corresponding expressions, are continually occurring both in the writings of the Evangelist, and also in the epistles. It is true that the formula or mode of using this expression is not always the same; that, while the phraseology, "It is written," generally occurs, yet on some occasions, the expression is rendered in this manner, "As the Holy Ghost spake by the mouth of David;" or, thus—"It is written in the prophet," or some such phraseology; but still the simple language, whatever form it assumes, is nearly the same. There is always a referring backwards to what occurs in the Old Testament Scriptures.

And this brings under your notice and mine, the very interesting fact, that while our blessed Lord was on earth, and working out the redemption of man, there were two grand proofs of his being the Son of God, and the Saviour of the world, to which he was incessantly pointing. One source of proof or evidence was in the miracles that he wrought, and the other source was the language of the Old Testament Scriptures. Blessed be God that he did appeal to these two sources of authority or testimony, because, if there had been merely the evidence of miracles, one grand evidence—that which comes down to us, and by which we are enlightened, strengthened, and comforted—would have been wanting. He pointed to the evidence of miracles during the whole period of his public ministry, after emerging from those thirty years of obscurity, in which his early life was spent. During the short period of his public ministry he was delivering discourses and parables, speaking as never *man* spake, opening the eyes of the blind, unstopping the ears of the deaf, enabling the lame to walk and the dumb to speak; nay, even from time to time raising the dead. He pointed to these miracles; they were performed in the light of day, and of them the Jews, and occasionally the Gentiles, were witnesses, and bore testimony, that he, who could perform such miracles, was no other than the Son of God.

Observe, these miracles were not independent of Scripture; they were sources of evidence, to which Christ himself was continually referring. I have no doubt that there is in your minds this one most interesting and comforting reflection, that when, on one occasion, John sent two of his disciples to Christ, to enquire "Art thou he that should come, or shall we look for another?" Jesus immediately wrought miracles of healing in the sight of those deputies of John; and, not satisfied with this, when he dismissed them to him by whom they had been sent, he said, "Tell John that the lame walk, the deaf hear, the blind see, the lepers are cleansed, the dead are raised, and the poor have the Gospel preached unto them; and in this way I give testimony of what I am." Now observe further in these words, Jesus was referring to the 35th chapter of the Prophecy of Isaiah, in which it is declared what the Lord God, when he shall make his appearance in the character of the Messiah, shall perform.

Thus Jesus combined the evidence of the two—the evidence of the miracles which he had wrought, with the evidence of the Old Testament Scriptures, which declared that he who should work such miracles, was the being for whom the Churches had, for ages, been looking; that he it was, who was described as "The desire of all nations."

As Jesus referred both to miracles and to the word of God, so did his apostles also. During the days of their flesh, they were enabled to work many miracles. We are told that, during the days of their flesh, they preached the future coming of his kingdom, the immediate coming of his kingdom, and in doing so they referred to the Old Testament Scriptures, as having foretold that event, and also his resurrection from the dead. When we read such sermons as that of Paul at Antioch, in Pisidia, we are struck by observing, that it is made up almost entirely, from beginning to end, of references to, or extracts from, the Old Testament Scriptures. This is the authority to which the apostle refers, and from which he draws his conclusions; this is the authority which, he assures them, points to Christ; and this is the testimony which he shews to have been fulfilled by and in him.

You remember that interesting fact, with regard to the Jews of Berea, they were said to be more noble than those in Thessalonica, "In that they received the word with all readiness of mind, and searched the Scriptures *daily*, whether those things were so." And in consequence of that searching of the Scriptures, the conviction that the Messiah had come, in the person of Jesus of Nazareth, was so strongly and overwhelmingly impressed upon their minds, that many of them believed.

But the apostles also wrought many miracles. We find in the Acts of the Apostles, an account of the miracle of healing, performed at the gate of the temple, on the man who afterwards followed the apostles to Solomon's porch, though he had been lame from his birth, and daily laid at the gate of the temple to ask alms. We read also of the sick being brought, and laid on beds and couches in the streets, and the shadow of Peter passing over them, and effecting their cure. I say that they wrought miracles, as a testimony of the divine mission which they had received from their glorified and divine master, for it was to the Old Testament Scriptures that they were continually referring; it was *their* testimony—the testimony of the Old Testament Scriptures—that they were continually bringing under the notice of their hearers. "It is written," or some corresponding formula, was what they were continually adducing. And as from their lips these references were continually falling, and through their lips reaching us, so when we read the Scriptures, we find those references abounding from beginning to end. You cannot read the writings of Paul, without seeing "It is written." God, who by the mouth of His servant David, has said, "Those things which God before had showed by the mouth of all His prophets?" All these we find, and in this way we discover that the spirit of the Scriptures was the spirit of his appeal; he believed what God had said in the Old Testament Scriptures, therefore he quoted them. We have the same sort of faith expressed in other words, "They believed, and therefore they spoke;" and hence we find, in the Apostles, an incessant reference to the Old Testament Scriptures, as not only one ground of testimony, but as the grand ground of testimony to the divine mission of their head, and of the mission which they themselves had received from him.

"It is written," therefore, is no vain term; it is a most important fact; it points to the grand source of the divine authority of Christ's mission; that grand source of it, that grand testimony, upon which it rested during his lifetime, and through which it has been transmitted to us.

Now, observe, I speak here decidedly and emphatically. I say that "It is written," shows us the grand authority which we have for believing that Jesus was the Christ. "It is written," is the grand reason that we have for the peace, that is spoken to our consciences, and for the hope of life everlasting, by which we are animated and actuated, in passing through this present world.

This leads me at once to what I have had chiefly in view; namely, to point out the grand uses to which the expression, "It is written," has been applied—the grand uses to which it has been turned—and the grand uses to which it will be turned by all who believe the truth. For instance, "It is written," occurs occasionally in the latter part of the Old Testament Scriptures, in reference to the former portion. In the Psalms we read, "In the volume of the book it is written." It only occasionally occurs in the latter part in reference to a former portion of the Old Testament Scriptures, but it is chiefly to be found in the New Testament Scriptures with reference to the Old. And this brings under our notice the glorious fact, that we possess evidence of Jesus being the Christ—that we possess a source of instruction, as to divine things, of which even the Jews themselves were destitute. Some, indeed, may be apt to envy the condition of the Jews, and to fancy that they had better means of approaching to, and understanding God, than we have. Certainly, it may be said that they had an external temple, occupied by an external priesthood, and in which external sacrifices were continually being offered. These struck the eyes, these affected the heart, these even enlightened the intellects of the worshippers, but what was the practical effect upon the Jews? Did it influence their minds to delight in the living and true God, and to go with delight to His temple, and to His services? So far from this being the case, we are informed, concerning the children of Israel, that while passing through the wilderness, they were continually proving themselves to be "a stiffnecked and rebellious people"—that they were continually provoking to anger the God of Israel, and that the consequence of their rebellious and provoking conduct was the cutting off of the ten tribes, and the carrying of them into captivity. And even after the return of the Jews from their captivity, their rebellious and provoking conduct continued, and we find them accused of abusing the altar of the temple. The prophet Malachi strongly remonstrates with them, and shows that the vilest practices and abuses were prevalent, not only among the people, but also among the priests. These apparent advantages, in the temple-worship, were not able to overcome the innate and powerful infidelity of the human heart. For ages before Christ came, the Jews had the Old Testament Scriptures in their hands, and had the means of ascertaining by reading them, how the God of Israel had dealt with their fathers; at all events, in the synagogue, every

Sabbath day, they heard the law and the prophets read; and yet, observe, they were, at the time that Christ came, so much in the dark, that in one of the passages of Scripture quoted in the 4th chapter of St. Matthew's gospel, we are told that Galilee was a land of darkness, where they sat in the region and shadow of death.

Well then, if this was the fact, what has been the consequence of our Lord's coming on earth? What grand effect followed from his fulfilment of righteousness, and his ascent to glory? What grand result has followed from the outpouring of his spirit upon his apostles and disciples, and from the preaching of the gospel forty years by them, not only in Jerusalem and Samaria, but unto the ends of the earth? What has been the result of all this? Why, it has been that they, among other things, obtained the power of committing to writing an authorized explanation of the Old Testament Scriptures. In the Acts of the Apostles and in their epistles, we have this authorized explanation transmitted to us, and therefore we have what the Jewish people never had. We have what is of far more value, and that of which the Jews were utterly destitute; we have a source of information peculiar to New Testament times, and in the possession and understanding of which we are peculiarly blessed.

I have more than once tried to draw your attention to the distinction between the Old Testament and the New. Both have equal authority, *as inspired;* both are equally inspired. But there is a difference, which consists in this, that the Old Testament Scriptures, at Christ's coming, had a veil thrown over them, by which they were rendered unintelligible: they *were* light, but the light was hid, in consequence of the veil, to which I have alluded. Since Christ came, however, the veil has been withdrawn: the veil is done away in Christ, and we now understand from the New Testament Scriptures, that the great subject-matter— the great spiritual subject-matter of the Old Testament Scriptures — is Christ himself; we now learn, that his coming, his suffering, his kingdom and the Church he was to set up, and over which he was to reign, constituted the great subject-matter of the Old Testament.

We learn, in fact, that the Levitical rites and ceremonies performed by the priesthood point to Christ himself, as the great high priest: the kingly dignity of David points to Christ as the great king of his Church; nearly all the prophetic writings point to him, as the great prophet: all the sacrifices offered, point to him as the great sacrifice; and, I say, we have now an understanding of the subject, which the Jews did not possess, and which, until the coming of Christ, they were unable to possess.

Here is a grand advantage—the advantage of possessing "It is written;" for by the New Testament Scriptures, we are enabled to understand what is written in the Old; yes, I repeat, we understand what is written in the Old, by what is written in the New: the one being a series of mysteries, the other an explanation, an infallible explanation, of those mysteries.

This leads me to the second advantage which we possess in, "It is written." Not only have we an inspired explanation, of inspired Scriptures, but we have, in the fact of possessing that inspired explanation, the best means of becoming acquainted with the divine character as therein revealed.

Atheists and Deists have professed to ridicule as absurd the idea of God committing anything to writing respecting Himself. I have often wondered what these men would be at. Are they so very ignorant as not to know the great difficulty with which an account passes from one hand to another without being mutilated and distorted? If God had left his character without committing it to writing, what form would it have assumed, long before it had reached our own times? The way in which the Jews distorted it, though it *had* been committed to writing; the awful way in which the Church of Rome, the Greek Church, and even Protestants have distorted the doctrines of God's Word, is an answer. If, with the written testimony before them, the whole nevertheless has been so distorted; if left to *oral* tradition only, how much more fearfully abused would it necessarily have been? Look at the heathen nations, and the manner in which they have distorted and still distort facts. You cannot take up the Metamorphoses of Ovid, or the Theogony of Hesiod, which treat of the genealogy and doings of the gods, without seeing that they all point to divine testimony continually. You cannot peruse the account of Deucalion's flood, or the labours of Hercules, without seeing that Deucalion points to Noah, and Hercules to Samson; and perceiving that they are fictions founded on facts contained in God's word, how wondrously distorted they have become in the hands of men, who had nothing but *tradition* to guide them to the relation of facts. If the Scriptures had not been written by expressly divine authority, in what state would divine truth have come down to us? It is difficult to say; and therefore, "*it is written,*" not only gives an inspired explanation in the New, of the inspired oracles of the Old Testament, but we have, in the fact of their being a surety and a certainty of what God has declared, an understanding of them, which, apart from such Scriptures, we never could have had.

See the providence of God, in the way that these Scriptures have come down to us. We know that, fearfully as the Jews violated God's law, and abused His testimony, still they never dared to change it. We are told by learned men, that they (the Jews) were extremely cautious about changing—even to the changing of a single point or letter. Hence the Scriptures, which bear testimony, even, against them and their iniquities, are brought down, pure and unmutilated, to the Christian Church. This is the advantage of having them written. So in New Testament times, though the Romish Church makes use of tradition, in order to keep the Scriptures from the laity, and declares that the priests alone are competent to explain them, still the Romish Church, with all its misdoings, has never dared to meddle with the letter of Scripture.

Thus then, in the course of God's providence, we have had transmitted to us, writings concerning God's character, which, only in that way, could have come down to us undistorted and unmutilated; and in the present Christian version, we have had the minds of our translators and compilers so *reverently* fixed upon their task, that, knowing that it was God who wrote, they have not dared to change it. We have, therefore, got our version of the Scriptures as nearly as possible, with very few exceptions, brought down to our own times, almost as pure as when it came fresh from the fountain of inspiration itself.

Then, last of all, by having the Scriptures in writing, we have God Himself speaking to us, just as He spoke to the prophets, apostles, and saints of old. Oh, this is a most glorious privilege, arising from the *writing* of the Scriptures—the writing of this book. Why, my friends, if a man had come to me with a message, and said; Thus saith the Lord, and yet in that message had pointed to tradition, I might have been suspicious, that his own folly was, in some way, mixed up with his message, and therefore I could not receive it, as God's word; but when I find that what our Blessed Lord said, when in the flesh, his apostles, inspired by him, had recorded; and when I find recorded what he spoke to the children of men; when I find him addressing me directly, through the medium of what is here recorded, I feel what blessedness it is, that I hear the same language, addressed to me by the Father of Spirits, that was heard by the apostles and the first believers themselves. The blessedness is, that I hear it, just as they heard it—that He speaks to me through His lively oracles and testimony. I hear Him and live; I hear Him and live, by the spiritual power that comes forth in His own adorable word.

I have been obliged to speak at such length upon the points on which I have already touched, that I cannot go on further, as I see that my time is expiring, but I have indeed much more to say, with regard to the practical application of the text to ourselves.

It will, however, be enough for me if I shall have suggested to you, the value of the formula "*It is written.*" The language of Christ and his apostles, "*It is written,*" is the infallible explanation of the Old Testament Scriptures. "*It is written,*" is the grand source of all information, and instruction, as it is the sole source of divine testimony, to your minds and mine.

The Lord bless what has been spoken, and may He bless the various exercises of this day, in so far as they have been performed agreeably to His mind and will.

SERMON IX.

November 5th, 1854.

It would have gratified me (if my eyesight had been sufficiently good) to have read the exact words of my text, and two other passages which are illustrative of it; but, I am afraid, I cannot. There is one passage which I wished particularly to bring under your notice. While our blessed Lord was in the flesh, we read of one going to him to solicit his intervention in the case of a disputed inheritance. You will remember, his answer was, "Who made me a judge or a divider over you?"

I should have liked also to read, at some length, the language of Christ at the bar of Pontius Pilate, when Pilate asked him, "Art thou the king of the Jews?" I should have dwelt particularly upon the words "My kingdom is not of this world. If my kingdom were of this world, then would my servants fight, that I should not be delivered to the Jews; but now is my kingdom not from hence." And so on. I should like to have read the whole of the passage, and to have brought under your notice other passages, in connection with it. But as I cannot do this, I would ask you, first of all, to refer to the 10th chapter of the First Epistle of Paul to the Corinthians, and the 15th verse, "I speak as unto wise men, judge ye what I say." And then I would ask you also to read the 4th verse of the 2nd chapter of the First Epistle to the Corinthians, where the apostle, speaking with reference to the first time he went to the Corinthian Church, declaring the testimony of God, says, "My speech and my preaching was not with enticing words of man's wisdom, but in demonstration of the spirit and of power." You may at once perceive the connection between the two passages to which I have referred, but perhaps their connection will appear more obvious as I proceed.

Since the period of the Reformation, there has been

no doctrine more insisted on, and more regarded as characteristic of Protestantism, than the right of private judgment. It is claimed by every sect of Protestants, and to claim it and act upon it, are regarded as the grand badges of distinction between free-born men, and the slavish subjects of the Pope of Rome. It is a doctrine claimed by me; it is claimed by you; it is acted upon by both of us. Still, however, strange consequences—practical as well as theoretical—have followed from this doctrine, or rather from the expression and application of it. We have, on every side around us, persons claiming the right of private judgment, and sitting in judgment upon the word of God itself. In Germany, they are rejecting whole books, and where the Scriptures are not rejected (but treated as worthy of some regard), there are men who reject their inspiration.

In some instances, where men have not gone so far as this, they, at all events, reject the doctrine of the "Manifestation of God in flesh;" they reject the efficacy of His "atoning sacrifice;" they reject the fact of "His righteousness being that alone in which the sinner can appear with acceptance before God." We find a Chillingworth, claiming and exercising this right of private judgment, and under the influence of it, at one time a professed member of the Church of England; at another time a professed Roman Catholic; at another time returning to the Church, with which he had been originally connected; and latterly, suspected of having no fixed religion at all. And we find still more eminent individuals—the celebrated Edward Gibbon, for instance, author of the "Decline and Fall of the Roman Empire," appearing first as a Protestant; then professing the Popish religion; and terminating, by throwing religion, of all kinds, overboard. We know that many other eminent men have been known to act on similar principles—and in a similar way—and we know that many men and women—not eminent—have acted and do act in a like manner.

You ask, why is this? They say, they were acting upon true Protestant principles; they were exercising the right of private judgment, that right, in the exercise of which Luther denounced the tyranny as well as exposed the corruptions of the Church of Rome. It is that by which our English and Scotch reformers overturned Popery in these realms; it is that, through the medium of which "Protestant" Europe has advanced in science and civilization, beyond its Roman Catholic compeers: and, they add, it is that which, as exercised by us, and by persons similarly circumstanced to us, will terminate in the subversion of every species of superstition (they, by what they call superstitions, too often mean God's own blessed truth, among the rest); it is that, through the medium of which every species of superstition will disappear, and the minds of men be emancipated from all human thraldom.

We stand aghast at this! Can such consequences, say we, follow from a true principle? Is the right of private judgment a Scriptural right? and if it be a Scriptural right, has it been rightly understood? Is there no sort of deception practised by these people upon themselves, and upon others, in reference to this matter? Let the thing be examined.

My dear fellow-Christians, I stand before you as one who has had this subject very much under his notice for a number of years. It has been the subject-matter of my most serious and Scriptural reflections. I stand before you, as one, who, in the light of Scripture itself, has been enabled to see (upon the whole at any rate), what the truth respecting it is, and who would therefore desire, distinctly and fearlessly, to proclaim it. I would observe, that like a number of other blessings, it has been much abused. False views of the doctrine of private judgment—have commonly sprung from our not distinguishing between truth and error—from not understanding our Lord's language when he said, "Give unto Cæsar the things which are Cæsar's, and unto God the things which are God's;" and which has sprung from our not understanding the value of the doctrine of Divine Inversion, that doctrine which shews the everlasting opposition which does, and which ever must subsist, between the things of men and the things of God.

The general result of my Scriptural investigation upon this subject has been—to speak paradoxically—the confirmation of the doctrine on the one hand, and the refutation of it on the other. I have seen it to be true, and I have seen it to be false; in other words—viewed in one light, and looked at under one aspect, it is true and gloriously true; viewed in another light and looked at under another aspect, it is false—it is only when we are enabled, in the light of God's blessed testimony, to understand where the truth lies, and are enabled thereby to lay down the line of demarcation between the true and the false, that the subject opens up to us in its true bearing, and that we find ourselves relieved from a network of difficulties, in which we were formerly entangled.

Well, then, the simple fact is, that the doctrine of the

right of private judgment, in matters of religion, is true, as regards man; it is false, as regards God. Let me try to bring the subject before you as pointedly as I can. In the first place, the doctrine is true, gloriously true, as regards man; I stand before you, asserting the doctrine of the right of private judgment, in matters of religion, in the highest sense of the term—as respects my fellow-men—but, in doing so, I go along with those only who assert this right on the same principles, and with the same object. Now, to comprehend what I mean by this, I understand that no tribunal upon earth—be it civil, or be it so-called ecclesiastical—has a right to summon any human being before its bar, to try and condemn him upon the score of his religious tenets. I am speaking now of religious professors as a whole; I am not speaking of the people of God in particular; but whether considered as such, or as holding some peculiar doctrine, they are not amenable to any human tribunal, on the score of religion. At the period of man's fall, when his conscience was stimulated into exercise, it became the province of God to deal with it, and it has been the province of God to deal with man's conscience ever since. Some will tell me, that there was one very remarkable exception. Well, I know there was, in the case of the Jewish people. They were a people, specially set apart by God. But then, you will perceive, from the nature of the exception, that they were a "typical" people. The Jews had divine views proclaimed to them. They had particular divine rules prescribed to them. They were not permitted to take different views, or to follow different practices from those that were laid down in the Old Testament Scriptures; this however was, not because *man* was to be their judge, but because *God* was their judge. The Jewish people formed a theocracy—that is, God was the immediate King of that people; over them God reigned, through the medium of direct manifestations, through the medium of Urim and Thummim; through the medium of communications made from time to time to the prophets. And therefore, while I admit that the Jews were amenable, as far as their consciences were concerned, to God,—or rather to the tribunals which God had set up, and which God had endowed with His Spirit (for even in these human tribunals God was still the actor); while I admit this, I observe that the Jews form an exception, but upon grounds which will only be understood by every Christian man; that is, upon the ground of their "typical" character.

Setting the Jews aside, however, I repeat, that no human

being is amenable to his fellow-men for the religious views he may entertain. These religious views constitute a matter between God and his own conscience, and when any human tribunal takes upon itself to judge men, in reference to religion—whether the tribunal call itself a secular court, or give itself the title of a Holy Inquisition—it is acting in the very teeth of God's word; it is forgetting the conduct of our blessed Lord, when he refused to become "a judge or a divider," or to intercefere in any secular matter, or in any respect whatever to act as one who passed judgment upon secular affairs. And, it shews ignorance also, for Christ declared that "His kingdom is not of this world;" which is manifestly true, because, if his kingdom were of this world, he would have employed servants to defend his cause; if his kingdom were of this world, he would have set up tribunals, civil and ecclesiastical, and would have ordered that the people should be judged through the medium of such tribunals. But his kingdom not being of this world, he will not allow, nor will he sanction, human beings acting, as if they had any authority—either of themselves, or from him—to interfere in the religious views and sentiments of their fellow-men.

Observe how I express myself. I am speaking now of religious views and sentiments. But, I do conceive the civil magistrate to have a right to interfere, where (under the pretence of religion) common morality is assailed, or the foundations of morality sapped and undermined. Human society is founded upon morals. Human society is maintained by means of a due regard to morals; the man who violates morals outrages human society, and violates his own conscience, and in so doing becomes amenable to the jurisdiction of the civil magistrate—therefore, where morals are concerned, the civil magistrate has a perfect right to interfere, because the interests of civil society are entrusted to his charge, and he is bound to see that morals are not violated; he knows that were a violation of morals tolerated, civil society would soon fall to pieces; and he knows that a just condemnation, for his neglect in the discharge of his duty, would necessarily and properly fall upon his head.

Well then, the grand doctrine is, that in so far as conscience—that is, the principles of religion—are concerned; in regard to no human being has the civil magistrate any right to interfere, for he is not lord of the conscience, and whenever he attempts to interfere with conscience, he steps out of his province, and usurps an authority that does not belong to him. Whenever men are guilty of what is unjust; whenever men are guilty of theft, or murder, or bear false testimony against their neighbours, or slander them, or commit any other offence against public morals, the civil magistrate has a right to interfere, and must interfere; and I, and every man, contending for the right of private judgment, in the fullest extent of the term, will go along with the civil magistrate, in endeavouring to put down every thing that is unjust, cruel, and impure; every thing that would attack the rights of property, and otherwise be inconsistent with the correctness of morals.

In the second place, as regards man, I assert the right of private judgment in matters of religion, peculiarly with reference to the Saints of God. I say with reference to them peculiarly, because, although a violation of the right of private judgment, with regard to mere professors of religion and unregenerate men, is wrong; they will take care to redress themselves in their own way. Take in modern times: the case of the Bohemians, who, because the clergy refused the cup in the Sacrament, rose in arms. Take our own country, where there was a great deal of this feeling exhibited in the reign of Charles I., which resulted in the Parliamentary wars. Take Scotland, where a great deal of what occurred with regard to the Covenanters, was simply a contest between the human conscience and the tyranny of interference with it, on the part of human authority.

The Church of God stands in a peculiar position, and we can understand why the members of the Church occupy a peculiar position with regard to their fellow-men. If I am not a Christian, any attempt to violate the right of private judgment arouses my resentment, and stimulates me to get others to join with me in conspiracy and rebellion against the civil authorities. Not so with the Christian. It is true that the Son of God has set him free, free from himself, and from human authority, in matters of religion. It is true that he has been convened before a far higher tribunal than that of men, convened before the tribunal of the Lord. It is true that he has been thus tried and pronounced innocent; yea more, pronounced to be just through the efficacy of that blood which cleanses from all sin. It is true that he finds himself one with Christ, and, as such, entitled to sit down with him upon his throne. It is true that he is not now in the position of a criminal, but in the position of a justified son, an heir of God, and a joint heir with Christ. Yet, as Christ was himself brought before a human tribunal, because he said he was the Son of God, so, mere men have in every age presumed to summon the people of God before human tribunals, and there try and condemn them. But no child of God, acting under the influences of Christian principles, will ever resort to force to maintain his creed.

Now, the people of God stand in this peculiar predicament. Knowing that Christ's kingdom is not of this world, knowing that the Lord of Glory himself, instead of employing force to defend his rights, submitted to be bound, submitted to be led and nailed to the "accursed tree," by his own creatures; for, "He was led as a lamb to the slaughter, and as a sheep before her shearers is dumb, so he opened not his mouth." They know that their business in this, as in all other respects, is to imitate their divine master; therefore, when they are brought before human tribunals, and are tried and condemned, for entertaining those religious views which Christ has committed to them; their business is to take it patiently, to receive it as coming from the hand of God, though through the instrumentality of man. They are at liberty, like Saint Paul, to plead their privileges, if they have any, and to rescue themselves from human thraldom by any lawful means; but, where this cannot be accomplished, and punishment cannot be avoided, on account of the unjust and unscriptural views of their fellow-men, they must submit to it patiently; they cannot oppose force by force, upon Christian principles; their business is, if it must be so, to yield themselves to that punishment, which men—upon mistaken principles—shall see meet to inflict upon them.

Persons so situated however, may make use of the right of private judgment. The more Christ shines into their hearts, manifesting the truth as it is in him, the more will they declare on every fitting opportunity what they have seen and been taught, and do it openly, honestly, and fearlessly; they know, that however man may condemn, God approves; they know, that though man may curse them, and visit them with pains and penalties, yet, that the Spirit of grace and glory rests upon them; they know, that in proportion as they profess God's truth, and in proportion as they suffer for that truth, they stand in the same predicament in which the Son of God stood; they know that they are acting upon the principle, that "Christ's kingdom is not of this world." In all this they are assuming that very right of private judgment which Christ himself assumed; and they are exercising that right in so far as man is concerned, as a duty, and what is far more, as a Christian privilege.

Now, I assert the right of private judgment, particularly for the people of God, because it is their prerogative to be set free by Christ from themselves and from the world; they are not persons to be judged by others, but persons to be the judges of others—"Know ye not that the saints shall judge the world?" They are not persons to be convened to man's bar; but, on the contrary, men are the persons to be convened to their bar; they are God's children and joint heirs with Christ, and overcome the world, even by his faith.

Peter and Paul and persons so situated have a rightful claim to exercise this prerogative; as taught by God, and strengthened by God, they are the very persons to claim the right of private judgment; as it is God's truth they hold and proclaim they are right, and the world is wrong. They labour under God, whom the world hates; they love God, and have a right to proclaim what has been made known to them, let the consequences be what they may. Observe, they have no more right than the world to say to another man; You must take my views. Do not mistake me, I am not claiming for the people of God authority to judge others in this manner. They judge the world after a very different fashion; they do not judge the world after an earthly fashion at all. No man is entitled to say to others —even though they be unregenerate men—you must take my views, any more than the civil tribunal has a right to interfere with the consciences of men in the way of inflicting pains and penalties upon them, on the ground of their religious sentiments. If any man dares attempt this, he does what Christ did not do, and he does what is inconsistent with true religion. His business is to proclaim the truth, and to proclaim it fearlessly, and, if necessary, to proclaim it by the force of argument, but he must leave the consequences of his appeals to the consciences of his fellow-men, with God; knowing that the moment he inflicts, or attempts to inflict, the slightest evil upon his fellow-men, for conscience sake, he is justifying the world in what it does, and is justifying the civil tribunals in their interference with the consciences of men. Therefore, no man acting under the influence of Christian principles, will ever in the slightest degree inflict any injury upon his fellow-men, on the ground of religion.

Now, having asserted the right of private judgment in these respects, that is, as respects man; having asserted this right for all my fellow-men, against every species of interference with their consciences, on the part of earthly tribunals—whether civil or ecclesiastic; having asserted it still more, for believers of the truth as it is in Jesus, having asserted their freedom to proclaim what Christ teaches, and as Christ enables them,—and this without in the slightest degree imposing any civil penalty on, or doing any civil injury to, their fellow-men;—having asserted these things, I go on to observe, on the other hand, what I do not contend for.

I loathe and abhor the doctrine of the right of private judgment, when it is applied to God,—for instance, where a man comes forward and tells me he has a right to judge God's Word.

Ah! and have there ever been such persons? Yes; such persons have existed, and do exist; and such persons are at the present time shewing the most outrageous insolence in their conduct towards the Most High! It is in this respect that Protestantism has run riot, and become rank. It is perfectly true that, of a revelation which falsely pretends to come from God,—human beings may be competent judges. If you present the Vêdas of the Brahmins to me, I have little difficulty in seeing that they are not from God, and I may do this without knowing God, because there is something in the nature of man which instinctively revolts from such doctrines as the Vêdas contain. Again, I have little difficulty, in looking over the Koran of Mahomet, in perceiving that it is merely a human composition. Men may sit in judgment, in all safety, upon that which pretends to be Divine, but which really comes from the hands of men. I believe there is little difficulty in proving the Apocrypha to be merely of human origin; and therefore, concerning this, I think we have a right to sit in judgment upon it. In the introduction to the book called "The Wisdom of Jesus," or "Ecclesiasticus," for instance, we find that the writer of it begs pardon for any blunders he may have committed. This condemns the whole book. In cases of this kind, we are perfectly entitled, as human beings, to sit in judgment. We are entitled to sit in judgment upon all human compositions *pretending* to be Divine.

Not so with God's Word—God's Word sets our judgment of it at defiance. It does not subject itself to us; it does not place itself at the tribunal of man's conscience. When God's Word comes home to us; whenever it is carried home to the conscience, in demonstration of the spirit and of power, it is as our judge: it does not permit us to judge it, and the reason is most obvious. When God speaks, He speaks as our mediator, and no creature whatever has any right to sit in judgment upon the sayings and doings of the Creator. Why, the very idea is preposterous, if you reflect upon it. When God speaks, and when God is heard speaking in His Word, the creature yields, or rather is made to yield, to it; the creature no longer sits in judgment upon God's Word, but finds that the Word of God has, as it should do, been sitting in judgment upon him.

Well then, we have the most perfect right to exercise private judgment, in matters of religion, as respects our fellowmen; but we have no right whatever to exercise private judgment as respects God, nor does the believer of the truth attempt to exercise it; but, in proportion as God's Word is made known to him, and is carried home to his conscience, in demonstration of the spirit and of power, in the same proportion is he made more submissive to it. This may be made to appear in several ways. In proportion as God's Word is made known to us, our own judgment is set aside and superseded by the judgment of God, which is heavenly and divine. Take an instance in proof of this. Naturally, I have no idea of any way of getting to heaven but by my own abstinence from evil, and by my own personal righteousness; but when the Gospel is revealed to me, I discover that I never could have got to heaven in any such way. I find that I am a guilty creature, possessed of no righteousness of my own, and that I stand condemned before God. The Scriptures shew me the Son of man, the Lord from heaven, who brought in everlasting righteousness, and that he who brought in that righteousness is my Saviour; and when my mind is opened to see this, God's judgment becomes my judgment, the views of divine truth that God presents to me through his word approve themselves to my enlightened mind immediately and gloriously; and, instead of, as formerly, my judgment pretending to condemn God's, my former judgment is superseded by God's, and in this respect His judgment becomes my judgment. It is true, the boldness and impudence of men have, in every age, stood up in opposition to such a glorious doctrine as this. It is true, men have said to me, it is a mere fancy of yours that any righteousness performed by another should become your righteousness before God; it would be far better to trust to your own human obedience, than to trust to the obedience even of him whom you call the Son of God. This is a specimen of man carrying out the right of private judgment, in a way not justifiable; it is making his own judgment a means of judging and condemning the views of God. And just so with regard to the grand doctrine of God manifest in the flesh. I have no idea of this naturally; my only idea as a creature is, that I must try to climb to the skies in some way or other. When I am told that God was manifest in flesh, and that God, in the person of His Infinite Son, appeared as man on the earth, fulfilled the law, magnifying it and making it honourable, I cannot realize his divinity, although I may admit his existence as Jesus Christ; and this is the case with the whole body of the Socinians, Arians, and Unitarians. But what is the case with those whose minds have been enlightened by God's word? They find that their former views were entirely erroneous; they find there could be no other plan of salvation but by the union of man with God, or rather, through the union of God with man; they find God's judgment condemning their original views, and they find God's judgment becoming their judgment, by trying and condemning their former natural notions; and thus, instead of using their private judgment in opposition to God, they rejoice to have God's public judgment made theirs; and they rejoice to see, that the manifestation of God in flesh, constitutes the link and the only link, by which the creature could be united with the Creator, and by which the guilty creature could have his sins purged away; and, through his union with the Creator, be raised to the position of a son of God, and an heir of glory.

And so, in other respects, just in proportion as God's mind is revealed to me, it becomes my mind; just in proportion as God's judgments are made known to me, they supersede my own natural judgment of things; and I find that I am not sitting in judgment upon God, but that God is sitting in judgment upon me, and trying and condemning all that is false and natural in me.

Well then, this is the first effect, in the light of which it plainly appears, that in the knowledge of what is heavenly and divine, we become acquainted with the fact that it is not the creature that is sitting in judgment upon the Creator, but the Creator sitting in judgment upon His creatures; we learn that it is the Creator giving His mind to the creature, and the judgment of the Creator becoming the judgment of the creature.

Then, let us remember this—that wherever Christian principles are possessed and exercised, there self-denial makes its appearance, and so essential to a Christian is self-denial, that Christ said, "Except a man deny himself he cannot be my disciple." There never has been, from the beginning of time, a human being one with Christ, who has not been a self-denying man more or less. The Redeemer himself practised self-denial; as we find from the 15th chapter of Romans. I have gone at length into the principle of self-denial, as respects Christ, on former occasions; and I shall perhaps refer to it on some future occasion as respects ourselves. Men naturally do not like to deny themselves—indeed, none but a believer can deny himself—and for an obvious reason. In the use of the lever, you require, not only the lever itself to be put under the weight to be moved, but you require a power to be applied to the lever, and you require also the fulcrum upon which the lever may rest, and by which you must operate upon the mass to be moved. "Give me something upon which to rest my lever," said Archimedes, "and I will move the world." Just so, says Christ, if there be given to you the knowledge of me, which is the earnest of the divine nature, then you can move yourselves, then you can deny yourselves, but not otherwise. Christ shewed the truth of this, when he said, "How can Satan cast out Satan? If Satan cast out Satan, he is divided against himself, how then shall his kingdom stand? And if I, by Beelzebub, cast out devils, by whom do your children cast them out? Therefore they shall be your judges." Human nature cannot cast itself out. I may oppose one earthly principle to another, but I am not denying myself; it is only human nature, under one of its aspects, which I am indulging; but to deny myself, I must have some higher principle: I must have something to rest upon, by which human nature may be moved and denied. And this is found in the knowledge and influence of the truth as it is in Jesus.

It is a blessed fact that Christ makes his judgment our

judgment; as he makes his views of things, our views of things; so, under the influence of the new mind communicated to us, we have the new heart,—in consequence of which we have the earnest of the Divine mind, and are enabled to deny man's mind; but, unless the earnest of the Divine mind be in us, the practice of self-denial is an utter impossibility.

Now, it is only the members of the Church who can deny themselves; and that merely in proportion to the extent to which the mind of Christ dwells in them, and operates upon them. And wherever the mind of Christ does exist, self-denial will be seen in the theories as well as in the conduct of such individuals. A Christian will not be found supporting theories of astronomy which contradict the word of God: he will not deny the facts of astronomy, but he will not support the errors of astronomers. While he admits every fact in geology, he will not maintain theories that contradict the word of God. Where there is Christian principle, there exists the earnest of the Divine nature, by which alone self-denial can be exercised. "I am crucified with Christ, nevertheless I live," is the basis of this doctrine; and the Christian's self-denial will shew itself by the manner in which he exercises the right of private judgment. Where God has spoken divine facts, and where God has made us acquainted with them, we will remember that the shortsightedness of men is never to be made the judge of the declarations and knowledge of the infinite God.

I see my time is nearly exhausted, and I must bring my observations to a close. Well then, you and I came into this world with Adam's mind; and have we the capability naturally of forming judgments of the Creator of Adam's nature? Certainly not. In matters of religion we have the judgment of Adam's nature superseded by God's judgment and revelations of Himself, in so far as these are made known to us, and we do not exercise any right of private judgment with respect to God, but are satisfied to see our vile judgment superseded by His high, heavenly, and wise judgment. We see the heavenly principle superseding human principles, and in that glorious state of existence to which we look forward at Christ's second appearing, when he shall come to conform us to Himself, all rights of private judgment, as respects God, shall be done away. Why? Because God's mind will be ours, in a way and to an extent, of which, in the flesh, we can have no conception. We shall bask in the sunlight of His divine knowledge, being enlightened by heavenly manifestations directly from Himself; and such will be the glory of this heavenly light and love; so completely shall our minds be conformed to the mind of the glorified Jesus, that every sentiment in opposition to God's views shall be completely swept away; our own natural ideas of things will be completely swallowed up in, and superseded by, those glorious views of his character and attributes which God shall then supply, and which, in the unstinted beams of His own divine and heavenly splendour, He will be pleased to communicate.

May the Lord bless what has been spoken, and to His name be praise for ever and ever.—Amen.

SERMON X.

November 12*th*, 1854.

It is more convenient to me to request you to turn up for yourselves the passages of Scripture which are to form the basis of the observations I am now about to address to you. Could I have seen easily, I should have read some Old Testament Scripture passages along with some from the New, but as I cannot do this, I shall confine myself to a few New Testament passages.

I will ask you, first of all, to look to the 1st chapter of St. Matthew's Gospel, towards the close, where the birth of our Lord is mentioned, and especially to the end of the 23rd verse, in which it is stated that his name shall be called Emmanuel, that is, God with us. I would also direct your attention to the 1st chapter of the Gospel of St. John, where we are informed, in the 14th verse, that the Word was made flesh. Observe, the Word, as spoken of in the 1st verse, "In the beginning was the Word, and the Word was with God, and the Word was God; the same was in the beginning with God." *Was God!* Observe that remarkable expresssion: by this Word were "All things made, and without it was not anything made that was made." In the 14th verse it is said, the same "Word was made flesh;" the Word became, or was made flesh, and dwelt among us.

Then look to the 3rd chapter of the First Epistle to Timothy, and the 16th verse; and in spite of all the Unitarian and German criticisms that have been made upon it, I have no hesitation whatever in reading it as it stands in the text:—"God was manifest in the flesh."

I might have called your attention to a number of other passages, such as that in the 2nd chapter of the Hebrews and the 14th verse: "For as much then as the children are partakers of flesh and blood, he also himself likewise took part of the same," and various Old Testament passages I might have brought in, but I think I have selected enough to induce you to pursue the subject further, through the medium of a copy of the Bible possessing marginal references. These will guide you to many other passages bearing upon those I have already alluded to. All such passages are from beginning to end combined with the 12th chapter of St. John's Gospel, 10th and 11st verses; and I have no doubt that on examination you will find them all pointing to, bearing upon, and proving one and the same thing.

Scripture abounds in paradoxes. A paradox may popularly be defined to be a statement of some fact which appears to contradict some other well-known and ascertained fact, and which appears, therefore, to involve an impossibility.

Paradoxes, as we all know, are not confined to the Scriptures. Several of my audience, I have no doubt, have from time to time looked into books of science, and even such as have not done so, may have perused popular works on geography and other subjects, which are commonly studied. In these you will find a great number of what are called paradoxes set forth. I have no intention to enter into these; but there is one fact that all of you are aware of. The earth to all appearance is at rest, but astronomers tell us that it is incessantly whirling round upon its own axis with most amazing velocity; and that it is not only turning round upon its own axis, but that every day it is making progress in its own orbit round the sun. There is something paradoxical in this at first sight, something contradictory and irreconcileable, between the apparently perfect state of rest of the earth, and the incessant state of whirl in which we are told it exists.

Then again, it appears paradoxical when we are told that there are persons existing in our world, whose feet are turned towards ours—and yet if this earth be a globe, as we are told by astronomers it is, it is obvious that such antipodes exist; that we are antipodes, or nearly so, to the people of Australia, and that they are antipodes to us; that is, their feet are turned towards us, and ours towards them. It appears extraordinary that this should be the case; but we know this, that by sailing some thousands of miles in one direction, we come to them upon the globe, and by continuing to sail in the same direction, we arrive again at the place from which we started.

And thus I might bring before you from popular works of science many things, either stated in a paradoxical form, or introduced as paradoxes to incite us to inquiry. Whatever may be the case with reference to human compositions on science, there is no doubt the Scriptures do abound in paradoxes—paradoxes of the most remarkable description, but paradoxes without which the Scriptures would lose one grand exhibition of their divine character and origin.

If Scripture presented to me nothing but what my paltry human understanding could grasp; if Scripture presented to me nothing sublimer and more profound than my every day observation presents to my view, it must be put upon a footing with the common shallow productions of the human mind; but coming as it does, from the Infinite Jehovah, it bears this character of its divine origin among others, that from time to time it suggests ideas far surpassing those which our minds or the minds of others have ever suggested; ideas studded and fraught with evidence the most intense and the most sublime, of the divine source from which they proceed.

What can be conceived more paradoxical than to be told that beings like us, who fret upon the fitful stage of time; that beings like us, who number at the utmost about three score years and ten, or four score years, and then return to the dust from which we were taken; that beings like us, whose days are spent in vanity, and who undergo numerous and incessant sufferings from the cradle to the tomb; that beings like us also live for evermore?—beings of a day, and also beings of eternal duration! Yet so it is, and the explanation is most satisfactory.

But at first sight the paradox is marvellous; it appears utterly impossible. Some human beings have tried to solve it on the principle of the natural immortality of the human soul. But men who have been taught the truth as it is in Jesus, see through the falsehood of this. Other men, of profound thinking in natural things, have seen reason to doubt the *fact;* but we realise it by our knowledge of the existence of two men; the first man of the earth earthy, and the second man the Lord from heaven. Man as one with the former finite, but infinite as one with man the Creator—in the one capacity the being of a day; in the other capacity the being that lives for evermore; not by some natural power or immortality of his own, but immortal, as one with Him who is the source of immortality, namely, the living and true God—Jesus Christ.

And so again, men are sinful here; we are told in Scripture that they are sinful. Ay! and we there find their character painted in the most fearful colours; but we are told also that the same beings are righteous—divinely righteous too—a paradox of the most remarkable description. So again, by knowing that men are sinful in the creature Adam, but not only sinless but divinely righteous in Christ Jesus the second man, the Lord from heaven, we are presented with another paradox. We are presented with the paradox that man is dead and yet alive for ever—dead in the creature, alive for ever in the Creator. We are presented with the paradox that men are weak, yet that they are strong—weak as creatures, yet strong as possessed of the strength of Jehovah himself.

And so I might go on, for the Scriptures are paradoxical from beginning to end, *and paradoxical because they are true;* —paradoxical, because they present to me and to you two distinct and opposite sets of views—views that are human, contrasted with views that are divine.

But I think the grand paradox of the whole is, that which I bring before you this morning. The paradox of a Being who is at once God and man—the infinite Jehovah, and yet apparently circumscribed by the form, and circumscribed by the mind of a creature.

Scripture is true: we rejoice in the knowledge of this revealed fact, for it is as revealed alone we know it; and we know that paradoxical as it is, it is true, and not only true, but possessed of unspeakable interest to us, for it is that which alone explains to us the phenomena of our creation and existence here below. It is what explains the phenomena of the entrance of sin and death into the world. It is what alone conducts us through the labyrinths of Providence—through all the intricacies of this world's career, and what alone makes the whole plan of God plain, and enables us to know that the child of earth is also the child of immortality.

Paradoxical! Yes: and it is this grand paradox which stamps Scripture to be what it is—the word of God. Impossible! I hear pronounced with a most singular tone of voice, by a certain number of individuals who, though they trample under foot the Scriptures and the grand truths they reveal, would, nevertheless fain be denominated Christians, at all events for the sake of the respectability of character which it confers. Impossible! A being, God and yet man? The thing is never for a moment to be thought of: it is an absurdity. Who told you so? What proof can you bring that it is absurd? Human proofs? Human suggestions? Human ideas? A whole mass of human systems and reasonings? This is admitted. What then? If you could bring us a proof from God himself that the thing was false, you would bring us an evidence of its falsehood infinitely more important than all the reasons which either your brains or the brains of others have ever suggested: let God say it is false and we are satisfied.

Impossible? What is impossible with God? Do *you* know the infinite one? Do you know what infinitude is? Before you pronounce anything to be impossible with God, you must be possessed of something like a divine nature.

But, say they, God has said there are some things that He cannot or will not do. We know that God says He cannot lie nor repent, and we are satisfied; for we know that He speaks a truth; but we cannot permit you to be the judge of what God cannot do; we cannot permit you to say that a thing is impossible with God; we cannot permit the creature in this or in any other respect to sit in judgment upon the revealed testimony of the Creator.

Impossible? Do you know that Jesus himself hath said, all things are possible with God? And do not some of you profess to believe in God's omnipotence—or, in other words —God's infinite power. And if I merely made the argument one to yourselves, I would ask you, How do you reconcile your denial of the possibility of the oneness of man and God, with the fact of your admitting God's omnipotence, and that with Him all things are possible? Oh, but, perhaps it may be said, the thing is a contradiction, an absurdity. What is a contradiction? Have we said, has any man in his sober senses and with his mind enlightened by the Scriptures, ever said that God in becoming man ceased to be God? If I, or if any one had said that, you might indeed charge us with absurdity. No: the infinite Jehovah hath manifested Himself as man; and again and again have I of late years brought under your notice the fact that as Jehovah is infinite in other respects, so He is infinite in His manifestations also; and His manifestation of Himself as man, is one perhaps the grandest of all His manifestations, still it is the manifestation of Jehovah—and Jehovah manifest as man, is still Jehovah.

There are perhaps persons present who know that there was one part of Scripture that was felt by one of the fathers of the Socinians—I think it was Faustus Socinus—the younger of the two—to be one of the difficulties in the establishment of his own system, and consequently in his denial of the deity of Christ; and that was the expression in the 13th verse of the 3rd chapter of John, where our Lord, speaking of himself, employs these remarkable words:— "Even the Son of Man which is in heaven." I think in the original the Greek participle is used—"he *being* in heaven," that is, the very person who was then addressing Nicodemus, represents himself as at that very moment existing eternally and gloriously in heaven.

Socinus felt the force of that expression: he could not get rid of it on the ground of any error in the manuscript, and has left it on record how he felt in rejecting it.

Further, we know this remarkable fact, because it is revealed, that Jehovah, the self-existent one, is also God the self-manifest one; and we know that it was as the self-manifest one that he appeared in flesh. Jehovah, the self-existent, is one with Jehovah the self-manifest one; and the self-manifest is one with His son, manifest in flesh. They are one. Jesus says, I and my Father are one. Therefore, it is not a creature that appeared in flesh: it is the Creator himself. And yet the Creator, appearing in flesh, did not cease to be God. He was God, and yet was one with him that was manifested—that is, God man appeared upon earth, and yet there was no interference with the unchangeableness of the infinite Jehovah: He was still what from everlasting he had been, and what from everlasting to everlasting he will be. He was merely manifest—manifest as man—manifest in the way of shewing to innumerable generations of the children of men his character, and thereby raising them to heaven along with himself.

A contradiction is something that involves an absurdity. I am aware it would be an absurdity if we were to speak of a *man* manifest in flesh. We should be laughed at by every sensible and thinking person. We may be told by an Arian, and we cannot dispute the fact, that it was not exactly a man that came in flesh, but it was some great and superior being—some member of the angelic host—some one who perhaps excelled the angelic host, as the head of angels. But we stop you and say, "Dear friend, we have no sort of idea of any value attaching to any creature manifest in flesh, and we might turn the tables upon you and say, that the manifestation of a creature for the purposes for which Jesus appeared, would be in our apprehension of things an utter absurdity. We cannot conceive of a being who is himself finite, performing a work which it was competent only for the Infinite to perform. We can understand the Infinite appearing circumscribed by the attributes of the finite; we can understand the infinite in that capacity, accomplishing the work which God's word represents Jesus as having done; but the idea of an angel or archangel coming in flesh for such a purpose, we not only reject as unscriptural, but throw aside as absurd." There is therefore no contradiction in the case, because he who appeared in flesh was God, and yet, in appearing as God manifest in flesh, he underwent no change; he was the same yesterday, to-day, and for ever. Therefore when you talk of the impossibility of this matter, we deny the competency of the creature to judge of what it is impossible for God to do; and we defy him—not on principles of paltry human reason, but upon principles of a higher kind—to prove the impossibility of the thing. And as he must deny the omnipotence of Jehovah in denying the possibility of this manifestation, we leave him to reconcile his own pretended admission of the divine omnipotence with his denial that God could become manifest as man.

Well then, what I bring under your notice this morning is this paradox, God-man; a paradox with which I became acquainted in early life—one which it has been my lot to think over, again and again, during the thirty or forty years in which my reflective powers have been exercised; it is one which grows upon me in beauty and importance the more I come to understand it; one which beams from every page of the sacred volume; one in which I have gloried while living, and one in which I will glory for ever. It is the truth of truths; without it Scripture would be a blank; with it, Scripture beams with light from beginning to end.

As to the texts I have selected, they appear to prove it in a manner the most satisfactory, in a manner the most distinct and uncontradictory. The name given was significant of the divine mind—the name given before his birth to the future Saviour of the world—Emanuel, God with us, is not such a name as we give to our children; not a name given by man to his fellow-man; but a name given by God to His Son, His well-beloved and only begotten Son.

And again it is proved by the 1st chapter of John. The Word (which word is expressly declared to be God) the Word was made flesh; that is, taking the two passages together, God was made flesh—appeared in the likeness of man.

Then again, I care not whether you take the passage in the 3rd chapter of the 1st Epistle to Timothy and 16th verse, with the translation given to it in our version, and which I believe to be correct, or whether you take it with the word which the whole Arian and Socinian body read, and for the Greek word θεὸς, you substitute ὅς. I care not whether you take the one or the other, because as Mr. Penn in a very beautiful criticism upon this text has shewn, if you were to look at the construction of the 15th and 16th verses of the 3rd chapter of 1st Timothy, and regard a certain portion of these verses as a parenthesis—he shews how they stand connected and why they are so—you would find that the living God still comes in as the party spoken of as manifest in flesh; you would find it is "the living God (then comes the parenthesis) who was manifest in the flesh." I have no hesitation in saying that I believe θεὸς is the word here meant, and "God was manifest in the flesh," appears to me not only as verbally recorded there, but to be the explanation of every other passage of the sacred volume where doctrines emanating from and founded upon it are involved.

There is one passage which I should have alluded to as a text, and which I should have liked to go over, had my eye-sight permitted, and that is the 6th chapter of Isaiah. It is short, but sublime and striking, and well calculated to excite reflection:—"In the year that king Uzziah died, I saw also the Lord sitting upon a throne high and lifted up, and his train filled the temple." Then he describes the seraphims before him and round about him with their wings:—"Above it stood the seraphims; each one had six wings; with twain he covered his face, and with twain he covered his feet, and with twain he did fly." And then the prophet proceeds to describe the language which fell from their lips:—"And one cried unto another and said, Holy, holy, holy is the Lord God of Hosts." And then it is said in the 12th chapter of John's Gospel, thus spake Esaias when he saw his glory—that is, Christ's glory, and spake of him. Thus then we have Jehovah himself spoken of as the Being whom Isaiah saw, this Jehovah being afterwards found incarnate in the person of Jesus Christ.

My dear, dear friends, the two terms, Lord and God, are not set down in Scripture for naught. Lord, Jehovah; God, manifest one; the self-existent one, Jehovah; the self-manifest one, God; for it is not a creature that appeared when Jesus appeared, but it was the Creator manifesting Himself to man. Jesus is the Creator manifest; not the Creator seen through the creature, but the Creator Himself seen, for he says, "He that hath seen and known me, hath seen and known the Father."

I never found my mind so powerfully impressed as when

reading that magnificent though brief chapter, the 1st chapter of the general Epistle to the Hebrews, and when I observed the striking climax by which the Holy Ghost ascends to the proof of the deity of Christ. After having shewn that he is the object of the angels' worship—"Let all the angels of God worship him"—after having shewn that the angels are God's creatures, and his ministers a flame of fire, and so on, he gives to the Son the character of God :—" Thy throne, O God, is for ever and ever ; a sceptre of righteousness is the sceptre of Thy kingdom." There is no such thing as a Unitarian ὅς, implying that this is not addressed to him ; it is addressed to him as God over all blessed for ever. But, not satisfied with this, the Holy Ghost goes on immediately to ascribe to him the still higher character of Jehovah. It is quoted from the 102nd psalm—"Thou, Lord (Jehovah), in the beginning didst lay the foundations of the earth, and the heavens are the works of Thy hands. They shall perish but Thou remainest ; and they all shall wax old as doth a garment, and as a vesture shalt thou fold them up, and they shall be changed ; but Thou art the same and Thy years shall not fail."

My friends, with such a remarkable passage as this before us, and with such a glorious description as that from Isaiah, proving that the being Isaiah saw in his glory was the Lord, as a priest on his throne in a priestly temple, and that that being was the Christ looked forward to for thousands of years with the eye of faith, can we entertain a doubt that Jesus was God with us? that God was manifest in flesh ? that the Creator of the world became apparent in the form of a creature, tabernacled among us for a time, and, when the purposes of his manifestation were accomplished, re-ascended to that glory from which he had previously descended?

God-man, is the language I employ, because it is the import of the language that God uses. Jesus, I say, was God. I have shewn that he is Jehovah too. I have shewn that he is the Lord God—the Jehovah God of the Old Testament Scriptures. You may perceive this proved in a remarkable way. When Paul was journeying towards Damascus, and breathing forth threatenings and slaughter against the Lord's disciples, a light, brighter than that of the noonday sun, shone round about him ; that light was immediately recognized by him, he knew that it indicated the presence of Jehovah, the God of Israel, and he knew that he stood in the presence of God. He had been brought up at the feet of Gamaliel ; and he knew that that bright light had travelled with Israel in the wilderness, and that it had dwelt in the temple; he knew that Jehovah was there; he is confounded and falls to the ground; a voice issues forth, "Saul, Saul, why persecutest thou me?" He is addressed in the Hebrew tongue—the tongue peculiar to the Jews; he is astounded at the thought of persecuting Jehovah, astounded as much as any Unitarian could be. God speaking, as if it were a Unitarian denying his deity; for in denying the deity of Jesus, they deny the deity of God; for he that honoreth the Son honoreth the Father, and alone is accepted with Jehovah; just so Saul is astounded when Jehovah asks him, "Why persecutest thou me?" But he is soon made to understand who the being is who speaks to him, for the language next is, "I am Jesus of Nazareth whom thou persecutest; it is hard for thee to kick against the pricks;" that is, thou knowest in whose presence thou art; as a Jew thou knowest that thou art convened, that thou art cited before Jehovah—Jehovah the God of Israel. Now I tell thee from this glory, that Jehovah, the God of Israel, and Jesus of Nazareth are one and the same person. Paul was at once confounded and delighted; he believed it; every doubt fled when Jesus himself condescended to speak to him; when he had proved by irrefragable testimony that the God of the Old Testament was the Jesus of the New.

Not more emphatically is it declared in the words spoken by Jesus, when he says, "I and the Father are one," than it was effectively carried home to the mind of Paul, that the God of Israel, and Jesus of Nazareth, are one and the same.

Well then, God was manifest in the flesh—Jehovah, God, —God and man were shewn to be one and the same. A most remarkable fact is here brought under our notice. After many years study in the schools of philosophy and human theology, I merely accustomed my mind to think that the word man was the name of Adam, and a term applicable to them who bore Adam's nature; and I do not mean to say that I am wrong, or that you are wrong in thinking so, for it is true in a certain sense; but I think the Scriptures, which teach us the true meaning of the name, give us a far higher idea of man than Adam and Adam's nature, or of any being possessed merely of Adam's nature.

I dare say you have observed that remarkable verse, the 5th, in the 2nd chapter of the First Epistle to Timothy, where it is written, "There is one God and one mediator, the man Jesus Christ," the word man being used and applied to Jesus. Now Unitarians say, Christ Jesus is here described as a man; and maintain that he is a mere creature. The emphasis upon *the man*, however, suggests a totally different idea to my mind, for *the man* stands between the Creator and the creature, like the days-man, laying his hands upon both—uniting both; and must have a different meaning from the word man as applied to you and me. It must have a superior meaning, and my mind is carried beyond the bounds of this diurnal sphere; it is carried into the regions of glory—carried up to Christ sitting upon his throne, and there I behold *the man*, not the man in the sense of a being in the Adamic nature, for though Christ took the Adamic nature, when he appeared in flesh, and sacrificed that pure and perfect body on the cross, yet, when he rose in the same body, he rose glorified, he rose in the character of the glorified man.

There is a corresponding text to those I have quoted, in the 15th chapter of the First Corinthians, where it is said, "The second man is the Lord from heaven;" taking these texts together, I perceive that the word man has the sense, not only of Adam possessed of Adam's nature and being, but has the sense of the second man the Lord from heaven, the Lord Jesus Christ, and also the sense of the Creator glorified; and I thus perceive that man, rightly understood in its fullest and highest sense, implies a being possessed of two natures; possessed of the nature of Adam, which is temporary, which is sinful; and a being possessed of the nature of Christ, which is everlasting, which is righteous, and which lives for evermore.

Here I come to understand that, in Scripture, man has actually a higher sense than merely that of a being possessed of Adam's nature. It is one of those words which in one sense are equivocal, and therefore requires minute Scriptural examination, in order to see when it signifies merely a being such as we are, clothed with infirmities—the being of a day; and when it signifies Christ, the second man, the being who descended from heaven to earth, the being who is the same yesterday, and to-day, and for ever; the being who is God over all, blessed for evermore. While in the higher sense I do admit that Jesus is man, it is in the sense of the glorified man that occupies the throne, and gives us to occupy the throne with him as one with him, and as clothed upon with his nature for evermore.

But when I said God-man just now, I was not speaking in the higher sense of the second man existing, as we know he did exist before his manifestation, as we know he does exist now glorified in the presence of the Father, but as made man, as conceived in a Virgin's womb; as he condescended to appear among us for a limited period, or when, to use the language of a beautiful phrase in John, "He was made flesh and dwelt among us;" when he took up a temporary abode amongst us, and we, as the apostle beautifully says, "beheld his glory, the glory of the only begotten of the Father, full of grace and truth;" God manifest, for God manifest is the Son, very God of very God, very light of very light. I do not like the phraseology of the Nicene Creed; but still it expresses a truth so far, that God, self-existent, is also God self-manifest. You will find the deep theology implied in that, not only laid down in John, but also expressed in the 1st of Colossians, the 15th to the 19th verses. There you perceive that Jehovah the self-manifest, is God, while God the Son, God manifest, is man.

We know that Christ appeared in flesh; we rejoice to know this; it is the fundamental truth of revealed religion. If any man deny Christ's coming in flesh, he is antichrist. Therefore, we know that Christ was in flesh during some thirty or forty years, somewhat less than 2,000 years ago, not indeed upon human evidence, but we know it upon the authority of God's inspired testimony.

A man. But say some here, what sort of a man? Ah! there's the rub. Blessed be God, he was not a man who came down arbitrarily from heaven, or made his appearance as Adam did; he was not a man who sprung out of the earth as some fabled monsters of antiquity did. No. He consented to be conceived, to be carried in the womb, to be born as human beings commonly are; he was a man who, while God was his Father, had a woman for his mother; a man who was bone of our bone, and flesh of our flesh; a man who had connected himself primarily with Abraham's descendants, for he came of the seed of David and Jesse, he came of the seed of Abraham, he came of the tribe of Judah. He was a descendant therefore of Israel, and consequently directly connected with the Jewish people. But Abraham was Adam's descendant, and therefore while he took hold of Abraham's, he also took hold of Adam's seed. You will find all this in looking over the genealogy of Christ; you will find that his genealogy is traced to Adam, and therefore to God. Our nature, therefore, he took hold of in coming in flesh.

Herein you will perceive there is at once a sameness and

and a difference; a sameness, for it was our nature that he took hold of. He was bone of our bone, and flesh of our flesh. The children being partakers of flesh and blood, he also took part of the same. Ah! what would have been his appearance in flesh to you and to me, if he had not appeared in the flesh of Adam and Abraham? He might have been an object of wonder, and the amazing tale of his history might have been the foundation of many a human speculation, and we might have philosophised and theorised upon it; but our belief would only have been the belief of the devils, whom we are told believe and tremble. His history is the more engrossing to us, because he was one with us. He took hold of us by the seed of a woman; that woman, the descendant of Eve; that woman, one peculiarly with Abraham's descendants; that woman, one with the family of man. A difference, for he differed from us in his being the second man, the Lord from heaven. He had no man for his father, but was conceived by the power of the Holy Ghost. The word of God was the principle of his existence: he was the Word made flesh; the Old Testament Scriptures were embodied in him.

Here is one grand distinction which lies at the foundation of your immortality and mine, that while you and I have two human parents, and in all respects human, the Son of God had only one human parent—the other was God himself. He thus came to unite the nature of man to the nature of God: he came to make himself for a time one with us in the nature we had in Adam, that he might make us one with him for ever, in that glorious nature which from everlasting belonged to him; for if he descended for a time into the sphere of humanity, it was that he might re-ascend, into the sphere of glory from which he had descended; and that he might reascend, not empty-handed, but carrying with him innumerable captives, captives of joy and triumph—clinging to his chariot-wheels, and rejoicing to be rescued and ransomed and redeemed by him, the mighty conqueror. Knowing that they were carried not back again to the gloomy dungeon from which they had been extricated, but knowing that from that dungeon he had released them and set them free; and knowing that he was carrying them to that throne upon which they were to sit with him, judging the twelve tribes of Israel.

There are some persons who think that God created man to be a sinner, and to die and pass away for ever; and they talk of God as the author of sin and death. Now, if God introduced man into the world as mere man, He was the author of sin and death; but that was not God's object. In Him we live, and move, and have our being, and if man appeared first upon the stage of time, and proved himself a being mutable and capable of sinning, what was God's object? It was that man might pass away, after death had done its office of punishing the being who had transgressed the divine command, it was that the true man might make his appearance, and magnify, and make honourable the law of God, and enjoy glory for ever through his fulfilment of it. And so it was, for God gave His Scriptures to the Son to be fulfilled by him, and he loved them, delighted in them, and fulfilled them; fulfilled them not as a slave, but like a free man, and so completely delighted in the fulfilment of them, that when he cried, "It is finished," he spoke words that come home to your consciences and to mine.

Here, then, is the true man and here is the true reason why Adam was created a mutable being; it was that this true man might come into existence, uniting himself to us in time that we might be united to him for ever; and we, as one with the false and shadowy man, are also one with him the substantial man. It is expressed in these words, in the 15th chapter, 1st Corinthians, that as we have borne the image of the earthy, we shall also bear the image of the heavenly.

I have been so absorbed with this delightful subject, that I could spend hours in speaking of it, and directing your attention to passages of Scripture in which it beams forth. Suffice it to have drawn your attention to this grand paradox,—Jesus, man; Jesus, God; Jesus man, one with us; Jesus was the true man that lives for ever, the true man in whom we also live for ever. And Jesus the true man came to rescue us, as one with the false and shadowy man, from the position in which we were brought by the entrance of sin; and he appeared as one with us and gave us an interest in his life, and, as one with him, an assurance also of enjoyment with him in all the glory and felicity to which by his own righteousness he hath risen.

Thus, then, God man, God one with man in the person of Jesus Christ, is the grand topic of the revelation of God; man one with Christ is the first, the constant, the heavenly source of all the joy and satisfaction we do possess or can possess, while sojourners here below, and is the earnest of that infinite joy which shall be ours when we escape from the earthly house of this tabernacle to our house which is above.

May the Lord bless what has been spoken, and to his name be praise for evermore.—Amen.

SERMON XI.

November 26th, 1854.

I will ask you to excuse my not reading the text, and request you to turn up your Bibles for a moment to the beginning of the 28th chapter of St. Matthew's Gospel. I may just remark, for I cannot read the words, that you will find there, an account of our blessed Lord having risen from the dead, on the first morning of the week; you will find the details concerning it, and if you have bibles with marginal references, you will find that they refer you to corresponding passages in St. Mark, St. Luke, and St. John; in St. John especially the resurrection of Christ is treated of with several additional circumstances, and also some facts are given to which the other evangelists have not made reference.

Need I tell you that the belief in the resurrection of our Lord from the dead was accounted a very fundamental part of Christianity? That you may have no doubt upon the subject, if you will just turn to the 4th chapter of the Acts of the Apostles, and the 1st and 2nd verses, you will find it there stated, that as Peter and John spake to the people, the priests, and the captain of the temple, and the Sadducees came upon them being grieved that they taught the people and preached through Jesus the resurrection from the dead: and if you will turn to the end of the 4th chapter of the Romans, you will find it said that Jesus was delivered for our offences, and was raised again for our justification. And, last of all (I might refer you to texts innumerable), by consulting the 15th chapter of the 1st Epistle to the Corinthians, you will find of what amazing importance the resurrection of Christ from the dead was considered, especially in that verse where it is said, "For as in Adam all die, even so in Christ," that is to say, in Christ risen and glorified, "shall all be made alive." In fact this chapter is one of the most extraordinary, interesting, and consolatory in its details of any portion of the sacred volume. Then, having asked you to look at these passages of Scripture, I shall now proceed to address you.

One morning in the spring of the year, and more than eighteen hundred years ago, a few poor women went early in the morning to a selpuchre, in the immediate neighbourhood of Jerusalem; so early was the time of morning, that the first streaks of dawn had scarcely begun to make an impression on the eastern sky; it was in fact rather the approach of day, than day itself. The sepulchre they went to was not like one of our graves, dug in the ground, where the body is deposited and covered up with earth, it was rather a hollow, hewn out of the solid rock, which, after the body had been deposited in it, was covered up by a stone placed against it; in the case before us, by means of a large stone, or piece of rock, which was rolled against it. In this sepulchre, two days before, a body had been deposited, but deposited under circumstances which required sudden interposition: and the women in question went under the influence of strong affection, that they might take out the body for the purpose of wrapping it up, and for the purpose in other respects of interring it anew in a more decent, and, in their opinion, a more becoming and satisfactory manner.

It would appear, that as they walked together towards the sepulchre, some conversation took place respecting the difficulty they should encounter in removing the large stone from the opening of the hollow rock in which the body had been deposited. They do not seem to have been aware of all the difficulties they would have to encounter; amongst others, that a small band of Roman soldiers had been stationed there, as was supposed, to prevent imposture; for we must bear in mind that the Jews had read in their own Scriptures, and had a certain understanding the language of the Prophet Hosea, 6th chapter, 2nd verse, "After two days will he revive us, in the third day he will raise us up, and we shall live in his sight;" and they had understood also something connected with the language of the 26th chapter of Isaiah 19th verse, "Thy dead men shall live, together with my dead body shall they arise;" and they laboured under the impression, or pretended to labour under the impression, that an effort might be made to fulfil this and similar language of the prophets; and therefore they had got the stone sealed, and a guard of Roman soldiers stationed near it. These things the women do not appear to have anticipated. They approached the sepulchre with sentiments of awe and singular affection, where a scene presented itself, for which they, and for which before it happened, none of the sons or daughters of men could have been prepared; the stone was rolled away from the sepulchre, and upon it sat a heavenly visitant prepared to meet them, and to afford them the requisite explanation. Before them was the hollow in the rock, or rather before them appeared part of the hollow, along with another part somewhat deeper in which the body had been laid, but no body was there; two heavenly visitants sat there—one at the head, and another at the foot—of the place where the body had temporarily lain. Astonishment, I may say stupefaction, seized upon them; they felt unable to account for what they saw. But they were speedily informed that he, whose body they had come to pay honour to, was no longer there; he had risen from the dead, he had fulfilled his own words, and the words of the inspired prophets. They were reproached for seeking the living among the dead, and were desired to go and give immediate information to his disciples of what they had seen.

After these remarks, need I say we are now speaking of the resurrection of Jesus, as the Christ, from the dead. He had, while on earth, told his disciples that he should be delivered to the Scribes and Pharisees, and by them be scourged and crucified, but that on the third day he should rise again; there was now before them clear and convincing evidence of his own language, and of the language of the Old Testament Scriptures with regard to him, having been fulfilled. Thus, simple is the history of this wondrous event as it stands recorded by the evangelists, but in its simplicity consists its truth, and consists also its great glory.

When men have to do with fictitious narratives, they are often sent forth with all the pomp and circumstance of words, and human fancy is largely drawn upon, in order to give to them a splendour and an attractiveness, which does not naturally belong to them. But the majesty involved in the resurrection of Jesus from the dead required no fictitious, or adventitious aid whatever, it was enough to state the facts; glory was in those facts; what is divine, constituted the very nature and substance of them, and therefore in this divine record the facts are barely stated, and stated without any of the trappings and ornaments of human oratory, and without any of the logic of human argument; they are stated as bare facts, related on the authority of God, and when manifested to the conscience by the Holy Ghost, they do their work. They produce a divine effect upon the heart and conscience; they raise man, dead in trespasses and sins, to newness of life, and they thus give the earnest of that heavenly blessedness which in due time shall be experienced by all who are one with him, who was first crucified, and then rose from the dead.

And why did he rise? He was God. Granted. I have tried to dwell at length upon the great, the glorious fact that Jesus was God, God over all blessed for ever. But simply considered as God, Christ could not have been an inmate of the tomb. No; he became man; God was manifest in flesh, and being of flesh and blood, aye, being of our own flesh and blood, he appeared as one with us upon this our earth, and we observed last Lord's day, in considering some of the leading features of his earthly career, that God in him had united himself to man: that he as man, as the second man the Lord from heaven, contained the whole human race in himself; and then we saw that this man had done what no mere man, no mere creature, ever had done or ever could do. We found him abstaining from all evil, washing his hands in innocency; we found him going about continually doing good, and we found him fulfilling the law of God externally and internally. By the very fact of his being the Creator manifest in flesh, he magnified the law and made it honourable—conferring such honour upon it as the obedience of all the creatures of the whole human race never could have bestowed upon it; for there was the Creator honouring his own law by yielding obedience to it—obeying it—not as Adam must have obeyed law when in Paradise, as a slave, but as a free man. How few understand this fact. When God said to Adam, "Of every tree of the garden thou mayest freely eat, but of the tree of the knowledge of good and evil thou shalt not eat of it, for in the day that thou eatest thereof thou shalt surely die." God addressed a being in the situation of a slave. When he spoke those words there was a threat given, and the threat is that of an absolute master to a slave. Jesus came in the form of a slave, or in the form of a servant, but Jesus, as God over all, was a free man—the true seed of Eve, the true seed of Sarah; he came free in reality, though he came in the form of a servant; and therefore he obeyed God's law, not in the spirit of a slave, but in the spirit of God's own Son—the true free man. He obeyed God's law, because he loved it; "Oh, how I love Thy law," he says; he loved its enactments, and he loved the very threats by which they were enforced. He loved it, and obeyed it, even unto death, his death being the grand and last command it enjoined. He offered up his holy, pure, human nature, the humanity which he had taken in connection with our humanity; the humanity that had made him one with us, and us one with him, he offered up as the sacrifice without spot to God, yet, bearing our sins, for he died the just for the unjust. He, therefore, in dying fulfilled the law of God; he left that law nothing to demand, he ended it as the law of God, as a law of ordinances, prohibitions, and commands, by the complete fulfilment of all its requirements; his last act of obedience to law being the sacrifice of himself. He conquered sin by the sacrifice of himself as the free offering; he put away sin by the destruction of the nature by which sin had been committed, and by the destruction of that nature, pure and spotless in himself personally—(for he was the pure and holy Lamb of God)—he hath taken away the sins of the world.

These, aye, and millions of other things which we cannot speak of, and which probably we could not conceive of, were accomplished by the manifestation of God in flesh—by the union of the Creator with the creature; for God, not man, was Jesus's Father, though a woman was his mother. He was God-man, and as man united to God he died; and thus man's nature ended as man's nature, in him, but ended in him that it might be reproduced as the nature of the second man, the Lord from heaven; so that the temporary man in him ended in the reproduction of the everlasting man; and this, that we as in him, might be conformed to himself for evermore; by his destroying in us the image of the earthy, and putting on us the image of the heavenly.

The man died. *The* man, observe, not *a* man like Adam, or like you and me. *The* man, the God-man, the man who is at once the Son of man and the Son of God. He died; his body was deposited in the tomb; but what tomb could hold the body of the king of glory? None. He therefore burst the bands of death asunder, it being impossible that he could be held by them, and on the third day, according to the Scriptures, and according to his own declaration, he rose triumphant from the grave; rose not directly to heaven, but rose to sojourn in his glorified humanity for forty days upon earth; rose, that he might convey instruction to his apostles and disciples; rose, that he might set his example still further before them; rose, that he might prepare them for the sufferings they were destined to undergo; and rose, above all, that he might prepare them for the discharge of that heavenly commission which he was so soon to give them, and which was to be sealed by the outpouring upon them of the Holy Ghost from heaven. And then after the forty days were expired, he took them to Mount Olivet, instructing them as he went along, shewing them that they must wait a few days longer before power from on High should come upon them; and after they had got to Mount Olivet, when his earthly intercourse with them had ended, while they beheld, he ascended to heaven. It was apparent that he was no mere man, that no trickery of any kind was played upon them; for, as he ascended, a cloud surrounded him, a cloud which from its very appearance made itself known to the Jews; the bright dark cloud; that cloud, the Shekinah, the peaceful emblem of the divine presence, received Jesus into it. The same cloud that appeared on Mount Tabor, the Mount of transfiguration, that same cloud received him; and God in the person of Jesus Christ ascended into glory. Thus Scripture informs us that Jesus rose from the dead, informs us of his forty days' sojourn upon earth; informs us of his ultimate ascension to heaven; and informs us further that from that heaven he shall yet come a second time to receive his people unto himself, that where he is, there they may be also.

And for what was this grand, this stupendous, this heavenly event, made to occur? God is not guilty of gratifying mere idle fancies; what God does, bears the stamp of divine wisdom as well as of every other divine and heavenly attribute. The resurrection took place, because the resurrection of Jesus Christ was indispensable to the important results at which God aimed, and which, through that event, He was to accomplish.

Remember who Christ was. He was not a being such as you and I are, children of a human father and mother; he had a human mother, but God was his Father; he was the Son of God. Remember that he came in a far higher capacity than Adam the creature had done. Adam the creature was made by this second Adam his Son, "For by him were all things made, and without him was not anything made that was made." Adam, the creature, in a certain sense had the whole human race in his loins; when he sinned, we therefore sinned, and died in him—became subject to death; but blessed be God, that the whole human race are summed up in the second man, the Lord from heaven; in him who was not merely the spiritual Abraham, but the spiritual Adam; in him who had man in him even upon earth, in him who hath man in him as one with him now that he has ascended to glory; for, if he made himself one with us for a time by assuming our flesh and blood, he hath made us one with him for ever by giving us to partake of his own divine nature.

He rose from the dead, and he rose not alone; he rose with us in him, he carried us up to himself as the subjects of his grace, the subjects of his triumph. In this he led captivity captive, shewing that as sin and death had led us captive for a time, he led them captive for ever, by destroying the power of both; by destroying the very existence of both; and he destroyed the power and existence of both, not in himself alone but in us.

This leads to the inquiry, what was the effect of the resurrection of the Son of God from the dead? Personally considered, he was saved or delivered. Delivered from what? Delivered from law viewed as a system of prohibitions and commands; for while he was upon earth law prohibited Jesus, the second man, from doing this or that, law commanded him to do this and that; and with law as a system of prohibitions and commands he constantly and perfectly complied, but when he rose from the dead he had nothing to do with law, for law was put under him. "God is love," and Jesus, as one with God, is love. Love without any regard to prohibitions and commands. While on earth obedience to law was manifest in the character, and in the work of the Son of God, but now that he has ascended to God's right hand, he is subject to no law: the only law he knows *is the law of love*—love which is God himself, for God is love. He therefore was saved or delivered from law in the form of prohibitions and commands, by his resurrection from the dead.

Again, he was saved or delivered from the necessity of bearing our sins and the necessity of putting them away. While on earth he was the man of sorrows and acquainted with griefs. Our sins were laid upon him. He was made sin for us, though he knew no sin, and the wrath of God rested upon his holy head as our representative. I say, he so bore our sins. But when he died he made an end of sin completely and for ever, he put it outside the pale of existence; it was thrown, as it were, by his death into the depths of the sea, there to be swallowed up and forgotten for ever. When he rose from the dead he was delivered from this bearing of our sins, from the necessity of making atonement for sin. Sin had come to an end in his atoning sacrifice, as it had in a certain sense previously come to an end in his conception, and in the whole course of his life: but sin ended completely and for ever in the sacrifice of the Son of God. He therefore rose, no longer with sin lying upon him, and with sin no longer requiring to be atoned for. He rose without requiring thenceforward to sacrifice himself any more for sin, after the one sacrifice had been offered and accepted by which it is put away completely and for ever.

Again, he rose from the dead saved or delivered from death; and, being raised from the dead, he dieth no more, death hath no more dominion over him. While he was on earth, he was saved or delivered from the moment of his birth. He came to his own, and, looking through the vista of years before him, he saw death upon the cross, in the far distant future: and to his own disciples he announced the fact, that "the Son of man must be crucified." And he saw that through those gloomy portals, lay the only way to the throne, that had been prepared for him of old. Therefore he required to pass through the valley of the shadow of death, but from the gloomy precincts of the king of terrors he saw that he should rise to his throne of glory. Therefore while he was on earth sin lay upon him, and to put away sin it was necessary he should offer himself a sacrifice for sin. But death was to him a voluntary act—I have power to lay down my life and I have power to take it again. That death was his Father's command—"This command have I received of my Father." And the accomplishment of the command he rejoiced to achieve. He knew that what his Father had ordered was right, and he loved the very stroke by which his connection with earth was to be severed. But having risen from the dead he was saved from death: he rose from the dead never to die again, but to live for evermore: he became the prince of life, having swallowed up death in victory and destroyed its very existence for evermore. The prince of life had been killed, but, in killing him death had sealed its own destruction.

Well, then, Jesus, as he rose from the dead, was delivered from obedience to prohibitions and commands, by which we commonly understand law. He rose as the living one, he was delivered from sin, he was delivered from the bearing of our sins, he was delivered from the necessity of making atonement for them, and he was delivered from death, for he, as the living one, swallowed up death in victory. He therefore rose from the dead no longer in the condition of one who is subject to law in the form of prohibitions and commands, in the condition of one who required to die for sin, in the condition of one whose death was necessary to life everlasting, but he rose as the loving, the righteous, the living one : he rose relieved from all the obligations that lay upon him while on earth, for he had discharged every obligation; he had confirmed the law by obeying it, and therefore all these things ended, not arbitrarily, but in consequence of law being dead, sin atoned for, and death swallowed up in victory. In consequence of everything being scripturally done, and because Jesus in dying and rising from the dead had performed all the conditions of his Father's commands.

But I said he did not rise alone, we rose in him. Who rose in him? Did the Jews rise in him? Yes. And, had they known the truth, they would have known that they had risen in him, and that all the earthly ordinances of Moses, the whole Mosaic economy having received its fulfilment in him, they were no longer subject to the law of ordinances. With reference to these the Apostle Paul says, "Touch not, taste not, handle not." They would have known this, and the result would have been that what was the case with a few believing Jews would have been the case with all, and while those few saw what had happened, and realised the blessedness of Jesus having fulfilled law, and relieved them from the law, and from all the obligations of the Mosaic dispensation, he being the antetype of the whole, the majority did not believe it, and the result is, that, though Moses's law is fulfilled to the uttermost, we see the Jews by their unbelief shutting their eyes to their real advantages, and putting themselves voluntarily under a law, under which God has not put them, seeing that having put Christ under it, and Christ having fulfilled it, the law has come to an end as being fulfilled in himself.

Here then, is a remarkable fact; a whole nation voluntarily submitting to a law and making themselves the slaves of a law that no longer exists, for it has passed away. And just so with regard to the great majority of the children of men. The gospel of Jesus Christ proclaims to you and me that we are set free from *law*; that we are righteous in God's own Son, his blood cleansing us from all sin, and that we are living in him in newness of life; and when this is seen by us the blessing is realised, just as it was by the believing Jews. The great majority of mankind do not see this, but are going about laying themselves under some law or other, generally the law of Moses accommodated to their own low conventional idea of right and wrong. They are still dead in their consciences, from which sin has not been purged away, and having sentence of death in themselves: they have their consciences telling them the wages of sin is death, and thus, like the Jews, they are shut out from the enjoyment of God's heavenly kingdom, shut out voluntarily and personally, God proclaiming the truth in His own way, and they turning a deaf ear to what he has said—turning their backs upon the declaration that life everlasting is given to them, saying, as it were, no, it is not thy gift, but it is to be earned by us in some way or other: and thus calling God a liar, and rejecting the assertion that this life is in His son. They shut themselves out from the mercies of God, and exclude themselves from the enjoyment of His everlasting kingdom.

But though this is the case, with an unbelieving world, what is the fact? Why, the fact as it has been given to be seen by us is, that when Jesus rose from the dead, having himself personally fulfilled the law — he rose as having fulfilled the law for us, and with us. Has law anything to say to him now with regard to life everlasting, as a law of prohibitions and commands? No: I point to law, my conscience rejoices in it, seeing that my Saviour hath magnified it and made it honourable, and has become the end of the law for righteousness to every one that believeth. It is true that the law of the spirit of life in Christ Jesus hath made me free from the law of sin and death. It is true that I am not arbitrarily set free from it, as if there were no principle in me, for the principle of love which is the principle of God—(for God is love, and he that dwelleth in love dwelleth in God and God in him)—that principle has taken possession of me, and of every man to whom the truth is revealed; and we have the mind of Christ in this, that as he has set us free from law, so we are influenced by the principle of love, by love to him who died for our sins, and who rose again for our justification.

Then as to sin, it is true that as Adam's descendants we are guilty, far guiltier than we have any conception of; and it is true that as God's word enters the conscience with knowledge and power, we discover many short-comings of which we were not previously aware—short-comings which our own selfishness would make us believe did not exist in us. But what of that? We see sin laid upon the adorable surety; we see him bearing it away as the scape goat into the wilderness, to be forgotten for ever. We know that a fountain is open in the house of David for sin and for uncleanness. We know that in Christ Jesus we have a fountain which cleanses us from all sin, and knowing this in the light of God's testimony, in the fact of the communication to us of the free forgiveness of sin, by the blood shed on Calvary, we find peace spoken to our consciences by it alone, completely and for ever.

And then as to death. We know that as Adam's descendants, our bodies are dead, because of sin; we know that they must undergo corruption, that in some way or other, they must return to the dust and be destroyed. We know this, but what of that? We know also that as Jesus rose from the dead, so shall we rise. We know that our body is sown in corruption, but we know also that it will be raised in incorruption, that it is sown in mortality, but will be raised in immortality. We know this, and possessing this knowledge, we have the principle of life everlasting already in us. We have the mind of Christ as to life and as to righteousness, for we are covered with the robe of his righteousness; we have also the mind of Christ as to love, we know that we are alive in him even now, for the spirit is life because of righteousness; but if any man have not the spirit of love he is none of his. We are, as Adam's descendants, going to corruption; sentence of death must be executed upon us, God having said, "Dust thou art, and unto dust shalt thou return." But He has shewn that in Christ we rose from Mount Olivet, and that with Christ we are seated at God's right hand: "When Christ, who is our life, shall appear, then shall we also appear with him in glory." We cannot with the form of our fleshly minds realize the glory awaiting us: "It does not yet appear what we shall be, but we know that when he shall appear, we shall be like him, for we shall see him as he is." We are thus the called and redeemed of the Lord; we are thus already raised in him, and when we go back to the facts that occurred at Calvary, or rather at the tomb on the morning of the resurrection, and when he, in the presence of his disciples, ascended from Mount Olivet, and a cloud received him out of their sight; when we consider these facts, we rejoice to know, as matters of revelation, that we are already raised above law in him, that we are already raised above sin in him, that we are righteous in him, that we are already raised above death in him, through our oneness with him, and we have in us, through the knowledge and love of himself, the earnest of all those heavenly and eternal blessings. It is not merely that we are saved and delivered; that is one thing, and a glorious thing—salvation is a most important doctrine, but it is that we are more than saved, we are raised in him to newness of life.

Oh, my friends, little did I know nearly thirty years ago, when I wrote my " Three Questions," the great value of the second question there raised. I had seen enough of natural theology to know that if Christ was merely restored to the state of Adam in Paradise, he merely died and rose again to restore us to a state such as Adam's in Paradise was, a state rendering us again capable of sinning and dying. I saw then, but how much more gloriously do I see now, that he rose, and raised us in him to a new life, not to the earthly Paradise of Adam, but to the Paradise of God. He, therefore, rose and raised us in him to a life that is heavenly and divine, and this by making us partakers in him of the divine nature; hence the absolute certainty of the blessing enjoyed by us; it is a present, an everlastingly present blessing. "Jesus is the same yesterday, and to-day, and for ever," and his people as one with him so far inherit this divinity; they are not God, but they have the nature of God, for they are partakers of that divine nature, and hence it is that they who believe have everlasting life. It is a present blessing, and constantly realised by us in connection with our knowledge of him who is the great I Am, the ever present one; He who lives without change, and with whom there is neither past nor future.

Well then, we are raised in him to love, to a love that puts law under foot, and triumphs over sin and death. By his obedience to death, we are raised above sin, and are made in him divinely righteous. We see sin put under his feet; as belonging to the nature of our Adamic existence. We see death, the result of Adam's sin, put under his feet, by his swallowing it up in victory. We are raised in him to the enjoyments of the earnest of the heavenly Paradise, and we are living with him as those who are strangers and pilgrims here below; with those to whom Adam's Paradise would be no gift whatever, because they are satisfied with nothing short of those blessings at God's right hand—those rivers of pleasure which flow there for evermore.

Is the resurrection of Christ then a trifling event? An event that could be realized by anything short of the Creator. Is it not manifestly an event which stamps the deity of Christ upon every thing connected with it? God interposed, the salvation of man is accomplished, divine blessings are the consequence ; and could any but God have procured such blessed results ? Ah! my dear friends, the salvation of Christ rises into an atmosphere—rises into a state of things infinitely beyond what the most cultivated intellect has any conception of ; it rises into the region of the heavenly and divine; it carries us by anticipation up to heaven, and the poorest, and the meanest of the children of Adam, knowing the truth as it is in Jesus, is already living in heaven by the earnest of immortality, while the greatest, the mightiest, the richest, the most distinguished in literature and science, are mere grovellers in the dust—parties destined to shew how worthless are all human attempts when the word of God has been neglected and trampled under foot; while the testimony of God concerning Christ has been regarded by them as a trifling matter, and while the testimony of man has been preferred to eternal life, the low condition of the sons of Adam has been preferred to the high condition of beings elevated by the resurrection of Christ to be the sons of God, and heirs of glory.

May the Lord bless what has been spoken, and to His name be the praise for evermore.—Amen.

SERMON XII.

Sunday, May 13th, 1855.

I would request you to refer to the two following passages, one contained in the Old, and the other in the New Testament Scriptures. The former in the 9th Psalm, and the 10th verse, "And they that know thy name will put their trust in thee;" and the latter in the 12th chapter of St. Matthew's Gospel, at the 21st verse, "And in his name shall the Gentiles trust."

I have brought these two passages together for a reason which will become immediately obvious. The text from which I mean to address you properly and particularly is that which is contained in the Book of Psalms, "And they that know thy name will put their trust in thee." The very language which I have now read, shews distinctly that the whole human race are not here spoken of. A limited number of individuals is brought under our notice. They only who know the name of Jehovah are those of whom the putting of trust in God is here predicated. Now who are these? Who are the limited number of individuals who know the name of Jehovah? At the time this Psalm was written, they consisted only—or almost only—of the descendants of Abraham according to the flesh. God had given to the descendants of that patriarch privileges of a most extraordinary nature. He had taken them as a peculiar people to Himself—He had separated them from other nations of the earth; He had given to them a law from Mount Sinai; He had conferred upon them institutions of a most valuable description; He had placed them in a land which He had prepared for them—and by having driven out their enemies before them, fulfilled the promises He had made to their forefathers; so that at the time this Psalm was written, they were manifestly monuments of the favour and grace of the Most High. Yet this nation, highly distinguished as it was,

was not made up as a whole of those who are spoken of in my text. Every member of Israel was not a believer in the God of Israel. All professed to be so, yet it was but few of that nation comparatively speaking who, with the heart, believed unto righteousness, and this upon a principle clearly established by the apostle in the Epistle to the Romans, namely, "They were not all Israel who were of Israel, but in Isaac shall thy seed be called;" that is to say, although the chosen people of God in Old Testament times were typical of the true internal and spiritual people of God in all ages and generations, yet, we are only to consider them as a nation, in their typical character.

Well then, looking at matters in this light, we discover that the persons spoken of in this Psalm at the time it was written were Israelites (generally at least), not all the Israelites, but a select body of individuals from among that nation, who, according to the divine purpose, and by God's Holy Spirit, had been illuminated from above. These are the persons here spoken of.

Now, some individuals present may be disposed to say to me, according to the phraseology that you have employed, you appear to confine salvation to a limited number of the Jewish people—you represent the inspired writer as speaking of all believers as existing among that nation only? Unquestionably, my dear friends, those who knew God's name at the time when the Psalm was written, were principally descendants of Abraham, but not so exclusively. When I look at the case of Melchizedec—when I look at the case of Job, I cannot help thinking that even at the time when this Psalm was written, there were some Gentiles according to the flesh who had become acquainted with the God of Israel; and who, in consequence of this, were partakers with Israel of spiritual and heavenly promises. And thus, I observe further, that the language of this Psalm is not confined to the period when it was written, or to any particular period. Although it was written about one thousand years before Christ came, it takes in every believer of the truth who had previously existed; and reaches forward from the time when it was uttered and recorded, to the period when the earth shall cease to exist—when its foundations shall be overthrown, and when with fire from heaven it shall be finally and thoroughly consumed. In a word, it takes in all those who have known Jesus—who now know Jesus, and who shall know the name of Jesus in every succeeding age. In proof that it was not confined to the period in question—if such proof were necessary, and I scarcely think it is—I say in proof of this, I have selected one passage as a specimen among many others in which the character assigned chiefly to a few of Abraham's descendants, at the time when the Psalm was written, is also ascribed to the members of the Gentile world—"And in his name shall the Gentiles trust."

These words are recorded in the Gospel according to St. Matthew, in the course of a reference made to a portion of the 42nd chapter of the Prophecies of Isaiah. They are not a literal quotation of the words of Isaiah, but their spirit and import, and sometimes even the very phraseology is given by Matthew very distinctly. It is true, that immediately after it had been stated that "A bruised reed shall he not break, and smoking flax shall he not quench, till he send forth judgment unto victory;" in the verse that immediately follows in Isaiah, there is different phraseology employed, from that which occurs in the language of my text selected from Matthew; but, if you look at that language as translated from the Hebrew, you will find that the import of the whole verse is emphatically and truly and beautifully given in the words, "And in his name shall the Gentiles trust." For independently of the preceding part of the verse, the words, "And the isles shall wait for his law"—which is the language of Isaiah—is evidently expressed in the New Testament phrase, "And in his name shall the Gentiles trust;" the isles being an expression frequently used by Isaiah, and very often occurring in the Old Testament Scriptures as significant of the Gentiles, and of the Gentile world; and the isles waiting for him is an expression equivalent to saying (as I find from consulting various passages), "The Gentiles shall believe or trust in him." Therefore I have no hesitation in saying, that the language as given by Matthew is a most admirable compendium of the more lengthened phraseology adopted by Isaiah; and be it always recollected, that as the same Holy Spirit speaks in the New, as spoke in the Old Testament Scriptures—so, as a matter of course, the same Spirit constitutes his own best interpreter. This being the case, the declaration, "In his name shall the Gentiles trust," is sufficient to shew us that the language employed by the Psalmist was not limited to the Jews of the time when it was written—or limited to the Jews of any age—but holds true of the believing Jews at that period, holds true of believers without any respect to kindred, tribe, nation, or tongue. Wherever there are human beings, be they Jews, or be they Gentiles, who believe in Christ Jesus—to whom the character of God, through His own well-beloved Son, hath been revealed, there are found those who trust in what he hath said—trust in his heavenly testimony, and who, trusting in that testimony, in due time will have their faith or trust swallowed up in the full fruition of the heavenly glory.

Having then brought in this phrase, "Gentiles," to suggest that there is nothing limited or confined in the phraseology adopted by the Psalmist—and having shewn from this verse—which is merely one specimen out of hundreds which I might have produced—having shewn from it, that the same trust in God which was peculiar to believing Jews, is characteristic also of believing Gentiles —having hinted that the privileges of the one, were also the privileges of the other, I now come back to resume the consideration of my first text properly and exclusively. "And they that know thy name will put their trust in thee."

Now, in this text, there are very clearly two things set before us. First of all, "Certain persons who know God's name," and in the second place, "The effect of this knowledge upon them, they put their trust in Him, who is made known to them." Let us briefly—and it must be in a cursory manner at the best—take up and consider in succession each part of this verse—in its literal signification —for I consider that the more we use the textual or literal interpretation of Scripture words, provided they are correctly translated, the better. It is not for us to deliver to you human essays, or bring you to the consideration of human theories—our business is to point your attention to the pure, infallible, and heavenly word of God.

"They that know thy name." Well, then, there are two things for our consideration,—" *know*," and " *God's name*." It is suggested by these words, as I have already hinted, that there are persons who do not know God's name. Ignorance of God's name characterises all human beings by nature— the knowledge of God's name is the result of God's purpose, and the effect of the illumination of the understanding by the Holy Ghost. Having made this simple remark, I would at once observe that I wish to draw your attention to a subject which I have not for a long period particularly dwelt upon—but which I think it is now necessary for me to impress decidedly upon your notice.

I have for a long time past observed among religious

characters a disposition to scoff at the theology of our forefathers. You know right well, that I am no apologist for that theology. I deem it to be in many respects defective, and in some respects repugnant to the truth of God's testimony. But the reverse of wrong is not always right. In our day it would appear that there are many who are bent upon flying from one extreme to another. Having detected some errors in the old Reformers, they have drawn the conclusion that nothing but error is to be found in their system. Now the fact is, that the Reformers erred, and erred in many respects—but those who pretend to be their correctors, would have us listen to them, whilst at the same time they have fallen into greater errors themselves. The Reformers fell into error, under the influence of the old scholastic theology, whilst our modern interpreters have fallen into error under the influence of German and Socinian theology. The only true corrector of errors of both kinds, is the Holy Spirit. It is he alone who can direct our attention to the testimony of God, and vouchsafe to us a clear and accurate understanding of it.

Now, the word knowledge is one of those about which errors have been committed, both by old Reformers and modern divines. According to the old Reformers there are two kinds of knowledge, there is head knowledge and there is heart knowledge—as if knowledge could really be connected with something more than the understanding. And on the other hand modern divines, looking to knowledge alone, set aside the principle of faith altogether, not understanding that there is a distinction between the knowledge that we may possess of the things of this life, and that knowledge which we receive of the things of the life to come. They tell us, Oh, it is all a mere matter of the understanding; and thus, between the blundering of the one, which makes knowledge to be the property of the heart, which in reality can only belong to the understanding; and the floundering of the other, which tries to bring down the knowledge of divine things to the level of the knowledge of human things; between these false notions, believers are apt to be led astray from the simplicity of the truth; but, setting aside human teaching, the blessedness of those "who put their trust in God" consists in being led by the spirit, through the medium of the word of God, into all truth. Now, without going at any great length into the subject, I will try to make myself understood by you, if it please God to enable me so to speak, and you to give me your attention, in such a manner as is necessary to the understanding thereof.

Those of you who have read Locke on the "Human Understanding," a work highly praised, and in many respects deservedly so, but a work in which God's character is ignored, and a system of theology suggested, which is opposed to God's word, may have remarked, that he correctly enough affirms, that natural knowledge is derived from information we originally receive through the medium of the five senses. We have the senses of seeing, hearing, tasting, smelling, and touching—no other, and it was an old maxim of the schoolmen, and not a bad one, that there is nothing in the intellect which was not previously in the senses. Natural knowledge, then, is derived, and is originally received from, what have been denominated, sensations. And a celebrated author has endeavoured to shew, that all knowledge comes under ten categories or heads, and one of the most celebrated men of modern times has only been able to improve upon him by making out twelve heads or categories. But it is enough for us to know that the knowledge we have naturally, is formed in us through the medium of, and from impressions previously made upon, our senses. Our senses are first impressed, then certain operations of the intellect or understanding follow, which result in knowledge—limited knowledge at the best, but increasing knowledge. Thus knowledge consists not only in what directly comes into our minds through the senses, but consists also in the operations of intellect upon itself.

But there is another kind of knowledge of a higher character, with regard to which divines generally have either no conceptions, or have erroneous ones. That is, the knowledge which respects God, Christ, and divine things. Now, this knowledge in one respect resembles the other, in that it is connected with the formation of the human intellect or mind. You and I are so constituted that we cannot rise naturally to any conception of things above man, or above the things of this world. When we think of God, we are obliged to clothe Him with a human form, and this in order to bring him down to our comprehensions. If we try to think of angels we clothe them also with the human form. So we try to think of heavenly glories by contrasting them with the things of this world: we compare them to mountains and hills, and verdant landscapes, and flowing streams, and all that is beautiful to the mind and vision, in order to have some ideas of them. The Word of God tells us that "it doth not yet appear what we shall be, but we know that when he shall appear we shall be like him, for we shall see him as he is" (1 John, 3, 2), but it does not tell us that there is a distinction between head-knowledge and heart-knowledge; it tells us something better—that as human knowledge springs from the senses and the operation of the intellect upon itself, so there is a knowledge that springs from faith, and that is the knowledge I want now to bring under your notice. But, say some persons, we do not understand anything about this, if there is faith in our minds it is the result of knowledge. No, my dear friends, faith that is the result of knowledge is merely human faith, and it is because so much of the faith that is in the world is merely human faith, that there is so little of the "faith that worketh by love," so little of divine principle obvious among the sons of men. They want to rest their faith upon knowledge, and hence they seek for evidences of Christianity, both external and internal, in order to reason themselves into a religion of some kind or other; but such a religion is not the religion of faith—it is not the religion of Jesus Christ. Whenever God enlightens our understanding through His own word—and that is the only medium through which such illumination is conveyed—wherever and whenever he does so, the principle of faith is thereby first imparted, and through faith, knowledge—heavenly knowledge—that knowledge which comes through the faith or trust that God speaks of in this text; and it is indeed a knowledge worth speaking of. Now, I do not speak thus, unadvisedly; for, some time after having been taught, scripturally, the doctrine of "Divine Inversion," through which I was astonished to perceive the blunders into which I had previously fallen, and that many passages in the Apocalypse which were previously dark, were opened up to my understanding; I observed the peculiar phraseology adopted by the apostle in the 11th chapter of the Hebrews, "By faith we understand that the worlds were framed by the word of God, so that things which are seen, were not made of things which do appear," which phraseology does not make belief subject to the understanding, but shews that by believing we understand. And, upon examination, I found this principle running through the whole of the Scriptures as applicable to divine subjects, and that faith is the only medium through which divine things can be at all understood. For instance, my conceptions are bounded by my knowledge, and at the best my natural conceptions of God do not reach beyond the human form, let me aggrandise that form as I may, but the knowledge I have by faith teaches me that God is a much higher being than man—that He does not bear the image of the earthly, but the image of the heavenly. I know also that the heavenly glory does not consist of hills, and valleys, and flowing streams, and so on : I know through faith that it consists of something infinitely greater and more glorious. This is the understanding which all believers have—an understanding which enables us to realise that which is heavenly and divine, infinitely transcending all that we have seen or can see —the eye not having seen, nor the ear heard, nor the heart understood, the things which God hath prepared for them that love Him. Here, then, comes out a remarkable fact, that while our natural understanding rests upon our senses —while all the supplies of that understanding are derived from our senses—on the contrary, that knowledge which is heavenly, springs from faith, and there can be no more heavenly *knowledge* in your mind and in mine than there is of *faith*. Remove faith and you remove all heavenly knowledge.

But I have another word to say on the subject. Human knowledge is not necessarily connected with any influence on the affections. That knowledge often does operate on the affections, I know, but it does not do so necessarily. I may know mathematics. I may have a tolerable acquaintance with the sciences. I may be well-versed in history, and many other things, and yet my affections may not be influenced in the slightest degree by them. So I may know many things about my fellow-men, or even things with regard to myself, that do not interest me. There are few things connected either with myself or my fellow-men, that are calculated to influence my affections. Now, let me draw your attention to a remarkable fact. Wherever faith is, it has the following properties, expressed in the 1st verse of the 11th chapter to the Hebrews, "Faith is the substance of things hoped for, the evidence of things not seen." Wherever faith enters into the mind it reveals God, not as an abstract being, but as *my* God ; it reveals Jesus Christ as *my* Saviour ; it reveals the supplications of Christ as heard on *my* behalf; it reveals life everlasting through him as freely conferred upon *me*, even through his righteousness ; so that the distinction between faith and human knowledge is, that wherever faith enters the mind, it enters as a principle influencing the affections. Hence the remarkable circumstance, that we can distinguish between human knowledge and its influence on the affections; and while our knowledge of religion is merely of a human character, we can do this—but, wherever faith is, the affections are necessarily influenced. Our hope is influenced, and our joy, our peace of mind, and our love to others, are influenced. Our affections are stimulated and called into active exercise, in proportion as our heavenly knowledge springs from faith; and they are regulated by the measure or extent of that faith; so that *all* heavenly knowledge is connected with the affections. Not that knowledge and the affections are one and the same thing, for that is an absurdity: knowledge and affection differ the one from the other. Thus I know that God is light, and that God is love; yet I cannot *separate* between light and love in God, although they are still distinct objects of apprehension. I know that love in God is different from light in God, nevertheless I cannot *separate* between the two. So, where faith is, it worketh by love, but you cannot separate in faith, between what you believe, and the understanding you have in what you believe. Well then, let me suggest these two things, for I have not time to dwell upon them longer. What I have thrown out is merely suggestive. First, human knowledge and human faith rest simply upon sensations, and upon the operations of the intellect itself; whereas heavenly knowledge is obtained through divine faith. There is no such thing as the attainment of heavenly knowledge, except through faith, and all understanding of divine things flows through believing what God has said. Then observe, in the second place, while human knowledge does not in the great majority of cases influence the affections in the slightest degree, in proportion to the amount of divine knowledge possessed, will the affections be necessarily stimulated; faith worketh by love, and constitutes in us the principle of love to God, and love to man—that love or charity, without which, as the apostle shews, we are but "as sounding brass," or "a tinkling cymbal." This faith, being of God himself, is to us the communication of the knowledge of God, and through it the enjoyment of those heavenly blessings, which flow from the knowledge of the character of God, as light and love.

"They that know thy name," that is by faith, "will put their trust in thee." Now, what is the name of God? The name of any one is that by which he is known and distinguished by his fellow-men. The name of God is that by which he stands distinguished from all other beings, and from every object of thought. Now, how does God stand distinguished from all other beings? By His name, Jehovah, the Almighty, the Creator, and so on. Very true, but is this all that is meant by God's name? Is it merely the use of words? No. God's name implies a great deal more—goes far beyond the mere distinctive use of the phraseology. The name of God implies what He is, and so exhibits His character; a being of infinite perfection. The name Jehovah implies that He is the self-existent one, and the author of existence in others;—the independent and the immutable. The name Almighty speaks for itself. Well, then, God's name signifies His revealed character, and as the Scriptures constitute the means by which that character is set forth and revealed, the Scriptures in one sense may be said to be God's name. Now, God's name is set before us in the Old Testament Scriptures, through the medium of narrative and of prophecy; but it is not set before us clearly, for there is a veil thrown over it; but when we come to the New Testament Scriptures, we find that God's name is revealed in Christ, and so clearly is God's name revealed in Christ, that through the medium of the New Testament Scriptures, the veil thrown over it in the Old Testament is torn asunder and done away, and in proportion as we are enabled to look into it by faith, we behold the unveiled face of Christ. Well then, the Scriptures are God's name, inasmuch as the full revelation of God's name is therein set forth; the veil thrown over the Old being done away—and God's revealed character set forth in the New Covenant without any doubt or mystery.

But God's name may be said to consist of His perfections as they are revealed in Christ Jesus, revealed in what Christ hath suffered—revealed in what Christ hath done—revealed in the perfection of God's justice—revealed in the perfection of His righteousness—revealed in the perfections of His love and wisdom—all of which are made known to us in His sending His own Son into the world to die for sinful men. That name is set forth in Christ, in the fact that "he hath magnified God's law and made it honourable;" that he hath put an end to sin and brought in everlasting righteousness; that he hath swallowed up death in victory, and has risen to God's right hand: that through him we might enjoy endless life in God's presence for ever and ever. Jesus, then, is the revealer of God's perfections; he is God's name. God's name was set forth in the Old Testament

Scriptures, but had a veil cast over it, which however did not prevent those who knew it from enjoying his salvation. But, having in the New Testament Scriptures Christ set before us, all the divine perfections of God are displayed; so that he that hath seen the Son, hath seen the Father likewise. He that hath seen and known Jesus, knows God's name, and hath seen all by which God stands distinguished from, and is made superior to, and supreme over all His creatures. And that which characterises His name is, that it sets Him forth as love—love in pardoning our offences—love in raising us from the dead—love in giving us life everlasting in His own dear Son. Well then, the name of God is all that he hath revealed in the person and work of Jesus Christ—which He hath caused to be recorded in that blessed Book. Those who know God's name, are those who believe in God's revealed testimony concerning Himself, and thus possess the only knowledge of Him, which can by any possibility be attained to. And "Those who know God's name will put their trust in him," and in every age have done so.

Now, observe what may be said respecting faith, trust, or confidence. It is no abstract principle. It does not lead me to believe that God loves another, but does not love me; nor lead me to look upon Him as a being I should dread and fear to speak of. In proportion as faith operates upon me, it leads me to Him, as my Father—leads me to see that I am one with Him, inseparably connected with Him, for time and for eternity. Whenever His testimony, as revealed in the person and work of His own Son, is made known to me, I necessarily know Him as my God; I obtain a view of His character, as revealed by faith; and the result is that I put my trust in Him.

Now comes a remarkable fact. Can any mere human being put his trust in God? I maintain that mere human nature never could trust in God—human nature never had confidence in God's revealed character. I do not say that my understanding cannot put confidence in the God and Father of our Lord Jesus Christ. What I mean is, that where the mind of Christ is,—where that earnest of the divine nature is, which exists in the hearts of all those who believe; wherever faith is,—that faith which is the substance of things hoped for, and the evidence of things not seen,—wherever that divine nature is, which clings to, and trusts in divine objects revealed to it; there are the persons who put their confidence in God, and own their relationship to Him. Faith then, necessarily implies knowledge of our connection with Him, who through faith is revealed; implies that he is the object worthy of our trust; implies our knowledge of the fact that he died for us, and that having died and risen again, he now lives for us—he inspires us with confidence and trust in himself; this faith produces in us such blessed effects, that we put our trust in him for time— we put our trust in him for eternity. It is thus that we find peace applied to our consciences by the blood shed on Calvary; it is thus that we realize the fact that eternal life has been freely bestowed upon us without money and without price, through Christ's divine righteousness. We have confidence that Christ hath put away our sins by the sacrifice of himself, and that he "is made of God unto us wisdom and righteousness, and sanctification, and redemption." And this, not on account of our superiority to our fellow-men, not on account of our being better than we formerly were; for, as the result of Christ's knowledge entering our minds, we discover more and more that evil is ever present with us; but we believe it because God has said it—it is His gift abounding through the divine righteousness of Jesus Christ; and we believe this, and put our trust in him for life everlasting. We also put our trust in him for the life that now is, as we do in regard to all spiritual blessings. Circumstances may occur to shake our confidence. We may not, for instance, have what we conceive to be the necessaries of life; still, in proportion as faith exists in us we are enabled to adopt the language of Job, "Though he slay me, yet will I trust in Him;" or the language of the prophet, "although the fig-tree shall not blossom, neither shall fruit be in the vines; the labour of the olive shall fail, and the fields shall yield no meat; the flock shall be cut off from the fold, and there shall be no herd in the stalls; yet I will rejoice in the Lord, I will joy in the God of my salvation" (Hab. iii. 17, 18). Believing what He hath said concerning Himself, and concerning the relationship in which He stands to us; we trust in Him, let Him do with us what He will, for we know that He will do all for our good as well as for His glory.

I had a vast deal more to say had time permitted, but it does not; and I would have you look into this passage and into all similar passages contained in God's word, which bring under our notice these precious truths. Wherever heavenly knowledge is, it springs from faith; wherever faith is, it influences us to love Him, who first loved us; and under the influence of that love, to trust in Him continually, not only for eternity but also for time. Thus, through difficulties, and trials, and dangers, we shall be so led till we attain to that blessed inheritance, where the Lord shall be our everlasting light, and sin and sorrow shall be known no more.

May the Lord shed his blessing on what has been spoken, and to his name be praise for evermore.—Amen.

SERMON XIII.

Sunday, May 20, 1855.

THE passage of Scripture from which I purpose addressing you at this time, is contained in the 5th chapter of Galatians. In the 6th verse we read:—

"For in Christ Jesus, neither circumcision availeth anything, nor uncircumcision;" then come the words of my text, "But Faith which worketh by love."

Faith, I am much afraid, is become a strange, and even a discreditable word among the professing Churches of the Lord. If we read the 11th chapter of the Epistle to the Hebrews, we find that in Old Testament times, Faith was the all and in all to the Saints; every word recorded in that sweet portion of the sacred volume, shews us that they "lived by Faith, walked by Faith, triumphed by Faith." At the period of the Reformation, Faith was one of the grand doctrines upon which Luther, Melancthon, Zuinglius, Calvin, and others, insisted; and it was by the proclamation of the wholesome truths which are connected with the doctrine of Faith, that these men would appear to have achieved their triumphs. In my native country, Scotland, and among the early Reformers of England, Faith was, at one time, particularly insisted on; and I have very little doubt, that it was the preaching of the power, and the value of Faith in this island, that was blest by God to the giving of such distinct and such powerful views of divine truth to the Scotch and English people, as have carried them down to the present day, and highly distinguished them from the other nations of Europe. But, alas! a change soon came over the spirit of the dream. Faith ceased to be the *grand* topic, on which divines insisted, and with which their people were pleased and edified. A new state of things followed.

Doctrines of human contrivance, old and exploded heresies, and views which dishonoured God, and could do no good to man, were gradually introduced. Faith, in a great measure, disappeared; and in the course of last century, a blight had come over, not only Europe, but over the Churches of our own island; "Ichabod," or "thy glory is departed," might well have been written, upon almost all of them. There have been some who have attempted a revival, as in the days of Wesley and Whitfield; and in more modern times, connected with the preaching of Chalmers, Guthrie, and others in Scotland, Faith has come to be more talked of, the value of Faith more frequently expounded, and numbers of individuals have appeared to rejoice in its light and to experience its power. But, again, a state of things has succeeded, in which Faith seems destined to be expelled, even from the pulpits, and places commonly understood to be Evangelical. The mists which arose in Germany; the locusts which from thence went abroad, have begun to overspread our own land. "Mysticism," a sort of Gnostic heresy, a disposition to substitute mere human facts and human reasonings for the word of God, has succeeded to a system which, with all its errors and mistakes, was in a spiritual, and even in a moral point of view, far superior to that which now exists. Instead of the value of Faith—instead of its necessity—instead of its triumphs—we are now doomed to hear of the superiority of our ministers—Established and Dissenting—in point of their literary and scientific knowledge: instead of the simple words, in which God's truth is declared, and the simple expositions, of which they alone admit, we hear nothing now but of Hermeneutics, Biblical criticism, and the power of reasoning, from the elaborate disquisitions of learned men. And instead of the minister being regarded as the servant of Christ Jesus, and the proclaimer of his name through the Scriptures, to those to whom the Scriptures are alone addressed, as containing all we know, or can know concerning salvation; instead of our looking to these Scriptures, as interpreted, not by human agency, not by human power, nor by human learning, but by that same Divine Spirit from whom they emanated; we now look to the learning, which is acquired in academies, we look to the powers of the vaunted human intellect, and look to uninspired men, to lead us on in our religious career, and to produce a Church unexampled in purity and glory. The result has been, that the doctrine of Faith has departed, coldness is becoming more and more apparent; and, just in proportion as men are followed for their classical and scientific attainments—in proportion as human eloquence is substituted for the simple declaration of the plain truths of God—in proportion as the itching ears of men seek after human novelties—in the same proportion will Christianity, among what are called Churches, deteriorate; and in the same proportion will it appear that through the insinuations of the old serpent, that tempted Eve, men have departed from the simplicity of the Gospel, and have been getting farther removed from the truth, as it is in Christ Jesus. In opposition to all this, and notwithstanding the contempt to which the confession may expose me, I declare, that, the doctrine of Faith is to me the dearest of all doctrines, or at least one of the dearest. By Faith, I mean simply, belief in the recorded testimony of God. Now, understand me. I am not going to treat you to any metaphysical disquisitions; I am not going to enter into any abstract explanations, with regard to Faith. Faith, or belief, simply signifies crediting; that is, the mind receiving as truth what is made known to it; and when applied to divine testimony, it means the seeing of that testimony to be true, in its own light, through the evidence conveyed into the understanding, by its Divine revealer. This is the simple meaning of the word Faith. And be it remembered, that this Faith is no unimportant matter. So essential is it to the existence of Christianity—to the existence of all religion—that, according to the highest of all authority, "Without Faith it is impossible to please God;" for he that cometh to God acceptably, cometh, believing that He is—that is, believing in the Revelations which He hath given in His word concerning Himself; and he in whom this belief of God's testimony is not, neither is, nor can be, accepted before God. Here then, is something to shew its importance. But there is something more. Another text in Scripture, in Habbakuk, a text, quoted several times in the New Testament, "The just shall live by Faith," is another most distinct mark of its true importance. "He lives," the just or righteous man lives, "by Faith;" that is where Faith exists, it exists as a principle of divine life; and as it can only exist, as a principle of divine life, where it is found, *there* is a germ of immortality; *there* is that germ or principle, which, in due time, shall expand into all the blessedness of heavenly sight and enjoyment; and this Faith is declared to be of the operation of God. Except where the spirit illuminates; except where the Word is introduced into the conscience, we understand that a pure Faith is not and cannot be. And it is God's peculiar prerogative to bring any individual, through the instrumentality of Faith, out of darkness into his marvellous light.

And, then, according to the Scriptures, how mighty have been the triumphs with which this simple, this despised, this *overlooked* principle, is inseparably connected. In that wondrous chapter, the 11th of Hebrews, we have a digest of this glorious subject. We are, therein, carried back to the days of Abel. We have the two brothers, Cain and Abel, contrasted; and the reason why the one—Abel—finds acceptance with God; and why the sacrifice of the other is rejected, is declared to be, that Abel offered *his* sacrifice, *believing* God's testimony, and as the result of so believing, he received the Divine approbation; while Cain, not believing what God had said, and venturing to present a sacrifice, which his own understanding merely had dictated, was sent away under the frown of God's disapprobation. Coming down the stream of time, we have our attention directed to Noah. We are informed of that, which enabled him to bear the scoffs and jeers and taunts of a Godless world, for a period of 120 years, during which time he was preparing the ark, by which himself and his family were to be saved from the flood; it was simply his *crediting* God's declaration, that He intended to bring a deluge on the earth; although I suppose that no sign of a deluge appeared for more than a century, after the divine declaration. All things went on as before; the husbandman sowed his seed, and the harvest waved over the fields; the enjoyments of life were not disturbed, and all things continued as they had been from the beginning of the creation. Still Noah wrought on with the ark; after having laid its keel, he went on to build it, plank after plank, until at last the whole was completed; the unbelieving world looking on, and scoffing at both the ark and its builder: scoffing too at God—if not directly —at least through His servant Noah, as it was through God's directions that Noah was acting. Noah's belief, as we all know, was justified by the results. Again, Abraham is set before us, as a wonderful instance of what Faith enables poor individuals, otherwise vile and worthless, to achieve. Abraham, born in Ur of the Chaldees —a land of idolaters—at God's command left his country, and his kindred, and his father's house, to go out, not knowing whither he went; at last he finds himself in the land of Canaan, which land God promises to give to himself and to his posterity, after the lapse of many ages. Faith in God enabled Abraham to obey His command, and fervently to believe the promise. We have various trials of his Faith recorded, out of all of which he came victorious. One you well know, that in which his fatherly heart was tried, by the command to sacrifice his son—that very son to whom the promises had been made, and through the life of whom alone, it appeared possible they could be accomplished. But he hesitated not—strong in Faith, he gives glory to God; and the son, by the same Faith, gives glory to God likewise. Both go up to the Mount—the father prepared to sacrifice, and the son to be sacrificed, in obedience to the divine command. The issue was, divine interposition; Abraham, "in a figure, receives back his son from the dead," and God commends his Faith by bestowing upon him the promise of blessings, even in this world, of the most glorious description. Following down the stream of time, in this same chapter, we find ascribed to the principle of Faith, all the actions, whether private or public, which the Holy Ghost has stamped with approbation. Joseph acted by Faith. Moses acted by Faith. Samuel acted by Faith. David acted by Faith. Jephthah acted by Faith. All these worthies acted as believers in the divine testimony; under the influence of that heavenly principle, they were carried out of themselves, and above themselves, and were enabled to set an example to the members of the Church of God in every succeeding age—an example recorded in God's word for their satisfaction, for their comfort, and for their edification. In more modern times, what enabled the apostles to triumph as they did? What carried them above fear of the Jews, and enabled them to encounter the vengeance of the Gentiles? What enabled them to bear stripes, and scourgings, and imprisonments, and tortures, and even death itself, undeterred? What made them go from country to country, exposed to privations and taunts, and obloquy on every hand? What, but believing the truth of divine testimony. It was Faith which encouraged them; it was Faith which made them triumph! But take a more glorious example still. Whence the triumphs of the Son of God? How was it that he from his birth, and throughout his wondrous life, achieved his triumphs? Why was it that he, the Lord of heaven and earth, condescended to visit this globe, and there suffered himself to be reproached by his own creatures, and even to stand as a criminal at their bar? Why was it that he suffered himself to be nailed to the accursed tree? It was through Faith; "I believed, therefore, have I spoken." Such were the words of the Son of God, recorded in the 116th Psalm; and as he believed and spoke, so he believed and acted; he was the author and finisher of Faith; and it was under the influence of this heavenly principle, that he "Endured the cross, despising the shame, and is set down at the right hand of the throne of God." Tell me Faith is a common principle; tell me it has been superseded by other principles. Nay, my dear friends, while we are in flesh and blood; while we are sojourners here below; while we see not the things of the heavenly glory; Faith is the only principle, by which they can be realized in our minds—"Faith is the substance of things hoped for, the evidence of things not seen."

Our desire, last Lord's day, was to bring under your notice a few of the grand and blessed consequences, of which this principle of Faith, this belief in the divine testimony, is necessarily productive. "They that know Thy name will put their trust in Thee," was what we found declared, and by speaking from that verse, our object was to shew, that from this principle of Divine Faith sprung divine-knowledge and divine-trust. Faith is, as it were, the root of all these. We observed that divine knowledge sprung from it, and we drew your attention to the distinction between human knowledge and divine knowledge, which from our pulpits are being constantly confounded. Human knowledge, we observed, rested upon the influence of the senses, or rested upon the dictations of the reasoning intellect; and we endeavoured to draw attention to the fact, that whatever we know naturally, we know by means of natural observation, or something of that kind; and observed that what passes for the religion of Christ, in our day, is nothing more than a series of human reasonings, which have been presented to us by human beings, like ourselves; hence the love for what are called "Evidences of Christianity." Not but that I know these evidences have their value. I know that when these are made use of, to stop the mouths of infidels, properly and judiciously, they have a tendency, in a certain degree, to do so—confounding such men on their own principles; but whenever these religious evidences are made use of to be the foundation of Christianity; whenever it is pretended that they strengthen confidence in God, I deny it. I deny that anything works Faith in us; that anything makes us acquainted with the true love of God; that anything brings us out of darkness into God's marvellous light, except His own Word, demonstrated by His own spirit; and that Word is so sweet, so bright and illuminating, and so glorious, that it sets at defiance all the facts and all the reasonings of men; and these facts and these reasonings can no more confirm my Faith in God's testimony, than they can shake it. Then, those who make human reasonings the foundation of their respect for the divine testimony, throw themselves open to the rebuke of the apostle; "Beware lest any man spoil you through philosophy and vain deceit, after the traditions of men, after the rudiments of the world, and not after Christ;" such men shew that they have been beguiled from the simplicity of the Gospel, by the teachings of the old serpent. This knowledge is founded upon what is conveyed by the senses, or derived from the reasoning intellect; but divine knowledge springs from divine Faith. It is not a knowledge of the heart, as distinct from that of the head, as I have already affirmed. I do not like this phraseology at all; seeing that human knowledge cannot be connected with anything more than the human understanding; but divine knowledge springs from Faith, as shewn by that wondrous expression in the 11th chapter of the Hebrews: "By faith we understand that the worlds were framed by the Word of God, so that things which are seen were not made of things which do appear;" it is not by understanding we believe, but it is by believing that we understand; that is, all our understanding or knowledge of things that are heavenly and divine, comes into our minds through believing them on God's testimony. And then it is a beautiful characteristic of the church in New Testament times, that it possesses a superior degree of knowledge to that which the church in Old Testament times did or could attain to. The Old Testament Church lived by Faith, miraculously begun, and miraculously supported; the knowledge it possessed at the beginning was very limited. It knew that a mighty deliverer was to come, to work out a deliverance, compared with which, no other deliverance could be spoken of; but who the deliverer was to be—how the deliverance was to be carried into effect—to what extent it would reach, was not known: the knowledge of these things was reserved for us, by the kindness of our heavenly Father. Therefore it is in New Testament times, that we are to look for more knowledge than was found in Old Testament times. Now, through faith we understand who Christ was; "The mighty

God;" we understand his relationship to Jehovah as His son; we understand how he hath accomplished the work of man's salvation, through his incarnation—through his obedience and sufferings—through his death and resurrection from the dead, and through his ascension to his Father's right hand; we understand many things with much more clearness than those most exalted in Old Testament times could possibly attain to. Therefore, unquestionably, the knowledge we have in New Testament times, infinitely surpasses that of Old Testament times. Well then, this knowledge springs from Faith, and it is because I believe God's Word, that I am led to the understanding of it.

I also drew your attention to the limits of the human understanding, with reference to divine things. We can never get beyond the forms of the human intellect. What I know of God, or of heavenly things here, I know by Faith. I have no conception of heavenly things, except by Faith; and I must wait till I am relieved of this burden of mortality, ere I can comprehend divine things as they are, and before my heavenly knowledge can be perfected; then I shall know, even as also I am known, and Faith will be absorbed in sight. We attempted also to shew, that from the same divine Faith springs divine trust. Why do I confide in my heavenly Father for salvation? Why do I know that when time ends, this mortal body shall be changed into the likeness of Christ's glorious body? Why do I know that this partial view of God shall be changed for a full and complete view of Him? I know it solely by putting my trust in what God hath declared. Why do I pass through the present world with certain confidence in my heavenly Father, that He will "never leave and never forsake" me? Because I put my trust in Him. I believe His testimony; my confidence in Him springs from faith in what He hath revealed. My knowledge, then, springs from my Faith. My confidence in God is the expression of my Faith; and my knowledge, as having the same origin, is the expression of the same Faith and trust; and just in proportion as it is given to us to believe God's testimony, in the same proportion will our understanding of divine things be enlarged. We shall have confidence in all the doings of our heavenly Father in our behalf, both for time and for eternity.

The words of my text tell me, it is "Faith in God's testimony that worketh by love." There is something energetic in regard to the phraseology, "worketh." It seems— if you will allow me to use the phrase—to be a favourite expression of the Holy Spirit. It occurs in many passages of Scripture. I think it occurs in Colossians i. 29, in Ephesians i. 11; it also occurs in 1 Thes. ii. 13, and in various other passages; in all of which it denotes peculiar work—work which is Internal; it not merely denotes the idea of working, but an operation or working which takes place in our own consciences—an internal overpowering, overcoming operation. Well then, this principle of Faith, as it has for its necessary results divine knowledge and divine trust; so it has for its necessary consequence divine love; that is to say, it operateth or worketh in us through the medium of love, and this upon the following grand principle:—What had God revealed Himself to be in His Word? Is He exclusively light; is He exclusively love? No! You, who have attended regularly here, or at any rate, such of you as are acquainted with the Scriptures, know that the same apostle John, who tells us that God is light, tells us also that *God is love;* that is, light and love, constitute God's very essence; in Him both are absolutely inseparable. But the words of my text shew me, that what they are in God himself, they are also in His people. No more can light be separated from love in them, than light in God can be separated from the love of God in Himself. As, therefore, God is light, He hath caused the light of the knowledge of Himself, through Faith, to shine into our understandings, and as God is love He hath shed His love abroad in our hearts, and both in connection with, and as the result of, this heavenly Faith. They exist together in the believer, as they exist together in God himself. And where there is knowledge springing from God's testimony, there will be found a working by love, too; a love directed towards God, and a love directed towards man. Our love is directed towards God in the fact that "we love Him because He hath first loved us;" we are drawn towards Him "with the cords of love, as with the bands of a man." We see a glory in Him. We taste a sweetness in Him. We feel an attractive power in Him, that draws us towards Himself; and, when thus drawn, our Faith trusts Him, not as an abstract being, but as revealed to us in His own Son. He presents Himself to us, embodied and revealed, in the person and work of His own dear Son. Our love to God, therefore, is love to Jesus Christ;—love to him, in seeing whom, we see the Father; love to him who came into our world to die for us, and to raise us from death, to life and immortality; love to Him who is continually, in His Church, overruling all things for their good as well as for His glory; and it is a love which leads us to prize Jesus in whom God is revealed, above all things beside. Jesus hath said, "He that loveth father or mother more than me, and he that loveth son and daughter more than me, is not worthy of me;" for wherever the love of God, in Christ Jesus, is, there Jesus becomes the supreme, I would say, the *alone* object of our deep and tender attachment; earthly things being loved only, in their connection with Him, and as the result of His own sovereign appointment. A most powerful instance of this love is given us by the Son of God himself, when He set His earthly relations in the back ground, while about his heavenly Father's business; and so with regard to all who believe. In every age this principle of love has enabled members of the Church of God to take joyfully the spoiling of their goods, and to bear the reproaches heaped upon them, and even to suffer death for Christ's name-sake; they have "had respect unto the recompense of the reward." As concerning Jesus, they could rejoice, and say, "whom not having seen we love—in whom, though now we see him not, yet believing, we rejoice with joy unspeakable and full of glory." Again, the love which they bear towards Jesus, they bear towards his Church. They, loving those whom they *have* seen, for Christ's sake, manifest thereby their love to Him whom they have *not* seen. How beautifully is this pourtrayed to us in the 25th chapter of Matthew, in the parable of the sheep and the goats; wherein it is shewn, that those who give unto Christ's people, give unto Christ himself, and thereby shew their love to him; and wherein it is likewise shewn, that those who manifest a want of love to Christ's people, manifest a want of love towards Christ himself. Therefore, be it understood, "Every one that loveth him that begat, loveth him also that is begotten of Him." They are all members of the same family; all heirs of the same heavenly hopes; and they will love, not in word only, but in deed and in truth. They will love in word unquestionably; they will address to each other words of comfort—words which manifest their attachment and affection towards each other; but, there will be something more. Christ says, "I was hungry and ye gave me meat. I was thirsty and ye gave me drink. I was a stranger and ye took me in. Naked, and ye clothed me. I was sick and ye visited me. I was in prison and ye came unto me;"—thus, with regard to members of the Church of God, there is something more than the mere address of words; something more than, "be ye warmed and filled; notwithstanding ye give them none of these things which are needful to the body;" but there will be the vivid, glowing testimony of divine love dwelling in their hearts by Faith, and the shewing forth of that love in their lives by what they do to the Church of God, and the testimony thereby given to the love which they bear towards Christ himself. Much more might be said on this subject, but I must be content with having addressed you simply and shortly from these words—I have hurried over them, touching, as it were, upon some leading facts, in order that you may, through the reading of God's Word, and the teaching of His Spirit, go deeper into the matter. Divine knowledge comes through Faith, and is of the operation of God. Faith leads to divine trust, and the principles of Faith and trust are shewn by the love we have to God in the person of His own Son, and through him to his own people. These are characteristics of the members of Christ's Church; where one heavenly principle is, there the other is; and where one is found wanting, there the other will be wanting also.

May the Lord bless what has been spoken, so far as consistent with His mind and will, and to His name be praise for ever and ever.—Amen.

SERMON XIV.

May 27th, 1855.

The words of my text will be found in the 13th chapter of the Epistle to the Hebrews, and the 5th and 6th verses, we there read, "Let your conversation be without covetousness, and be content with such things as ye have," then follow the words of my text, " For he hath said, I will never leave thee nor forsake thee," so that we may boldly say, "The Lord is my helper, and I will not fear what man shall do unto me."

When reading these gracious and precious words—words full of the strongest divine consolation — three preliminary ideas suggest themselves to our minds. In the first place—that language addressed to one or two believers may have, and even must have, a reference to others. The words of my text when originally uttered by Jehovah, were addressed first to Moses, and afterwards to Joshua, his successor. Moses was reminded that God would neither fail nor desert him, while engaged in the very arduous task of rescuing the children of Israel from Egypt, and carrying them through the wilderness to the promised land ; and after God had referred to what he had done in the case of Moses, Joshua is encouraged to expect the same protection and support at the hands of the Almighty, which his predecessor had received. From the quotation and application of the passage in the Epistle to the Hebrews, it evidently appears that words originally addressed to Moses and Joshua, were not intended to be confined to them alone ; and they are therefore quoted by the apostle with reference to believing Hebrews, and with reference to believers in every succeeding age. And this, let me observe, furnishes us with a key to the understanding of many other passages, and enables us to take comfort to ourselves from many other declarations of Holy Writ, which like that now before us, were originally addressed to others, but which in their divine import refer to ourselves, as well as to those to whom they were originally addressed.

The second consideration suggested to us is—that language which had a reference to circumstances of one kind, not only *may* have, but in the course of God's providence really *has* a reference to other things and to other subjects. For instance, when these words were uttered originally to Moses, God was referring to the protection which he had extended to his servants in the land of Egypt, and in the wilderness—referring to the protection which Moses himself had received at His Almighty hand, when engaged in conducting the Israelites from the land of Egypt, and out of the house of bondage, into the good land prepared for them. When originally addressed to Joshua, they had reference to him as destined to complete what Moses had begun. After the death of Moses his wonderful predecessor, Joshua was to carry the Israelites over the River Jordan, introduce them into the promised land, and so lead them, as to overcome all their enemies. These then were the circumstances to which these words in Holy Writ, originally had reference. But you will observe, as employed in the New Testament Scriptures, they refer to New Testament times. They refer in the first place to all the circumstances treated of in the preceding and subsequent portion of this chapter; to the bringing of the Old Testament Israel to believe in Christ Jesus; to their being brought out of the former or old dispensation into the new one—to their being enabled to go without the camp, bearing Christ's reproach, and to their being enabled to set at defiance, all that their Jewish countrymen and unbelieving rulers, or others, could do unto them. They referred in fact to what would be their privileges when, having turned their backs on the old dispensation, they set their faces Zionward, and followed Christ Jesus in the track and path which he himself had pointed out to them—and not only had they reference to these Hebrew believers, but they have a reference to the case of believers in every age—to the fact of their having, by faith, been brought out of a world that lieth in wickedness—out of what Bunyan calls the "City of Destruction," brought out of the state of nature in which we are all naturally, a state of ignorance, of sinfulness, of death—and introduced into the kingdom of God's dear Son, a state of marvellous, supernatural, and glorious light.

Now referring to these, the language implies that what was the privilege of Moses, and what was the privilege of

Joshua, is your privilege as believers also; as they in their straitened circumstances were protected by the Almighty, as they were enabled to surmount all the difficulties which they had from time to time to encounter, so you, believing in Christ Jesus, animated by the principle of hope in him—having his love shed abroad in your hearts—are under the same protection, are sustained by the same Almighty arm, and are as safe from all enemies—and as they were enabled to complete the work respectively given them to perform, so you also, protected by the Almighty, shall be guided "through faith unto salvation, ready to be revealed in the last time."

There is a third consideration suggested to us in the words of my text, and that perhaps the most important of all. We gather from these words and their application, the complete oneness of Christ and his Church, and the complete oneness of the members of the Church with each other. The oneness of Christ and the Church are never overlooked. The fact is, these words are primarily and principally addressed to the Church's Head, and were primarily and principally realized in him—and as addressed to him and realized in him, they are addressed to every one of the members of his Church, and realized in them also. Christ and his Church are one, and unless they be viewed as one, it is impossible for us to receive consolation from the promises made originally to the Church's Head; but let that oneness be recognized—let it become a fixed and stable principle in our minds—as it is one of the grand principles of Holy Writ—then we shall hear the Holy Ghost addressing our Divine Head—and hear him addressing us as one in him, as established in him, and as saved in him with an everlasting salvation.

I observe also that there is suggested to us the oneness of the whole Family of God. It is suggested by this most sweet promise, made to Moses and Joshua, and through them made to believing Hebrews, and believing Gentiles. How can this happen? Simply because the Church constitutes the one body of the Divine Head, all the members mutually existing in each other; therefore, the promise made to one is virtually made to all—and really made to all; for blessings of a spiritual description belong not to one member only, but to all the members of Christ's Church in common; whether these blessings be temporal or spiritual, to promise them to one, is to promise them to all the rest.

I thought it proper before advancing more particularly to the consideration of this passage, to draw your attention, in a preliminary way, to these three things. *First*, to the fact that what was addressed to Moses and Joshua, is addressed to all other believers. In the *second* place, to the fact that a promise which originally respected circumstances of one kind, is here represented as also having a reference to circumstances of another kind. And in the *third* and last place, to the fact of the unity subsisting between the Church's Head and the Church itself, and the unity subsisting among all the members of the Church—such a unity as renders a blessing or promise to *one*, a blessing and promise to *all* the others. Having made these remarks then, let us proceed. It is clear at a glance that the words of my text divide themselves textually into two parts.

1. The divine declaration.
2. The practical conclusion deduced from it.

The two parts are the *one* in the 5th verse, "I will never leave thee, nor forsake thee;" and the *other* in the 6th, "So that we may boldly say, the Lord is my helper and I will not fear what man shall do unto me." In the first place we have the divine declaration. Now, permit me, not in an offensive way, but with an especial, particular, and personal, but, at the same time, affectionate application, to the conscience of each individual, to treat of the precious words which constitute the first portion of the text. The language is not "I will never leave *them*, I will never forsake *them*;" the language is not, "He will never leave them nor forsake them," language which would have been equally true, and, in certain respects, equally valuable, but which would not have been equally personal. The force of the language consists in the use of the first personal pronoun, "*I*," and the second personal pronoun "*thee*," that is to say, it is a direct address from one being to another, and couched, too, in language of parental love and encouragement. "I will never leave *thee*, I will never forsake *thee*." And who are the parties speaking and spoken to? Are they ordinary individuals? Is the subject treated of an ordinary one? Most assuredly not! He who speaks is the everlasting God, the Almighty, the Creator of the ends of the earth, the Being to whom we owe our existence, and the Being by whom we are constantly upheld and sustained.

The words "He," "I," refer to none other than the Sovereign of heaven and earth, to none other than "He," who hath revealed Himself in His Word. "*He* hath said," and when He speaks in the first person "I," He comes forward in His personal character, and as the personal character of God is Jesus Christ—(for "he that hath seen and heard him, hath seen and heard the Father"),—when God says, "I will never leave thee, nor forsake thee," it is God speaking to us through the person of His own Son, and that in the most endearing and affectionate language in which He could address us; speaking to us through His word—that Word which is emphatically called "the Word of power"—that Word which shewed itself to be a Word of power when creation started into being at its Almighty fiat, saying, "Let there be light, and there was light;" that Word which shewed itself to be a word of power, when Jesus stood at the grave of Lazarus and said, "Lazarus come forth," and he that was dead came forth, bound hand and foot, with grave clothes; but, above all, a Word which shewed itself to be a word of power, when, having gone forth and having taken effect, a child was born of a sinful woman, the Son of God himself started into being, a loving, powerful, and Almighty Saviour.

It is indeed a mighty power that speaks in the Word, it is the Everlasting, Living, Almighty God, speaking with a power which, when He willeth, not even the most hard and flinty heart can resist. When He who speaks with the word of power, speaks thus, "I will never leave *thee*, nor forsake *thee*," to whom is He speaking? My dear Christian friends—let me rather say in the singular number —my dear Christian brother or sister, is He speaking to others, is He speaking to believing Hebrews, who died hundreds of years ago? Is He speaking to men of preceding generations? Or, rather, is He not speaking to all the children of faithful Abraham, to those who have faith in His testimony in every age? Yes! He is speaking to every believer, to every believer that has lived, to every believer that is living, and to every believer that ever shall live on the present earth, and to none beside. If you read, meditate on, and understand the import of the parable of "the sower," contained in the 13th chapter of St. Matthew, and elsewhere, an explanation of which Christ himself has given, and, if you understand the import of the language contained in the 6th chapter of Isaiah, to which reference is made by St. Matthew, you will perceive that all human beings naturally have eyes, but the majority of mankind see not with those eyes, the things that are heavenly and divine; all the human race have ears, but the majority hear not God addressing them in His most precious Word; all have the gift of natural understanding, but with this understanding the majority perceive not the precious testimony which in God's Word is laid before them, and enforced upon their notice. Thus to the great majority of the human race, God speaks as though He spoke not; they not having eyes to see, ears to hear, or hearts to understand.

Yet there are some—there ever have been a few—to whom His truth is carried home to the conscience with power—and that because God himself goes forth with it, and gives effect to it. There are a few who have ears given them to hear, and do hear the voice saying, "This is the way, walk ye in it," and who do walk in the way that voice points out. They *hear* that voice, especially in the language of my text, saying, "*I* will never leave *thee*;" "I Jehovah," God revealed in Christ, "will never leave thee;" "I Jehovah," God revealed in Christ, "will never forsake thee." They hear Him addressing them individually and personally, and comfort is thereby imparted to their minds. With that comfort strength is also given to them, and they joy in the Lord their strength, they grow stronger by the heavenly declarations made to them, and by the effects of which they are productive, and thus they go forward, strong in the Lord and in the power of His might.

Is this thy experience Christian brother or sister? Believe me, I know well, unless God hath spoken to thy conscience through His Word, there is no spiritual connection formed between Him and thee; it may be however, that while He hath revealed Himself to thee in Christ Jesus, and hath caused thee to hear Him speaking in the Scriptures, it is possible that this particular portion of Holy Writ may not have been felt to be addressed to thee; for God does not carry home *all* His testimony at once to the hearts and consciences of His people; He is continually giving them more light, and adding grace to grace, and strength to strength; still, if the truth, as it is in Jesus, has obtained a footing in thy mind—if the mind of Christ Jesus—without which no one can belong to him—is thine; if the mind which is connected with faith is thine, then this passage is addressed to *thee*, as well as to all other believers—addressed to thee in the most direct form, in which any passage of Scripture can be. God is not speaking to others only, but to *thee*, and blessed be His name, when what he says comes home to the conscience with power, we hear Him speaking, we hear Him saying, "*I* will never leave thee, *I* will never forsake thee." Thus we find ourselves strengthened amidst all our weakness, and comforted amidst all our sorrows. We have consolation imparted to us, giving us to rejoice with joy that is unspeakable and full of glory, and have also imparted to us, by the influence of the Spirit, spiritual strength, spiritual power, and spiritual life.

Now, what is it God does say; what is it that is spoken directly to thy conscience, beloved Christian brother or sister; what does God here say to thee, "I will never leave thee, nor forsake thee?" Let me not indulge in empty rhetorical distinctions—let me not say that *leave* means something ordinary, or something extraordinary,—let me not say that *leave* means to quit for a time, or to quit ultimately and for ever; but let us quietly, calmly, and with the aid of the Old Testament Scriptures, to guide us, look at the words as they lie before us.

Well then, these words are not tautological, there is a distinction between the meaning of "leave" and "forsake," and the distinction is this. The use of the latter word gives a greater force and strength to the promise, than is implied in the single word leave, which goes before. It is believed, and rightly so, that when God made a promise to Abraham, and confirmed it by an oath, the oath was a climax to the promise, and the stronger of the two. So here, God says, "I will never leave thee nor forsake thee," and in this light, while the promise of never leaving us is most precious, the promise never to forsake us is still more precious.

In the first place, "I will never leave thee." How suggestive are these words of the divine kindness, as it has ever been evinced by God towards His people while sojourning in this vale of tears. God never left Moses, He never left Joshua, until He had fulfilled the promises He had made to them respectively. And upon the same principle, for He is truth itself, He will never leave us. Not that we deserve this kindness, for as we had no right in ourselves to that everlasting life which God has freely bestowed upon us, so we have no right to the continuance of earthly blessings; just as, while we were yet sinners Christ died for us, and while we had not the shadow of a claim upon God's favour, that favour was bestowed upon us, not for works of righteousness which we had done, but according to His own mercy; so upon no ground but that of His own character, does He continue the manifestation of His loving kindness towards us; and on this ground alone He will never leave us.

With reference to ourselves, personally and individually,

the words, "I will never leave thee," obviously mean, I will never leave thee to thyself. O how precious is this. Are you Christ's, then you will understand, that to be left to ourselves would be the most dismal and dreadful calamity that God could inflict upon us. We are naturally dark and full of hatred to God, and to be left to ourselves would be to be left to the reign of darkness and enmity. But God does not act in any such way towards His people. Having brought us out of darkness into His marvellous light; having delivered us from a state of hatred, into a state of love towards Him, even for the love wherewith He first loved us; He keeps us in that love. He may for a time leave us to the stirrings of evil in our own hearts; He may leave us to suffer the feelings of remorse to which such evils necessarily give birth; but He is all the while abiding by us: He is watching over us, protecting us from ourselves; and when the evils of our own hearts have been suitably and to the proper extent displayed, He reveals Himself with that language of love which is peculiarly His own, and then the rebuke comes home to the conscience, with a severity which all the language of hatred, and all the language of condemnation, never could have produced. What was it that stung the hearts of Joseph's brethren? Was it that he spoke to them harshly? was it that he charged them with having countenanced the taking of his cup? No! but when he said to them, with all the language of endearment, "I am Joseph, your brother," it went to their hearts, they were overwhelmed with anguish, they were stung with remorse, they felt their great crime, and prostrated themselves before him. So, when the Lord shews us that He has not left us to the evil of our own hearts, but has taught us for a time with severity for our good; when He gives us to hear His voice speaking within us, "It is I, be not afraid," His loving kindness beams upon us, and we are overwhelmed when we think of the infinite love against which we have rebelled by our misconduct.

And as He watches over us, and does not leave us to ourselves, so He does not leave us to the devil, or to a world that lieth in wickedness, or to any enemies from without. When evil men would corrupt us, He is watching over us to put the corrupting influences aside; when evil men would overwhelm us, He is strengthening us to overcome by His might; and in all the varied circumstances of human life, weak as we are, He shews us His Almighty strength, He is manifesting His strength in our weakness, giving to the "worm Jacob" to "thresh the mountains and beat them small, and to make the hills as chaff." And if we should be overwhelmed with poverty, He is still with us, suggesting to us, "I am thy portion, I am thy exceeding great reward;" suggesting to us that while we are but earthen vessels that can easily be broken, He the Lord is "the same yesterday and to day, and for ever." Even when it was permitted in the case of the *martyrs*, that they should be taken and tortured, and torn by wild beasts, and put to death, even then He was with them, whispering, in most powerful accents, "Fear not them that can kill the body, but cannot kill the soul." It is true, that by these trials thy body may be brought down to the grave, but "I am with thee" in all these trials of thine, for I have promised that when thou passest through the waters, I will be with thee, and through the rivers, they shall not overflow thee; when thou walkest through the fire thou shalt not be burned, neither shall the flame kindle upon thee. I am still here; if they take thy life, it is only that thou mayest ascend in the fiery chariot to the enjoyment of my presence, and to "the glory that I have prepared for thee before the foundation of the world." I will not leave thee, for thou art Mine, and being Mine,— *one with me*,—thou art bound up in the bundle of life with the rest of those who are dear to Me. This sweet promise, then, is addressed to us individually by our Divine Head.

But He that hath said, "I will never leave thee," hath said also, "I will never forsake thee." These words go to the bottom of the matter, banishing all doubt or hesitation with reference to the future. Shouldest thou say, "I may go on for a time, but the period may arrive when I may be so left to myself as to depart from God, or I may be so overwhelmed by poverty, or afflictions, or family difficulties, that I may be apt to charge God foolishly, and so subject myself to be forsaken." No, says God, thou art in my hands; though thou art weak and foolish—though thou art prone to depart from Me, the living God—yet it is I who uphold thee, and thou shalt never be forsaken by me. What He hath said, He will perform; and, as He hath said He "will never forsake thee," for that reason thou art especially safe. Thou wilt never be allowed to come down to the position of those who are excluded from His kingdom, because that kingdom has been prepared for thee from the foundation of the world. Those whom He loveth are those whom He "hath loved from everlasting," and whom He loveth, He "loveth to the end." He loveth thee to too great an extent ever to forsake thee. Our greatest extremities and trials are only permitted for a time, in order that through their instrumentality, we may be led to perceive the evils of our own hearts, and though we may be sorely tried for a time, yet will He not forsake us. Having loved us from everlasting, He loves us to everlasting; the love being all on His part, the mercy being all on His part, the security being all on His part, and, although we are weak in ourselves, we are strong in the Lord and in the power of His might—strong in the purpose which He purposed in Himself, before the world began—strong in the fact of the unchangeability of His character, "the same yesterday, to-day, and for ever;" and who hath said, "because I change not, ye, the sons of Jacob, are not consumed;" the reason why you are not utterly forsaken is, because I am not what you are; what I purpose is not what you purpose; because "I am what I am," in Me you are secure for ever.

Having laid down this blessed declaration, then, "I will never leave thee, I will never forsake thee," God himself speaks directly to the conscience of each individual believer, and is heard by the consciences of those to whom He speaks, they having ears to hear and hearts to understand.

Then comes the second part of my text, "Therefore I will boldly say, the Lord is my helper, I will not fear what man can do unto me." This is the conclusion deduced from the promise going before. As "the Lord will never leave nor forsake me, I will boldly say the Lord is my helper." This language is very expressive, but it does not express a boldness founded upon self. This boldness God rebukes. It is not the boldness of the Pharisee rejoicing in his self-righteousness, or that of the Sadducee rejoicing in the power of human reason; such boldness God will not justify, as shewn in the case of the Pharisee and the repentant publican. No! the boldness here spoken of is a boldness of a spiritual description—it is a boldness which responds to the Divine testimony, as well as being founded upon it, and is the legitimate result of receiving that divine testimony; for if a man hears God saying "*I* will never leave thee, *I* will never forsake thee," he will lose his timidity, and draw the conclusion that the Lord will perform what He hath promised: the ground of this boldness is heavenly and divine; where belief responds to the divine testimony it is a bold belief—it is a divine belief, and corresponds to the testimony

P

upon which it rests. So there was no timidity with our blessed Lord, although he was meek and lowly in heart, still, where God's honour was concerned, he was confident, and shewed what the divine testimony was in him, by the confidence and certainty with which he acted. Knowing that he came from the Father, he declared, "If I should say I know Him not, I should be a liar." He knew Him, and therefore boldly declared that knowledge, and acted accordingly. And one of God's followers, speaking under the influence of the same boldness, said, "I know whom I have believed, and am persuaded that he is able to keep that which I have committed unto him against that day." Therefore this boldness is not founded upon self, it is not founded upon our own righteousness, but it is connected with the knowledge that we are weak, sinful, dying creatures, having no strength in ourselves, and liable every moment to depart from God; it is a boldness founded upon the fact of God having said, "I will never leave nor forsake thee;" it is founded on the testimony of Him who is "the faithful and true witness." I have not *man* sustaining me; I have no mere *creature* throwing his protecting arms around me, but I have the Almighty God delivering me from this present evil world, enabling me to surmount every difficulty, and carrying me onwards to glory. Having "God," then, "for me, who can be against me." He is the Lord of Hosts, and the Lord of all the creatures marshalled against me—therefore, as a conclusion, I will not fear what man can do unto me. Let me be placed in circumstances however alarming; let me be exposed to dangers from which I see no earthly means of obtaining relief; let me even be brought to the gates of death, still I will not fear, for God hath declared that "all things work together for good to them that love Him, and are the called according to His purpose;" thus even death itself is reckoned in the catalogue of blessings by those who are secure in Christ Jesus, the Church's divine head. The Creator is mine, and He not only gives me to know that He is mine, but He also gives me to know that He will raise my mortal body and fashion it like unto His own glorious body.

I have perhaps hurried through these verses, but in them we have one of the most sweet and precious addresses ever uttered by God himself to His believing children; and on their part, we have language and determination corresponding to the address—language which shews that the joy of the Lord is his people's strength, animated by which they go forward "strong in the Lord and in the power of his might."

May the Lord bless His Word and make it effectual to speaker and hearer, and to His name be praise for evermore.—Amen.

SERMON XV.

Sunday Morning, June 10th, 1855.

I DESIRE this morning to bring the following texts of Scripture under your notice, and to address to you a few words founded upon their statements. In the first place, I must refer you to the 15th chapter of St. Paul's First Epistle to the Corinthians, and the 32nd verse, you will read the following words:—

"What advantageth it me if the dead rise not? let us eat and drink; for to-morrow we die." Then turn to the 49th verse of this same chapter: "And as we have borne the image of the earthy; we shall also bear the image of the heavenly." And, last of all, permit me to direct your attention to the passage contained in the 5th chapter of the First Epistle of St. John, and the 11th verse: "And this is the record" (or testimony, or witness bearing) "that God hath given to us eternal life, and this life is in His Son."

In these *three* passages of Scripture, we have brought under our notice two distinct principles of action, by which human beings while living in the flesh, may be influenced. The one, the human principle, "Let us eat and drink, for to-morrow we die;" the other, a divine principle—or rather *the* divine principle—"This is the record that God hath given to us eternal life, and this life is in His Son,"—or, "As we have borne the image of the earthy; we shall also bear the image of the heavenly." We have thus set before us in God's own words, and in express contrast, these two principles, that we may look at them, and see them standing separate and apart, the one from the other. Before I proceed any further in the observations it is my purpose to submit to you, I may observe with regard to the human principle, that for a very long period of my life I have been aiming to distinguish more and more between the various principles of human nature, and have frequently asked myself, "What are the grand principles of human action?" And especially, "What are those principles by which human beings are actuated and practically influenced, while destitute of the knowledge of the living and true God?" I have wished to ascertain what these are; not by consulting philosophers—not from the pages of historians or poets—but from the language of inspiration itself. I have for years been satisfied, that if we are to know ourselves, and to know human nature as it really is, it must be from the pages of Holy Writ that the required information is to be gathered. It was said of our Lord, when he spoke from the Mount, and delivered those sayings which stand recorded in the 5th, 6th, and 7th chapters of St. Matthew—"That he taught the people as *one* having authority, and not as the Scribes;" and so we may say with regard to God's word; every delineation of human nature which is contained therein, comes home to us with authority. The word of God does not use the language of doubt and hesitation—it does not speak as if the mind of the speaker had been baffled in his researches into the principles and motives of human action, but it speaks with knowledge—with firmness—with power; it tells us at once what man is—it throws open his heart—it makes us acquainted with the motives of his conduct—it delineates the whole of humanity in a form, at once condensed, and yet complete; and thus brings us into an acquaintance with ourselves and with others, thoroughly satisfactory in its nature; and which, from no other source than God's word can by possibility be derived.

Now, while searching the Word of God, and examining its contents, with the object of obtaining clearer and more satisfactory views of the leading principles of human conduct; I found it convenient, first to look at the catalogue of human principles with which God Himself hath seen meet to furnish us; to apply these first to the Jews, and then to the Gentile world, and then to ascertain their application to ourselves. I am not going to dwell upon this part of the subject, with which you must be quite familiar, as I have so frequently brought it under your notice on former occasions. Suffice it to say that, according to the Apostle John, "all that is in the world," is summed up in these words, "the lust of the flesh, the lust of the eyes, and the pride of life."

It is generally supposed that an allusion is made in these words to fleshly desires, covetousness, and ambition. I do not agree with this common interpretation put upon the passages. That fleshly desires, covetousness, and ambition, are prominent features of human nature no one can dispute; but an examination of the characteristics of the Jewish sects, together with an enquiry into the nature of Christ's three temptations, through God's word, would lead to the belief that the words have a different and a far higher meaning than is generally assigned to them. Unquestionably, under the head "lust of the flesh" is included every sinful and inordinate desire; but by "lust of the eyes," something totally different is meant from what is commonly supposed. For years I have seen men prone to indulge in the use of their intellectual and reasoning faculties, to an extent which is not warranted by God's word. They glory in these, and in that which results from them, and place both as superior to God's testimony, and are found sitting in judgment upon God's testimony by means of them. Jesus in his temptations, however,—particularly in the *second*—showed that he could not be influenced by any appeal to the reasoning faculties, however close or cogent such reasoning might be, when he had *God's word* for a guide.

Satan, in his temptation of Christ, quoted a passage of Scripture, "He shall give His angels charge concerning thee, and in their hands they shall bear thee up, lest at any time thou dash thy foot against a stone;" but the Son of God, seeing that the suggested ground of action was an express divine prohibition, repelled the temptation by replying, "Thou shalt not tempt the Lord thy God." The "lust of the eyes," or a reverence for the reasoning faculties, was therefore not in him. In him, God's word was triumphant—triumphing above human reason, or the results of human reason.

Then with regard to the "pride of life;" from a careful investigation of the 3rd chapter of St. Matthew, and of other parts of God's word, I believe these words to have a direct reference to the religious principle, which exists in human nature. I am not speaking of that spiritual and *heavenly religious* principle, which is found to exist in the children of God, but of that *natural religious* principle, which was stimulated and brought into action in Adam himself, through transgression—a subjective-religious principle which is stimulated into exercise by the teaching of parents, and of those under whose care we are placed—stimulated into exercise by our acquaintance with the world, by our listening to preachers, and attendance on what is called the preaching of the Gospel. I am speaking of that religious principle common to the natural and fleshly conscience found in every human being, and of the tendency of which few are aware. This *natural religious* principle does not, as some suppose, tend to the worship of God; but tends to the worship of *self*, to the worship of Satan, and to the worship of the creature.

In these words, a reference is made to the third temptation of our blessed Lord, in which Satan offered him all the kingdoms of this world, provided he would fall down and worship him, to which the Son of God replied, "Get thee hence, Satan: for it is written, thou shalt worship the Lord thy God, and him only shalt thou serve," and in Him, God's word was again triumphant. This brings out an important fact, the fact that all human beings are influenced by a "*natural religious*" principle, which leads them to the worship of self, instead of the worship of God. "To their (own) net they offered sacrifice, and to their (own) drag they burnt incense," is the language of the Prophet Habakkuk, and so it is with men naturally in all ages. As worshippers of self, they are their own god, and are brought into the position which Eve anticipated when tempted by the serpent, that of becoming "as gods knowing good and evil." This "pride of life" is the highest rank and dignity that the fleshly mind of man *can* assume. This principle is manifested in those who, like the monks of "La Trappe," spend days and nights in vigils, and fastings, and self-inflictions, and so on. Even amongst those calling themselves Christians, this principle of self-worship is often brought into full operation. But a right understanding of the Scriptures shews that the true worship of God is entirely opposed to this principle; this principle of self-worship is the highest ground that human nature can assume, and will ever be antagonistic to God's worship. It is an exhibition of the pharasaically religious character, being the highest religious form in which human beings naturally can appear—it is that in which the Apostle Paul appeared, when endeavouring to work out his own righteousness; and it is the highest in which any human being ever has appeared. It is the understanding of this, that shews me that there were among the Jews, three classes of individuals naturally—leaving out of view, for a moment, those who possessed the principle of faith, who formed a distinct class. Taking then the ordinary classes of the Jews, there were in the *first* place, the mass of the common people, who were influenced by mere earthly motives and considerations, and who acted therefore simply under the influence of the flesh. In the *second* place, there was a higher class who studied the sciences, and studied the Scriptures in a scientific point of view—who believed, like many in modern times believe, that only five Books of the Scriptures should be regarded as genuine; and took away, even from these, everything of a divine import, endeavouring to confine their meaning to this present world; these were men of refined intellect and cultivated taste—men who were of a superior grade in society—men who delighted to cultivate their reasoning faculties—and these men were known by the name of Sadducees. Then there was a *third* class, men of superior character, who devoted themselves to the external observances of all religious duties and ceremonies, who gave tithes of all they possessed, and made other sacrifices—men of enlarged principles, who appeared to be devout and holy, who appeared to endeavour to act conscientiously at all times and in all respects; these were men who studied the *letter* of Scripture, and had attained to a very considerable measure of acquaintance with it, and these men were known by the name of "Pharisees." Some individuals have most absurdly tried to divide the Jews into four classes, bringing in the Essenes; but these Essenes, I believe to have been nothing more than one of the most rigid of the Pharasaical sects. I have never been able to distinguish more than these *three* classes of Jews, namely, the low, or common people, who delighted merely in fleshly pursuits; the more intellectually cultivated part, who prided themselves on their reasoning faculties; and those who were characterised by a high tone of religious sentiment, and who prided themselves in their religious superiority over their fellows.

Having discovered these three classes existing among the Jews, I extended my enquiries to nations of antiquity, having regard especially to those of Greece and Rome; and in the course of a tolerably long life, spent among books, I have been led to perceive that these *three* classes existed among all the cultivated nations of past times, and I am satisfied it will be found by those who study the subject, that in proportion as nations have become cultivated, these three classes will be found to have existed among all the nations of antiquity. In the first place, I have found among the Greeks and Romans, the great mass of the common people, and among all classes, from the highest to the lowest, those who were indulging in the "lusts of the flesh," those who were not only grossly vile, but were characterised by great avarice, ambition, and so on; all of whom came under the category of those who exhibit in full operation the "lusts of the flesh." Next, I have observed the cultivated classes. All of you will doubtless be aware that the finest specimens of human composition have come down to us, firstly, from Greece, and afterwards from Rome. These have been transmitted to us as models, and have attracted the notice of all men of cultivated intellect. Now this class formed a considerable portion of the population both of Greece and Rome. Then there was, in all these nations, a class of religious men such as we find in existence among the followers of Buddah, Confucius, Pythagoras, Zoroaster, and so on. They were, to a certain degree, devout, attentive, worshippers of the gods —men who cultivated what were then deemed exercises of piety—and amongst them doubtless were sincere men. After considering these matters, the question arose in my mind, "How could individuals, constituted as these were, without the knowledge of the living and true God, pass their lives in any degree of comfort?" "How could they disguise from themselves the blackness and darkness that lay before them as to futurity?" "How could they, under the circumstances in which they were placed, find *any comfort whatever?*" I have found an answer to these queries, in the discovery of a principle which appears to me to have had very little attention bestowed upon it by religious men; but which is one of the most remarkable principles of our common nature; I mean the principle of "Desperation." It has obtained different names according as it appeared among different nations. Among the Turks, for example, it was called "Fatalism." Still it was always the principle of "desperation," the principle which first appeared in Adam and Eve, the moment they transgressed, and before the promise of a great deliverer was made to them; it was a principle made manifest among the Jews, but which appeared more prominently in the Gentile world amongst the cultivated nations of antiquity. Now this principle of desperation appeared in two forms; in the first place it appeared as a sort of blind acquiescence, on the part of the majority, in their circumstances, or, in things as they were. When I think of the deplorable condition of the Roman and Greek people, and of the vast number of slaves that existed among them—when I think of the cruelties they practised on the helpless and the conquered—I have often asked myself what species of comfort could the majority of these people realize under circumstances so dark and forbidding? The only solution I have been enabled to give is this—that they seemed to think themselves forced to take things as they were—and to acquiesce in them, because they could not help it; they gratified their appetites—pursued their respective businesses—were quiet under ordinary circumstances—and turbulent under extraordinary ones. In the great majority, you could not fail to see this sort of blind acquiescence in things as they were, the spirit of desperation appearing to actuate them, that spirit leading them to make the most of this life, as circumstances gave them opportunity; but this appeared in a very extraordinary form, when they were subjected to trials and privations, and to death itself. When we look, for instance, at the state of the slaves among the Greeks and Romans—when we look at the cases of those who were brought forward in gladiatorial shows—to slay each other in various forms—when we look at the many scenes of wanton cruelty practised on the slaves, we see in these heathens a sort of desperate acquiescence in the circumstances in which they were placed—a feeling that they *could not* help themselves, and so became resigned to their fate, and to the circumstances by which they were surrounded.

But the spirit of desperation did not *always* shew itself in this acquiescent form; strange to state, it sometimes shewed itself in deeds of daring and violence, and acted upon the principle, "We are here placed in such evil circumstances, that we cannot be worse; let us enjoy life while we can, and as long as we can; and, if we cannot do this without acts of violence, let us make some bold and even desperate effort to free ourselves from our present situation." Another view of this spirit of desperation was exhibited among the higher and cultivated classes—who were in possession of leisure and wealth, and among those who enjoyed the highest honours of state. I have been struck to observe that most of these, although highly cultivated, were "Epicureans," both in principle and practice. All acted on this principle—"Let us enjoy ourselves to the utmost." We find our years are passing away, and grey hairs are stealing on us; the world is slipping from beneath our feet; let us therefore enjoy it and its pleasures as long as we can, and to the utmost of our power. Even those called the *religious* classes were not destitute of this feeling, for an examination into their religious ceremonies, as well as their private lives, will shew that they were often to be found acting upon the same principle that the apostle speaks, of when he says, "Let us eat and drink, for to-morrow we die." "Let us eat and drink—let us indulge the passions—let us make the most of the present time—and live as well as we can;" was the principle of many, who made religion a cloak for carrying on their licentious practices. Thus, this principle is perceived to have existed in two aspects among these people. In the first place, it was shewn in a blind acquiescence to their fate; and in the second place, in a desire to enjoy life to the utmost of their power. These are the two grand features which, even in their own works, the highly-cultivated nations of Greece and Rome present to us. Therefore, the apostle did not use any imaginary language when he said, "Let us eat and drink, for to-morrow we die," he quoted their own language, he alluded to their own practices, while affirming, that if the resurrection of the dead was denied; then, indeed, these wretched men *were* correct. I will not enter further into this subject. "The lust of the flesh—the lust of the eyes—and the pride of life," are made manifest in *all* human beings, their ordinary operation being seen in the common people, their peculiar operation in literary men, and their highest in *very religious* men; these are the grand characteristics of human nature, whether presented before us in its lowest or highest aspect. And in each of these three forms, it will be perceived that the principle of desperation reigns triumphant, this being the grand principle which men have pressed into the highest services of human life.

The principle of desperation is one which has been very generally overlooked, and I have brought it in for the purpose of contrasting with it, the grand principles of the divine nature as laid down in my other two texts.

Now, looking at these two texts, "This is the record that God hath given to us eternal life, and this life is in His son;" and, "as we have borne the image of the earthy, we shall also bear the image of the heavenly;" I say, looking at these two texts, it will be perceived that *the first* points out as a grand principle of the Divine nature, a something that is freely bestowed upon us by God himself; and the *second* points out the form in which the blessing is bestowed. I desire to look at these matters *scripturally*, and I always think it desirable to have God's words brought prominently and distinctly before our eyes. There are some persons who think that grace is derived, not from God's testimony, but from the exercise of human reason—from the dictates of the human mind, from the influence of our own hearts, and so on; but the testimony borne by God to the conscience of every individual whom He has seen meet to enlighten is, "He that believeth hath the witness in himself:" that is, it becomes a witness to him, and this witness testifies that "God *hath* given to him eternal life." God *hath* given—not *may* give—but *hath* given; it is thus a matter of present possession and of present enjoyment. "He that believeth hath everlasting life;" he hath it, not in consequence of being better than his fellow-men—not in consequence of any superiority over his fellow-men—not because he has any *right* to possess it—but because God hath chosen freely to bestow it; and, just as we have received human blessings without any right on our part to possess them, so do we receive all things pertaining to the life of godliness, without any right or claim to them on our part; and we can have no right to possess them at any future period of our lives any more than at present. Eternal life is God's gift bestowed sovereignly and freely at first, and it is a gift bestowed sovereignly and freely still. Any other ground of hope might cause us to doubt, to hesitate, and to despair. Well, then, "God *hath* given to us eternal life"—hath given it to every believer of the Truth—hath given it to him through faith in God's own testimony,—and wherever there is a true belief in God's testimony, there will be found eternal life—that life which is in His Son. But this life is not the life that Adam possessed naturally—a mere *creature* life. God has not—blessed be His name—given us such a life through His Son, but has given to us a divine life—given to us the highest life—given to us the life that God himself lives—given to us a life that involves everlasting blessedness—a life which is the perfection of knowledge—a life which is the perfection of love. This life consists in seeing the Infinite Jehovah as He is—in loving the Infinite Jehovah as He is; it is therefore the enjoyment of God, as what He is revealed to be—and that enjoyment is by seeing Him revealed as light and love, which constitutes God himself—for He is light and He is love. Thus eternal life is given to us—life here and life hereafter—through the manifestation of Himself, and it is through opening the eyes of our understanding that we are made to love Him, as having first loved us.

And then it will be observed that, this life is in His Son, not in the mere creature, such as Adam was—not in you nor in me. It is not an angelic life that is given us: that would come short of the divine intention;—no; it is a life given to us in God's own dear Son, who came down to save us; it is a life given to us in Jesus, who died for our sins and rose again for our justification, and ascended again to God's right hand. It is a divine life that comes to us through Him, and through Him we are made partakers of the divine nature. He hath brought in a life of which he Himself is the author; and this precious truth, carried home to the conscience, sets us free from every doubt, and even from the fear of death itself.

The principle of desperation is connected with, and belongs to, every human being; but the divine principle is only connected with the manifestation of the truth as it is in Jesus; and through the manifestation of this divine principle, we know what God is, and what we are in Him. It is thus that we rejoice in Him with joy unspeakable and full of glory; we know that "God is not a man that He should lie, nor the Son of man that He should repent;" what He hath said He will do; having given to us eternal life—having given to us all things pertaining to the life of godliness now—He will carry us through this present evil world, so that, when death overtakes us, it shall be to exchange a world of sorrow and of sin, for a heaven of joy and love, where we shall see His face, and enjoy heavenly blessings at His right hand for evermore.

Then observe the form in which the blessing is conveyed. God gives us, not the image of the earthy, but the image of the heavenly. Whenever some men, calling themselves Christians, treat of a future state, they treat of it as if it were to be a sort of repetition of our present life. How fallacious! Has Jesus—the second Adam, the Lord from heaven, merely risen from the dead to restore us to an Adamic paradise? It cannot be. No; when Christ comes, "this corruptible shall put on incorruption, and this mortal shall put on immortality;" we shall then be with Christ, and see him as he is,—and we shall not only see him as he is, but we shall be conformed to our Head, conformed to the glorious body of the Son of God.

I might, if time had allowed, have said a great deal more. I would, however, ask you to contrast the operation of these principles—the operation of the principle of *human* nature—that principle of "desperation," which runs throughout human nature, and which acts so powerfully on the mass of human beings; with the operation of those sweet principles conferred by God himself, through the manifestation of His own Son, consisting in the manifestation to us of eternal life through him, conforming us to our divine Head here and hereafter, and thus giving us to rejoice in full hope of the glory of God.

May the Lord bless what has been spoken, so far as consistent with His Word and will, and to His name be praise for evermore.—Amen.

SERMON XVI.

Sunday, June 17, 1855.

THE passage of scripture, from which I would now address you, is contained in the 8th chapter of St. Paul's Epistle to the Romans, and at the second verse.

"For the law of the spirit of life in Christ Jesus hath made me free from the law of sin and death."

So close is the connection subsisting between passages of Holy Writ—and so close especially is the connection that exists between the wonderful reasonings of the apostle Paul, that in order to the understanding of the passage, which I have read as my text, it is requisite to consult, not only the preceding context, but the whole of the preceding part of the Epistle; and it is also necessary to make ourselves intimately acquainted with the verses that follow in this most important chapter. If I remember rightly, the celebrated Locke dwells much in his work, "On the Reasonableness of Christianity," on the impropriety of being guided in our reading of the Scriptures by the simple division into chapters and verses. Locke in this was right. I am not much in the habit of agreeing with him, as to his views on theology, which appear to me to have been dreadfully defective—if not altogether opposed to the mind of God—but so far as the fact is concerned, that the Scriptures must be looked at apart from any reference to their division into chapters and verses, I am decidedly at one with him. In the course of a sermon on such a subject as that which I am about to bring before you, it is impossible for me to take into view, or bring under your consideration a very large portion of this epistle; but it may be proper to observe, that the verse that immediately precedes, and the two verses that immediately follow, are absolutely necessary to be taken into account, in order to obtain a full and correct understanding of the words of my text. In the verse that precedes, the apostle states, that "there is no condemnation to them who are in Christ Jesus, who walk not after the flesh, but after the spirit." And he gives the reason of there being no condemnation to such persons, in the words of my text. And again, he explains the words of my text in the third and fourth verses, and these verses, taken together, imply, that out of Christ Jesus —or rather to us as mere descendants of Adam—there is nothing but condemnation; but that in consequence of our connection with Jesus Christ, condemnation is out of the question; and the reason is, that the whole weight of condemnation has fallen upon our devoted and glorious Head; and having been borne by him thoroughly and completely, has been withdrawn from us; and through his finished work, we are set free. The fact is, apart from Christ, there is in the mind of man, when his attention is called to the subject of religion, nothing but a sense of condemnation. Guilt entered into man's mind when Adam transgressed; the sense of guilt has descended as an heirloom to each one of us; this sense of guilt can be called into exercise by a variety of means, and this sense of guilt we cannot get rid of thoroughly, except by the introduction into our minds of a principle, by which guilt is superseded and swallowed up, and that principle can be none other than the one which is referred to in the language of my text.

Not to detain you any longer with prefatory remarks, because the words of my text suggest to us so much, as to render it difficult to give even a very meagre illustration of them. I would observe that they bring under our notice clearly, and decidedly a contrast between two laws, "the law of the spirit of life in Christ Jesus, and the law of sin and death." There is no occasion for me to dwell upon the ordinary meaning of the word law. The common sense of mankind comprehends it; but it may be requisite to observe, that the word "law," is used in one of the cases spoken of in our text, in a sense peculiar to itself. Although I am not going to enter into the subject, it is requisite by the way, to allude to it. When "the law of sin and death" is referred to, a law is spoken of which may be broken, and which has been broken, "in that it was weak through the flesh," as the next verse shews. But when the other law—"the law of the spirit of life in Christ Jesus," is spoken of, there is reference made to a law which never was violated— a law which is absolute and imperative in its commands—a law which is always and necessarily obeyed. The one is merely a law of "prohibitions" and commands, and stands in opposition to, and is violated by, human nature; the other is a law of principle, a law, the implantation of which in the mind is the communication of the divine nature, and, like all divine principles, carries along with it its own accomplishment. Not, however, to dwell upon these matters in a general way, I would just divide the subject, as the text itself does, and call your attention first to the law of sin and death, so that you may thereby understand what that is, from which by the law of the spirit of life in Christ Jesus we are set free.

Well then, in the first place, what is meant by the law of sin and death, is to be gathered partly from this epistle, and partly from the rest of scripture. The apostle Paul, who wrote this epistle, was a Jew—a descendant of Abraham, according to the flesh, and as such was the subject of two laws, and both of these, when examined into, are found to be "laws of sin and death." As a Jew he was subject to the law of Moses; as a man he was subject to the law—or rather, he was in him and one with him who was subject to the law, given and broken in the Garden of Eden. Now, looking at the law under these two aspects, I say Paul had been subject to the law of Moses as a descendant of Abraham: he was born under the law; he was circumcised; he was brought up in the knowledge of it: he had been trained up in obedience to it; he tells us he was devoutly attached to it—and, having been a Pharisee in the strictest sense, he attained to the greatest proficiency in the knowledge and practice of the doctrines held and maintained by that particular sect. Now, this law of Moses was a law of sin and death. It was a law that brought to light continually the transgressions of those who were subject to it; it exposed transgressors to various punishments—and even, in many cases, to corporal punishment. We know that, according to the word of God, where there is no law, there can be no transgression; and consequently, where there is a multiplicity of laws, there must be a multiplicity of transgressions. Now the law of Moses contained laws almost innumerable—or, at all events, laws exceedingly numerous; and according to the number of these laws, was the capability and possibility of transgressing them. We know as a matter of fact, that by the Jews they were broken from the very first. We have furnished to us, in the five books of Moses, proofs of their transgressions in the wilderness; and in subsequent books we have complaints of their transgressions in the "Promised Land;" and other books carry down the transgressions of the Jews to the very last of the prophets. So multiplied were their transgressions, that in the 1st chapter of Isaiah they are spoken of as "thoroughly diseased," as a polluted body, "having no soundness in it from the sole of the foot to the crown of the head, but being full of wounds and bruises and putrifying sores;" the result was, that instead of the law having justified the Jewish people, or any member of that body, it had brought them all in as cursed; as it is written, "cursed is every one that continueth not in all things written in the book of the law to do them." It had been to the Jewish nation in general, and to every member of it in particular, a law of sin and death—it had convicted each one of numerous transgressions, and it had shewn him that he was justly deserving of death.

Now under the Jewish law, the Apostle Paul, as well as all other Jews, was brought up. But I go on to observe, that he was also in Adam—the common progenitor of Moses and all mankind; that he had in him been subject to the one law of prohibition, which having been violated, was proved to be a law of sin and death likewise. And looking at him in these two capacities—as subject to the law of Moses as a Jew—and subject to the law given to Adam in Paradise as a man—he being a son of Adam—looking at him as standing guilty and dying in these two violated laws —we have a clear idea of what was the condition of every descendant of Abraham according to the flesh, by nature. But, my dear friends, we have more. We have an idea also of what was the state of every Gentile, for although it is very true that the Gentiles in general, and you and I in particular, were never directly subject to the law of Moses— although it is true, the only law to which we are subject, is the law given to Adam in Paradise, which having been violated by him, was violated by us in him, so that it became in this way to them and us, a law of sin and death—although it is true, that we die exclusively on the ground of Adam's one transgression, as our transgression—yet at the same time, it is a remarkable fact, recorded in the 2nd chapter of the Epistle to the Romans—and recognised in various other parts of the Scriptures—that men may render the law of Moses their law, by making it a law unto themselves; and thus increasing their condemnation by bringing themselves into the position of the Jewish people, and becoming voluntarily subject to a law under which they were never placed by God Himself. To me, one of the most extraordinary circumstances connected with modern times—not merely to be seen in the Church of Rome—but in Protestant Churches, is this, that over the Communion-table they have the Ten Commandments printed. Now, if it were merely to allude to what the consciences of men naturally dictate to them, as shewing things that ought to be avoided, one might not object to it; but when we recollect that these Commandments are placed there as rules to which Christians are to be subject, and to be obeyed by them under pain of damnation (for such are the views entertained on the subject), we wonder at the parties who can be guilty of such a piece of folly—for it is shewn by the apostle expressly, in the 5th chapter of the Epistle to the Galatians, that to be subject to the law of Moses in one respect, is to be subject to it in all; therefore, all such parties in making the subjection of men to the Ten Commandments a condition of salvation, virtually place themselves under the law of Moses, as if that law had been actually given to them, and thus introduce into their consciences additional condemnation.

Such was the condition of all Jews; as Jews they were subject, in a twofold sense, to a law of sin and death—subject to the law of Moses as such—and subject to the law given to Adam in Paradise. Both were laws of prohibition—both condemning when violated—and both bringing in death, as the inseparable portion of condemnation.

I observe also, that Gentiles were similarly situated. For although never directly under the law of Moses, which was given to the descendants of Abraham according to the flesh exclusively; yet, even before Christ came, numerous Gentiles —especially those of Greece and Rome—had voluntarily become subject to the law of Moses, had joined the Synagogue service—and become proselytes to the Jewish code. Indeed, such is the beauty, force, and power of the Ten Commandments, or law of Moses in general, that it not only forces itself upon the approbation of Gentile consciences, but has compelled the great majority of the Gentiles—ignorant of the Gospel, to make themselves voluntarily subject to its precepts, and to seek for life everlasting by relying on a fixed compliance with its demands.

Now in addressing you, my dear friends, I address parties to whom the law of Moses has necessarily commended itself by its simplicity, beauty, and power—and there are none of us who have had that law brought home to our consciences, but have felt that, even while transgressing it, it had a right to our obedience. Who then are set free from this law? Are any? Are the majority of those called Christians set free from it? My dear friends, if we consider what was our own case before the Gospel was revealed to us—if we look around us on the whole mass of human society—if we consider the ordinary dogmas of religion that are prevalent, we must say, that while we know it to be the portion of some, it is at the best, but the portion of a very few, to be set free from this law of sin and death. The law of Moses commends itself to your conscience and to mine, but it commends itself by condemning them; but we enjoy the glorious privilege of knowing the Gospel, by which freedom from this condemnation is revealed to us, and the means by which that freedom is conveyed; but the majority of professing Christians still profess to live under the law of Moses, and therefore continue under its curse, preferring to look to and rely upon it for salvation, rather than to being saved through the work of Jesus Christ on Calvary, and completed by his resurrection from the dead.

In the blessed passage now before us, the apostle says, "The law of the Spirit of life in Christ Jesus hath made *me* free from the law of sin and death." Here then is one individual, who, whatever may have been his former state and condition—however strong or desperate the bondage under which he had laboured, and however much he might at one time have hated the Gospel scheme of salvation—here is one individual who declares in the spirit of truth and faith, that he had been set free from the law of Moses—and from the law transgressed by Adam, completely and for ever. And he not merely proclaims to us, that he had been set free, but he tells us, when and how; and he speaks of a privilege not peculiar to himself, but one which he shares with all the people of God in every succeeding age.

The law of the Spirit of life—now, this must be explained in connection with what follows—"The law of the Spirit of life," or "of the life of the Spirit." Who, or what is the Spirit of life? I am afraid the word Spirit is used by many of us more in a technical sense—than from any real understanding and comprehension of its Biblical import. To the Scriptures themselves we must look, if we would understand what it means. We discover from the language of the Old Testament Scriptures, and from the conversation which Christ had with Nicodemus, recorded in the 3rd chapter of St. John's Gospel, that the word Spirit has reference to "breath or wind," it is connected with both words in the original.

Now, in this and other passages, especially in passages where a contrast is intended, to what does the word Spirit refer? In the 2nd chapter of Genesis we are told, that "God formed Adam out of the dust of the ground, and then breathed into his nostrils the breath of life, and man became a living soul." Was this breath of life, the spirit of life that is here spoken of?   No; but it was a beautiful type of it; it was a type of a far more glorious antitype.   The spirit or soul, breathed into Adam, was the type of that heavenly spirit—that everlasting spirit—which, wherever it is breathed, communicates—not life in word—not the life that Adam possessed—but communicates a life everlasting. Therefore, the Spirit of life here, is not the spirit of human life—but its antitype—it is the spirit of a divine life—it is a principle which knew no beginning, and knows no end.

But to be more specific.   To what does this word spirit more particularly refer?   It refers to God's word, which in one sense is the breath of God's spirit—which in another sense, is that through which God communicates life everlasting, to any of the children of men. Looking at God's word, we find that "*Spirit*" is always connected with divine efficacy; it was God's spirit which moved upon the face of the waters, when they were created; it was God's spirit which went forth with the word, "Let there be light, and there was light;" it was God's spirit which went forth with the word, "Let us make man in our image, after our likeness;" with God's spirit divine efficacy is connected, even in natural things ; for it was God's spirit which breathed into Adam even the inferior principle of natural life.

But God's spirit has assumed a higher aspect through the medium of an individual who differs from and is superior to Adam. There once appeared upon earth a Being who derived his origin from no man. He was born of a Virgin—the Spirit of God, for the first time appeared, forming a Being in the likeness of sinful flesh, but who was not sinful, or even capable of sinning.   What a beautiful emphasis there is in a passage, contained in the Evangelist, St. Luke, 24th chapter, 5th verse—where the women having gone to the grave in which Jesus had for a time been laid, are asked, "Why seek ye the living among the dead?"   The fact is, the whole of the human race are dead; for, although God created Adam naturally as a human being, He created him pure and innocent, but he fell from that state, he involved himself in guilt, he involved himself and his posterity in death—and death swept over the whole human family; and every human being who now comes into the world, comes into it stamped with the impress of sin and of death. Some are taken away in old age, others in youth, and some at their birth, but all are swept away by the one destroyer, after having spent a longer or shorter period on earth.

But with respect to one Being, the principle of life appeared in him from his very conception—not the principle of a human life—not the principle of a dying life, but the principle of a heavenly and everlasting life. He was from his very conception the living among the dead; he was *the Word* of God embodied—the spirit of the Lord dwelt in him without measure; there was in him divine life from his very origin, and throughout the whole of his earthly career, divine life was manifested in him in the form of human life. That living principle in him triumphed over all sin, as it ultimately triumphed over death; that living principle in him triumphed over all opposition; that living principle in him appeared in the form of intense and perfect love to his heavenly Father; appeared in the form of entire obedience to His most holy law, and appeared in the ultimate sacrifice of himself. Then, this living one, thus being clothed in flesh, who was conceived by the Spirit of life—and in whom the Spirit of life dwelt from his very origin—this Being triumphed over death; he threw of his connection with mortality—he changed mortality itself into life—he arose from the dead in his own appropriate character as the living one, as the Prince of Life. Thus it is that he imparts the principle of life to others—he imparts his own life—not the life of Adam, but life in a crucified and risen Saviour.

"The Spirit of life." This Spirit of life then, is the Word of the living God. Now, if there is one fact that has become more plain to my mind than another, it is the awful state into which the Church of Christ—as it is called—has fallen, by giving to human writings a power and authority in religion which is due only to the Word of the living God. Now, I may speak—others may speak—we may speak logically and correctly—but we speak merely as human beings; our words have no divine power, and are attended with no divine efficacy; but the Word which emanated from God himself—that Word which was given by Him to inspired prophets and apostles, and stands recorded in the Holy Scriptures—that Word has in it the principle of life—the principle of everlasting life—and this Word shewed that it possessed this principle when it took effect in the conception of our blessed Lord. I do not say that this was the first proof of its efficacy, for it had shewn its efficacy in every preceding age, in the faith of the prophets, patriarchs, priests, and others, but it was the grand proof of its efficacy.

No doubt, in the case of the prophets and patriarchs there was an exhibition of the power of the divine Word, for it was through that Word that faith in them was engendered and maintained; but never was its wondrous efficacy displayed fully, until that Word took effect in the conception and birth of our Lord—until that Word shewed itself, as constituting the very substance of his mind. For our Lord had no views arising from what is commonly called "common sense," or views derived from the prejudices of the world; our Lord's views were all derived from God's Word, and were all attuned to God's Word. He was *the Word*; and, if you want to know what is the meaning of the Old Testament Scriptures spiritually, look at the character of Jesus Christ as it stands recorded in the New Testament Scriptures, and you will find that the Old Testament Scriptures were in him embodied. The 119th Psalm is a most beautiful epitome of the fact now stated; for, from the beginning to the end of that psalm, Jesus is opening up his mind, and shewing, that by the pages of Holy Writ he was influenced, and that what he aimed at was always according to God's Word. In Christ there was nothing derived from man in the way of ideas or notions, or with regard to the objects at which he aimed; all was strictly impressed with his firm belief in what God had said; he believed it with reference to men, and he practised it under the influence of the Spirit by which it was dictated.

Well, here you perceive the grand power of God's Word. Christ was the eternal Word made flesh. He was the everlasting Word as embodied in the Old Testament Scriptures; so that, when you look at Jesus Christ, you look at the Word which was with God, and came from God—and was, from the beginning, with God.

Now, that Word exhibited as the Spirit of life in Christ Jesus, acquired a most extraordinary power. Jesus arose from the dead and ascended to God's right hand. He poured out his Spirit, on the day of Pentecost, on his assembled disciples; the Spirit of life came down from him, and was shewn in the form of the Word which the apostles proclaimed; and the living power which had lain latent in the Old Testament Scriptures, now became procreative through the medium of their voices, and the writings they have left on record. Jesus shewed his almighty power as the Spirit of life, in the effects produced by Peter's sermon, by which thousands were converted; he shewed it in Jerusalem, and in Samaria, and he shewed its wondrous efficacy in the Gentile world, and has been shewing it for eighteen hundred years, seeing that by its instrumentality sinners in every age, have been brought out of darkness into his marvellous light.

In the case of Jesus himself, the Word of God came home as "law:" it was the law of the Spirit of life in him. Our blessed Lord was not created as you and I are—he was not set free from the law of sin and death; he came into the world subject to law; he was made under the law. The Spirit of life therefore came to him under the circumstances to which I have alluded, as "the living among the dead," it came to him saying, "Thou shalt love the Lord thy God with all thy heart, and with all thy soul, and thy neighbour as thyself;" it came to him exacting the most perfect obedience; not one jot or tittle of it was to be left unfulfilled by him; and all was required to be fulfilled by him, under the influence of the same Spirit by which it was dictated.

Although our poor paltry minds, conversant only with human subjects and taken up with human affairs, will turn to anything rather than this; there is not a more wondrous subject for our consideration than Christ's obedience to the law of the Spirit of life. This law finds in every human being a law opposed to it—the law of human nature—but in Christ it found a principle ready to comply with it. He loved it, as it is written, "O how I love Thy law;" therefore it was the Spirit of life to Christ Jesus; and it is the law of the Spirit of life to us, as in him and one with him. I am afraid, my dear friends, that this principle is not only boldly set aside by the Church of Rome, but is generally set aside by Protestants and Dissenters also.

We are one with Christ Jesus. Just as decidedly as Adam's violation of the prohibition in the Garden of Eden was our violation of it as in him and one with him, so is Christ's obedience our obedience. His obedience to the law of the Spirit of life is our obedience; and the Gospel, or "Glad tidings," opens up this fact to us—shews us that Jesus having fulfilled the law for us—having died for us—and risen again for us—we are so inseparably one with him, that his righteousness is our righteousness—and his life is our life.

Well then, this law of the Spirit of life in Christ Jesus, does not come to us in the form of a law of prohibition or command, which we are to fulfil—but it comes to us in the form of the manifestation of a law fulfilled, and fulfilled by him who is our divine and heavenly Head, and so fulfilled that no part of it remains to be fulfilled by us. "He has become the end of the law for righteousness to every one that believeth."

Is the eye of thy understanding opened, my dear Christian brother? Hast thou been brought out of the kingdom of darkness into the kingdom of God's dear Son? Then thou beholdest thyself one with him most sweetly, one with him everlastingly. But observe what follows. It has set thee free from the law of sin and death. Formerly, thy conscience was accusing thee of sin, and the word of God told thee that thou didst die in Adam, the common ancestor of all men; thou wast trembling like a guilty slave before one whose character was mistaken by thee for that of a tyrant; thou wast trying to get rid of the gloomy circumstances in which thou wast placed; thou wast perhaps plunged deep in anguish and despair—and it may be, that unable to derive any comfort, thou wast perhaps giving way to the indulgence of thy lusts, until brought into a state of desperation; but it was revealed to thee by a divine power, that Adam was the figure of him that was to come; it was revealed to thee that God had thee in everlasting union with himself before Adam existed, and but for which everlasting union Adam would never have existed; it was revealed to thee that Jesus' righteousness was a divine righteousness, that hath swallowed up sin, and put away the sin of the world; it was revealed to thee that the blood of Jesus Christ cleanseth thee from all sin; and thou now beholdest thyself, no longer exposed to the consequences of Adam's transgression; thou seest thyself clothed in Christ's divine righteousness—one with him—no longer dying but divinely living—thou findest in thy mind, by sweet experience, that thou art set free from the law of sin and death—and not only so, but findest that in Christ thou art virtually set free from this present evil world, and art living in the earnest and foretaste of the life to come; and all this through the mind of Christ Jesus being revealed to thee, not in the sense of a law of commands or prohibitions to be fulfilled by thee; but in the sense of all prohibitions and commands fulfilled by thy divine Head; thou thus seest thyself set free, and art given to rejoice with joy that is unspeakable and full of glory.

Well then, "The Spirit of life in Christ Jesus" hath brought us into a state of freedom, a freedom that exacts no conditions on the part of the creature, and depends on no conditions to be fulfilled by the creature, but springs solely from the knowledge of the divine and glorious facts revealed to us, that God is shewing forth His love in Christ Jesus, proclaiming peace on earth and good-will towards men;

speaking peace to our consciences by the blood of the cross; and shewing us that although sooner or later death must perform its office, that we have died and risen in Christ Jesus, and shall live and reign with him for ever, and all this is accomplished by the Spirit of life in Christ Jesus.

Thus then we are one with God in Christ Jesus, and are made partakers of the earnest of the Spirit of life. We are set free from the law of sin and death, and like the eunuch of Ethiopia go on our way rejoicing, finding the joy of the Lord to be our strength. And what God hath done man cannot undo. Man may tell us of our guilt, but we point him to Christ, by the shedding of whose blood we are cleansed from all guilt. Man may tell us of our dying in Adam, but we point him to Christ, as he in whom we are alive for evermore

Now, wherever this knowledge is possessed, it is productive of effects; for, as God hath given to us eternal life in His Son, so we shall shew our love to him, and to those who bear His image, by doing good to all men as the Lord hath given us opportunity.

May the Lord bless what has been said, so far as it is agreeable to His word, and to His name be praise for evermore.—Amen.

SERMON XVII.

July 8th, 1835.

The passage of Scripture from which I would this morning address you, is contained in the 45th chapter of the Prophecies of Isaiah, and at the 22nd verse—"Look unto me, and be ye saved, all the ends of the earth."

"Look unto me." You are aware, my dear friends, that the language of Scripture is, "It doth not yet appear what we shall be." While in this fleshly state, we are not possessed of capacities enabling us to see and hear God, as He is—I mean fleshly capacities. And hence it is that, in addressing us on Scriptural topics, God speaks to us through the medium of the capacities we have, suggesting thereby that there is a far higher mode of becoming acquainted with Him than any which we can possess while we are sojourners here below. You know, for instance, that each human being is characterised by certain senses. These have been commonly called the five *external* senses. There is the sense of "sight," the sense of "hearing," the sense of "smelling," the sense of "taste," and the sense of "touch." Now, as we have no *real* mode of understanding God, as He is, God addresses us with reference to spiritual topics through the medium of these five senses; sometimes as in the text, he speaks to us through a reference, to the sense of sight, "*Look* unto me;" sometimes with reference to the sense of hearing, "Blessed are they that *hear* the word of God, and keep it," and in other passages, "They shall *hear* and understand." Then again we have a reference to the sense of *smelling,* the offering of Christ is spoken of as a sweet smelling savour. And again, we have the command, "O *taste* and *see* that God is good." And then again, we have the command to "*lay hold* of the hope set before us," with reference to the sense of touch. Now all these figurative expressions are explained by Scriptural terms, constantly occurring in the New Testament Scriptures, and with which, no doubt, the majority of you are quite familiar—I mean the word "faith," and the word "believe." Now we must never attempt to explain the word "believe," by these figurative terms—but always explain the figurative terms by the words, "to believe;" and my authority for this, is Christ's own language; for if you read with care the 6th chapter of John, you will find that figurative language is often applied by Christ, both with reference to spiritual food, and to our partaking of it; and you will find also that it is explained, more than once, by the fact, that it is through our believing, that *that* food is appropriated, and becomes conducive to our spiritual sustenance and nourishment. Then, in the words of my text, the language, "*Look* unto me," is equivalent to saying, "believe on me," because it is through "believing" that we look to him, who is the blessed and glorious speaker.

It will occur to every individual, at all interested, in knowing the mind and will of God, that He who here speaks is Jehovah Himself. The context shews it. "By Myself have I sworn, saith the Lord," and the whole scope of the chapter in which the words occur shew it; the whole scope of the Prophecies of Isaiah, and the word of God throughout shews, that it is not a mere creature, but the Creator himself, who says, "Look unto me," that is, "believe on me, all the ends of the earth."

But who is this Creator? Who is He, who, thus, in terms so *emphatic*, and yet so affectionate, addresses us? Is it one who ever stood to us in a peculiar relation—who was brought very near to us—who was "bone of our bone, and flesh of our flesh?" Yes; it is He who speaks, for this is one of the numerous passages of Scripture, in which we find *one* portion of the word of God, serving as an inspired interpretation of another. When you and I come to the New Testament Scriptures, and read the solemn, impressive, and most instructive exhortations, which were addressed by the apostle Paul to believing Jews, we find towards the close of the Epistle to the Hebrews, the following emphatic declaration—"Looking unto Jesus, the author and finisher of our faith." "Looking unto Jesus," carries us back to the words of my text, "Look unto me," and enables us at once to perceive that He who speaks in the Old, is He of whom mention is made, and to whom our attention is called, in the New Testament Scriptures; and that to "Look unto Jesus," that is, "to believe on Jesus," is a realization of the words of my text. This, I regard as the correct interpretation of the words, "Look unto me;" but we have not only this, we have the very name of Jesus himself given us, as an authority for it. You will recollect that before he was born, it was declared, "his name should be called Jesus," because he should save his people from their sins. He, who is *Jesus*, should do this. But what does the name Jesus mean? You are aware that the Hebrew word, "Joshua," and the Greek word, "Jesus," correspond; and there is no occasion for me to state what lexicographers or the dictionaries say on this point; for, if you read with care the 4th chapter of the Epistle to the Hebrews, you will find the explanation in the following words; "If Jesus had given them rest, then would he not afterwards have spoken of another day." Now, the "Jesus" spoken of in this passage, is "Joshua," so that Joshua in the Hebrew, corresponds with Jesus in the Greek; and as Joshua signifies "Jehovah, the Saviour;" Jesus, of course, has the same signification. Therefore, "Looking unto Jesus," is looking unto Jehovah, the Saviour; "Look unto me," and the words immediately added, "and be ye saved," clearly proves this to be its meaning. Thus then, in the single word, Jesus, or Joshua, "Jehovah the Saviour;" you have the import of the Old Testament phraseology, "Look unto me, *Jehovah*, and be ye saved," "Look unto him," that is, "believe on him"—"believe on him," in the two capacities here spoken of. "Believe on him," as what he is, "Jehovah, the I AM, the self-existent one," the Being who conversed with Adam in the Garden of Eden; the Being who conversed with Abraham, Isaac, and Jacob; the Being who became known by His name "*I am*," in the "*burning bush;*" the Being who has come down to us, as the "I am," in the person of Christ Jesus, who is "the same yesterday, and to-day, and for ever."

I very seldom trouble you with discourses about the "Trinity," or the "Trinity in Unity," as I am not fond of using phrases, however correct they may be, on the whole, but which are nevertheless of human origin; but while I wish to avoid unnecessary phrases, as much as possible, still *the great fact* of Scripture is, that "God was manifest in the flesh, for the salvation of man." It was not a creature, it was not the highest of creatures, that was born of a Virgin, and for a while sojourned on earth, expired on the cross, rose from the dead, and ascended to glory; it was God himself, the mighty, the everlasting God, who condescended to appear in flesh, to save us from our sins, and to save us from this present evil world. And any person who comes short of recognizing in the Son of man, and the Son of God, the person of the speaker, throughout the Old Testament Scriptures, the person of Him who said, "Let there be light, and there was light;" the person of Him who said, "Let us make man in our own image, after our likeness;" the person of Him who, in every other respect, is brought under our notice throughout the Old Testament Scriptures—any one, I say, who fails to recognise in Jesus of Nazareth, the God of the Heavens, and the God of the whole earth; that person misses the fundamental truth of revelation, can never have peace spoken to his conscience, or be enabled to rejoice in the Holy Ghost.

My dear brethren, I say these things, not as distrusting you, but as the expression of my own sympathy for the truth, for, the more I know of the Scriptures, the more I perceive therein the *Deity* of Christ set before my eyes, and made manifest to my understanding, and find it to be the grand, triumphant, cardinal truth of Scripture. "Look unto me," in my character of Jehovah, the self-existent one; and "Look unto me," in my character of Jehovah, the "Saviour." Your consciences may have been filled with fearful anticipations; you may perhaps have been striving, by many efforts, to relieve yourselves from your unhappy position; you may perhaps have betaken yourselves to theological physicians, but physicians of *no value;* you may have been endeavouring to heal your wound yourselves, or you may have asked them to attempt the cure of it, but hitherto *all in vain;* for the ulcer breaks forth afresh, and perhaps when, for a time, it has appeared to be healed over, it again breaks out, and you feel all the terrors and alarms of a guilty conscience. Now, Jesus is the Saviour. What the *creature* has not done, and cannot do—what cannot be effected by yourselves, or by others, has been accomplished, and gloriously accomplished too, by the Son of God. He came in human flesh, to bless you, and to save you. He came not to bestow upon you the Adamic nature—for he was not a man of the earth, earthy, like Adam—he was the second man, the Lord from heaven; and he came to make you partakers of his own divine nature; he came, not to restore to you the image of the earthy, but to make you partakers with him of the image of the heavenly. He saves you from yourselves, as well as from sin and from death. He saves you from self, by making you one with himself, and a partaker of his own divine nature. For, says the apostle, "I am crucified with Christ, nevertheless I live; yet not I, but

Christ liveth in me." The principle of creature-self is nailed to the cross of Christ, with all that appertains to nature of Adam; and we know that we are crucified with Christ, and yet, that in him we are alive, are partakers of his divine nature, and are destined to the enjoyment of his bliss and immortality.

To the salvation of Jesus as "Jehovah, the Saviour;" reference is made in the words of my text—we know Jesus through looking to him, through believing on him—and the enjoyment of this knowledge, speaks "peace to our guilty consciences," and inspires us with "joy that is unspeakable and full of glory."

"Look unto me," "look unto Jesus," "Jehovah the Saviour." But how? Here again we are left at no loss as to the meaning upon this point. The majority of mankind do not look away from themselves, and are merely considering and asking, "What shall we eat, and what shall we drink, and wherewithal shall we be clothed." Some may be immersed in suffering and sorrow, but at the same time so ignorant of the Saviour, that earthly considerations alone can occupy their minds; so that, looking away *from* themselves is not their characteristic, or within their power. And, painful to state, looking from self to God is not a characteristic of those who are cultivated in mind, or professedly *religious;* for men of cultivated intellects, who have a tendency to be religious, too often look to their own minds, and their own intellects, rather than to what *God* hath said. And even men of a decidedly religious turn of mind, instead of looking to Jesus, are looking to themselves, looking to human authorities, to what *this* man or *that* man has uttered, asking what "Baxter" said, and what "Henry" said, and what other eminent men have said; and are guided and influenced by their declarations. Now, with reference to these things, the tendency is to idolize human reasonings, or human works; this is not looking to God, but making a god of something else. But the most painful view is exhibited by those who are the most religious, after a certain fashion. We have two specimens of these characters furnished to us in the Word of God, one of which is given by Christ himself in the 18th chapter of Luke—"Two men went up into the temple to pray, the one a Pharisee and the other a Publican. The Pharisee stood and prayed thus with himself: 'God I thank thee that I am not as other men are, extortioners, unjust, adulterers, or even as this Publican. I fast twice in the week; I give tithes of all that I possess,'" and so on.

We find that the Pharisee was exceedingly self-complacent at discovering in himself, as he thought, a character of superiority over his fellow-men; and especially over the wretched Publican, who was then his fellow-worshipper. You will find another instance in the person of the apostle Paul, before Jesus of Nazareth met him on the way to Damascus, and, by shewing him his Glory, overcame his opposition. It appears to me that the character of the apostle Paul, previous to his conversion, was that of a Pharisee of the most pure and conscientious description; far more so than any other that I know of. He appears to have been a just man, and to have acted conscientiously up to his own profession, and yet, all that he did—like the Pharisee I have just spoken of—stamped him as a blasphemer and injurious. Both of these were men, who, in their Pharisaical character, looked not to God, but to themselves; and in this I perceive the manifestation of self, in its highest form. And in the Christian Church, so called, men are continually asking "What do you feel," and "what do you think," and "are your desires right with God;" not looking unto Jesus, to ascertain whether these thoughts or feelings, or desires, are opposed to God; or whether there is in our fleshly minds anything agreeable to God. Persons of this description feed on their own delusions, and are turned aside from the simplicity of the truth as it is in Jesus. My dear friends, in all these various forms, whether in the form of indifference as exhibited on the part of the world generally, or in a disposition to refer to human beings and human works, instead of to the Word of God; or in a disposition to find something in ourselves, or something in *others*, by which to gain the favour of Heaven, men shew that they are not "looking unto God."

But there *is* such a thing as "looking unto Him," and this is brought before us in a most simple manner. It is brought before us and carried into effect in the same way as when God said, "Let there be light, and there was light;" —as when God said, "Let the earth bring forth every living thing after its kind, and the earth brought them forth accordingly;"—as when God commanded the earth to bring forth grass, the herb yielding seed, and the fruit tree yielding fruit after his kind, they sprang into existence, covering the earth with verdure, and adorning it with foliage,—as when God said, "Let us make man in our image," and man was made. And wherever the Word of God goes forth, it necessarily takes effect; and thus when God says, "Look unto me, and be ye saved," there is the same power in that Word, as was in the

'Omnific' Word, through which creation started into being. It is true, that that Word does not take effect in every one, because that Word is not addressed to every one. God hath said, by the mouth of Jesus Christ, "*He* that hath ears to hear, let *him* hear." There is a destined generation in the world, to whom these words are addressed, and in whom, *as* so addressed, they do, in due time, necessarily take effect. As certainly as light sprang out of darkness, so certainly is every "destined heir of salvation" made to hear the words, " Look unto me ;" and is also made to hear all corresponding words, such as, " Ho, every one that thirsteth, come ye to the waters ; " and all the precious testimonies, borne by God himself, throughout the Scriptures, they " hear ; " and with that " hearing," their souls are made alive. They " behold the Lamb of God that taketh away the sin of the world ;" they behold God's character revealed in him ; they are thus carried out of themselves and carried upwards, and there is thus realised in them that blessedness revealed and promised in the text.

But again, the power goes forth *with* the Word; the power is carried into effect *by* the Word. And this leads me to observe, that we are not commanded to " look " vaguely ; the word " look " implies " believing " to salvation. The testimony, to be *believed*, is recorded in the Scriptures, both Old and New ; it is nowhere else to be found ; but it is to be found there, certainly and exclusively. When Jesus Christ —who is God—says, " Look unto me," He says, " Look unto me, as revealed in my Word," and when God's power is put forth, the exhortation is complied with by those to whom it is addressed ; by all those who have ears to hear, eyes to see, and hearts to understand. And when we hear God speaking in His Word, we are made acquainted with what we could never have known otherwise ; we are made acquainted with the glorious character of God, manifested in the finished work of Christ Jesus, and are made partakers of life everlasting.

Well then, we are enabled to "Look to Him" who speaks ; our attention is directed to the testimony given concerning Him, and towards Jesus Christ as the true interpreter of that testimony. For, from the declaration of Christ himself, we know, that " no man knoweth the Father save the Son, and he to whom the Son hath revealed Him ;" and the Son reveals Him through the written testimony, and through it *only*. I am afraid we overlook the fact, that when our Lord was in flesh, and when conflicting with the Pharisees and

Sadducees, he did not refer to human reasonings to prove what he advanced. You will find Christ continually referring to "*It is written;*" to the written testimony of God, which was embodied in himself, and which he came to fulfil to the very uttermost. And in the preaching of the apostles, as recorded in the Acts of the Apostles, we find that it is to the Word and to the testimony recorded in the Old Testament Scriptures they invariably referred. "Who by the mouth of thy servant David hast said," and, "as it is written in the Scripture," and so on. Thus the head and the members both referred to the Word of God as the only source of divine knowledge, and the only ground of divine confidence. So has it been with the Church of God in every age; and those brethren of Berea, did not more clearly shew that they were more noble than those of Thessalonica, in that they received the Word with gladness, believing in the Scriptures, by which they learned that Jesus was *the* Christ, than all believers shew *their* superiority over the world, by having the eyes of their faith directed to God's written testimony, and in proportion to the degree in which they are made to understand it—in proportion as the light of the New Testament Scriptures is brought to bear upon the Old—in that same proportion do they grow up to the stature of men in Christ Jesus, and are thereby enabled to go on strong in the Lord, and in the power of his might.

"Look unto me," that is, "Believe on me," is the language of Jehovah, Jesus. It is his language calling upon us to direct our attention to God, and to himself, as the manifestor of God; for "he that hath seen the Son, hath seen the Father;" calling upon us and directing our attention to the Word of God, as that through which both he and the Father are made known; as that by the understanding of which the Spirit of God dwells in our hearts, and manifests in us the fruits of which it is productive, teaching us that "we should live not to ourselves, but to him who died for us and rose again." Thus, "Look unto me," is God's commandment; not in the sense of a commandment to be obeyed by us in our fleshly capacity, but in the sense in which light sprung into existence at the Almighty fiat of His word, and power going forth with the Word. In the sense by which, when Christ said to the man with a withered hand, "Stretch forth thine hand," and he stretched it forth, and it was restored whole like unto the other, so the command, "Look unto me," is followed by our looking unto Jesus; power goes forth with the Word, so that we who were formerly ignorant of God, as manifested in Christ Jesus, and looking to our peculiar idols, and endeavouring to establish our own peculiar views, now have "the eyes of our faith directed towards Jesus; in him the glory of God becomes manifest; in him all the brightness of God's perfections shine forth; in him there is an overwhelming fulness of the divine perfections by which we are drawn to him "with the cords of love as with the bands of a man,"—we are drawn towards him, who first loved us—and thus we are led to look upon him as all our salvation and all our desire.

This leads me to observe, that in the words of my text it is said, "Look unto me, and be ye saved." It is again the same command, accompanied by the same power, as we have been treating of; it has a relation to, and is embodied in, the word Jesus, "Jehovah, the Saviour." Those to whom it was addressed originally, were ruined in a two fold sense; ruined as men, as descendants of Adam, who had forfeited this present life through sin; and again as Jews, who, in consequence of transgression, had in a great measure forfeited the privileges of Judaism, and were about to forfeit them entirely, by crucifying the Lord of Life and Glory. Here the words of my text speak by anticipation, as if the crucifixion of the Lord Jesus *had taken place*, and in saying, "Look unto me, and be ye saved," intimates that entire ruin, both as Jews and men, had already come upon them—as men, having forfeited their natural existence in Adam; and as Jews, being deprived of the Old Testament institutions. But this ruin falls, not only on them, but on the whole family of man—it falls on the Gentiles, as well as the Jews; and the text intimates that both Jews and Gentiles are now saved, in one common salvation—salvation from this present world—salvation from the nature of Adam—salvation from sin and death—and that, through the second man, the Lord from heaven, they are introduced into the realms of bliss and glory.

But the words of my text bring me somewhat nearer home; they bring me to the consideration of them with reference to ourselves, as the inhabitants of this present evil world. And what every believer of the truth, knows and understands by them is, that they realize what is our condition by nature. By nature we do not know God—we do not *love* God, for "the mind of flesh is enmity against him, and is not subject to His law, neither indeed can be." Well, this is our condition naturally. We are ignorant of God, and *opposed* to God, and this springs from the fact, that by nature we are selfish; and, being selfish, have a disposition to self dependency, and to make *self* our God; for we are all naturally self-worshippers. But the moment the truth as it is in Jesus, shines into our minds, that moment we are so far saved from the ignorance that is in us; and in proportion as that truth shines into our minds, we are saved from the actions of our fallen natures, for observe, the same word which brings us out of the *kingdom* of darkness, is that which gives us deliverance from the *works* of darkness, throughout all our subsequent career. As we are delivered from ignorance, so are we delivered from enmity. We are, by nature, lovers of ourselves, and of this present evil world—we are lovers of pleasure, rather than lovers of God; but as soon as the truth enters into our consciences with power, we are saved from the love of *self*, of *sin*, and of *the world*. We are made to experience the love of God, as having first loved us; and are made to manifest a disposition, "to do good unto all men as we have opportunity." Thus is realized our deliverance from darkness and enmity.

Passing by the illustration of other facts, I come to the conclusion of my wondrous text, "Look unto me, and be ye saved, all ye ends of the earth." Now had not you and I texts like this to refer to, in the Old Testament Scriptures, how could we, being Gentiles, have the presumption to think that *we* could have any interest in Old or New Testament blessings; the Jews were God's favoured people, and only by becoming Jews could any blessings of this kind have become ours. But we rejoice in the fact, that Christ came the "true Abraham," the Father of "the true seed in Abraham," "born not of corruptible, but of incorruptible seed, even by the word of God that liveth and abideth for ever." We rejoice, in one word, that he came in flesh, to bring his people to himself, out of every kindred, tongue, people, and nation. Therefore, the address of my text, and the addresses of similar portions of Old Testament Scripture, are not to the Jews exclusively, but to the Gentiles also; for "the middle wall of partition" between Jew and Gentile has been broken down, so that both are placed on the same footing, and both have access by one spirit unto the same Heavenly Father.

This then is your grand prerogative, and is proof that this passage of Scripture has reference to you, as "the ends of the earth." It addresses Jews, and addresses Gentiles: it addresses you and me, and whenever it is given us to hear the words so addressed to us, our souls are made alive

—for the power of God goes forth with them—so that we, who were formerly darkness became light in the Lord; and "we love God as having first loved us." Christ, "the way," goes before us, we learn to walk in it and follow Him, until at last the way results in the enjoyment of life everlasting.

I now hope that I have brought before you the import of the words of the text; and I also hope, that you will not fail to look into this blessed portion of Scripture for yourselves. I would have you look into the word of God, to ascertain whether what I have said is true. You will perceive that the Saviour is Jehovah—Jehovah who was made manifest in the flesh—you will perceive, that Jehovah speaks with power, and leads us to look to him, through the medium of his word—we believe in him as our Saviour—a Saviour from ignorance—a Saviour from self—a Saviour from the present world—a Saviour from sin—a Saviour from the guilt of sin, and from the power of sin—and a Saviour from death. I might have gone much further into this matter; but I have contented myself with throwing out a few scattered obervations.

Well then, we look to Jehovah, as he is revealed in his Word. And the parties who are called upon to look to Him are not Jews or Gentiles, but "all the ends of the earth," including you, me, and all that believe that in God's testimony exist all God's promises.

May God bless what has been said, giving to you and me to look to Him, " as He is revealed in His word," that thereby we may have the power of His life realized in us, crucifying the flesh, and living not to ourselves, but unto Him alone, and to His name be all the praise for ever and ever.— Amen.

SERMON XVIII.

July 15, 1855.

Had it been consistent with the present defective state of my sight, I should before addressing you this morning, have read portions of two chapters of Holy Writ. I should have read to you a large portion of the 7th chapter of Daniel, and likewise a large portion of the 7th chapter of the Acts of the Apostles. May I respectfully entreat you to read these chapters for yourselves, in order to see the correctness of what I am about to advance, in so far as it is agreeable with God's Word, and to enable you to detect any inconsistencies or inaccuracies with which, as a fallible being, in addressing you, I may be chargeable. The passage from which I would address you, is contained in the 7th chapter of the Acts of the Apostles. As far as I can recollect the words contained in the 55th and 56th verses, run thus:—

"But he, being full of the Holy Ghost, looked up steadfastly into heaven, and saw the glory of God, and Jesus standing at the right hand of God. And said, Behold, I see the heavens opened, and the Son of Man standing on the right hand of God."

There is nothing new expressed by me, when I observe, that no book contains more touching and affecting passages —viewed merely in a natural light—than do the Scriptures of Truth. Often have men of refinement, and literature, and science, dwelt upon the story of "Joseph and his brethren," as it stands recorded in the book of Genesis, and have contrasted the simple pathos of the narrative as there related, with the more diffuse form in which the same story is told by Josephus. And again, how few men, who possess any sensibility at all, can have read the account of the last moments of a sufferer, greater than Joseph or any other mere man—I mean the account of the sufferings of the

Son of God in the garden of Gethsemane and on the cross—how few men, I say, possessed of any sensibility, can have read these without feeling affected to a degree, which many of them may possibly be unwilling to admit; for it is a well known fact, that many men of professed infidel sentiments have acknowledged, that in reading the narratives given by the Evangelists, concerning the sufferings and death of Christ Jesus, have found themselves affected in the highest degree. But putting aside what has been remarked concerning "Joseph and his brethren," and the "sufferings and death of the Son of God," there is another most touching passage of scripture—the one which I have selected for my text. Stephen, who forms the subject of this passage of scripture, is only brought under our notice in a very few parts of Holy Writ; his name, so far as I recollect, is not mentioned at all, until spoken of in the 6th chapter of this Book, and his death and burial occupy the termination of the 7th and the commencement of the 8th chapters. His history, however, brief as it is, is most affecting and most instructive. He is presented to us as full of the Holy Ghost; he strenuously resisted the unbelieving Jews; and he speaks with a power which even the greatest of them found themselves unable to gainsay or resist. His language, his strenuous opposition to Judaism, and his success in making converts, at last brought down upon him the resentment of the Jews. He is then brought before the Sanhedrim, a council composed of the high priest and other priests, when a very extraordinary physical circumstance is recorded as having taken place. Looking at the face of Stephen as he stood at their bar, ready to answer the charges brought against him, they beheld his face as it had been the face of an angel; and when at last, according to the Jewish law, an opportunity was given him to make his defence, he makes it in a style of genuine simplicity; he makes it in a style, and exhibits a power, which every man possessed of the slightest knowledge of Christianity, must feel in a moment to be heavenly and divine. He appeals to and reasons from Old Testament Scripture, in so far as it has respect to the origin of the Jewish people, and God's dealings with them, from the very beginning. He goes over the history of Moses, at the same time briefly sketching the subsequent history of the Israelites, down to the days of David and Solomon. The great object which he had in view, obviously was, to shew that there is no tendency in the nature of man, and that in the Jews as possessed of that nature, there was no tendency to believe in the divine testimony; but that, on the contrary, wherever man's nature merely is concerned, there is, and always will be, an exhibition of unbelief, and necessarily of its effects. He shews that although the Jewish people, in the person of Abraham and of his immediate descendants, had been the objects of special divine favour, scarcely had one or two generations passed away, when, with the oppression to which they were subjected by the Egyptians, came great forgetfulness of God on the part of that people, together with great unbelief in his promises. He speaks of Moses, to whose laws they, before whom he stood, professed such attachment, shewing that even he was rejected by that people; his divine commission trampled under foot, and the question put to him, "Who made thee a prince and a judge over us?" He shews that after God himself had interposed directly, and given a divine commission to Moses by the mouth of the angel from the burning bush, to bring the children of Israel from the land of Egypt, even then but a temporary and very reluctant obedience was rendered to him by the Israelitish people; he shews that from time to time it was made manifest, even to the very last, that his authority was opposed by the unbelief of their hearts, leading them into the most wayward and refractory behaviour. He shews them that Moses, of whom they now professed to boast so much, was once the object of detestation and distrust to their forefathers. He hints that the same feeling prevailed at subsequent periods of that nation's history. He shews that the prophets, commissioned and sent by the Holy Ghost to proclaim the truths which God gave them to deliver, instead of being received with respect, and their messages believed and obeyed, were resisted by their forefathers with every species of contempt and cruelty, and that not by way of exception, but as a general rule; that therefore from the days of Abraham down to the days of Solomon, they had proved themselves to be a stiffnecked and rebellious people, and full of unbelief so far as the testimony of the Holy Ghost was concerned. After a few words with regard to David and Solomon, referring to the house that David desired, but was not permitted, to build, the privilege of erecting which was reserved for Solomon—after hinting that this house could not be the true house in which God dwelleth, and taketh delight in for evermore—he then speaks of the existence of another house —that house or temple to which Christ alluded when he said, "Destroy this temple, and in three days I will raise it up," referring to the temple of his own body—after alluding to these things, being filled with the Holy Ghost, and constrained to bear testimony against his own people, for whose salvation he ardently longed, he then cries out to them, not under the influence of creature feeling, but under the influence of strong feeling impressed upon his mind by the Holy Ghost, "Ye stiff-necked and uncircumcised in heart and ears, ye do always resist the Holy Ghost; as your fathers did, so do ye." I have been shewing you that your forefathers in every age resisted those prophets whom ye now pretend to honour, and the charges they brought against them, ye are now bringing against me: your course of procedure towards me is an exhibition of the same principle on which your forefathers acted towards them. "Which of the prophets have not your fathers persecuted? and they have slain them which shewed before of the coming of the Just One, of whom ye have been now the betrayers and murderers?" Oh, how effective must this harangue have been! He quoted from their own scriptures, and proved, with irresistible evidence, to their own consciences, that what their forefathers had been, they were. And what was the effect? The same as when Peter and the other apostles stood before the council, and in answer to the high priest said, "We ought to obey God rather than men. The God of our fathers raised up Jesus, whom ye slew and hanged on a tree. Him hath God exalted with His right hand to be a Prince and a Saviour, to give repentance to Israel and forgiveness of sins;" and, "when they heard that, they were cut to the heart and took counsel to slay them." And the same council, after hearing the address of Stephen, "were cut to the heart and gnashed on him with their teeth." The anguish of their consciences was great, and they could not help giving visible expression to it. Stephen, however, filled with the Holy Spirit, looked up steadfastly to heaven, and a miracle was wrought; the heavens were opened, and the glory of God became visible to his illuminated eye; he saw Jesus standing on the right hand of God, and the impression it made on the mind of this holy man was so strong and keen, that he could not help exclaiming, "Behold, I see the heavens opened, and the Son of Man standing on the right hand of God."

Now at the time when this vision was vouchsafed to Stephen, the New Testament Scriptures, in the fulness of their apostolic testimony had not been given; there was not therefore that full manifestation of the Son of God which we, through the medium of the New Testament Scriptures, thoroughly enjoy. In order, therefore, to the full enjoyment of Stephen in preaching the Gospel of Jesus Christ, as well as in enduring suffering on account of it, a miracle behoved to be wrought on his behalf; and God, who never worked miracles unnecessarily, but always worked them where they were necessary, saw meet to work the miracle which is here referred to; the eyes of Stephen were enlightened, and heaven, as it were in all its fulness and glory, was opened to his spiritual vision.

Now let us try and if possible understand the matter. There is this difference between fanaticism and divine reality: fanaticism mistakes impressions made upon the senses, for divine impressions, under the influence of that deceitfulness of the heart which God hath declared to surpass all human comprehension. But there was no fanaticism here; there was an immediate divine work, and an effect corresponding to that work; Stephen was enabled to behold heaven, as far as it is possible for man in flesh and blood to be enabled to do so. Of course he could not see it, as he was destined soon to do, when they who stoned him had deprived him of his earthly existence, when the veil of flesh being completely withdrawn, the glory of God should be seen by him as it actually is; he saw not the mere emblem, but the reality, or at all events, such a manifestation was made to him through a physical medium, that he saw, as it were, the Shechinah, the visible emblem of the divine presence; he saw the glory of God, and saw that Jesus, whose glory he had been striving to promote, standing at God's right hand, in the exercise of that power in heaven and earth with which he had been invested by his resurrection from the dead; he saw something like what was subsequently vouchsafed to the Apostle Paul, when he was caught up to the third heaven, and heard things which were not lawful for man to utter—things which it was impossible to express through the medium of human language; and very probably saw those things which did not require any peculiar revelation, and which are brought down to our apprehensions through the medium of allegories. But Stephen saw not these things with his carnal vision, but with the eye of faith; and they were vouchsafed to him for the purpose of sustaining him, and in the manner best calculated to sustain him in the fiery conflict in which he was about so speedily to be engaged. He had been already encouraged by his faith, the Holy Ghost had been bestowed on him in no ordinary measure—that

Holy Ghost which always speaks and bears witness through God's written testimony, and is never to be found apart from that testimony—that Holy Ghost dwelt in him most powerfully, and had led him to speak with confidence and power against the unbelief of his own countrymen; and as the same holy and heavenly Being had enabled him to sum up what they and their forefathers had done, in a manner which the Sanhedrim felt that they could not resist—so that same Holy Ghost now came forth in all his glory and fulness to sustain him in the awful situation, humanly speaking, in which he was placed, to sustain him by carrying him, like Elijah in his triumphant car, from earth to heavenly glory. Stephen was not as a dying warrior, who endeavours to revenge himself upon him, by whom his body has been pierced. He has no feeling or desire to be avenged on his conquerors; but his feelings were those of love to God, and love to man—feelings of love even towards his very enemies. For like Him, whose first martyr he was—like Him whose spirit dwelt in him in such fulness—while the stones were pouring upon him in murderous volleys—and his executioners surrounded him on every side—like Him whose he was and whom he served, he cries, "Lord, lay not this sin to their charge," and fell asleep. There is something most exquisitely touching in the simple record of the last discourse and martyrdom of Stephen, and I have felt that the whole subject breathes a holy fervour, combined with great simplicity, which shews us that where God chooses that His Spirit should operate, it brings us powerfully under its influence, as is manifested in the case of Stephen, as recorded in that glorious portion of Scripture contained in the words of my text. It was Stephen's faith in Jesus, in Him whom the Jews crucified, and whom God had raised from the dead, that enabled him previously to act the part he had done, and now bore him triumphantly through this trying conflict.

Well then, let us look at what these words imply; let us ask ourselves have they any reference to us; let us endeavour to extract what bearing they have upon our own individual minds and consciences. There are two things expressed, in the narrative. In the first place, we are told, in the 55th verse, that Stephen saw the glory of God, and Jesus standing on the right of God; and in the second place, we have his own language, in the 56th verse, "Behold, I see the heavens opened, and the Son of Man standing on the right hand of God."

In the first place, then, Stephen saw the glory of God.

Now, allow me to say, that what Stephen saw, by means of a miraculous or extraordinary vision, every believer of the truth —of that truth which is embodied in the New Testament Scriptures—sees with an ordinary vision—they all see the glory of God as with open face revealed in the Scriptures, and without the manifestation of this, and the state of mind with which it is inseparably connected, no man can belong to Christ Jesus the Lord. It will, no doubt, be said to me by some, and said boldly, none of us ever saw the glory of God —none of us ever saw the Shechinah, the visible emblem of the divine presence. It was one of the characteristics of the Shechinah to appear in the form of fire descending from heaven, and consuming the sacrifices, as at the dedication of the temple, when the priests could not enter the House of the Lord, because the glory of the Lord had filled it, and the children of Israel saw the fire come down, and the glory of the Lord upon the house. In the case of Stephen, we have the Shechinah presented to our spiritual vision. And it must be borne in mind that the Shechinah was a pillar of cloud, as well as of fire, as is proved in the case of the Israelites when passing through the Red Sea; to them it presented its bright side, whilst it presented its dark side to the Egyptians. And here we perceive that inasmuch as whilst the Jews, as Jews, were under a cloud of darkness, Stephen, on this remarkable occasion, beheld the bright side—the glory of God. But to understand clearly what is meant by the Shechinah, or visible emblem of the divine presence, take Stephen's Old Testament interpretation of it, " the glory of God." The great characteristic of this glory is brightness, it is light as contradistinguished from darkness; it is the kingdom of light, the kingdom of God's dear Son, into which all the followers of the Lamb are introduced. Be it recollected, my dear friends, you can no more understand passages like these, than you can understand the relation that the New Testament Scriptures bear to the Old, unless you bear in mind that these Scriptures speak of earthly things and of heavenly things, of the earthly man and the heavenly man. " The first man is of the earth, earthy ; the second man, is the Lord from heaven; as is the earthy, such are they also that are earthy ; and as is the heavenly, such are they also that are heavenly." Well then, some persons suppose that such a state of things as existed in Paradise, is to be restored at a future period, but such persons never understand and never feel what is implied in the words of the text. Now I have often endeavoured to bring under your notice from a very remote period of my ministry, that the paradise of earth was but the symbol of the paradise of God—that at the best Adam's possession was but an earthly paradise, and once forfeited was never to be restored, but all this was subservient to the introduction of the people of God into a Paradise which is heavenly and everlasting. For, from the beginning of Scripture to the end of it, there is a contrast drawn between earth and heaven, between that which is natural, and that which is supernatural.

Well then, Stephen saw the heavens opened, which implies an elevation not to a paradise of earth, but to the paradise of God. This was intimated to Adam immediately after the fall, was reiterated on subsequent occasions, and constitutes the glory of the Gospel when thoroughly and perfectly made known. Therefore, there is a distinction between heaven and earth running throughout the Scriptures, and as there is a distinction between the one and the other, so there is a distinction observed between earthly and heavenly dispensations. It is so when comparing the dispensation of Moses with that of the Lord Jesus Christ, and concerning the former it required the veil to be withdrawn before its brightness could appear. Its import was not generally understood—Christ said unto Nicodemus, "If I have told you of earthly things, and ye believe not, how shall ye believe if I tell you of heavenly things," as if he had said, "There is still a veil thrown over heavenly things which will require my death and resurrection from the dead, before they can be thoroughly understood." Now here, as well as in other passages, particularly in the 9th chapter to the Hebrews, where mention is made of a worldly sanctuary as emblematical of the heavenly, we have brought under our notice, the Mosaic dispensation viewed in relation to what it fore shadowed; so that although the earthly no doubt contained more or less of what was heavenly, still it was a mere symbol from first to last; it was perfectly true, but it was only an earthly system consisting of earthly ordinances, and promising earthly rewards as the fruits of obedience; and the great majority never saw further than this, never looked through the veil, through that which was earthly, to something heavenly afterwards to be revealed; they could not see the heavenly things themselves; they had to wait for Christ's coming, and the consequences flowing from it, before the veil could be withdrawn; and only a few were led by faith to observe, that all these earthly ordinances were a series of mere emblems, shadowing forth the realities, to which they were subservient.

Looking at the matter in this light, we see the two dispensations of Moses and Jesus Christ, standing to each other in the relation of an earthly and an heavenly dispensation—the dispensation of Moses being earthly, and emblematic of the dispensation of Jesus Christ—the latter being the substance of the emblems, with which the Mosaic dispensation abounded. Now this dispensation of Christ Jesus, is a heavenly dispensation; it is that which Christ came on earth to set up, it is that which, by the instrumentality of apostles and evangelists, has been set up, and which it is our privilege to enjoy.

Now, my dear friends, having made these preliminary observations, I may remark, that as believers of the truth as it is in Jesus, we all see the heavens opened, but we do so on the principle revealed and declared by Christ himself, that the least in the kingdom of heaven is greater than any of the Old Testament prophets. The Old Testament prophets saw not the opening of the kingdom; even John the Baptist, who stood at the very threshold of that kingdom, saw it not; but all afterwards, however mean their condition, however low their attainments—I say, all who were born afterwards, and made acquainted with the nature of this kingdom, have privileges greater than any member of the Old Testament Church enjoyed, inasmuch as they all see the heavens opened, and thus see the glory of God.

But to connect my former remarks with what I am about to bring under your notice. I must observe that the Shechinah which dwelt in the Cherubim of old—that pillar of cloud and of fire that went before the Israelites in their path through the wilderness, was the symbol of God's written testimony concerning His own Son. We know from the language of Ezekiel in the 1st chapter of his prophecies, that in the midst of that Shechinah dwelt the figure as of a man; and in the Shechinah as manifested to Peter, James, and John, on the Mount of Transfiguration, dwelt the God of Israel; for when Moses and Elijah appeared speaking to Christ, a bright cloud came down, and a voice came out of the cloud, shewing that the speaker was the God of Israel, the God of the Old Testament Scriptures. And again, when Saul was converted on his way to Damascus, in that same bright cloud which almost overwhelmed him, and those that were with him, appeared Jesus of Nazareth, proving that Jesus of Nazareth, and the God of Israel were one and the same person. Thus, whether spoken of by Ezekiel, or by the evangelists with reference to what occurred on the Mount of Transfiguration—or spoken of with reference to Saul—in the same bright cloud was Christ Jesus, dwelling in light ineffable and full of glory. What then were these things but the opening up of the Old Testament Scriptures. We find that the moment the Holy Ghost opened up the Old Testament Scriptures—no sooner was the veil withdrawn from them—than Jesus Christ appeared, shining forth in all his splendour and glory; and as Jesus dwelt as in a bright cloud under the Old Testament dispensation, so in these Scriptures, Old and New, Jesus now dwells as the sun in the midst of the firmament, diffusing light to all around him, shedding light into the minds of his chosen ones, by means of the Scriptures; so that when these Scriptures are opened up to their minds and their understandings, they are taught what they declare; they then find, in the language of the 119th Psalm, that Jesus is the Sun set in the firmament; and find the language of this Psalm carried home to their consciences, in all its significancy and power; they find that just as Paul was made submissive to him who spoke from the bright cloud, so in proportion as the word of God, which is Spirit and Life, is introduced into their hearts, they are taught to live, not unto themselves, but to him who died for them and rose again. The word of God is quick and powerful, inasmuch as it is sharper than any two-edged sword; it was that Word that gave birth to Jesus Christ himself, who was conceived by the power of the Holy Ghost, and has also given birth to the whole of the spiritual kingdom connected with him. And I say, that in these Scriptures Jesus dwells—from them he shines, and they constitute the power by which the new creation is formed, carried on, and perfected.

But remember how these Scriptures correspond to what constituted that cloud which presented its dark side to the Egyptians, but its bright side to the Israelites. Is not this the character of the Scriptures still? Are they not a savour of death unto death to some, and a savour of life unto life to others? While they shine forth brightly in Jesus of Nazareth as our God and our Saviour; while they enter into our minds, making us willing in the day of God's power, as having his love shed abroad in our hearts by the power of the Holy Ghost given unto us; while they constrain us to rest on him with all confidence, love, and faith; in the case of the world, instead of the Scriptures being seen to proclaim Jesus as their Saviour, as their light, as their life, and his righteousness as their righteousness; the men of the world are trying to extract some ground of hope out of themselves, something by which they hope to be supported in the hour of death; something which they desire to find in their own hearts—their guilty consciences, not resting satisfied with what God in the Scriptures imparts to the minds of His people.

Well then, the Scriptures are the heavens thus opened to us; even while in the flesh, "the glory of God" shines upon us; and Jesus, the substance of that glory, is made manifest to our minds through them.

Thus, every believer of the truth in reality has his eyes directed towards the heavens, and he sees them opened by the death, resurrection from the dead, and ascension of Christ Jesus to God's right hand; and in proportion as these Scriptures are more and more opened up to him, is he carried on in his spiritual career; and while sojourning on earth in the flesh, he is made to enjoy in anticipation, the glories which they reveal of the heavenly state.

But I observe that as Stephen beheld the heavens opened, and saw the glory of God—which heavens are opened to us in the Old and New Testament Scriptures, the substance of which is Christ himself—so he beheld Jesus, also standing at God's right hand. The declaration of this truth—a most glorious truth—could not fail to be most offensive to those to whom he addressed himself, for if he was right, they were most fearfully wrong. Were Stephen right, the Sanhedrim of the Jewish nation, and the Jewish nation itself had committed the most traitorous of all crimes and offences against God. Stephen declared he saw the Son of Man standing at God's right hand. What was the import of this? Were the Jews—the members of the Sanhedrim especially—not acquainted with the phrase, "Son of Man?" They could not but know that by the "Son of Man" was meant the Messiah. They were all acquainted with this. Therefore, when Stephen uttered this language, they could not but recollect, that in the 7th chapter of Daniel, the very phrase itself was applied to the Messiah, when brought before the Ancient of days to have given to him dominion, and glory, and a kingdom, that all people, and nations, and languages should serve him—an everlasting dominion which should not pass away or be destroyed.

Now it will be recollected by the majority, that a very few

days before, they had brought this very same Jesus to their bar, and accused him of blasphemy; and that they so hated him, that they had hired perjured witnesses to bring about his condemnation; and they understood that this same individual Stephen was applying the words of the Prophet Daniel, testifying that henceforth they should see the Son of Man, who had stood at their bar as a criminal, seated on the throne of his glory, and that they themselves should stand as criminals before him, and by him be condemned. Therefore, when Stephen said, "I see the Son of Man standing at God's right hand," what was the effect on their minds? Why, they felt that, according to this man's statement, the "Son of Man,"—the Messiah spoken of by Daniel—had already appeared in flesh; and Jesus of Nazareth, whom a few days ago they had crucified, as a blasphemer, was that Messiah. This man, he tells us, is now, elevated to his throne; this man, he tells us, is the Messiah, of the Old Testament Scriptures; he tells us, that in condemning and crucifying him, we have been his betrayers and murderers; he tells us, that this is he of whom the vision treated, and, if what he says is true, that Being whom we have condemned is seated on the right hand of power and majesty, ordering all things after the counsel of his own will. How could Stephen's words have been uttered without their being deeply and keenly felt; it could not but be galling to them to hear that this same Jesus, whom they had crucified, then sat at God's right hand, in the exercise of all power in heaven and in earth. Yet so it was. That same Jesus, who in the Jewish estimation, was not a learned man like the Scribes, or like those who stood forward as men of letters, and well versed in the arts and sciences; that same Jesus, who, in their estimation, was one of the most low, and one of the most despised among men; that same Jesus, who had been crucified by them, and who had ever exhibited a course of conduct totally different from that which the great among the sons of the earth had exhibited, and whose chief followers were made up of fishermen and tax-gatherers; that same Jesus, who had declared that publicans and harlots should enter the kingdom of heaven before Pharisaical and self-righteous men; that same Jesus, whose whole course of conduct was so entirely different from what was to have been anticipated by worldly wisdom, and worldly sagacity; that same lowly Being, whom the Jews had rejected and crucified, was actually elevated to a throne infinitely higher, and infinitely greater, than that which any earthly monarch ever possessed, or ever can possess. There he is standing at God's right hand, the King of Kings, and Lord of Lords, and as such he is presented to us in God's Word; it was not only told to the Jews, but it is told to you and to me, that we are not to ascend into heaven, that is, to bring Christ down from above; or to descend into the deep, that is, to bring up Christ again from the dead. But what saith it? The word is nigh thee, even in thy mouth and in thy heart, that is the word of faith which we preach, and there it is for your good and mine, who believe on his name.

How sweet the thought, that the lowly Being whom man despised, and whom the nations rejected—the Being who expired on the cross—was God's eternal Son, manifest in the flesh; was the man who came to bear our sins, and to bear them away for ever; was the man who came in the greatness of his might, travelling in the greatness of his strength, to conflict with enemies before whom the greatest of the human race had fallen, and ever must have fallen. This lowly Being, having the strength of the Almighty, conquered sin, and conquered death, destroying both, by his own resurrection from the dead, and ascension to God's right hand; and having done so, and having risen to his throne, leading captivity captive, has carried you and me with him, as tokens of his everlasting and glorious triumphs.

Thus he who sits at God's right hand is one with us; he is the second man, the Lord from heaven; and he hath raised us to newness of life, that the blessings he enjoys may be enjoyed by us also; having sat down on his throne, he gives us likewise to sit down with him on his throne in glory. Even here we have the earnest or foretaste of these heavenly blessings, and how much greater will be our enjoyments, how much higher our privileges, when, having got rid of flesh and blood, and of this present evil world, we shall see him as he is, and enjoy him for ever.

I have thought it proper to bring these things under your notice, not to detract from the miracle wrought in the case of Stephen; for be it remembered it was a miracle, wrought for a special purpose, as was afterwards made manifest, but I have done so to suggest to you what the opening of the heavens is, even upon earth, and this through the medium of the Scriptures revealing Christ Jesus, in whom the glory of God is seen, and from whom it shines. For there is no source of divine light and glory revealed save the Scriptures, through which the Holy Spirit speaks, and by which the Holy Spirit breathes; and these Scriptures revealing Jehovah the Saviour, the poor crucified one, as the glorious king, shining as in the Shechinah of old, revealing to us that he is one with us, and we one with him; and that he is giving us to rise with himself, by the way of manifestation now, and is preparing to give us with himself the fulness of enjoyment for evermore hereafter.

May God bless what has been said, and to His name be the glory for ever.

SERMON XIX.

Sunday Morning, October 7th, 1855.

May I ask you to read for yourselves, for I confess I am unable to go through the whole of the passage, the first verses of the 3rd chapter of the epistle to the Galatians, and I shall stop till you have read through the first five verses, commencing, "O foolish Galatians," (pause).

Understanding you to have read through those verses, I may state that the one from which it is my intention to address you this morning is the third verse: "Are ye so foolish? having begun in the spirit, are ye now made perfect by the flesh?"

I am not aware that I have anything personal in view in selecting this text as the subject matter of my present address. The fact is, the human heart in myself, and as it is represented in the Word of God, is becoming more and more in the light of Christ's testimony, the subject matter of my consideration, and I am having more and more deeply impressed upon my mind the force of Jeremiah's words: "The heart is deceitful above all things and desperately wicked; who can know it?" I am becoming more and more satisfied that the deceitfulness of the human heart is a fact which believers of the truth cannot too frequently keep in view, not so much with reference to the belief of the truth—because where the truth is believed, we know it to be believed; it is in us a light shining in a dark place; it is Christ himself seen by us as all our salvation and all our desire—but while the human heart remains, its deceitfulness as one of its leading characteristics still remains, and we are more or less the subjects of delusions, and against these delusions we cannot be too much or too continually on our guard.

The Word of God is full of exhortations, addressed to

believers of the truth. "Let him that thinketh he standeth take heed lest he fall"—not fall into everlasting condemnation, but fall into transgressions that would dishonour his Christian character. And again, "Walk circumspectly, not as fools, but as wise, redeeming the time, because the days are evil." Now, recollecting the deceitfulness of the human heart; recollecting that it is so desperately wicked, that God alone can thoroughly understand it; recollecting that it can only be understood by us in proportion as the light of God's word in Christ Jesus is conveyed into our hearts and consciences, I desire to call my own attention—for I do not want to say to you what I am not addressing to myself—and to call yours to several other passages of Scripture, especially to those in which believers of the truth are exhorted at all times to be on their guard against the deceitfulness of their own hearts, as well as against the deceitfulness of the hearts of others.

There are few portions of Holy Writ more useful than the Epistle to the Galatians. It is useful not only for its sweet and powerful statements of divine truth, but it is useful also for the valuable hints which it gives us as to one form of the operation of the deceitfulness of the human heart, and of the deceitfulness of the workings of men, whereby we are apt continually to be led astray from the simplicity of the truth as it is in Christ Jesus.

It is enough in the preliminary part of my address to observe, that the Galatians constituted one of the numerous peoples, or nations, who dwelt between the Euxine, or Black Sea, and that portion of the Mediterranean which lies to the East and which is commonly denominated the Levant. It may also be added that it has been supposed by some writers, that judging from their name, they came originally from Gaul, or ancient France. Be that as it may, it appears that the apostle Paul, at a very early period of his ministry, had carried the truth as it is in Jesus into their provinces, that he had found them benighted, and that he had been the means of causing the light of the knowledge of the glory of God in the face of Jesus Christ to shine, not merely upon their dwellings, but into their very hearts and consciences. And it appears further, that he was received by them with a most hearty welcome; they rejoiced, or appeared to rejoice, for a time at least, in the glorious light which he was the means of shedding and diffusing among them. He tells us in one of the chapters (the 4th) that so ardently disposed were they towards him, and so dear was he to them at one time, that they would have plucked out their eyes in testimony of the regard which they cherished towards him. But it appears that in process of time several Judaizing teachers made their way among these Galatians. Need I now describe who and what these Judaizing teachers were, especially after the numerous occasions on which I have had to revert to the subject already? They were parties who professed to believe in Jesus as the Messiah, but who, not having the least idea that the dispensation of Christ was inconsistent with the dispensation of Moses, continued and were desirous of perpetuating Moses' dispensation, along with the dispensation of Christ Jesus. They were of the same spirit that Peter evinced on the Mount of Transfiguration, when he said, Lord, let us make here three tabernacles, one for Thee, one for Moses, and one for Elias, that is to say, he expected the permanency of the persons of Moses and Elijah, as well as of Christ; and so these Judaizing teachers expected permanency for the dispensation of Moses, and this in connection, as they alleged, with the dispensation of Christ Jesus; and, under the influence of this fundamental error, they declared that it was necessary for all believers, and even Gentiles, to be circumcised, and to keep the law of Moses.

You are aware that, as related in the Acts of the Apostles, when the question was referred from Antioch to a convention, or assembly of the disciples and elders of Jerusalem, a decision was come to totally adverse to the views of those Judaising teachers — namely, that instead of being subjected to the yoke of Moses' law, it was declared that to that law they were not to be subject; at the same time a few necessary things were prescribed, things without attending to which there could be no union between the Jewish and Gentile believers; but with this exception they were declared to be free from all obligations to the law of Moses, and they were declared, not in any way or respect whatever, to be subject to its prescriptions and ordinances. It would appear, however, that in addition to this declaration of the apostles and elders, an express and divinely written epistle was required in the case of the Galatian converts, and which is, through them, addressed to all Christians in every succeeding age. It seems that the Galatian converts, once so zealously affected towards Paul, were in their folly, just as greedy to listen to the Judaising teachers, as they had previously been to listen to the apostle of the Gentiles, and to listen to their instructions with as implicit credence; and not only so, but they proceeded to act upon them. They went about being circumcised, thus professedly subjecting themselves to Moses' law, and thus drawing down upon themselves the blame and reprobation which are contained in this epistle, in which they are made clearly and distinctly to understand, that in the course of conduct they were then pursuing, they were most unmistakably nullifying the work and faith of Christ; that they were going back to a law which in Christ Jesus had been fulfilled; that they were taking upon themselves a yoke which neither the Jews of their day, nor their fathers, were able to bear; that they were destroying, as far as they could, the work of Christ, and this by setting up works of their own; and setting up a system so completely antagonistic to the system of Christianity, that it was absolutely impossible to reconcile the one with the other. Therefore the apostle shews, throughout the epistle, that if they were to continue the servants and friends of Christ Jesus, they must immediately and unhesitatingly throw aside the new and false gospel to which they had declared themselves subject, and return to the faith they had abandoned, and shew their contrition by subjecting themselves anew to apostolic authority, by receiving the doctrines they had temporarily laid aside, and by rejoicing in Christ Jesus, and in him alone, to the condemnation of the law and to the condemnation of the works of the flesh.

Let what I have now stated suffice as a kind of introduction to the words of my text, and to our consideration of them. These words are, "Are ye so foolish? having begun in the spirit, are ye now made perfect by the flesh?"

"Are ye so foolish?" There are two things, in regard to the natural mind of man, which are particularly conspicuous in the language of Holy Writ. The first is man's ignorance of God naturally; and the second is the folly of his conduct naturally, in regard to God and divine things. Here I beg not to be misunderstood; I am not speaking of human ignorance or human folly as to the things of this world at all. Let it always be borne in mind, that men who are ignorant of the Gospel, and who act foolishly in regard to it, may be men of the strongest natural intellects, and men of the highest scientific attainments; for the experience of the apostle was that few that are rich, few that are great, few that are noble, few that are exalted in any respect above their fellow-men, are called to the profession and enjoyment of the everlasting Gospel of Christ Jesus:

and I am sure I can speak of it as my own experience—and those that have had much acquaintance with the world will perhaps be induced to agree with me—when I say that the greatest and mightiest men whom it has been my privilege to know, have been parties either indifferent to, or openly hating, the Gospel of Christ. I have mixed with a few individuals who have ranked high in the world's estimation, by some of whom the Gospel, or something like the Gospel, has been professed; but in the great majority contempt for it, secret or avowed, or more avowed than secret, has been obvious in the whole tenor, tone, and temper of their lives and conversation.

Now, I am not speaking of such people at all; they may be wise as to this world; their wisdom may have been followed by the acquisition of wealth, or by the acquisition of fame; they may have risen to the highest rank in human society; they may have been hailed and esteemed for their benevolence and their liberality, and for other virtues which rank high, and deservedly rank high, in the world's estimation; but such individuals, if they be ignorant of the Gospel, rank amongst those whom Scripture calls fools—that is, as to divine things; and however great their worldly prudence and worldly wisdom may be, they come under the lash of many Scripture censures. The Word of God declares, " I will destroy the wisdom of the wise, and bring to nothing the understanding of the prudent. Where is the wise? Where is the scribe? Where is the disputer of this world? Hath not God made foolish the wisdom of this world?" 1 Cor. i. 19, 20. And in every age has God acted upon this principle. The wise of this world concurred in the rejection of the Lord of Glory: the wise of this world concurred in his crucifixion; and the wise of this world in every age have trodden in the footsteps of those who have gone before them. They have rejected Christ, and have preferred other gospels to his Gospel, or have been contented to remain indifferent to the subject of religion altogether. There are, no doubt, men, useful men, and men entitled to sincere respect among them; and let us never refuse respect to men when they act with propriety in their several spheres of action. But they are not the parties I am speaking of: or rather, it is not in reference to their worldly wisdom or folly that I am now addressing you. Remember, that I am speaking to you of the ignorance and folly of men as to divine things, and it is in regard to them in this respect that the words of my text speaks, " Are ye so foolish, having begun in the spirit; are ye now made perfect by the flesh?"

The first thing to be observed in regard to men naturally is, that as they come into the world, they are ignorant of divine things altogether. Christ alone had the mind of God by nature. He was conceived, and born the Son of God. Human beings, however, come into the world without any divine principle whatever. Except you are pleased to call their principle of conscience a naturally divine principle. No doubt it is so in one sense, and that is in making us conscious of sin, and death, and guilt; but it is a conscience which knows nothing of Christ Jesus or of God, as made manifest through Him. This total ignorance of human beings concerning God, and divine things as they come into the world, is the subject-matter of incessant and innumerable passages of Scripture. In one passage we are informed that mankind are "alienated from the life of God through the ignorance that is in them, because of the blindness of their heart," 5th chapter of Ephesians, 18th verse; and words similar to those which I have quoted from the 1st chapter of the Epistle to the Galatians are to be found in many other passages of Scripture. If you read the 3rd chapter of Romans carefully, you will find in the catalogue of the natural characteristics of mankind, given from the 11th to the 18th verses, ignorance of God and divine things clearly pointed out.

Well then, one grand characteristic of the human mind, naturally, is ignorance of God and divine things—not ignorance of what the claims of conscience demand—these claims, all educated worldly men, in whom the power of conscience is strong, understand and feel—but ignorance of God's real character, ignorance of Him as love, ignorance of Him manifested as love in Christ Jesus, and this through ignorance of the nature and operations of Christ's work, and from the fact of its never having been applied by the Holy Ghost to their consciences. This is the ignorance of which I speak— not ignorance of it theoretically, but ignorance of it as God's subject, as God's truth dwelling in their minds—that is the ignorance of which they are guilty. Combined with this ignorance, there is in all human beings naturally, folly. I am not speaking of folly as to this world, but of folly as to divine things. No man ignorant of the Gospel can act wisely as to that Gospel.

Now, a want of wisdom which springs from human ignorance, or the folly manifested in human beings as to divine things, shews itself in a variety of ways, but in three ways principally. It shews itself, in the first place, in the rejection of divine things by the great majority of those who hear of them by the hearing of the ear.

Now, what are really divine things? The first is, that God is in Christ Jesus reconciling the world unto Himself. What God has declared, is, that He loves us, and hath shewn His love to us in Christ Jesus the Lord; by sending him into the world, by his atoning sacrifice, by his resurrection from the dead, by his ascension to the right hand of God, he has proclaimed himself the free forgiver of all offences committed against him. Who believes this truth, or professes to believe it? Not one man in a thousand. But the Gospel, say some persons, makes itself professed on every hand. Men say that Christ is their Creator and their Saviour too! Yes, in words I admit; but do they either understand or believe what they say? Try them. Suppose me to say to one of such persons, you know that Christ is your Saviour. Well then, you know that God so loved the world that He gave His only begotten Son, that whosoever believeth in him should not perish, but have everlasting life. You know that eternal life is God's gift; and knowing it to be so, you know that it is given to you, given to you freely, without money and without price, you know it to be yours. "I am not so sure of this." What! I am afraid you don't believe God's truth, you don't believe God's testimony. "I should believe it if I found some change taking place in myself, or saw some difference in myself." My good friend, according to your own testimony, you are walking in darkness; it is not Christ you are looking to, it is not by his righteousness, and life, and love, that you are enlightened and animated; it is not Christ as your Saviour that you are looking at, and in whom you are rejoicing; you are striving to convert him into an instrument of self-righteousness, who has left a something to be wrought out by yourself. You prove to me that Christ is not your hope, and cannot be, for you are seeking to find a fancied righteousness in yourself. Now, however refined may be the mode of expressing yourself, Christ is not your hope, *self* is your hope; therefore, you are in the most refined of all ways, abusing the Gospel and shewing your folly as to divine things. Now, I have taken a favourable view of things, because the great majority of those who profess to believe the Gospel tell me, that what they hope for is to be saved, provided they are good, provided their actions are agreeable to God's law; in other words, it is self which they clearly and openly proclaim to be the foundation of any hope they possess or affect to possess.

I might go through a variety of cases, in order to shew you that the great majority of the human race evince their folly with reference to the Gospel; and in cases where men profess to believe it, it is clearly a something which is not Gospel, a something which does not afford them consolation in any shape whatever.

The folly of a great number is shewn, not in a direct rejection of the Gospel, but in a ready reception of what appears to them to be Gospel, without understanding what they say or whereof they affirm; and thus they merely profess to receive the truth. Our Lord has anticipated such characters in the case of the stoney-ground hearers. There is a profession, but the seed has no depth of earth, no real root; they have heard something, and have attached a human meaning to it, and it has for the moment occasioned joy to their minds; after a time, something arises which brings to light what the nature of their belief is, and prove the fact of its being a mere profession. Their folly is shewn by their professing to believe what in reality they do not believe; and this because they do not scripturally understand it. And their folly goes on to shew itself further in their rejection, after a time, of that in which, for a while, they had appeared to rejoice.

The folly of men is shewn in the fact of what I have, to a certain degree anticipated, namely, in a turning back from a profession of the Gospel; in which, for a time, they have appeared to rejoice. This was a thing very common in the apostles' days; many are spoken of as having forsaken Christ, and returned to the world. In the 6th chapter of John, when Christ began to speak of the necessity of his suffering, many of his disciples went back and walked no more with him, because they found it a hard saying. And so you find the apostle speaks, not of Galatians only, but of others who had forsaken them, because they were not of them. Their folly is shewn in forsaking that very profession which they had made, or appeared to have made. I might bring out their folly further, by observing that it arises from that ignorance of divine things that dwells naturally in the human breast, and their ignorance is connected with want of prudence and want of wisdom in regard to divine things. This is true in several respects. I have endeavoured to abridge the subject with a view to my being understood, but there are other ways in which the folly of fleshly mind is evinced as to divine things.

Thus the folly of men is shewn in professing to believe a truth which they never understood, and this leads me to speak of the grand and too common exhibition of folly on the part of many who once professed to believe the truth. It is a painful circumstance to think of, but I remember more cases than one, of individuals who, before I left my native country, had made great professions, but who, in a future period of their lives, openly denied them and returned to the world; and, what was still more painful, in some respects, by their flagrant misconduct, brought an evil reproach upon that blessed truth which, for a time, they had professed to believe.

Well, I confine myself to this, "Are ye so foolish?" as an address made to the Galatians originally, with respect to their ignorance of divine things, and with reference to certain effects flowing from that ignorance. That grand folly to which we now direct attention, is the fact of their withdrawing themselves from the profession of a faith in which at one time they appeared to glory.

Now, this leads me to the substance of my text, namely, having begun in the spirit, are ye now made perfect by the flesh? Before I advance, it becomes necessary to say a word or two to you respecting flesh and spirit; for, unless you have a clear and complete understanding of these terms, you will be liable to mistake my meaning altogether.

Firstly, *flesh*. There is no difficulty in understanding what this is. In the lowest sense of the term it means the human body as consisting of flesh and bones. But putting aside this obvious meaning of the word, I observe, that flesh signifies human nature generally, that is, the nature of Adam generally. Some will perhaps say, that flesh does not signify the nature of Adam until *after* the fall. I beg pardon, before the fall the nature of Adam was a fleshly nature—but as created by God it was a pure and innocent fleshly nature. God had organized a fleshly body out of the dust of the ground, flesh therefore is Adam's body, or, rather, Adam's nature which includes the Adamic or earthly mind. Of this we require no better proof than that given us in the 8th chapter of Romans. I might have contented myself by referring to the Epistle to the Galatians only, but some of you may prefer to take the 8th of Romans with it, where we have not only flesh set before us, but the mind of flesh, and that mind of flesh connected with flesh itself. Fleshly mind is inseparable from fleshly body, and this fleshly mind is there contrasted with spiritual mind, contrasted with spiritual mind in itself, and in the consequences to which it leads. Well then, in general, flesh signifies human nature—human body and human mind. Of course, human body and mind, as formed in flesh, because ever since Adam's transgression, in no other point of view have the body and mind of man ever been presented, except as guilty mind connected with dying body.

But flesh signifies more. Flesh, in many passages of Scripture, clearly signifies the dispensation of Moses, or the Old-Testament dispensation. Now the reason of this is very plain. The Old-Testament dispensation was set up, not for individuals in their spiritual or heavenly capacity, but for individuals existing in flesh, existing in a natural capacity, and was set up for temporary and earthly purposes. It was set up for spiritual purposes in the sense God gave it; that was, as emblematic of what was spiritual and heavenly, and as pointing to a future and a higher dispensation. But in itself it was a dispensation connected with flesh, or with this present world; a dispensation of which every individual became a member, merely by his fleshly descent from Abraham. Flesh is, in many parts of Scripture, applied to the Old-Testament dispensation; and there are numerous passages in this very epistle in which it has, and can have, only that meaning. To dispose of this part of the subject, flesh signifies Adam's nature, whether his nature of body, or mind as connected therewith and dependent thereon; and it signifies also the dispensation of Moses, as a fleshly or earthly dispensation.

On the other hand when we look to Spirit, the first thing that demands our attention is, who and what is Spirit? Well then "God is Spirit," but is there nothing more specific in the word Spirit? Yes, the Lord Jesus Christ is Spirit, and if we desire to know what Spirit is, our attention is specially directed by the New Testament towards Christ. Recollect the impressive language of the 15th chapter of the 1st Epistle to the Corinthians, where it is said the first man Adam was made a living soul, the last man Adam was made a quickening spirit; that is, a life-giving spirit; an idea repeated in more than one place in the New Testament Scriptures. Again, in the 3rd chapter of the 2nd Epistle to the Corinthians it is expressly stated "the Lord is that Spirit." And you may also read the striking passage in the Book of Revelations, the 22nd chapter, "the Spirit and the bride say, Come;" that is, the bridegroom and the bride say, Come.

I might multiply instances to prove this, but I think it is enough to have pointed your attention to one or two significant passages, as decidedly shewing that Spirit, means the second man, the Lord from heaven, and in him is realized, and by him exhibited.

Further, Spirit signifies the dispensation which Christ has set up; it is spirit or spiritual life as contra-distinguished from flesh, or that fleshly dispensation which was set up by Moses. Now, I must draw your attention to a fact which I have reserved till now. Among other meanings, Spirit has the signification of substance as contra-distinguished from shadow. Flesh is shadow, the dispensation of Moses was a shadow; but Spirit is substance, and Christ is the substance of the first Adam. The first Adam was a shadow, the second Adam a substance. Christ is the substance of the Old-Testament Scriptures they are all realized in him, every type and every figure is realized in him, every promise is realized in him: He is, as Spirit, the substance of the Old-Testament Scriptures. Therefore, if I am asked what the dispensation of Christ is, I say it is a substantial dispensation—a dispensation heavenly and divine; and, as heavenly and divine, is calculated to exist for ever.

But there are many circumstances connected with Christ's dispensation—which is a spiritual dispensation, and to which I want to allude, but as briefly as possible.

In the first place, it is opposed to the dispensation of Moses. You recollect that statement in the Galatians, "The flesh lusteth against the Spirit, and the Spirit against the flesh, and these are contrary the one to the other." Here, then, is a grand fact with regard to Christ's dispensation, it is entirely opposed to the dispensation of Moses.

Again, in the second place, the spiritual or substantial dispensation of Christ as opposed to the dispensation of Moses, is the superior.

Read with care, when you go home, the 3rd chapter o. the 2nd Epistle to the Corinthians, where you are told that whatever glory the Old-Testament dispensation might have, it had no glory in this respect, by reason of the glory that excelleth. There the superiority of the spiritual dispensation of Christ is most clearly expressed.

And, in the third and last place, not only is the spiritual antagonistic to the earthly dispensation and superior to it, but it supersedes it, just as the light of the sun dispels the darkness of the night: just as before the glories of the day, the shadows of night and the shadows of the morning flee away, so before the substance—that is the spiritual dispensation of Christ Jesus—the shadows of the Law flee away. If you want to see this thoroughly illustrated, read with care the Epistle to the Hebrews, from beginning to end, in which the Old-Testament dispensation with all its rights and ceremonies, is shewn to be a mere dispensation of shadows of which Christ and his dispensation, the spiritual dispensation, constitute the substance.

I have passed over many things in order to suggest some others to your minds in regard to Spirit. Spirit is Christ himself; "the Lord is that Spirit." It is the dispensation which he came to set up—the heavenly and divine dispensation—the substantial dispensation as contrasted with the shadowy one. But Spirit is more, and the very context will show it to be more. Spirit points to the effects of the dispensation which Christ set up. These effects were to be partly miraculous and partly common; they were to be the outpouring of spiritual gifts upon the earlier believers of the church. These gifts we know were poured out richly and amply upon the apostles, and also upon the members of the New-Testament Church. Every man had a dispensation of the Spirit to profit withal. And we know that the members of the church were bound together by the miraculous outpouring of the Spirit, and by the spiritual gifts that were vouchsafed to its members, and then there is the grand effect of the gift of the Spirit. This consists in the manifestation of the truth simply, and the confidence thereby implanted in the believer's mind through the New and Old-Testament Scriptures, made to be understood by their divine and Heavenly Author. This is the grand dispensation of the Spirit: this is the grand effect of the Spirit with which you and I have to do. It is owing to the Spirit of the New-Testament Scriptures throwing light upon the subject-matter of the Old, that Spirit which is Christ himself, carrying home his truth with power to our hearts and consciences, that you and I understand anything respecting this subject. That is Spirit in its heavenly operation, and this is the grand effect of the Spirit in every age of the Church of God. This is Spirit; it is the understanding mind whereby men see and enjoy the earnest of everlasting life.

I have now given you the meaning of flesh, and leave you to fortify yourselves by an examination of the scriptures. I have also given you three grand meanings of Spirit, Christ himself, and the effects of the Spirit upon the Church. And here comes the complaint, "Are ye so foolish having begun in the Spirit, are ye now made perfect by the flesh?"

Having begun in the Spirit, while the apostle preached the truth as it is in Jesus, to these Galatians, they had professed to receive Christ as having died for them, and as having risen again on their behalf. They professed to receive those blessings simply through the work which Christ had finished on Calvary, and purely as God's gift, and as having no right to them themselves, but as receiving them purely by the sovereign favour of Jehovah.

Well, now, in every age there have been individuals declaring that God hath revealed himself to us through His Son, that God hath given us life everlasting in His own Son, and that all the spiritual blessings, of which we are possessed, have come to us by His free and sovereign grace. And, as it happened to the Galatians, so in many cases has it happened to individuals. When the truth was first proclaimed to them, they received it with joy and professed it with decision; and in this way they appeared, if not to themselves, certainly to others, to be the recipients of those glad tidings, through which everlasting life is conveyed to the guilty children of men.

But what was the case with those who professed to recognise Christ the Lord and his spiritual dispensation, in its antagonism, to the dispensation of Moses, and as superior to, and superseding it? What was the ultimate effect in the case of the Galatian converts? That they desired to be made perfect by the flesh. Previously they heard the word with readiness, but when the Judaizing teachers came among them declaring the necessity of their being circumcised and keeping the law of Moses if they would enter into the kingdom of God, the consciences of too many of them which had been but partially awakened, or perhaps scarcely, if at all enlightened; many of these too greedily drunk in the delusive language of those favourers of a law which Christ had already fulfilled and put away; and the result was, that many who had once idolized the apostle, the very men who had shewn towards him warm and apparently enduring attachment, these men abandoned their former profession, joined the party of the Judaizing teachers, adopted their views of the necessity of receiving Moses' law, and became the bitterest opponents of that pure and heavenly gospel which the apostle delighted alone to preach, and in which they themselves had, for a while, apparently delighted to believe. And have there not in every age been instances of men who have at one time professed to receive the gospel in all its purity, and in all its simplicity, and who rejoiced in Christ Jesus as all their salvation and all their desire, but who, after a while, from one cause or another, have returned to the world, and in regard to the gospel, have become as if they had never professed to believe it? Look at the great number of evidences in the world of men, who, after professing Protestantism, have been converted to Popery in our days. That is an extraordinary instance of men going back from the liberalizing professions of that Church, to one which delights in a profession of bondage. I do not now speak of men going back from any denomination of congregationalism to Protestantism for the sake of the loaves and fishes, or for the sake of worldly rank and worldly emolument, though this might be introduced as one of the numerous tendencies of men going back; but, I speak of men professing to believe in the gospel; of men professing to believe that God hath given them eternal life, in and through His love manifested in Jesus His Son; of men professing to rejoice in Christ Jesus and yet having no confidence in him; of such, men, after a while, becoming luke-warm as to their former profession. They walk no more with those who continue to adhere to it, but ultimately, perhaps, turn their back upon it; and, what is still worse, finally deny and trample under foot, and hate that simple gospel, in which they once professed to believe. In the parable of the sower, our Lord has forewarned us of such results, and intimates to us the feebleness of our minds.

The fact is that Christ is not only he who enlightens, but he who supports his people. It is he who conducts them through the dark and devious paths of the world, and brings them through the difficulties and dangers by which they are surrounded, and to which they are continually exposed. It is he who keeps them by faith unto salvation, and he well knows that were it not for this, they would be ready at any moment to deny the precious and everlasting truths of the Gospel. There is in no human breast a disposition to continue believing. There is in us a heart of unbelief, continually tending to turn us from the living and true God. It is in Christ Jesus that we are made to believe; it is in Christ Jesus, and by him alone, that we are kept believing; it is he who keeps our eyes directed towards him. It is he who gives us more and more to see the beauties and the glories of his revealed character, and to rejoice in him more and more unto life everlasting.

Too often men first grow lukewarm, and then turn their backs upon their previous profession. From time to time men who once appeared to delight in that Gospel in which Christ is all in all, and in which his blood is found to speak peace to the guilty conscience—to cleanse it from all sin, and finally, and in a heavenly sense, to inspire the believer with joy; if such men are found afterwards professing to think that something more and something else than Christ is required: if such men are found to wonder at their delusion in having ever ascribed to Christ alone the power and the glory of salvation; if this circumstance happens from time to time, and if the hearts of believers are filled with anguish on this account, they are made more and more in the light of the Gospel to see their own weakness and inability to stand fast in the Lord. They are made to see the necessity of their being upheld by that blessed Spirit which enlightens and supports them. We know this from God's Word, and we know it also from the selfishness of the human heart, which will from time to time make its appearance, and in this respect I speak of myself as well as of others. The Lord keep both you and me looking to the simple facts which are revealed concerning Christ Jesus the Lord:—looking to the facts revealed in Scripture concerning his atoning sacrifice and its completeness, respecting our forgiveness in and through him, respecting our hopes of eternal life in him, and giving us to see the fact, that if we were but left to ourselves, we could not stand even for one moment. Our weakness is shewn to be his strength—"My strength is made perfect in weakness." Well then, we are upheld, not by our weakness, but by the same good pleasure, the same sovereign grace by which, at first, we were enlightened, and we shall be carried forward, step by step, until at last, we shall appear before our Saviour in his own kingdom, with exceeding joy.

May the Lord bless what has been spoken, so far as consistent with His Word and will, and to His name be praise for evermore.—Amen.

SERMON XX.

August 23rd, 1857.

ALLOW me to draw your attention to a passage contained in the First Epistle general of Peter, the 2nd chapter, at the beginning :—

"Wherefore, laying aside all malice, and all guile, and hypocrisies, and envies, and all evil speakings; as new-born babes, desire the sincere milk of the word, that ye may grow thereby, if so be ye have tasted that the Lord is gracious."

There is nothing more remarkable in the heavenly testimony, particularly in the New Testament Scriptures, than the distinction incessantly laid down, between the old man and the new man; and the reiterated exhortations given to put off the old man with his deeds, which are corrupt according to the deceitful lusts, and to put on the new man, which after God is created anew in Christ Jesus, in righteousness and true holiness; and in the passage I have selected for my text, we have a specimen of an exhortation of this kind.

You may recollect that a few Sabbath days ago, I drew your attention to the close of the preceding chapter, where mention is made of the people of God being born again, not of corruptible seed, but of incorruptible, even by the word of God which liveth and abideth for ever. On that occasion we drew your attention to the distinction between the birth from Adam and the new birth from Christ Jesus, the one earthly in its nature, and the other heavenly; we spoke of the word of God as meaning, not only God's testimony, as recorded in the Scriptures, but as meaning Christ himself, as the true and embodied word; and we drew your attention to the fact that the word—that is, the Gospel, or glad tidings contained in the New Testament Scriptures—is a proclamation of Christ as the subject-matter of those Scriptures. It is he who is preached unto you, it is he who is spoken of to you as the subject-matter of the Gospel, and before I proceed further, I really must take the opportunity of saying, that if I have committed the mistake (and it is a mistake too commonly made), of presenting the Gospel in the form of law, and not in the form of what it really is, I would wish to correct it. Let me not be misunderstood. The meaning of the word Gospel, is simply "Glad tidings."

I am afraid that from the necessary and incessant tendency of the human heart to view religion under the aspect of law, or to take a view of spiritual things as conditional, I say, I fear there is a tendency to use such language as would seem to imply, that in some way or another, there are certain terms to be complied with, and certain conditions to be performed, before we can obtain an interest in the work of Christ Jesus the Lord. Now, nothing can be more adverse, not only to the spirit, but to the letter of God's Word, than any such idea. This is the Word which by the Gospel is proclaimed, and the Word always comes as glad tidings—that no law is required to be obeyed by us, that no conditions are required at our hands, that the law of God received its complete fulfilment in Christ Jesus the Lord; that he became the end of the law for righteousness to every one that believeth; and that every condition was fully and thoroughly fulfilled by him when upon the cross he said, "It is finished; Father, into Thy hands I commend my spirit." I say, every condition was then complied with, and the Gospel, therefore, declares to us that God's law has been completely satisfied by the person, and in the work of Christ Jesus, and that every condition of life everlasting was accomplished when he bowed his head and gave up the ghost. This is the grand subject brought under our notice; it is the word of God proclaimed as just what it is, "glad tidings;" glad tidings of peace on earth and good will to man, on the part of Him who alone can proclaim these glad tidings and carry them into effect. And when the Gospel does take effect in the heart and conscience of any individual, it is as a manifestation to him that God is gracious and merciful, long suffering, and of tender mercy; that God hath forgiven his iniquities for Christ's name's sake, that God in Christ hath raised him to a new life here, and that God will ultimately bring him in Christ, to the full enjoyment of a heavenly life hereafter; and these things he has proclaimed by the Gospel of glad tidings. But wherever the Gospel, or glad tidings, have been carried home to the conscience by the power of the Holy Ghost, they are of the nature of a spiritual and heavenly principle, and like every other divine principle, they are productive of effects exactly corresponding to their nature; and just as Adam and the life that Adam was possessed of, was characterised by certain effects, and certain manifestations, so, Christ and the life he is now possessed of are characterised by certain other effects, and by certain other manifestations, and the difference between them has no limit, for, "Flesh lusteth against the Spirit, and Spirit against the flesh, and these are contrary the one to the other." The result is this, that where the Gospel, that Gospel of which we have been speaking, that Gospel which makes known to us God's Word, that Gospel which makes known to us Christ as the embodied Word, that Gospel which reveals and opens up to us that eternal Word of which Christ is the spirit and the substance, I say, wherever that Gospel enters the mind, and takes effect upon the conscience with power, it sows the seed of a new, spiritual, and heavenly existence; it enters the conscience as a new and divine principle, and is immediately productive of certain new and divine effects.

These effects have a two-fold character, they are in the first place indirect, and in the second place direct. The indirect effects are manifested in their operation upon our fleshly natures, they tend to and issue in the complete crucifying of the flesh with its affections and lusts; their direct influences being manifested in causing our affections to be set not on things on the earth, but upon things above, where Christ sitteth at the right hand of God.

Now, in the passage before us, we have most clearly manifested what the indirect influence of Christianity is; we have a distinct reference to what it effects in the way of controlling, crucifying, and destroying certain earthly affections; those earthly affections which belong to our Adamic nature, and which are characteristic of us as the descendants of him that sinned and died. And we have a view of certain direct effects of Christianity alluded to in the second verse; and we have also a reference to the parties to whom this exhortation is addressed, namely, those who have tasted that the Lord is gracious; so that we have three grand topics referred to in the text, namely, the indirect effects of spiritual things as a principle; then, certain direct effects of that principle alike new, simple, and powerful; and then the parties to whom the exhortation is addressed, and through whom alone it can be carried into effect.

In the first place, let me speak of the indirect effects. "Laying aside all malice, and all guile, and hypocrisies, and envies, and all evil speakings." Now you are not to understand that in this first verse every characteristic of human nature is enumerated, but quite the reverse. There is merely a selection made of the characteristics of human nature, and these are alluded to, not as exhausting the subject, but merely as affording specimens of what human nature is; specimens of what the affections are, which under the influence of Christian principles are to be crucified, and are crucified and destroyed.

You will observe that there are five things selected and enumerated. You will observe they are all distinguished as human, and they are all to be found working in ourselves continually and incessantly. Further, you will find them all opposed to those qualities which were manifested in Christ Jesus, and which are recorded concerning him in the New Testament Scriptures.

In the first place, laying aside—the meaning of which is to crucify, or to put away from us—all malice—you may translate it, if you will, wickedness; the term malice, however, is a very proper and an adequate representation of what is meant by the word here employed. Now, there is nothing that men, particularly those who have been brought up in refined society, and who are possessed of naturally amiable dispositions—are more disinclined to admit than the malice that naturally exists in the human mind, and is ready on the first opportunity to make itself manifested; and yet there is no truth more certain, and none which our Christian experience makes us more aware of, than that we are by nature hateful, and hating one another.

If there is brotherhood required for any particular purpose; if it be necessary for some immediate object of society that men should combine together, they may do so, and profess the utmost respect for each other; they may even appear to cherish a strong and lasting attachment to each other, and be ready to a certain degree to do good to each other; but if we were capable of going to the bottom of their hearts, if we were possessed of such observing powers as would enable us to look into the depths of their hearts, and the hearts of those with whom they are conversant, nay, even when listening to the language which men sometimes use with respect to each other, even towards their chosen and bosom friends, it is astonishing how much we may discover of the malice latent in the human breast, and which is at any moment ready to gratify itself at the expense of the sufferings of another. This malice comes out in a great variety of forms. It may appear in speech, in thought, in act, or it may appear in a disposition to do an injury to our fellow-men whenever an opportunity occurs, but whether that opportunity occurs or not, the principle is in us, and that principle springs from the selfishness of the human mind, operated upon by our fallen condition. Satan has taken possession of our hearts, and only waits for the opportunity to cause our native selfishness to appear in all its diabolical and hateful malignity. A veil, however, is thrown over it, but it is a veil that can at any moment be withdrawn, and then the words of one of our poets, which occurred to me just now, are verified, and that hateful thing, a naked human heart, appears in its native character.

Look at Christ, on the other hand. There is no malice in him. He is love and loving. If ever a being had occasion to cherish a feeling of enmity towards others, it was the Son of God. He was hated without a cause. He came to do good to others, and they did evil to him; and the more his love was made to appear, the more their hatred was manifested towards him; and yet, instead of their increased enmity to him, their causeless hatred to him, and opposition to him, drawing forth anything like enmity from him, even on the cross in his death agonies, when they were mocking at his sufferings, and glorying in the indignities they were heaping upon him, even then he could say, "Father, forgive them, for they know not what they do." He came to seek and to save that which was lost. He came, not to condemn the world, but to save the world. He came as an emanation of love and mercy—of love and mercy amazing and unbounded. I might dwell on this, but I merely throw out the hint, of the love of Christ as opposed to the malice of man.

And then, guile. I may just observe, that in man there is, owing to his native temperament, arising perhaps from his position in life, or perhaps, as some will be disposed to say, from the necessities of the case, there is a covert tendency to deceive our fellow-men—an inborn inclination to take advantage of their simplicity, in order that we may turn it to our own account. This is a principle of human nature, and is generally exhibited in the form of cunning—in the form of that cunning which stands connected with the disposition to take advantage of each other.

Now look at Christ again. With regard to him it is said that he knew no guile, "he knew no sin, neither was guile found in his mouth;" the grand characteristic of Christ Jesus is, that he was truth itself.

Not to dwell further upon this, let us look at the term hypocrisies. As the second term, guile, refers to our disposition to over-reach others, so does this third term refer to our disposition to deceive others. And I think it not only refers to our disposition to show off ourselves as different from, and superior to what we really are, but it refers to our disposition to put on a mask to hide our disposition, and thus exhibit ourselves to the world as what we are not, or, in other words, to profess with our lips that which our hearts neither believe nor feel. This is referred to by Isaiah when he says "This people draw nigh me with their lips, while their hearts are far from me." This is another exhibition of the disposition of man not to appear to his fellow-men in his true character, a disposition to deceive others by pretending to be what he is not, either intellectually, morally, or both, and this principle is no doubt carried out in the form of craft or guile. We do not always choose to appear what we are, we cannot afford to appear as what we really are.

I have no wish to enter into many particulars, but if we have studied the character of Christ, we must have been often struck with the difference that subsists between him and ourselves. We find that in him there was a constant exhibition outwardly of what exactly corresponded to the inward disposition of his heavenly mind. Both completely agreed, and squared with the laws and demands of his Heavenly Father.

Look at the next thing—envies. There is not a more powerful principle of human nature than that of finding fault with our superiors, and endeavouring to draw them down to our own level; a disposition to abuse and misrepresent them, whether rightfully or wrongfully, and thus reduce the estimation in which they are held by their fellow-men. This is a strong disposition of human nature. In passages innumerable in the New Testament as well as the Old, it is spoken of, and James says "The spirit that dwells in us lusteth to envy." He strongly condemns it, and draws the attention of the Church to the fact that it cannot be too watchfully guarded against.

Again look at the Son of God. There is not the least exhibition of this in him. When a kingdom was offered to him, did he accept it? No. He had no feeling of envy towards those who were above him. There was in him no envy of the Rabbins and Scribes and Pharisees; no envy of the Roman procurator, or of his authority. He envied no one. He refused the kingdom, why? Because he had something better in view, and therefore he trampled all earthly grandeur under foot as worthless. He knew perfectly well its true value. He knew that life itself was but a bubble. He knew that earthly reputation was but a bubble. He knew that let him obtain all the kingdoms of the world, they could not, in the first place, satisfy him, and in the second place, they could not last. He knew what was far better when he said "Thou shalt worship the Lord thy God, and Him only shalt thou serve." He was influenced by one heavenly principle. The principle of envy was an entire stranger to his breast, he knew nothing of it. To every manifestation of it he was opposed. When the young man, excited by envy, desired him to speak to his brother to divide the inheritance with him, he said, "Man who made me a judge and a divider over you."

Then there is evil speaking or accusations, or whatever may be meant by the term employed. Our disposition is continually to bring accusations against our fellow-men. I have often found it working in my own mind, and we shall find it a characteristic of each one of us. It is one of the strongest and most marked characteristics of human nature. You remember how this is corrected in Jude, where we are told that when Michael the Archangel was contending with the devil, he durst not bring a railing accusation against him, but said, "The Lord rebuke thee." This is a remarkable fact. Even to Satan, bad, vile, diabolical as he was, the utmost the angel said was, "The Lord rebuke thee." But human beings bring accusations against their fellow-men. They bring accusations against their brethren in the Lord Jesus Christ, and against those to whom the utmost tenderness should be exhibited.

Now, on the contrary, see how Christ treats these accusations. If he brings an accusation it is not a false one, but one that comes home to the consciences of those whom he accuses. When the woman taken in adultery was brought unto him, he said, "He that is without sin among you, let him first cast a stone at her." And in this way he goes to the bottom of the hearts of his pharisaical hearers, and proves the correctness of what he says by turning their very consciences inside out, shewing them up to themselves, and making them feel that his words were true. In Matthew you find innumerable instances of the self-conviction, which his statements carried home to the consciences of his hearers, because those statements were always founded in truth: but it was for the good of those whom he addressed that even these accusations were brought; for, in general, instead of uttering accusations, there flowed from his lips the words of grace and of heavenly consolation. He came to speak of life everlasting conferred freely, not upon the worthy, but upon the unworthy. While we were yet enemies he died for us, and hence his language exactly corresponded with his purpose, it was the language of mercy, pardon, and grace.

Well then, look at these five things. They all belong to human nature. We are here exhorted to put away all malice, guile, hypocrisy, envies, and evil-speakings, as things belonging to our Adamic nature. We are to put them away, but not as a ground of hope and trust in God. We are not to do this in order to attain eternal life. We are not addressed to this end, but are addressed as persons who have obtained eternal life; as persons to whom the mind of God has been made known, and, therefore, as persons in the possession of God's favour—not as persons to be possessed of it, but as being already possessed of it. We are exhorted to put away these things, and thus indirectly manifest that we have the mind of Christ, by the crucifying of these things.

In the second place, let me direct your attention to the effect that is produced in the believer's mind. "As new born babes, desire the sincere milk of the word that ye may grow thereby." There is so much contained in this verse that I fear I should far more than exhaust your time and patience, were I to go fully into it. Permit me however to observe, that these words stand intimately connected with a verse in the previous chapter: "Being born again, not of corruptible seed, but of incorruptible, by the word of God which liveth and abideth for ever." Believers are represented as children brought into Christ's spiritual kingdom, having first been brought out of darkness into God's marvellous light; and you will remember the words of Christ, "Whosoever shall not receive the kingdom of God as a little child shall in no wise enter therein."

Observe then, the persons addressed are persons thus begotten again, born into Christ's heavenly kingdom, and are addressed as those who have become possessed of the earnest of the divine nature. But this view has so frequently been the subject-matter of our reflections, and so often enlarged upon, that I will say no more, but leave you to a further examination of the Scriptures for your own satisfaction. "As new-born babes, desire the sincere milk of the word that ye may grow thereby." There was a time when I held a very different opinion from what I do now, as to what is meant by babes in Christ, and I am not going to deny that there was a great deal more ignorance in my early opinion than I imagined. I had come to fancy that in the divine life there are little children, and young men, and fathers, in a sense in which I am afraid these terms are too commonly understood.

Now, that there are such differences I cannot dispute, but I suspect they stand in just the reverse order from that which even believers of the truth are disposed to ascribe to them. I suspect that little children in divine life are too often to be found among those who fancy themselves to be fathers. I am afraid that the very self-conceit of the minds of such persons indicates the instinct of their nature, which is to continually think of themselves more highly than they ought to think, and thus they attain to but a low growth in the divine nature. If their state in the divine life were an exalted one, instead of thinking highly of themselves, they would think the very reverse.

Again, with regard to young men, supposed to be strong in the Lord, I am afraid that these young men in the divine life, too generally think themselves old, and when exposed to temptation, are made to feel the weakness of their faith, by finding themselves incapable of holding fast by the shield of faith, the helmet of salvation, and the sword of the Spirit, which is the word of God; and who, consequently, too often fall away even before the very slenderest temptation, thus shewing, that instead of their being strong in the Lord, they are at the best but weak and feeble in regard to spiritual things. Then as to fathers. I find there are few who, in consequence of having the spirit of Christ bestowed upon them freely, and dwelling in them richly, have their minds so brought down and subdued as to be fixed upon Christ only, and have such a view of themselves, as to be actually able to look upon themselves, and the vileness and abomination they are continually discovering in their own hearts, and who find their only pleasure is in looking to Jesus, and deriving all their comfort and all their consolation from him, and from him alone. I fear that this is but a very small class.

I will tell you what has occurred to my own mind; it is this: there is no doubt that there are such distinctions in the divine life as children, young men, and fathers, and I think that all these characters are applicable to believers of the truth as it is in Jesus. They have the characters of children as possessed of simplicity of mind, receiving the truth with ardour and intense love, because it is as little children that they enter into the kingdom, and as little children that they are kept in it. Again, they are young men in so far as they are strong in the Lord, and manifest a vigour of spiritual principle in being able to stand in the evil day. Every circumstance in which a believer is able to resist and overcome temptation, is a proof of the vigour or youthfulness of the divine mind existing in him; and in proportion as our minds are made to take in divine truth, it grows up in us, and stands in connection with a love of divine truth that humbles us and makes us feel our fallen condition. In proportion as we are taught divine truth, we are made to know our own weakness, and our own ignorance. Then as fathers, we are continually looking to God as revealed in Christ Jesus, to Him who is the same yesterday, to-day, and for ever.

Looking at the words, "As new-born babes," in this light, they may be considered as addressed to every believer of the truth. We are all therefore addressed as babes, and one of the direct exhibitions of the existence and influence of divine and heavenly principle is, that we are made to know that we are not called upon to do anything; but as new-born babes we desire the sincere milk of the word, just as a new-born babe shews a want of its natural nourishment, and as new-born animals of every description shew the tendency of their nature, by desiring to receive that nutriment which God has provided for them through their mother.

There is something rather striking in the language of the text, so that I am induced, with a view to our understanding it better, to call your attention to a passage, which occurs in the 12th of Romans, and the first verse. There can be no doubt about the translation of the word rendered "milk" in the text, nor any doubt as to the term "milk of the word:" but the same word translated milk in the passage before us, is used as an adjective in the Epistle to the Romans. In the 1st verse of the 12th chapter of Romans, the word is translated reasonable, "presenting your bodies a living sacrifice which is your *reasonable* service."

It has been said that this translation of the word in our text would give us, "desire the sincere and reasonable word," yet I do not think that is the translation; I think our translators are nearer the meaning of the original. Perhaps they are mistaken in the passage in Romans, and I suspect it; I have a strong suspicion that the translation, "which is your reasonable service," is not quite correct. I suspect it means "which is your service *according to God's reasonable word.*" It is the service which that word indicates and prompts to; it is no doubt reasonable in a logical sense. And it is more; it is a service to which we are prompted by the reasonable word of God. I think our translators have taken a nearly correct view of the passage in Peter, "Desire like new-born babes, the sincere milk of the word that ye may grow thereby."

The word of God is represented as having the character of strong meat, and so it has. You may remember that in the 5th Hebrews we are told that "Every one that useth milk is unskilful in the word of righteousness, for he is a babe. But strong meat belongeth to them that are of full age," shewing that the word of God has the character of strong meat as well as milk. Milk, however, is one of the characteristics of the word of God; and, just as the milk that flows from the breast of the mother, gives nourishment to her infant, so the word of God is as milk to the Church —the true Church of God—the Church as built upon the foundation of the prophets and apostles. The seed of the word is that by which we are begotten spiritually—begotten again to a new and divine life; so the milk of the word is the nutriment upon which we live, the nutriment by which we grow, the nutriment by which we are carried on unto life everlasting.

Observe further, this nutriment is kept pure only in the divine mind. The moment it passes through the alembic of the human mind, it produces spiritually some vile disease. New-born babes do not desire to have the truth distorted by human reasons, they desire the pure milk of the word of God—that word of which I have been speaking—that word first proclaimed enigmatically in the Old Testament Scriptures, but from which the veil is now withdrawn—that word which reveals to all the destined heirs of salvation, **the finished work of Jesus Christ, through the New Testament.**

Desire it, that ye may grow thereby. This brings under your notice and mine the fact that there is a real growth in Christian things. I cannot dispute that there are children, young men, and fathers in the divine life, and that there are consequently in the Church of God some who are children, some young men, and some fathers; because the expression intimates that there is a growth in heavenly and spiritual principle on the part of the people of God, and the word shews how the growth takes place. It is not by cultivating human literature or human science, but by advancing in divine light. The growth is connected with the sincere, the pure, the uncorrupted milk of the word. It is connected with that, and that only, and we grow thereby, hence the growth is very slowly carried on, and slowly completed.

But "that we may grow." This contains a hint that the only way in which our growth in the divine life can take place, is by the divine word entering more and more into our understandings, taking increased hold upon our hearts and consciences, thoroughly overcoming them, and so completely superseding our earthly nature, and in proportion as that word takes hold of us becomes in us the growth, the spiritual growth, by which we advance from children to young men, and from young men to fathers. Observe, this growth is through the word of God, that word of God first introduced into the conscience by God Himself, for while the Holy Spirit is the only competent teacher of the word—the Holy Ghost always teaches through the word—the word is the only medium of communicating, carrying on, and perfecting the divine life.

If so be ye have tasted that the Lord is gracious, I have only time to remark that this exhortation is not addressed to the world in general, but to believers exclusively, to those who have already tasted and become children like the newly-born infant that has tasted its maternal nutriment. If the word has made known to you and me that God is gracious, and by His grace and mercy hath freely forgiven us all our iniquities for Christ's sake, and by this knowledge has given us to taste the value of His word as heavenly milk, and the desire to partake of it more and more, for as a child who has once tasted the mother's milk continues to desire it more and more until the time of weaning arrives, so do we who have first tasted that the Lord is gracious, go on to desire more of the sincere milk of the word as the only principle of our spiritual growth—as the only source of our heavenly nourishment.

I have been obliged to hurry over the subject. It is enough if I have thrown out such suggestions as shall lead you to look into this matter for yourselves. May the Lord lead you to a careful examination of the subject in connection with the facts spoken of in the preceding chapter, and enable you to ascertain that God is gracious, and so bring you, through the medium of the gospel of Christ Jesus, from darkness into light, and from the power of Satan unto God, and bring you to know and to comprehend His mercy, and His love as embodied in Christ Jesus; and having brought you to the knowledge of Himself, lead you to shew forth the influence of divine principle in the crucifying of the flesh with the affections and lusts, and in the putting away of all malice, and all guile, and hypocrisies, and envies, and evil speaking.

May the Lord lead you more and more to the love of, and a desire for, the sincere milk of His word, and to His name be praise for evermore.—Amen.

SERMON XXI.

Sunday, April 25, 1858.

PERMIT me to draw your attention at this time to the three following texts of Scripture. You will find the first in the 8th chapter of St. John's Gospel. The Jews had said to our Lord, as recorded in the 57th verse of the chapter, Thou art not yet fifty years old, and hast thou seen Abraham? His answer is contained in the 58th verse—" Verily, verily, I say unto you, before Abraham was, I am." Along with this take the 20th verse of the 18th chapter of St. Matthew's Gospel—" For wherever two or three are gathered together in my name, there am I in the midst of them." Take also along with these passages the 18th verse of the 28th chapter of St. Matthew's Gospel—" And Jesus came and spake unto them, saying, all power is given unto me in heaven and in earth."

Sometime ago I drew the attention of my friends to what appeared to me to be some valuable, interesting, and edifying facts, concerning the Lord Jesus Christ; and I have frequently spoken of truths revealed in Scripture, such as, that God is the ever-present one—that He is the I am—that He is everywhere, in all places of the earth, and at all times; and also that power appertains to Him in the highest degree; or, as it is sometimes expressed, He is omniscient, omnipresent, and omnipotent. It will be in the recollection of those who are in the habit of attending here, that I have endeavoured from time to time to fix their attention upon the fact, that whatever is said in regard to God, is said also of Jesus Christ; and that we can only understand the divine attributes of God as they are displayed and revealed to us by our divine Redeemer; and that I have endeavoured to draw your attention to this fact also, that Jesus is the true I am, and that we can only know Jehovah himself as the I am, as He is revealed in Jesus Christ.

Again I have drawn your attention to the fact that Jesus Christ exists everywhere—that there is no circumscription of his being, and that Jesus Christ is therefore the true and omnipresent God. And I have also drawn your attention to the fact, that Jesus Christ is possessed of all power, has all things entrusted to his hands, and is in the exercise of sovereign dominion; and, therefore, that we can only understand what the possession of the highest power of omnipotence is, by observing it as displayed in, and exercised by, our Divine Lord.

Now I want to remind you of these things, because I have a strong suspicion that there is a tendency amongst mankind, and particularly among those of a philosophical turn of mind, to think of God *abstractly*; if they are led to think of Him as a Being that is ever living, as a Being who is everywhere present, as a Being who is possessed of *all* power, I suspect it is only in an abstract sense they do so.

I have drawn your attention to the fact, that abstract disquisitions are not to be found in Scripture; the revealed truths of Scripture are (to use a particular phrase) concrete. They all refer to one and the same individual, and we can never understand them abstractly, but only as they are exhibited in, and verified by, the person and character of Christ Jesus.

Permit me to remind you of this. You and I know nothing whatever of Jehovah as the I AM, except as revealed in His own Son. We know nothing of any omniscient, omnipresent, or omnipotent Being, except as revealed in the person and character of the Lord Jesus Christ. "He that hath seen me," says Christ, "hath seen the Father." Christ is expressly called the image of the invisible God, therefore, you and I are not permitted to go abroad in search of these things. We are not permitted to consult our own imaginations, or our own reasonings, with a view to ascertain how God is possessed of such attributes. We are commanded to look to Christ, and if we are led by faith to look to him, we can then understand what the attributes of omniscience, omnipresence, and omnipotence are; and these can never be understood spiritually or scripturally in any other way.

Having thus made a general reference to what I have formerly brought under your notice; I would now observe, that I have a particular object in view, in bringing a similar subject under your notice this morning.

It may be remembered by you that I have twice or thrice —not uttered apologies for popery—for I had no intention to do that, but twice or thrice I have thrown out hints that even the errors of popery, gross, delusive, and abominable as they are, may be found to have had something like a divine origin,—not that the errors themselves had a divine origin, but what are fundamentally divine truths, have, under the influence of human error and human fallibility, been brought out in the form of caricatures; and an examination of some of these as exhibited by popery, may with the divine blessing suggest to us what the real truth, what the heavenly doctrines are, which have been so awfully and so profanely abused.

Now, on one occasion I think I hinted to you that the doctrine of purgatory is in reality derived from the doctrine of purgation of the conscience by the blood of Christ; and from a misapprehension of the 3rd chapter of the First of Corinthians, where mention is made of a man being saved "yet so as by fire;" and also from a misapprehension of the doctrine that "God is the Saviour of all men, but especially of them that believe." This doctrine of purgatory, I believe to have attained to its present monstrous form, through the medium of the misunderstanding of the true doctrine, that the only purgation of the conscience, the only thing that really cleanses man from guilt, is the blood that was shed upon Calvary.

Again, I think I have drawn your attention to the Popish doctrine of supererogation, or the doctrine which supposes that there are certain works over and above what the creature is required to perform, and which may consequently be set down to his own account, or if not to his own account, to that of others. I think this doctrine most awful, abominable, and profane; and yet, it appears to me to have had its origin in the true doctrine laid down in the 6th and 7th of Romans, where it is shewn that when we believe the truth as it is in Jesus, and have our consciences set free from guilt, and are made to enjoy the consciousness of that peace that passeth all understanding, we then perform works not unto ourselves, but unto God; we live not to lay up for ourselves, but out of a good conversation we shew our works, with meekness and wisdom, and this to the glory of him that died for us and rose again. Now this doctrine, misunderstood, perverted, and misapplied, by the mere fleshly mind of man, has led to the monstrous doctrine of supererogation as we see it displayed in the Church of Rome.

Again, the doctrine of penance has clearly a reference to the doctrine of repentance, perverted by the same false tendencies, the same ignorance, and the same opposition to God on the part of the creature, that is displayed in the other figments of the Romish Creed. It is quite clear that believers bring forth works, or fruits, meet for repentance, but these fruits do not result from having certain convictions derived from a mere creature like ourselves; or from having received absolution on condition of performing certain works prescribed by him as a penance. These fruits are the effects that are brought forth by every believer whose mind is changed in its views of what God is, changed in its views of self, and who now perceives that he has righteousness and life in Christ Jesus, and that it is to the grace of God alone that he is indebted for salvation, peace, and joy. And the believer of the truth being made to perceive these things, his mind becomes changed in its principles, changed in its aims, changed in its pursuits; and thus the fruits of repentance are fruits brought forth, not only corresponding to, but produced by, the changed mind of which we are made partakers by the Holy Ghost.

I need not go through some other Popish doctrines that I intended to speak about, which may be characterised in the same way, as perversions in one form or another of true doctrines. I may remark, that you will find a truth lying at the bottom of every perversion of the truth—not that the Popish doctrines are true in themselves, for, as presented by the Romish Church, they are the grossest falsehoods. What I mean to say is, that there seems to lie a foundation of truth at the bottom of all of them, that they are all truths turned into falsehoods by the ignorance or by the hostility of the mind of man.

I have of late been led to think a good deal of two forms of error that exist in the Romish Church, and with which it is probable most of you are familiar; and I have thought it right, after having reflected upon them myself, to turn your attention to those solutions of them which appear to me to be the true ones. There is a foundation of truth in both these forms of error, but in both the truths are disguised. Though falsehoods as held and practised by the Romanists, there are really truths suggested by them, and the question is, what these truths are.

Roman Catholics—and, I am sorry to say, there is a class of Protestants who sympathize with them, and seem to be partakers with them in their evil deeds—I say, Roman Catholics make use of the crucifix in their devotions, and say that it is not the mere ivory, wood, or stone, but Jesus himself, whom they profess to regard as present in the particular crucifix, towards which their devotions are directed, and that, therefore, it is the person of Jesus who is present in the crucifix, whom they say they worship, and not the crucifix itself. This is the apology they make, but you and I know they practise an awful delusion in so doing.

And in regard to transubstantiation. You and I know that when the priest reads or says "This is my body," in the consecration of the mass, they maintain that what was formerly bread and wine are substantially changed into the body and blood of Christ; though the accidents, as they call them, of bread and wine remain, they say the substance has passed away; the substance is no longer bread and wine, the substance is the body and blood of our Divine Redeemer; and they ascribe a sort of ubiquity or everywhereness, if I may use the term, to the body and blood of Christ; so that wherever the mass is duly offered up by the priest, there the body and blood of our Divine Lord are.

Now I shall confine myself this morning to these two things—the worship of the crucifix which they profess to justify, by the idea that it is Christ who is present in it, and whom they worship; and the doctrine of transubstantiation which they profess to justify by the assumed or supposed ubiquity or everywhereness of the body and blood of Christ.

And now let us ask ourselves, are there revealed to us in Holy Writ any doctrines, and doctrines too of an edifying character, which misunderstood, misapprehended, and misapplied, by the fathers of the Catholic Church have led to these blunders? Are there any real Scriptural doctrines by which we Protestants may, and not only may, but, if God be teaching us and God be influencing us, by which we must continually profit?

I shall now direct your attention to what the doctrines are, which the Romish Church, having misapprehended, has misapplied and brought out in the shape of those two practical delusions to which I have just referred. I will take them in succession. You will observe that one of our texts is, the declaration of Jesus, "Before Abraham was, I am." Now, bearing in mind the fact that Jesus is God, and as God became man, that in him God and man were united, and that in Jesus, God and man were united as the "I am," and also bearing in mind the fact that Jesus was expressly called man during his abode upon earth, I now ask what does "I am" imply? It clearly implies the sinking as it were of the past and the future; it expresses the past and future as swallowed up in the present. You and I know that God has no past existence, properly speaking, and can equally have no future. When He appeared in the burning bush to Moses his language was "*I am.*" When speaking of Himself in the New Testament Scriptures, it is very true that Jesus says, He is the Being that was, and the Being that is to come, as well as the Being that is; but then again it is also said of Him that He is the same yesterday, and to-day, and for ever. But when the past and future are spoken of by Him, it is evident that the terms have a reference to the human mind—to our modes of conception and comprehension. Men live in the past and future. The past and future belong to the human mind, and when God in the person of Jesus Christ, says, that He is He that is past, or that He is He that is to come, the two forms of expression are merely accommodations to our modes of thinking, for in reality the proper appellation of Jesus Christ is " I am," and that appellation he took to himself in one of the passages which forms part of my text, " Before Abraham was, *I am.*"

" I am " implies what you and I cannot thoroughly conceive of. If we say we do, we profess to do that for which our present faculties do not qualify us. Remember the apostle's words, " It doth not yet appear what we shall be, but we know that when he shall appear, we shall be like him, for we shall see him as he is." We have no power of conceiving what Jesus is now, in his ever-present and unchangeable existence; but while we cannot conceive of this, we can believe it, for it is easy to believe that Jesus is the " I am;" it is easy to believe that he is Jehovah, the ever-living and unchangeable God. Has it ever occurred to you that as the " I am," there is an ever presence communicated to his abode on earth, and especially to his sufferings in the Garden of Gethsemane, and on the cross? Let me not be mistaken in this. I do not say that these things have a present existence in an earthly sense. They have not, and never can have. They are events that occurred eighteen hundred years ago, and cannot be repeated. It is not in this sense I say so; but what I mean is, that Jesus is the ever-present one, the I am, God, Jehovah; and the events to which I have referred, occurred in the earthly history of Him who is the " I am."

This being the case then, when they are presented to your minds and mine by faith, there is in a certain sense a presence communicated to these events as they were realised in the person of Jesus. The facts are to us historical, and occurred eighteen hundred years ago, but by faith we can have them brought before us, as if we saw them actually transacted; and when the eyes of our understanding are opened by the Spirit of God, we are enabled to realize in Christ Jesus the "I am," are enabled to recognise in him the character of "God over all, blessed for ever;" and enabled to believe in him as having appeared in flesh; as having wrought out our salvation; as having offered himself a sacrifice for sin; as having died and risen again from the dead, and ascended to God's right hand. We are made to perceive that he is the I am, and are enabled to bring before our minds, or rather, we have brought before our hearts and consciences, events that took place eighteen hundred years ago, and realise them as if present. We are enabled to enter into the Garden of Gethsemane, and there, as it were, to behold the Son of God withdrawing himself from his disciples; to observe his agony; and to see the sweat, as it were, great drops of blood falling from his sacred temples to the ground. We are enabled to hear him, as it were, utter the words, "Father, if it be possible, let this cup pass from me, nevertheless not my will, but Thine be done." From the Garden of Gethsemane, we follow him to the cross. We behold him stretched thereon, and nailed thereto. We behold that great darkness which overspread the land, and continued for hours. We hear the language of the malefactors. We hear his own blessed language. We observe the fulfilment of the 22nd Psalm, and of other passages of ancient prophecy in his case. We hear him utter the agonising cry, "Eli, Eli, lama Sabachthani?" "My God, My God, why hast Thou forsaken me?" And still more, we hear, when the appointed period arrived, those glorious words uttered by him, "It is finished," when he dismissed his spirit, and, for a time, yielded to the power of death. And all these things are brought before us as if they were present. We behold the Lamb of God crucified for us; crucified for sin, and taking away sin by the sacrifice of himself.

Observe then, that this ubiquity or omnipresence is realised in every age, simply by the fact that he is the "I am" —that there is with him neither beginning of days nor end of life, and that as being the "I am," there is communicated even to his earthly existence, and the sufferings he underwent upon earth, such a presence, as is brought home to our hearts and consciences, when by the power of heavenly faith they are realised in us.

I am not speaking of this as a theory. I shall shew you

what I mean by it. But first let us look at the facts, and observe what the Romanists teach their congregations. We appeal not to the imagination, but to the facts that stand recorded in Scripture, concerning the Lord Jesus Christ. To these facts there is a presence given in our consciences, and that it is the "I am" of whom these facts stand recorded in Scripture. There is an annihilation of time altogether in regard to them, when He who is the "I am" is concerned.

And so, further, I have said that ubiquity or omnipresence belongs to the Lord Jesus Christ. Now, you and I know this to be a fact, wonderfully brought out in the Old as well as in the New Testament Scriptures; we know that Jesus, who appeared in flesh, is the "I am," we see him in the garden of Eden, we find him in the camp of the Lord's host when he appeared to Joshua.

But to pass by the Old Testament manifestations of him, to which I have so frequently alluded, let us look at what is said in regard to him in the New Testament—especially after his resurrection from the dead. We observe that in the case of Peter and John at the beautiful gate of the temple, when they commanded the man, lame from his mother's womb, in the name of Jesus Christ to rise up and walk, immediately the man stands up: his feet and ankle bones receive strength; he walks and leaps and praises God.

Again, after the dismissal of the apostles Peter and John from the council, when they gave utterance to that wonderful, divine, and glorious prayer, recorded in the Acts of the Apostles, 4th chapter, in which there is a quotation from the 2nd Psalm, we find the house shaken in which they were assembled, and a visible testimony was borne to the presence of the Lord Jesus Christ.

Again, when Stephen delivered that wonderful speech at the bar of the Sanhedrim, which drew forth the bitter and cruel hatred, not only of the members of the Sanhedrim, but of the Jews who were assembled; when they were cut to the heart, and gnashed upon him with their teeth,—he, being full of the Holy Ghost exclaimed, "Behold! I see the heavens opened and the Son of Man standing on the right hand of God."

And again, we know that on another occasion, when Paul was going towards Damascus, breathing forth threatenings and slaughter against the disciples of the Lord; that at noonday—and you may conceive something of the brightness of a Syrian noonday sun, from what we have seen of the sun's brightness in this colder climate,—there shined round about him a light brighter than the sun. It was at once recognised by Paul as the Shechinah, or visible emblem of the divine presence. He at once recognised the presence of the God of Israel; and still more, when he heard the voice saying, "Saul, Saul, why persecutest thou me," and said, "Who art thou Lord?" he was immediately made to recognise the presence of Jesus, and was made to perceive that the voice of Jesus of Nazareth, and the voice of the God of Israel, were one and the same.

Well then, here again was his ubiquity made manifest, and so, in the words of the text, "Wherever two or three are gathered together in my name, there am I in the midst of them," to bless them and to do them good. Jesus is everywhere present. There is no possibility of such a thing as the confining or circumscribing of him by space any more than by time; nay, even within his heavenly abode, he is above space, as he is above time.

I am reminded of several other things, which I cannot touch upon. These two things however are brought under our notice. Jesus is the "I am," and he is everywhere present, and with him there is no past and no future, and there is no possibility of confining Him to any particular place. But, let us take into consideration another view of his character, and forming one of my texts. "All power is given to me in heaven and upon earth."

Well then, he is possessed of all power. Let me not be misunderstood in this. If I were to say that imagination was to be regarded as an element in what I am about to speak to you, I should be guilty of something, quite as gross, if not of the same nature as popery. If I were to say we really make present the death of the Son of God, present as to time, and present as to space, I should be substituting the imaginations of our minds for historical facts, left on record by the Holy Ghost; but I say no such thing. What I am reminding you of is, that Jesus is the ever-living one—that Jesus is the ever-present one, and I observe that that very eternity of the Lord Jesus Christ, and that very ubiquity of his is, in one sense, imparted presence; in one sense imparts presence to what he was in flesh, and to what he accomplished therein, and realises what he says in a remarkable passage—"I am he that liveth, and was dead, and behold I am alive for evermore." In this passage he connects the events of his life upon earth, as a sort of episode, with his everlasting existence in glory.

Let us recollect these facts, not forgetting that they occurred eighteen hundred years ago, at a distance of three or four thousand miles. Without forgetting these facts I observe, that it is the ever-living, the ever-present one, who died eighteen hundred years ago—who died on Calvary. And I have hinted that these are truths which lie at the bottom of those Popish doctrines to which I have been directing your attention, but which have been grossly perverted in coming down to our time through a period of hundreds of years.

Is there no real value in the knowledge of the fact that Jesus is God? that he is the I am? that he is the ever-present one? Most assuredly it is a remarkable fact, that the historical records of the death and resurrection of Christ from the dead, are made by the almighty power of which he is possessed, to bear upon our consciences as if they were actually present — present as to time and present as to space, and when the Holy Ghost in every age of the Church —and remember that the Holy Ghost is the spirit of the Lord Jesus—opens the eyes of the understanding of any one to receive the truth concerning Christ, when the principle of faith enters into our consciences with power, then doth Christ immediately appear as if he were present, both as to time and space, and the glorious events of his life enter into our minds with all the power they had eighteen hundred years ago. The lapse of time has not taken away the efficacy of Christ's blood. He was the Lamb that was slain from the foundation of the world, and his blood operates in every age, and operates with the same grand, glorious, and divine efficacy; and therefore, when the Holy Spirit opens the eyes of our understandings, and we are given to believe in the death which Christ underwent for the sins of the world, that moment the blood shed on Calvary enters into our consciences with all the power, and with all the divine efficacy that it ever had or can have, and speaks peace to those guilty conciences, purging them from all sin; and, when this blood is sprinkled upon our hearts and consciences, it speaks better things to them than the blood of Abel. Now, this is the power of which I have been speaking—the power of the Holy Ghost put forth through Christ's death; yes, and made present to us, and powerful and efficacious within us.

In the same way in regard to the resurrection of Christ from the dead, that power of his resurrection to which our attention was directed two Lord's days since. That event, though it occurred eighteen hundred years ago, and in a far distant country, is brought into our consciences with present power, and present efficacy, and we find ourselves raised from death in trespasses and sins, to the new life upon which Christ himself hath entered. We are made to sit with him, even here, in heavenly places, and are made to experience the anticipation of resurrection with him from the dead, to the glory of his and our Father.

This is the remarkable circumstance connected with these events. Historically they are past; historically they are not performed in Great Britain; but then Jesus is the "I am;" and Jesus is everywhere present; and when the truths concerning him,—the truth of his incarnation, the truth of the perfection of his character upon earth, the truth of his having been obedient unto death; and the truth of his death and resurrection from the dead are made apparent by the power of the Holy Ghost, that is his own power, for "all power is given unto him in heaven and in earth,"—I say, when these truths are by that power made to enter into our consciences, there is no oldness found in what occurred on Calvary. There is no want of life found, as in the history of worldly events, where from lapse of time these events lose their influence, not only upon the memory but upon the understanding and will; on the contrary, what happened eighteen hundred years ago, is found to have the same power to enlighten, the same power to save, the same power to quicken, the same power to influence us, to live not unto ourselves but unto God, which it ever had. The same power which the sacrifice had when it was offered, and the same power which the resurrection had when Christ ascended to God's right hand, they possess now, and will continue to possess until time shall be no more. This power is present, and present it will always be, ever powerful to purge, ever powerful to speak peace, to impart life, and to raise us above the world; and thus raising us to a position at which nothing but what is heavenly and divine could enable us to arrive; and which results in our being made to live not unto ourselves but unto him that died for us and that rose again.

While therefore we condemn the conduct of papists in looking to Jesus as present in the crucifix, and while we condemn as profane the making his body and blood to be every where offered up, and while we reject as a species of profanity these practices, let us recollect that, according to the 10th Hebrews, the true sacrifice once offered could never be repeated; and let us bear in mind that in the deity of the Lord

Jesus Christ we have these facts prominently brought before us; that as God, he is ever present, at all times and in all places; and that to him is intrusted "all power, both in heaven and upon earth;" and that in these sublime facts, misunderstood, perverted, and misapplied, lie those abominations of the Romish Church to which I have referred.

Let us ever recollect, that Jesus, the ever-living, and the ever-present one, has all power, and is in the exercise of sovereign dominion; and that the events which occurred in his own personal history, in a far distant part of the world, are brought, by the mighty power of the Spirit, to bear with a present power and a present efficacy upon our hearts and consciences, giving to us life from the dead, even life with the glorified Jesus—life by anticipation here, and life into the full enjoyment of which we shall enter, when time to us shall be no more.

May the Lord bless what has been spoken, and to His name be praise for evermore.—Amen.

SERMON XXII.

November 28th, 1858.

ONE of the passages which I have selected as texts on the present occasion, will be found in the Epistle to the Hebrews v. chapter, 8th verse. "Though he (that is, Christ) were a Son, yet learned he obedience by the things which he suffered." And I would wish you to take with it another portion of this wondrous Epistle, namely, the 11th chapter, 6th verse, "Whom the Lord loveth He chasteneth, and scourgeth every son whom He receiveth."

Few topics are more insisted on, especially in the New Testament Scriptures, than the conformity between the Divine Head and His divine members in their religious experience, and yet few topics have been less understood, and, I suspect, are less attended to than this. While it is expressly declared that "if we suffer with him we shall also reign with him," and while it is also declared that "it is only through much tribulation we can enter into the kingdom of God," human nature, shrinking as it does from suffering, and cherishing a selfish desire to obtain exemption from all that would distract or disquiet, is apt to cherish the hope that it may be different with ourselves, and that we may quietly and without trials go forward to the end of our career—that we may be exempt from those sufferings which have been the experience, I may say the privilege, of the saints of God in every age. Our heavenly Father, however, loves us too dearly to permit such a state of exemption from suffering, as that which our selfish natures are too apt to long for; nay, our heavenly Father, loving the head, loves the members too dearly, and is too desirous of promoting their conformity to His Son, for Him to suffer them to pass thus easily through the world. Blessed be His name, conformity to the Son, by anticipation here and in glory hereafter, is one of the grand principles of divine revelation, and when understood and carried home to the conscience, when made to be experienced in all its blessedness, even upon earth we are made to say, because we feel it along with our Divine Head, "It is good for me that I have been afflicted, that I might learn Thy statutes." "Before I was afflicted I went astray, but now have I kept thy word."

My Christian friends, after a good deal of reflection upon the passages which I have selected as texts for this morning's consideration, I felt I should perhaps preach to you a more efficient sermon, if, instead of going over details collected in my own mind, and arranged by my own reflections, I should try to bring some marked and prominent passages of the heavenly testimony to bear upon your consciences, and with a view to the bringing about of this, I have selected two of my texts; but I have in my mind, and, were I able to accomplish it, I should bring under your notice several more. I shall allude to a few more, and I have in view two particularly, which I wish to bring under your notice, as indicating conformity between the Head and its members in sufferings, a conformity leading to one and the same glorious result; for, whether the Head or the members be tried, the "divine glory" is the result; and this being the case, there must be something peculiarly sweet and delightful in the consideration of such a fact, to the experienced and Christian mind.

Well then, there are two passages which I want particularly to bring under your notice as exemplifying conformity between the Head and the members in sufferings. The one is that recorded concerning our Divine Head, when led up into the wilderness to be tempted of the devil, which you will find in the 4th chapter of St. Matthew's Gospel; the other is what is said concerning Paul, as recorded by him in 12th chapter of the Second Epistle to the Corinthians.

If you reflect upon the matter, taking Scripture for your guide, you will find that sufferings have been inflicted upon the people of God for various causes, and for various special objects. You will find, for instance, that they were inflicted on account of misconduct. If you go back to the 24th chapter of the Second Book of Samuel, you will find that David, though he was a man according to God's own heart, was tempted to number the children of Israel, and this in opposition to the dissuasion of Joab and of many of his leading friends and supporters; and as the result, an awful calamity befell the nation over which he presided, and consequently befell himself. He was, in the presence of his people, most grievously punished for the sin, which in the very teeth of expostulation, and in the teeth of his own conscience, he had committed. And we know that what happened to David, also happened to Moses. You will remember his transgression before the waters of Meribah, and the effects of that transgression, in excluding him from the earthly Canaan. Throughout the Scriptures, the chastisement of believers for misconduct is brought before us prominently and practically; and then, it is also brought before us with equal prominence, that all these chastisements, for whatever cause they are inflicted, have God's glory and the good of God's people, for their object. Look at the case of Job. Nothing could be more remarkable than what is said with regard to him. He was perfect and upright, feared God, and eschewed evil; there was no fault to be found with him; but in consequence of the suggestions of Satan, he is delivered over to him, to be tried with sufferings of the most acute kind, both in his family and in his person; the result being that Job is carried through them all, patiently and triumphantly, and his latter end is blessed more than the beginning.

Whether we look at the case of David, of Moses, or of Job, whether we regard their sufferings, as the effects of the divine displeasure, or as inflicted with a view to the trial of their faith; in each case we see the truth of the language, that "He chasteneth us for our profit, that we may be partakers of His holiness," and that his own glory may, by the means of those sufferings and the way in which they are endured, be the triumphant result.

But I confess it is not with a view to these things alone that I have brought this subject before you this morning. It is true, that God does chasten His people for misconduct. It is true, that He does chasten them, that through the medium of patience under their sufferings, through the medium of their being upheld by His heavenly truth, He may glorify Himself, as well as benefit them. That is true; but I have been struck by another feature of this subject brought before my mind in the heavenly testimony. It is only lately that it has struck me with such force, and I now want to bring that particular feature under notice. There is a conformity between the Head and members in sufferings, but there is also conformity in another respect, which probably may have occurred to some of you, but which as I tell you has only recently occurred to my own mind in a very peculiar and emphatic manner. I have observed, in the case of the Lord Jesus Christ, that after he had been baptized, and after he had received that most remarkable attestation to his divine character, "This is My beloved Son in whom I am well pleased," he was immediately led into the wilderness, there to be tried by, and to pass through, a series of the most severe temptations, from which temptations he emerges most triumphantly. Again in the case of Paul I have been struck by the fact, that he had revelations of the most remarkable nature made to him; and immediately after, he was subjected to trials of the most keen and pungent nature, through which he was carried in a remarkable way, the result being, as in the case of our Blessed Lord, the glory of our heavenly Father.

First let us look at the two cases, and make a few observations on the remarkable conformity between them; and then let us observe, the important application of them to the case of all Christ's people. In the first place, look at the Head, and I must be brief, and leave you to examine the subject more carefully for yourselves—after you leave this place. I say look at the Head; and in doing so, take the end of the third with the six verses at the beginning of the 4th chapter of the Evangelist St. Matthew, and you will find the following things: Jesus is baptized. He comes up out of the water, and in so doing, the Holy Ghost from heaven descends upon him, and a voice issues from the excellent glory, saying, "This is My beloved Son in whom I am well pleased." Oh, think of what such an attestation as this was to his rank and character, and to the love borne by God to him. How markedly was it pointed out to those with whom Jesus was externally associated, that he was none other than the Son of God. But remark what immediately followed. This attestation was not subservient to what a worldly-minded individual would have thought, or subservient to his becoming the inheritor of great wealth, or to his gaining an earthly throne.

As soon as this great attestation to his rank and character has been borne, he is immediately carried into the wilderness, to be tried and tempted of Satan. And observe, the temptation consisted of three parts. He was first tried to show that there was nothing of "the lust of the flesh" in him. He refuses to command stones to be made bread, and thereby remove his confidence in God to confidence in the creature; the very sin which Adam and Eve committed. He declares that man was not to live by bread alone, but by every word that proceedeth out of the mouth of God." There was therefore no lust of the flesh in Christ Jesus, proved by the result. He is then tried to show that there was nothing of the lust of the eyes in him. He is carried to the pinnacle or wing of the temple, and he is there commanded, or rather, it is suggested to him, by the infernal agent, to throw himself down, and the 91st Psalm is quoted as the sanction for his doing so. Jesus again shows that "the lust of the eyes"—that is, a disposition to trust in human reasoning on Scripture was not in him, for instead of complying with the suggestion as to the angels being commanded to bear him up, lest at any time he should dash his foot against a stone, he showed that he lived by the express command "Thou shalt not tempt the Lord thy God." He showed that he did not live or attempt to live by inferences or conclusions drawn from human reasonings, but by the express declarations of divine truth. And then again when he is taken up into an exceeding high mountain and shewn all the kingdoms of the world, and the glory of them, and the tempter says "All these things will I give thee if thou wilt fall down and worship me," he saith unto him, get thee behind me Satan, for it is written "Thou shalt worship the Lord thy God and Him only shalt thou serve." Thou shalt not worship Satan the creature in any form, was proved to be the grand characteristic of Christ Jesus, and temptation, no matter how attractive and seductive, met with no response in him. Therefore, the pride of life, that grand failing by which we are, in our imagination, pharisaically carried above our fellow-men, and led to look upon ourselves as better than our fellow-men—that principle was not in Christ Jesus. The result shewed that no pride of life, nor any other earthly principle had a place in him, as was the case with Adam when he fell from his first estate. The Lord Jesus could be exposed to every species of temptation, without the temptation having any power over him. Instead of its having power over him, he had power over it. He was God manifest in flesh, and being so, he overcame the temptation of the devil, and thus triumphed over him. Even before Jesus came to the cross he shewed he was the power as well as the wisdom of God; and the glory of his Heavenly Father was the result of the trials, or rather series of trials, to which he was subjected, after that most extraordinary instance of divine love which had been shewn to him at the river of Jordan.

In the next place look at the Apostle Paul. He at first avoids stating that he was the person of whom he was speaking, though it comes out afterwards, when he says, he knew a man in Christ about fourteen years ago, whether in the body, he could not tell; or whether out of the body, he could not tell: God knew; he knew such a man carried up to the third heaven. And in a subsequent passage he says, he was taken up into paradise where he heard words, which it was impossible for any man to utter much less to explain: such were the words he heard, that it was not in his power to repeat them. I have very little doubt, —although I do not mean to say that others may not differ from me—still I have very little doubt in my own mind as to the meaning, comparing one part of Scripture with another. I understand the language of the Divine writer to mean, that the first heaven was the degree of divine manifestation that was possessed by those who lived under the Old Testament economy; that is, the heaven from which the New Testament Church was excluded; so the second heaven is the degree of divine manifestation that is vouchsafed to the people of God in New Testament times, and which they enjoy through the medium of the record of the New Testament Scriptures, the writings of the evangelists and the apostles, which writings throw light upon the Old Testament Scriptures. Now, this is what I understand by the second heaven. And when he says he was carried up to the third heaven, I understand him to mean the highest degree of divine manifestation, that is, a perception of the state of things which belongs to the saints when the earthly house of this tabernacle shall have been taken down, and when they shall be clothed upon with their house which is from God. I understand that to be the third heaven—a state of things not realised by believers of the truth upon earth; a state of things which we do not find any record of having been realised, except in the case of St. Paul, here alluded to; or it may be in the case of John, as recorded in the Book of Revelation, which may have been the introduction of John into the third heaven. I do not know in the New Testament record of any other distinct intimation of a human being—a being in flesh, having been carried up into the third heaven, that is, into a perception of the future enjoyment of God, except Paul, and that only on the one occasion to which he here refers.

Now, observe the remarkable coincidence in this case between the head and the members. There is bestowed upon Christ a very remarkable attestation, while upon earth as to his divine character and mission. Just so, after he has ascended to glory, his servant Paul is carried up to him, and remarkable manifestations and communications are made to him, so great and glorious that it was impossible for any human being to speak of them, or to convey a knowledge of them, the human mind not being qualified to receive them; and not until our bodies and minds are entirely conformed to the body and mind of Christ shall we be capable either of expressing or understanding the things of God. You observe, in the case of our Lord, that after the remarkable manifestation made to him, he was carried down into the wilderness to be tempted; and just so, we observe in the case of Paul, that after that most remarkable privilege had been conferred upon him of being carried up to the third heaven, lest he should be exalted above measure, there is sent to him a thorn in the flesh, a messenger of Satan to buffet him.

I am not going to enter into any merely curious enquiries as to what this thorn in the flesh was. Many theologians have made an attempt to explain it, in which they may have succeeded, or they may have failed. It is enough for me, that God, in the case of His beloved apostle, with a view to prevent his exaltation above measure—to prevent that effect of which those who know the truth may have some idea, sends him this messenger of Satan to buffet him. Believers of the truth, know that every thing that is divine, has of itself a blessed and heavenly effect, yet through the weakness of flesh, through our nature being ignorant and opposed to God, the fleshly nature of man actually takes occasion from things that are heavenly and divine to exalt itself—and is apt to forget God—and in various other ways to shew that fleshly nature is unchanged and unchangeable—that it is a nature ever and thoroughly opposed to God.

I need not dwell upon this. If you will look at the facts recorded in the New Testament, you will find instances of persons who were exalted to office in the Christian Church, and who manifested a tendency to magnify—not the divine nature—but to make use of that which is heavenly and divine, for the purpose of promoting mere earthly purposes, and for the exhibition of earthly principles and earthly motives. With a view to prevent this, he sends this thorn in the flesh to buffet his apostle. And observe the blessed effect. The apostle instead of following out the evil suggestions of this messenger of Satan, and instead of being led into unbelief in consequence of it, immediately repairs to the throne of his heavenly Father, and asks to have it removed. He feels his own weakness; he feels that he is unable to conflict with Satan; he has not confidence in his own strength, and he goes to him who alone is capable of removing it, and asks him to remove it. Observe the answer, and how instructive it is, "My grace is sufficient for thee; for my strength is made perfect in weakness." The temptation, whatever it may be, is not immediately removed according to the prayer of the apostle, but another view of the divine character is given him; and he is not only made conscious of his own weakness, his own inability to conflict with this adversary by his own strength, but there is opened up to him a view of what God's love, and grace, and strength are. It is suggested to him, that however unable he may be to conflict with the temptation, there is a power in God vouchsafed to him—a power which will enable him successfully to conflict with it and to overcome it. And this is conveyed to him, not in connection with any latent strength in himself. He did not discover it, for in connection with the discovery of his own infirmities, in connection with the fact of his own weakness, he could not have discovered it. He was thoroughly ignorant. But it was this weakness of the creature, it was these very infirmities of the creature which gave occasion to God, through him, as a creature weak and infirm, to manifest what the power of God is, and to manifest the truth of that beautiful principle laid down in the 8th Psalm, and quoted by Christ himself, "Out of the mouth of babes and sucklings thou hast ordained strength;" and to afford another illustration of the principle brought out in the 1st chapter of the First Epistle to the Corinthians, that "God hath chosen the foolish things of the world to confound the wise, and God hath chosen the weak things of the world to confound the things which are mighty; and base things of the world, and things which are despised, hath God chosen, yea, and things which are not, that he may bring to nought things that are;" in other words, that by this very exhibition of weakness on the part of the apostle, there is afforded a glorious opportunity for the manifestation of the power, of the glorious power and might of his Divine Redeemer. And you will observe, that the result was a declaration on the part of the apostle, that he would thenceforward glory in his infirmities—not in the infirmities themselves, but in them as affording an opportunity for the manifestation of what God is—as affording an opportunity for a manifestation of that glory, which redounds to God from the members of His Church, in time and throughout eternity.

Now, my dear Christian friends, before I proceed to

a short application of the truths which I have brought under your notice, I may observe, that I have passed over many cases of the sufferings of God's people, which you will find alluded to in other parts of the divine testimony. I have shewn how sufferings were inflicted upon Moses, David, and Job; but I have tried to confine your attention to an important and most wonderful view of the reason why God afflicts His people, the view of His bringing out conformity between the Head and the members. The Head had a divine attestation given to him while in flesh, and it was followed by exposure to the keenest and most pungent trials. Then the great apostle of the Gentiles—the chief of saints, and the chief of sinners—had some extraordinary revelations made to him, in which he seems to stand unique, and these were immediately followed, as in the case of our Blessed Lord, by trials of a severe and pungent character.

Observe what follows in both cases. The divine glory was promoted. In the one case, when temptations from without were offered, it was that the glorious and divine nature of the Redeemer might defeat the devil at every point, and shew the tempter that if he was strong, in coming into contact with the Son of God, he came into contact with one stronger than himself, and one who could spoil him of all the armour in which he trusted. Look at the case of the great apostle of the Gentiles. He has a large manifestation made to him which might have exalted him above measure, but with a view to prevent any undue influence or operation of fleshly nature, there was given to him a thorn in the flesh to buffet him. And observe the blessed result—the glory of God, the manifestation, not of the power of the creature, but of the power of the Creator. The manifestation of the infirmities of the creature, affording a splendid opportunity for the manifestation of the loving-kindness and power of the Creator.

Now let us briefly look at these truths with a reference to ourselves. They appear to me full of meaning, and full of sweet and powerful application. All those who know the truth as it is in Jesus, know that they acquire that knowledge, not because they are superior to others naturally, but because God has been pleased to reveal it to them, according to the counsel of His own will. In one part of Holy Writ, the 13th chapter of the Acts of the Apostles, it is said, that all who were destined to eternal life believed; and therefore those to whom the truth is made known, believe it simply because it is God's purpose that the eyes of their understanding should be opened, and that they should be brought out of darkness into marvellous light, and there is no other reason to be assigned for this but God's good pleasure.

Mark what would follow if sufferings were not sent to believers. I am not forgetting what is said regarding Christ. In him it was merely to bring out and manifest his divine nature. The Apostle Paul's sufferings were sent to him that he might not be exalted above measure—that God might, in his case, exhibit His heavenly power as contrasted with human weakness. All believers of the truth have tasted this doctrine, which is both heavenly and divine, and are made partakers of privileges by which they become heirs of God, and sons and daughters of the Lord Almighty, and which give to them a priestly and royal character. Although this is their privilege, and they are directly influenced according to godliness, yet all those to whom this manifestation is made are still in flesh—a flesh derived from Adam—a flesh ignorant of God—a flesh opposed to God.

Observe, this fleshly nature exists in all of us, and the tendency of it is to abuse our heavenly privileges just in proportion as they are possessed by us, and just as God's word dwells in us richly with spiritual understanding. There is a tendency to bring forth good in so far as the divine nature operates; yet human nature is stimulated by the effect of increased divine manifestation to shew more decidedly what it is; to shew itself in its thorough opposition to God, and in opposition to godliness. Now, it is when placed under circumstances like these, that we perceive the beautiful application of the language of my texts and the two passages I have referred to.

We perceive that it becomes necessary for the good of all Christ's people, as well as for God's glory, that they should be subjected to trials, to make them feel how weak they are, and to bring them to the throne of their heavenly Father; to bring them to an increased sense of dependence upon Him, and to an increased desire to receive those things which are capable of sustaining them, and which alone can sustain them in the time of need. I have no hesitation in saying that this is the case with all the people of God in every age. God knows we are but dust. As a father loveth his children, so the Lord loveth them that fear him. He not only corrects us for our misconduct, but he also anticipates as it were our wrong-doings. His aim is to prevent them. He is desirous that His children should not be puffed up or walk unseemly; that they should not expose themselves, **or** the cause in which they profess to believe and to rejoice, to the attacks of a world that lieth in wickedness. Therefore with a view to their benefit as well as His own glory, He sends a thorn in the flesh, the messenger of Satan, to buffet them with trials, and where these trials are sanctified to them as the trials of Paul were to him, the same blessed result follows; they are made conscious of their infirmities; they are brought to the throne of the heavenly grace to ask that the trials may be removed; or, bearing in mind the case of Paul, they go to that throne and ask that, if they are still to be subjected to these trials, God's grace may be sufficient for them, and that it may be given in sufficient measure to uphold them, and enable them to overcome them. What they desire is a grace, not consisting in anything fanatical, but a grace consisting of increased manifestations of the divine character, and of increased intimations of the divine love; a grace consisting of an increase of that joy in which their strength alone consists, that joy in the Lord, which is the source of all divine strength.

I have no hesitation in saying, that when the mind of the believer is brought into this state by the operation of the power of God's grace, the operation of heavenly truth, the operation of the Spirit through love and through the truth, then, by the increased discovery of evil views and evil tendencies in himself, he is made conscious of his dependence upon divine strength and divine grace, and has this sense of dependence cultivated in him, and brought into operation more and more, and thus through infirmities and distresses for Christ's sake, though weak in himself, he becomes strong in the Lord and in the power of His might.

In the case of every believer the same blessed result follows as in the case of our Lord and his apostle Paul. The divine glory is promoted; God's strength is made manifest in their weakness; the power of heavenly truth to enlighten them, and the power of heavenly love to enable them to live not unto themselves, but unto him that died for them and rose again, are brought out in strong relief.

The subject on which I have been speaking has of late been very much before my mind and operating upon it, and I have thought it might be advantageous to you as well as to myself, to bring it under your notice, not by making statements of my own, but by a reference to the facts recorded in Scripture, the truth of which we all experience in passing through this present world. We are but human beings, and in everything sin, and come short of the glory of God, and the Lord will and does chasten us, His beloved children. And it is because He loves us that He chastens us, and many valuable results are produced by temptations assailing us, and when we are brought out of them like gold tried in the fire, God is thereby glorified.

In conclusion, I have brought under your notice facts of which you will find many similar instances recorded in the heavenly testimony. I have selected two remarkable—to me most remarkable ones. Christ and the attestation to him from heaven, followed by the strong and pungent temptations to which he was exposed, and the glory of God being promoted by his coming out of them triumphantly. And then a circumstance of a similar character occurring in the case of his beloved apostle Paul, and followed by a series of trials of the most severe nature, in which he is led to appeal to his heavenly Father and to the power of His grace, thus shewing God's strength perfected in His weakness, and this weakness of the creature made subservient to the manifestation of the power and wisdom of the Creator. And observe, all believers of the truth are brought through faith into the possession of privileges, and into the possession of a wisdom superior to that of the world around them. This tends to God's glory. We know that what is born of the Spirit is Spirit, but then as believers of the truth, we know that we have not the Spirit without measure; we have still the Adamic nature, and against the workings of this Adamic nature in His people God provides as in the case of Paul. Lest they should be exalted above measure, He sends various trials, and blessed are they who, in the event of these trials being inflicted, find them made subservient to a sense of their weakness and dependence upon God, and the means of taking them to the throne of grace, and as the blessed result, are made to perceive God's strength manifest in their own weakness.

I have tried to speak of these things in the simplest manner I can to you. May the Lord lead you to a further consideration of them, and to the many subjects that stand connected with them, and may He bless what has been said, and to His name be praise for evermore.—Amen.

SERMON XXIII.

January 2, 1859.

I HAVE selected two passages of God's Word, contained in the New Testament Scriptures, from which to address you at this time. The first you will find in the 17th chapter of the Acts of the Apostles, and the 27th and part of the 28th verses, "That they might seek the Lord, if haply they might feel after him, and find him, though he be not far from every one of us: for in him we live and move, and have our being." The other passage is contained in the 10th chapter of the Epistle to the Romans, and the 8th verse: "But what saith it? The word is nigh thee, even in thy mouth, and in thy heart: that is, the word of faith, which we preach."

I am not assuming a great deal when I assert, that there is not a single human being present, who has attained to years of maturity, who has not been conscious from time to time, of a sense of distance and alienation from God. To express myself in another form, if there is one principle of human nature connected with religion more remarkable than another, it is the fact that every human being naturally conceives God to be at a vast distance from him; at such a distance that he deems it to be difficult, if not impossible, for him to get over it; that is to say, the feeling produced by the sense of God being at a distance from us is that we either cannot approach Him, or, if we do, we are able to do so only with the utmost difficulty, and after incessant efforts, mistakes, shortcomings, and disappointments on our part. I shall express shortly and simply what I want to bring under your notice this morning by observing, that the principle of human nature with reference to God is to regard Him as standing at a great, or perhaps I should rather say, at an infinite distance from us; the principle of the divine nature, on the contrary is, that God is near to us —aye, infinitely nearer than, even with the clearest views and apprehensions of His divine character, we are capable of conceiving Him to be. Distance from God is, therefore, a feeling of human nature : nearness to God, or rather God's nearness to us, is the grand principle of the divine nature. Now let us look at and examine these two things separately, with reference to the opposition of the one to the other.

In the first place let us look at and examine that feeling of distance from God, which is characteristic of human nature. Now, this feeling of distance from God is both general and special, and we may understand the subject better by considering it under both these aspects. Our feeling of distance from God, or rather the feeling that God is at an infinite distance from us, is a general one. No wonder that such a feeling should exist in, and be exhibited by, human nature, for if we look at the subject from below, that is, from the platform of human nature, it is but too true that there appears to be an infinite distance between the creature and the Creator.

Some time ago I drew your attention to what occurred in the plains of Shinar, to the attempt made by man to build a temple which should reach to heaven; and I pointed out the failure of man in that attempt, and that he was not one whit the nearer to God when the temple had been reared to its apex, than he was when he laid its foundation-stone. I endeavoured to shew you that, in that fact, we have the foundation of all Socinian or natural views of God, which suppose that the creature may, from the mere platform of human nature, rise up to the apprehension and enjoyment of the Creator. Every such view involves a positive falsehood, for the creature can never, in his own apprehensions of God, rise one whit above himself, however refined may be his intellect, and however deep and profound his cogitations, and, when he has finished, he has only arrived at creature views of God after all, leaving him as far from God when he has finished as when he began.

Looking at the matter from this point of view, the creature dwells in the finite and the indefinite. The mind of man is at best but indefinite in its views and apprehensions of subjects of all kinds. God, on the contrary, dwells in the infinite, and He being infinite, if we look at Him from below, we can never rise to a true apprehension of Him, for it is impossible that the mere creature can ever pass over the gulf that separates between the finite and the infinite. The finite is but a shadow, of which the infinite is the substance, and this is a gulf over which no creature ever threw a bridge; hence, of all the absurdities that human nature ever attempted, the greatest is the absurdity of man attempting by his own power and might, to rise from the mere foundation of creature nature to the glorious super-scripture of the divine nature.

Now, viewing the matter generally, we find that this is actually the case with regard to man, when brought to reflect even superficially upon the subject of which we are speaking. There is in every man who thinks about God, but who is really ignorant of what God is, an idea naturally that God is at an infinite distance from him; so distant, that, if his meditations are carried out legitimately, and if he is led to reflect upon principles, which he may have borrowed from revelation without being aware of it, the more he thinks of God, the more will God appear to be distant from him, so that the profounder the cogitations of such an individual are, the less near to God does he find himself to be, or likely to be, and this feeling of immense and infinite distance from God is strengthened in his mind by such questions as: If God can be reached, how am I to reach Him? If He is to be found, where is He to be found, and how can I find Him? What steps must I take to find Him? What walk, what course of conduct must I pursue? Where are the tracks of God whereby I may come nearer to Him than I now am? These questions, and such as these, enter into the thoughts and puzzle the minds of reflecting individuals, and they are led to say, Where am I to find Him? Is He above or below? Is He on my right hand or on my left? What is the track that I am bound to follow, and what is the path that will conduct me to Him? I say, not only is there a deep and growing sense on the part of thoughtful human beings of their infinite distance from God, but this feeling is complicated and strengthened by such questions as those I have mentioned. Such is the general feeling of man of the distance of himself from God and of the infinite distance of God from him. Passing by the subject in its general form, let us deal with it in a more special way.

This feeling of distance from God existing in man's mind is connected with two facts. In the first place it arises from the sense of guilt, and in the second place from the question as to how the law of God—man ignorant of the truth always supposing himself to be subject to it—is to be thoroughly fulfilled and exhausted.

Now, let us look at the subject in these two respects. We shall find that they not only increase and develop, but that they bring out the sense of man's distance and alienation from God more distinctly and thoroughly than from a general point of view it can be made to appear.

Look first at the sense of guilt. There is a sense of guilt in every human being which has come down to us as an heirloom from Adam. There is a principle of conscience existing in man capable, at any time, of being roused and stimulated into action. This principle of conscience exists in the child, and requires to be stimulated, in order that its existence may become manifest. It is stimulated and brought into action by a variety of causes, and the sense of guilt enters the consciences of all human beings, whether educated or uneducated, whether civilized or savage, and is stimulated more or less as persons grow up in life, according to circumstances. Where nothing but the principles of heathenism exist, it will probably be stimulated in a very minor degree. In Old Testament times, when the law of Moses was viewed as a series of obligatory commands and prohibitions, it exercised a powerful influence over the minds of those who were subject to that law and a sense of guilt was stimulated in a high degree: but in us to whom God is savingly made known through the medium of the Scriptures Old and New, there exist clearer views of human nature, and now the sense of guilt is capable of being stimulated in a greater degree than before the coming of Christ and the preaching of his gospel. Connected with the sense of guilt, and the condemnation that follows, there is a deep and a growing sense of God's distance from us. The more the mind of man tells him he is guilty, the more profound his sense of the violation of God's law, internal and external, the farther removed does God appear to him to be, and the more inaccessible His throne, and consequently the sense of punishment, the sense of alienation, and the sense of distance, are increased and strengthened more and more; this sense of distance from God leading (unless God, in the course of His providence interpose in some way or other) to a feeling of despair, or even to a feeling of desperation itself. This is one of the most remarkable features of the human mind connected with the feeling of distance between man and God. The feeling of man naturally is that God stands at a great and immeasurable distance from him, that guilt is interposed between him and the love and regard of his Maker. This guilt in his mind brings along with it the fear of judgment, that is, the fear of punishment; and the fear of punishment can never exist in any of our minds in connection with views of God as near to us, as ever present with us to bless us and to do us good.

Now, it is possible to conceive that this sense of guilt, involving as it does a sense of distance from God, may for a time be overcome, and we know that from time to time it is overcome, and the result is that our consciences, which at one time have been condemning, are at another time excusing us; and when the sense of guilt has, in one way or another, been temporarily overcome, there is some sort of self-satisfying feeling introduced into the mind that God, after all, may not be so very remote from us as, when labouring under a strong sense of guilt, we supposed Him to be. We may however imagine some such case as the following to have occurred. A long night of suffering connected with a sense of guilt and with the idea of God being at a great distance from him, may have been passed by some individual, and followed by some sort of delusion, (and it is possible for the mind to be labouring under strong delusions,) by which he is led to think or hope that God, after all, may not be so remote from him as he had supposed.

Take the case of a thoughtful and reflective individual, who has been trying to get rid of a sense of guilt by external obedience to law, and who finding this impossible, asks himself: What if after all I should be required not only to get rid of previous guilt, but to obey God's law to the uttermost, in order to recommend myself to His favour, and to be brought nigh to Him who appears so remote from me? If this feeling exists in the mind of any one, and still more if it grows and increases, there will be a greater sense of alienation and distance from God on the part of such an individual, than in the case of one who has deluded himself into the belief, that he can be brought nigh to God by his external conduct; but in the case of an individual who has fancied he could say, like Paul, "that as touching the law of righteousness he was blameless, that every one of God's commandments he had observed from his youth up," there should be introduced into his mind a suspicion that something more than abstinence from external evil was required, if, for instance, as in the case recorded by Paul in the 7th chapter of Romans, "Thou shalt not covet," should be introduced into his conscience with power, or if Christ's sermon on the Mount should take a deep hold of his mind, then he begins to discover that God requires a little more than external abstinence from evil—something more than an external compliance with the commandment. He discovers that there must be purity of mind, there must be abstinence from the evil thought, there must be a disposition to obey God internally, as well as the appearance of obeying Him externally. This is a fruitful source of the sense of alienation and distance from God on the part of man, and if this self-righteous principle be carried a degree further, without the knowledge of the Gospel, it would, I suspect, generally result on the part of individuals of a highly conscientious character, either in madness, or in some act of desperation, as we know from time to time actually to have taken place.

Well then, I have sketched as briefly as I can what is the state of man's mind naturally, and what are the views of human beings acting in the light of human nature in regard to God. God generally appears to be a Being at a great distance from them who "seek Him, if haply they might feel after Him, and find Him;" and when besides this general idea of distance, they are perplexed by the sense of guilt and evil doing, it adds to the sense of distance from God; and when still further, the individual is a man who conscientiously endeavours to obey God's law, internally and externally, as a ground of acceptance with God, and is made to discover that all his efforts to overcome evil, even externally, much less internally, have failed, and that evils are continually recurring which, from time to time, he had supposed himself to have overcome—then I can understand that the sense of distance from God on the part of such an individual is more and more fearfully increased, and may run to such a length, and attain to such a magnitude, as to involve his destruction.

Now, having briefly looked at these facts, let us turn to what God says concerning Himself, and the views He presents to us of His own character. Let us look at what the Divine nature is, as contrasted with the views taken of it by human nature, and depend upon it, the grand general principle involved in God's Word is, that man's views of God naturally, are always found to be the opposite of what God's views of Himself actually are.

Now I have selected two texts with a view of bringing under your notice and illustrating what I have to say in reference to this subject, and this for an obvious reason, that the one text respects mankind in general, and the other text has a bearing upon believers of the truth in particular. This will afford an opportunity of drawing your attention to the subject as respects the world, and as respects the Church of the living God

In the first place, as respects the world. If you look at the 17th chapter of the Acts of the Apostles, you will find that Paul had gone to Athens in consequence of having been obliged to quit Thessalonica; and while waiting for Timothy, whom he expected to join him there, he went into the market-place or forum, where he found a number of individuals prepared to discuss with him those very doctrines which it was his privilege, as well as his duty, as an apostle of the Lord Jesus, to proclaim. It appears that he had there excited such an interest in the minds of the novelty-loving Athenians, that, not satisfied with meeting him in the market-place and there discussing with him, the Epicureans and Stoics either dragged him or persuaded him to accompany them to the Areopagus, the hill on which the Temple of Mars stood, and in which the courts of justice were held. Having brought him there, and placed him in the Areopagus, or Temple of Mars, in the presence of an assembly of the judges, or leading individuals of Athens, they then asked him, "May we know what this new doctrine whereof thou speakest is? For thou bringest certain strange things to our ears: we would know therefore what these things mean?" The apostle, taught by God, and inspired and influenced by the Holy Ghost, seized upon the opportunity, and preached that brief but wondrous sermon; which we find recorded in the latter part of the 17th chapter of Acts.

He begins by telling them that they were too superstitious, too much given to the worship of idols; he tells them that among the many inscriptions he had seen, as he walked through the city, there was one, "TO THE UNKNOWN GOD," and upon this fact, assumed as a text, he builds a splendid argument, one so clear and cogent, so irrefragable, so irresistible, that no individual, taught by the Holy Ghost, can have perused it without feeling the force of it. He tells them what this unknown God, whom they ignorantly worshipped, declares unto them. Having referred to God, as the Creator of the heavens and the earth, having founded the argument that He by whom all things were made, and upon whom all things depend, could not Himself be bounded by any being or set of beings, he then proceeds to carry the matter home to the hearts and consciences of the Athenians. He proclaims to them the doctrine, that mankind in all previous ages had been seeking after God, if haply they might feel after Him and find Him, and then declares to them that glorious truth, "He is not far from every one of us, for in Him we live, and move, and have our being." These words were addressed by him, not merely to believers of the truth, but to all his auditory. He expressed sentiments in which all who listened to him were concerned. For in Him, whether believers or unbelievers, we all live, and move, and have our being.

Now I think our translation is an admirable one, " We live in Him," that is, we perform all our actions in Him—nay, we have our very existence in Him. Observe, how completely this language of the Apostle Paul runs counter to the ideas of God to which I have just been directing your attention—to those ideas of God that are characteristic of human nature. Man naturally conceives God to be at an immense distance from him, at such a distance as can only be overcome with the utmost difficulty, if it can be overcome at all. The apostle at once attacks this idea, and says, so far from this view being true, God is not far from every one of us. On the contrary, He is very near us, aye, as close as it is possible to conceive Him to be. The proof of this is, that "in Him we live, and move, and have our being." Can I or any other human being be at a great distance from Him in whom we live? No; therefore we must be infinitely near to Him, and He to us.

But further, we move in Him; every thing we perform, is performed in consequence of our dependence upon Him. We depend upon Him for our daily bread. We are told that a sparrow cannot fall to the ground without His interposition, and that the very hairs of our head are all numbered; that is, every action and every circumstance of our lives, as well as life itself, is dependent upon God.

The language of the apostle to which I have referred, is proclaimed to his heathen auditory, and is consequently applicable to all human beings naturally. This is a remarkable fact brought under your notice and mine, as contradicting man's natural feelings and ideas with regard to God; so far from there being an infinite distance between the creature and the Creator, there is the closest union, and intimacy existing between God and man, for "in Him we live, and move, and have our being."

It is a singular circumstance, with regard to human beings, that, from time to time, in connection with revelation, some idea of a union with God, seems to flash across their minds, the thought that God is not so far from them after all. But this is checked by the natural views and tendencies of the human mind, and the man who at a particular moment may have cherished the idea that God is not far from him, may, by the consciousness of guilt, and his conscious inability to live to God, be led to think that God is at a great distance from him. It was this feeling of distance from God, among other things, that led the Athenians into heathenism—that led them to make statues to God, as if by so doing they could attain a means of closer approach to deity. It is this same feeling that makes the Roman Catholic fear to approach God, except through the medium of his priest, his saint, or the Virgin Mary. There appears to his mind to be such an immense distance between the creature and the Creator, that the only way in which he can come to God is through some creature medium.

The apostle proceeds to shew in what follows (and blessed be God's name, there is a most wonderful reference to this tendency of the human mind, and the consequent necessity of the manifestation of His own Son), that God was fully aware, from His knowledge of man, and of man's heart, that there was a necessity for a mediator between man and Himself, and while He overturns all creature mediums, such as the human mind suggests, He brings forth His own Son, a Being who is at once God and man, the mediator between God and man, and shews that in him, He is a God near at hand, and not afar off.

Now, you will observe, that in that wondrous sermon, the apostle after having drawn the attention of his hearers to the circumstance that even his heathen auditory were near to God, though they were ignorant of the fact, proceeds to point to Jesus Christ, and to the day of the New Testament dispensation, in which he was to judge the world. He calls the attention of his auditory to this fact, as the true medium of Divine communication, as the true way in which the Creator is shewn to be near to the creature, and the creature near to the Creator. At this point he is interrupted, and his argument is broken off; the Epicureans and Stoics mock and jeer; they cannot understand the value of the Divine declaration he is making. It is enough for us, however, to have seen in this language of the apostle, the nearness of God to His creatures, set down as a point of prime importance.

From this, important as it is, I hasten to my other text, the grand object I had in view in bringing these truths under your notice. My second text has to do, not with heathens or the world in general, but with the people of God in particular; God is in reality near to all His creatures, for "in Him we live, and move, and have our being," yet the creature naturally is not aware of this fact. The sense of alienation and distance from God exists in his mind, and until the revelation of God in Christ shall have been made to him, he prefers his own notion of being at a distance from God, to God's declaration that He is near to him. So much for creature ignorance of God, so much for the men to whom it has not been given to believe in God's revealed character.

In my text from the 10th chapter of Romans, the apostle says, "The word is nigh thee, even in thy mouth, and in thy heart: that is, the word of faith, which we preach." What a most interesting truth is here brought under our notice. To be nigh or near, is a relation of God with regard to all creatures, but it is here shewn with regard to believers, that to be nigh or near to God, is to have the knowledge of the fact realised in them. It is not merely a divine fact proclaimed by the apostle, but it is a great divine fact of which they are themselves cognizant, and in which they find themselves interested. The apostle had shewn immediately before that by the righteousness of faith, God is never seen to be at a distance. The language of faith is not, "Who shall ascend into heaven? that is, to bring down Christ from above; or who shall descend into the deep? that is, to bring up Christ again from the dead." This is never the language of faith, because Christ hath already been raised from the dead, and is now seated at the right hand of God. Not only was this the language of Jews then, but it is the language of Jews still, always expecting and looking for the Messiah to come down from above. It is the language of unbelieving men of all nations. They never believe the revealed fact that the work of salvation hath been accomplished, and represent the work of Jesus Christ as a work yet remaining to be performed.

In opposition to this, look at the language of our text. "What saith it? The word is nigh thee." The doctrine proclaimed in the 17th chapter of Acts, is carried home by the Holy Ghost with power and effect, not to the consciences of an unbelieving world, but to the consciences of all believers of the truth. The word is nigh thee, that is, the word of faith proclaimed by us apostles; it is in thy mouth, and in thy heart. In this way it is near; it is not a word that tells you to go and seek the Messiah in the flesh; it is not a word that carries you into the depths of Hades to bring up the Messiah from the dead. It tells you that he has already appeared in flesh, it tells you that he has risen, that the work he came to perform has been accomplished by him, and that it is a work in which you yourselves are personally interested. The word is nigh thee, even in thy mouth. But it is more, it is not only in thy mouth —for if it were merely so, thou mightest, like the parrot, express what we have been uttering, and never be a whit the better; but it is in thy heart. Oh! my Christian friends, in this there is a nighness of God to the creature, in the highest degree, and which is realised to the fullest extent in which it can be realised while we are in flesh. Blessed be God, that while the minds of men naturally view Him at a distance, it is the privilege of all believers of the truth to have carried home to their hearts and consciences the knowledge of the fact that He is near to them, so near to them, that by His testimony introduced into their hearts, and the blood of His own Son sprinkled upon their consciences, they are made pure, and have their consciences cleansed from all sin.

Not only is the blood of Christ sprinkled upon their consciences, and peace spoken to them thereby, but they have the answer of a good conscience by the resurrection of Jesus Christ, they know that he who died for them remained not under the power of death, but on the third day burst the gates of death asunder, and rose again, raising them in him to a new and divine life. They find themselves no longer old, but new creatures, possessed of the earnest of a new creation, possessed of that faith which is of the operation of God. The word is thus not only in their mouths, but it exists in their very hearts. It is the very principle of their consciences; it is the earnest of life everlasting in them, and thus they are brought into the closest proximity to God; nay, they are brought into complete union with God, even in this present world, and while passing through it to glory. What is said in regard to believers of the truth? "Ye are the temple of the living God," and God dwells in them, and walks in them. Can there be any closer connection than this dwelling of the Creator in the creature. Not only does He dwell in you, but you dwell in Him, there is a mutual indwelling of the Creator in the creature, and of the creature in the Creator. Can you conceive a more intimate union than this, the creature brought into oneness with the Creator by the purgation of the conscience, through the introduction of the principle of life everlasting by Christ Jesus.

These are the truths brought out in this simple and beautiful passage. "The word is nigh thee, even in thy mouth, and in thy heart, that is, the word of faith which we the apostles preach;" the word which, being proclaimed, is believed by us; which, being believed by us, realises the fact of God's nearness to us, and our nearness to God; and which destroys the sense of distance and alienation which exists in the human mind naturally, in connection with a sense of guilt, and a sense of inability to act up to the divine commands. We find that God was, in Christ, reconciling the world unto Himself, and hath laid our iniquities upon the Son of His love, who died for us and rose again; and we find that in him we have salvation and eternal glory; we find that in God is realised all our hope, and all our desire; and we find that from Him, and out of His fulness, and through His grace, there is bestowed upon us a righteousness, even divine righteousness, which we vainly attempted to attain, but which is ours in Christ Jesus; we have bestowed upon us even the life of God Himself, so that already in Christ Jesus we, who were formerly bearing the image of the earthy, and feeling at a distance from God, are now bearing the image of the heavenly, and as such, know that God is near to us, and that we are brought near to Him in His own Son, so near that God dwells in our very hearts, and that we have the earnest of the Holy Spirit in us, the first fruits of life everlasting; and we know that the period will soon arrive when these earthly bodies, connected with our Adamic descent, will be laid aside, and we shall be clothed upon with our glorious bodies fashioned like unto the glorious body of the Son of God, and enter into the fulness of enjoyment of his presence for evermore.

I have not time to enlarge upon the subject. There are two or three topics I should have liked to notice, but it is, perhaps, enough for me if I have suggested a contrast between God's distance from man, or rather man's sense of distance from God, and of God's views of himself; shewing that He is near to each of us, near as proclaimed in His Divine testimony, but near, in a higher sense, to His own people, for by faith He is dwelling in them as temples of the Holy Ghost, so that He dwells not only in their mouths by their profession of Him, but He dwells in their hearts by their belief in Him, and by the hope they cherish of His second advent when He shall appear again without sin unto salvation, to be glorified in His saints, and to be admired of all them that believe. Blessed be His name in having brought us to a knowledge of our nearness to Him, and our oneness with Him.

May the Lord bless what has been said, and to His name be praise and glory for evermore.—Amen.

FUNERAL SERVICE.

February 22nd, 1858.

LET us pray.

We draw near Thy throne, heavenly Father, recognizing Thee as our God and our Father in Christ Jesus, and as in Him, the Father of mercies, and the God of all consolation.

We come before Thee, as the creatures of Thy Head, as creatures sinning, creatures condemned, creatures dying. We remember that we are guilty, in that we have committed innumerable transgressions—personal transgressions; that Thou canst not look upon us in ourselves, but with abhorrence, and that Thou, as the expression of Thy justice, hast assigned to us the "wages of sin, which is death." But we come before Thee, not merely recognizing our sinful character and condition, but rejoicing to know that all this had been foreseen by Thee, and all the consequences of this our condition, amply provided for, in that covenant of grace and scheme of mercy, which was made from everlasting, in the councils of peace, between the Father and the Son; and this is shewn to be the case by the promises made, immediately after man's transgression, and by these promises being put on record in the Old Testament Scriptures, and finally it is shewn by the advent of Thine own Son in the flesh, who came to obey Thy law, and to bring in everlasting righteousness; who came to put away sin by the sacrifice of himself; and, having risen from the dead, to introduce a new, glorious, and divine system, by which we—who have a fleshly and creature existence, in the first Adam—are made partakers of the divine nature, in the second Adam, who is our heavenly and glorious Head. We desire to recollect, that we appear before Thee, under peculiarly trying circumstances. We have before us the body of one—the child of a sorrowing mother, and she a widow. We recollect that Jesus is not now in flesh, as he was when he commanded the son of the widow of Nain to stand up, and delivered him again to his mother; but we remember that the same Jesus is now exalted to glory—that he is possessed of all power, both in heaven and on earth; and that among the other prerogatives, of which he is possessed, is that of raising the dead; that is, not as in the case of the widow of Nain, by the restoration of this mortal life, but by raising the dead to life everlasting—to the possession of life with himself, in the realms of bliss and glory, for ever and ever.

Oh, how sweet this consideration! How delightful to know, that that same power which hath consigned our deceased young friend to death and the tomb, hath also provided for us an escape from the grave, a resurrection from the tomb, by the swallowing up of death in victory, through our divine and heavenly Head; and though we shall never see this accomplished with our bodily eyes, yet we know, by faith, that the period is approaching when that same Jesus, who himself rose triumphant from the dead, shall come again by his own mighty power, and shall present us pure, and possessed of a glorious body, before the presence of his Father, with exceeding joy.

We know that we live now, not by sight but by faith; but our faith is not in the word of man, but in the Word of God—in the Word of Him who cannot lie; and we therefore know, that whatever obstacles may intervene, and whatever appearances may suggest to the fleshly mind, yet the period will come, when the language of the apostle of Jesus shall be thoroughly accomplished; when "this corruptible shall put on incorruption, and this mortal shall put on immortality," and when, removed from a scene of sin and suffering, and woe and death, to one where these are utterly unknown, we shall enter into the joy of our Lord, and possess the glory and the happiness of heaven, for ever and ever.

We would at this time consider the case of the bereaved widow; we would enter into her habitation this morning; we would sympathize with her, as being ourselves also in the body. Lord, in her case, do Thou help and sustain her, speak to her in accents of peace and consolation. Do Thou direct her to Thy heavenly testimony—to its precious declarations, and to its heavenly promises. Do Thou make her to find, that while all things—human, are not only transient but treacherous—that while no hope can be reposed in a system, which is contradictory and conflicting; yet Jesus Christ is the same yesterday, to-day, and for ever; that all the promises he has made, are like himself—sure and certain; that although time may bring along with it no consolation for the bereaved mother; and, although as regards human efforts, most miserable are all our attempts at consolation, yet God hath spoken, His word hath gone forth, and the period shall come, when she shall see again him with whom she has parted in the image of the *first* Adam, clothed upon with the glorious image of the Son of God.

Oh, may she be comforted by such hopes and promises; and may she be comforted with the prospect of an interminable union with all the members of her family; with her dear departed husband, and with others, who have gone before her. May these hopes be shared by all the surviving members of her family. Oh, may these hopes of the Gospel be conveyed to her, our bereaved friend, and to her family in their present affliction.

Lord, be with us in meditating on Thy word. May we enjoy its consolations and divine promises; and Thine be the power and the praise, and the glory, through Christ Jesus.—Amen.

Had I been possessed of eyesight, I should—as is customary on such occasions as the present—have read, word for word, the language of the 15th chapter of St. Paul's First Epistle to the Corinthians. It is now out of my power to do so, and I hope therefore that you will be satisfied with some general, and a few special references on my part, to the contents of this most interesting, instructive, and consolatory chapter.

You remember, then, that it consists of several parts, and that it advances by a series of gradations. There is first of all, the great general doctrine, upon which all the particular spiritual arguments and conclusions are founded, and from which they are deduced. You have laid down, the broad and substantial fact, that Jesus, as the Christ, died, was buried, and rose again on the third day, according to the Old Testament Scriptures; the evidence of what should happen, thus concurring with what actually took place, in the case of our divine Redeemer; and then, to the evidence of an exact agreement, between the Old Testament Scriptures and the matter of fact, there is added the evidence of those who met him and consorted with him after his resurrection; and of his being seen by above five hundred brethren at one time. The apostle dwells upon these as matters of fact, and as laying the foundation of all that follows, in the subsequent part of the chapter.

From the 12th verse downwards, the chapter proceeds to speak of the resurrection of Christ, with reference to the resurrection of the dead; and the apostle then proceeds upon the grand principle, that the resurrection of the Head is, and must be, inseparably connected with the resurrection of its members.

It proceeds, first,—negatively, by supposing some to be of opinion that there is *no* resurrection of the dead; from which, as he shews, the inference follows irresistibly, that in that case there was no resurrection of *Christ*; for to deny the resurrection of the dead, is equivalent to a denial of Christ's resurrection. "If it be preached to you that Christ rose from the dead, how say some of you, that there is no resurrection of the dead?" "For if there be no resurrection of the dead, then is not Christ risen; and if Christ be not risen, then is our preaching vain, and your faith is also vain."

He proceeds still further, to shew that it being laid down as a fact, that there is no resurrection of the dead, then, not only is our faith vain, but those who are fallen asleep in Christ, are perished. He goes on to close the argument by saying, "If there be no resurrection of the dead, then are we who believe in the resurrection of Christ, of all men the most miserable." Such is the way in which the apostle states and proposes, the negative form of the argument, namely, that to deny the resurrection of the dead, is at once to deny the resurrection of Christ himself.

From the 20th verse downwards, he states the case, positively, draws from it the requisite conclusions, and points to that glorious summary of divine truth, in regard to the dead; which the fact of Christ's resurrection and our resurrection in him, necessarily involves. "But now is Christ," that is, the Anointed one, "risen from the dead, and become the first fruits of them that slept; for as by man came death, by man came also the resurrection of the dead." By man the creature, came in the one; by man the Creator, came in the other; "for as in Adam all die, even so in Christ shall all be made alive."

The apostle here stops to point out the *order*, in which this grand fact is carried into effect—"but every man in his own order, Christ the first fruits, afterwards they that are

Christ's, at his coming. Then cometh the end, when he shall have delivered up the kingdom to God, even the Father, for he must reign until he hath put down all rule, and all authority, and all power; for he must reign until he hath put all enemies under his feet. The last enemy that shall be destroyed, is death; he hath put all things under his feet, but when he said all things are put under him, it is manifest that he is excepted, which did put all things under him; and when all things shall be subdued unto him, then also shall the Son himself be subject unto Him that put all things under Him, that God may be all in all."

After having thus stated the order in which this grand fact shall be carried into effect, the apostle then proceeds to a sort of episode, in which he sets forth the absurdity of denying the resurrection of the dead, and yet continuing the practice of baptism; for baptism implies, that if the party goes down under the water, he is in that case brought under the power of death; and it is from out of the water, that he rises to the possession of life again. To baptize therefore, under such circumstances, is to perform a rite, which contradicts the assertion of those who deny the resurrection of the dead.

The apostle also shews, various other consequences that follow. He shews that all his own trials and struggles would have been in vain, if the dead rise not. He shews too, that the proper conclusion—the practical conclusion—in connection with this doctrine of the denial of the resurrection of the dead, would be to adopt, and act on, the Epicurean principle, " Let us eat and drink, for to-morrow we die;" and then gives a very broad hint, that such language, amongst professed believers, shewed that all of them had not the knowledge of God, and declares that he spoke this to their shame, and to the shame of the Church, which could tolerate such a principle, as would render all their preaching vain.

Having disposed of this argument, he then proceeds to meet broadly the question, " Some will say, how are the dead raised up, and with what body do they come?" as if they had said, we desire some further and more minute information on this subject. The apostle at once meets this question, by a charge of folly against those who bring it; " thou fool, that which thou sowest is not quickened unless it die; and that which thou sowest, thou sowest not that body that shall be, but bare grain, it may chance of wheat, or of some other grain." He thus brings under notice, what every agriculturist, and indeed what every person, possessed of common sense, must have observed, namely, that the seed that is put into the ground, is not that which comes up; but that it is that which comes from the seed, that comes up—*not* the seed itself; and this illustration he applies to the resurrection of the dead. "God giveth it a body as it hath pleased him, and to every seed its own body;" for we commit to the grave, a body connected with Adam—a body that is dead—but we reap from it, a body connected with Christ—a body that lives for evermore.

He then proceeds to illustrate this by a reference to the diversities of bodies that exist. "All flesh is not the same; there is one flesh of men, another of beasts, another of fishes, and another of birds. There are also celestial bodies and bodies terrestrial;" and he hints that among celestial bodies, there is a great variety of glory—that "the glory of the sun differs from the glory of the moon; and the glory of one star differs from the glory of another."

Having suggested this very interesting and valuable fact, that when we sow grain, we reap not the seed which we have sown, because that seed dies; but that we reap something inseparably connected with it, and springing from it. Having stated this, and pointed out that in regard to bodies celestial and terrestrial, there ever has been, and ever must be a marked and decided difference; having pointed to these facts, he then proceeds to meet the question more closely, "so also is the resurrection of the dead." There is a something raised—the same with, and yet different from, what is sown; there is something in the celestial form, in which it is raised, in which the body differs from the terrestrial form, in which it had previously appeared. "It is sown in corruption, it is raised in incorruption; it is sown in dishonour, it is raised in glory; it is sown in weakness, it is raised in power; it is sown a natural body, it is raised a spiritual body." Here then is something raised proceeding from what is sown; something which is connected with, and yet which differs from, that something which is sown, and which dies, and from which springs up something else, which lives for evermore. It is a body derived from that which is sown; and yet this body is raised in a form capable of living for evermore; which, in the natural or soulical state, in which it originally appeared was impossible. There is a soulical body, and there is a spiritual body. "The first man, Adam, was made a living soul, the last Adam was made a quickening" (that is, a life-giving) "spirit." And then follows the declaration, "howbeit that was not first which is spiritual, but that which is natural; and afterward that which is spiritual." And he then still further points out the distinction that exists between them, in these very remarkable words: "the first man was of the earth, earthy;" (which may be seen by referring to the 1st chapter of Genesis, and there reading the account of his formation) "the second man is the Lord from heaven;" (which you will perceive by consulting the 1st chapter of St. Matthew, and reading an account of *his* advent) "and as is the earthy, such are they also that are earthy; and as is the heavenly, such are they also that are heavenly." The descendants of the earthy man, correspond to the earthy man; the descendants of the heavenly man, correspond to the heavenly man himself. Still this does not prove the matter thoroughly to our understandings and experience, nor does it supply the crowning elevation of our hopes, but the next verse does, "and as we have borne the image of the earthy, we shall also bear the image of the heavenly." He then reasons, "Now this I say, brethren, that flesh and blood cannot inherit the kingdom of God; neither doth corruption inherit incorruption." I never meant to say (as if he had expressed himself), I never meant to say, that that which is earthy, and belongs to the Adamic man, is raised to the participation and enjoyment of the Divine nature. "Except a man be born again, that is, born from above, he cannot see the kingdom of God;" for as the earthly nature of man is fitted for his earthly situation only; so it is only by the earthly nature being superseded by the heavenly nature that man becomes fitted for the heavenly state. "Behold, I shew you a mystery, we shall not all sleep, but we shall all be changed in a moment, in the twinkling of an eye, at the last trump: for the trumpet shall sound, and the dead shall be raised incorruptible, and we shall be changed; for this corruptible must put on incorruption;" that is, with reference to the body, "and this mortal must put on immortality;" evidently with reference to the mind, the two parts of man being composed of body and soul; "so then when this corruptible shall have put on incorruption, and this mortal shall have put on immortality;" in other words, when he who was originally corrupt—after the image of Adam—shall be fully and for ever re-created; when the image of the earthy shall be exchanged for the image of the heavenly, "then shall the saying be fulfilled, death is swallowed up in victory." This being the case, there is an elevation of believers in the truth, to a blessedness and glory, far surpassing—and infinitely superior to—that which Adam naturally enjoyed, and which none of his posterity are capable of enjoying in this world; is it not plain from this, that instead of death achieving a conquest over us, we really achieve a conquest over death. It is true that death may temporarily reign over us; but we ultimately, and for ever, reign over it; the result being therefore, that in exchange for this temporary triumph of sin unto death, we obtain an everlasting triumph over sin, unto eternal life; and, instead of being cast down, when we lose a friend, or when we view the prospect of our own dissolution, we have the more reason to triumph, that in Christ Jesus we are made more than conquerors; and, we may, and will, exclaim, "Oh, death where is thy sting," "Oh, grave" (or Oh, *Hades*) "where is thy victory?" That is, *Hades* has a reference to the death of *soul*, corresponding to that which "*grave*" has to the death of the body. "The sting of death is sin, and the strength of sin is the law." Where there is no law, there is no sin. The law was given from Mount Sinai; and this is the law in which justice and mercy completely manifest the condemnation of Adam, and those possessed of Adam's nature. He points to the only source of "victory" over sin and death, over the original law, and over the law given by Moses: "Thanks be to God, that giveth us the victory," over all Christ's and our enemies, "through our Lord Jesus Christ. Wherefore, my beloved brethen" (and this is the practical conclusion, deduced from the whole), "be ye steadfast, unmovable—(not acting as those, who are merely passing from stage to stage, and are consigned to the 'grave')—'always' (should the state of your mind correspond to the state of him, with whom you are made partakers) 'abounding in the work of the Lord.'" And why? "Forasmuch as ye know, that your labour shall not be in vain in the Lord."

I would—before dismissing you from this place—briefly, as I have no wish to detain you longer, in the present severe state of the weather,—I would ask you (especially those connected with the deceased) to bear in mind the language of God's express declaration, by the mouth of His inspired apostle; and to recollect that no man can add to that, which God hath so clearly, and perspicuously, and emphatically he declared on this all-important subject. In what I have just now read, he directs your attention, and mine—not to the creature, but to the Creator—to God's triumph through

Christ Jesus, over sin and over death. He directs our attention to the fact, that although under present circumstances, we are witnesses in the case of our young friend, of the temporary triumph of sin reigning unto death; it is, that it may be succeeded and superseded, by the still greater triumph of Grace, reigning through righteousness, unto eternal life, through Jesus Christ our Lord. He therefore points you and me for consolation, in this chapter, not to any human circumstance; not to anything connected with our present transient condition; but points us to Christ Jesus, and to his grace, whereby we triumph over sin, with a present triumph, the knowledge of which exists in the hearts and consciences of all believers; for it is a divine fact, and one known to each one of us, to whom " the Truth has been carried home with power," that we are already risen, and are already received in heavenly places, and that the power of the Resurrection of Christ Jesus hath been already put forth; and that we have been thereby made partakers of the glorified mind of our heavenly and divine Head. And he also reminds us, of the important fact, that as death assailed the mind of Adam, and was followed by the corruption—or death—of the body; and, as that body became dead, because of sin, yet the Spirit, in us, is life, because of righteousness; "but if the Spirit of Him, that raised up Jesus from the dead, dwell in us, He who raised up Christ from the dead, shall also quicken our mortal bodies, by His spirit that dwelleth in us;" which declaration is also made in another epistle, where it is said, "that He will change our vile bodies, and fashion them like unto his own glorious body, by that mighty power whereby he is able to subdue all things unto himself." And this is our consolation, that, "as we have borne the image of the earthy, so also, shall we bear the image of the heavenly;" that as our dear, departed young friend has been with us, but a few short years; and as he has, almost at the very outset of human existence, been removed from us, bearing the image of the first man Adam, so—as interested in the death of Christ, and washed from sin in his precious blood, and clothed upon with his divine image—he shall yet appear before the throne of God, there to see Him, and enjoy His presence for ever. And while we thus venture to look forward, through the revelation of the Truth as it is in Jesus—through the work of him that died on Calvary, and that rose from the dead; and while we look forward to that work being carried into effect, in the case of our young friend, let us unite in tenderest sympathy with his mother, in tenderest pity for her, a widow, now also deprived of a child of her strongest affections. And may it be our earnest desire, and our urgent entreaty at the throne of the heavenly grace, that to her may be imparted that strong consolation and that good hope, which the Word of God alone can inspire, and which, when communicated by the power of the Spirit, raises us above the various trials and painful bereavements of this present world, and gives us to reap an abundant harvest of joy, and to anticipate the blessings of that period, when the sorrows of time shall be exchanged for the happiness and glory of eternity.

May the Lord bless and preserve us, and to His name be praise for evermore.

At the grave-side, Dr. Thom, in earnest prayer to God, on behalf of the bereaved mother, and surviving family and friends, besought God that He would comfort them in their present bereavement; and touchingly referred to the time, when the relations and friends of those assembled on that melancholy occasion, would lament over them, as they were now mourning the loss of him, over whose tomb they were standing; and he also prayed that when the time of their dissolution arrived, they would be found with him in the realms of glory, where the now weeping widow, with her departed husband and son, as well as their relations and friends, and the strangers present, would be united for ever.

WORKS
OF THE LATE
Rev. DAVID THOM, D.D., Ph.D.

1. —REMARKS, by the Rev. David Thom, Minister of the Scotch Church, Rodney Street, Liverpool, on a Series of Charges recently preferred against him, before the Reverend the Presbytery of Glasgow, by certain individuals connected with the management of the said Church. With a copious Appendix. 1825. 1s. 6d.

2. —MEMORIAL submitted by the Rev. D. Thom to the Presbytery of Glasgow, regarding the Theological Points of his Case. Second Edition. 1825. 8d.

3. —A LETTER to the Rev. Richard T. P. Pope, adverting to some important mistakes committed by him in his recent controversy with the Rev. Thomas Maguire. By Observer. 1827 1s. 6d. (*Out of Print.*)

4. —THREE QUESTIONS PROPOSED AND ANSWERED, concerning the Life forfeited by Adam, the Resurrection of the Dead, and Eternal Punishment. 1828. 2s. 6d. —The same Work, second edition, altered, enlarged, and improved. 1825. 5s. (*Both out of Print.*) Third edition. 1849. 2s. 6d.

5. —RECENT CORRESPONDENCE, between the Presbytery of Glasgow and the Rev. David Thom, occasioned by a second interference on their part with him. 1828. 8d. (*Out of Print.*)

6. —THE MIRACLES OF THE IRVING SCHOOL shewn to be unworthy of serious examination. 1832. 1s.

7. —THE ASSURANCE OF FAITH; or, Calvinism Identified with Universalism. 1833. 2 vols. 8vo. 21s. (*Out of Print.*)

8. —WHY IS POPERY PROGRESSING? 1835. 1s. 6d. (*Out of Print.*)

9. —DIALOGUES ON UNIVERSAL SALVATION, and Topics connected therewith. 1838. 5s. (*Out of Print.*)—The same Work, second edition, with additions, 3s. 6d. 1847.

10. —DIVINE INVERSION; or, a View of the Character of God as in all respects opposed to the Character of Man. 1842. 10s. (*Out of Print.*)

11. —THE THREE GRAND EXHIBITIONS OF MAN'S ENMITY TO GOD. 1845. 10s.

12. —THE NUMBER AND NAMES OF THE APOCALYPTIC BEASTS, with an explanation and application. In two parts. Part I., the Number and Names. 1848. 12s.

Such of the preceding works as are not out of print, may be had of H. K. Lewis, 15, Gower-street North, London.

Edited by the Author.

13. —WITHOUT FAITH WITHOUT GOD; or, An Appeal to God concerning His own Existence, &c. By the late John Barclay, A.M., Pastor of the Berean Assembly, Edinburgh. With a Preface by the Rev. David Thom, Minister of Bold-street Chapel, Liverpool. 1836. 2s. 6d.

14. —THE RESTORATION OF ALL THINGS; or, the Recovery of the Whole Human Family out of their Fall. By Jeremiah White, Chaplain to Oliver Cromwell. With an Introduction by David Thom, D.D. 3s. 6d.

www.ingramcontent.com/pod-product-compliance
Lightning Source LLC
Chambersburg PA
CBHW030556300426
44111CB00009B/1001